"I've played accordion in seventeen countries, and if there's anybody who knows more about accordions and their history than Bruce, I've never met them."

Geoff Berner, novelist, songwriter, and klezmer punk accordionist

· ·

"*Accordion Revolution* is an inspirational guide to the accordion's deep and shadowy past."

Skyler Fell, Accordion Apocalypse Repair Shop

· ·

"Triggs is the closest I've known to a human encyclopedia of all things accordion. He's been slaving on this book for as long as I've known him, and I'm very excited to see it finally coming into existence."

Jason Webley, songwriter, vagabond, cult leader, eater of artichokes

· ·

"A worthy redemption for an instrument that has always been far more beautiful and complicated than its reputation might have you believe."

Brooke Binkowski, accordionist and award-winning media fact-checker

· ·

"The most extensive research into accordion music across all genres that I know of. Triggs has painstakingly unearthed details but made it accessible to everyone. If you love music, check this out."

Alex Meixner, polka's ambassador for the new millennium

· ·

"I give it five out of five bellows-shakes."

Renée de la Prade, producer, Accordion Babes Pin-Up calendar

· ·

ACCORDION REVOLUTION

BRUCE TRIGGS

ACCORDION REVOLUTION

A People's History of the Accordion
in North America from the
Industrial Revolution to Rock 'n' Roll

Demian & Sons
PUBLICATIONS

Copyright © 2019 by Bruce Triggs

All rights reserved. No part of this book may be reproduced, stored in a retrieval system or transmitted, in any form or by any means, without the prior written consent of the publisher or a licence from The Canadian Copyright Licensing Agency (Access Copyright). For a copyright licence, visit www.accesscopyright.ca or call toll free to 1-800-893-5777.

ISBN 978-1-9990677-0-0 (paperback)
ISBN 978-1-9990677-1-7 (ebook)

Every reasonable effort has been made to contact the copyright holders for work reproduced in this book.

Demian & Sons Publications

Produced by Page Two
www.pagetwo.com

Cover design by Peter Cocking
Cover illustration by Michelle Clement
Interior design by Taysia Louie

www.accordionrevolution.com

Dedicated to Alice Hall, Leon Sash, Viola Turpeinen,
Julie Gardner, and all the heroes of
the Accordion Revolution.
And to my family and accordion friends
who made this project possible.

Contents

ABOUT THIS BOOK'S TWO VERSIONS: Working on this project I struggled with two contradictory goals: I wanted to create an enjoyable, readable book for music fans, whether accordionists or not. But I also hoped to include detailed annotations to inspire future research. The idea of academic and popular versions of the book, sharing the same main text, sprang from this conflict. The only difference between the twin versions is the hundreds of pages of footnotes and the extended bibliography included in the annotated version.

Information on the fully annotated/referenced version of *Accordion Revolution* is available at **www.accordionrevolution.com.**

Preface: Reopening the Accordion Case

THERE IS AN accordion-shaped hole in the history of popular music. This book charts the rise and fall of this missing squeezebox from its birth in the Industrial Revolution until its popular explosion and dramatic collapse in the mid–twentieth century. As the instrument returns from obscurity today, it's time to reclaim this history.

Accordions arrived in North America in the arms of immigrants, and intermixed with just about every culture on the continent. Popular music embraced them from the beginning. Accordionists stepped onstage in some of the first minstrel shows and continued all the way to the opening days of rock 'n' roll. They appeared in big band orchestras in the 1940s and in ethnic bands across the Midwest. They backed Hollywood movies and broadcast weekly on the *Grand Ole Opry*. No genre was secure from the squeezebox invasion.

Like the electronic and digital revolutions to come, the accordion changed the culture of music. Less experienced players could and did drown out masters of other instruments who couldn't compete with the mass-produced newcomer. Accordions were everywhere, and marginalized populations often led their expansion. Women, African Americans, European immigrants, Mexican Americans, and working-class people of all ethnicities embraced the instrument. Their joys, struggles, and refusal to be silenced are at the core of the accordion's story.

A few well-known names appear in this book, but the vast majority of the artists who spurred the accordion's popularity are unknown today. Instead you'll find new and unfamiliar tales from genres you may already love. We also delve into the origins of once-obscure styles like zydeco and Irish traditional music that have gained international attention and helped restore the accordion's reputation with modern listeners.

The squeezebox reached people in all corners of the continent, from Inuit musicians in Canada's Arctic to West Coast session players recording TV commercials. In Annie Proulx's 1996 novel *Accordion Crimes*, a little green accordion travels through a hundred years of comical, poignant, and occasionally brutal history. Many people play it as it passes through one immigrant culture after another. Accordions enriched North America, and reflect the dramatic changes over the last century and a half that shaped music, people, and the world.

The book is arranged roughly chronologically, with sections divided by culture and genre:

Part One · The Dawn of the Accordion Revolution, describes how the instrument was born and raised until it was old enough to head out on its own. It also introduces the absurd variety of instruments within the accordion family.

Part Two · The Golden Age, recalls the half-century when accordionists were stars rather than punchlines—when they commanded stages, screens, and hit records, and when millions of people welcomed them into their homes.

Part Three · Roots Music: An Outsiders' Canon, delves into genres that stayed true to the accordion while the mainstream forgot it. It reveals why zydeco, Irish music, Jewish klezmer, and Texas/Mexican border accordions have become key to the instrument's revival of popularity.

Part Four · American Wheeze: An Alternative Pre-history of Rock, explores the accordion's role in the origins of what became rock 'n' roll. Here you'll find African American "windjammers," legions of little-known country music accordionists, and an only slightly tongue-in-cheek exposé of the folk revival's attempts to suppress the squeezebox in the mid-1960s.

Part Five · The Accordion Exile in the Age of Rock. The final section relates the dramatic story of the accordion's downfall. We examine the cascade of causes that united to banish the instrument from the spotlight for four decades. Finally, we briefly introduce the accordion revival of the late twentieth and early twenty-first centuries, starting in lively ethnic music communities (see Part Three), followed by more and more eruptions into popular music.

After its long dormancy, it is a fascinating time for the accordion in North America. In the 1980s, the instrument began a slow, steady re-insinuation and has stealthily penetrated the worlds of folk, rock, electronica, and even hip-hop. Young singer-songwriters are creating new accordion music based on pop and punk models. Skilled ethnic, classical, and jazz players are using the instrument to display their chops. Accordion music is more diverse than at any time in its history. Our goal is to share the backstory of this vibrant renaissance.

This book shrank as it grew. It started as a short "beginners' guide" to historic and modern accordionists around the world. As the manuscript expanded to more than seven hundred pages, the focus had to narrow to North America. Material for a volume on modern artists split off and may follow.

Due to time constraints and my own limitations, many significant artists and areas of the accordion world didn't find their way into these pages. Experts especially may be unsatisfied with the depths I've dedicated to particular styles or regions. I even belatedly realized I'd overlooked several entire accordion genres and cultures within the bounds of North America.

For example, the Basque *trikitixa* button accordion reached rural areas of the American West (where it emerged in Bernardo Atxaga's 2003 novel *The Accordionist's Son*). An entire other book needs to be written on accordion music from the Caribbean. *Merengue típico*, with its blazing button accordion, has a strong presence in the Dominican communities of the eastern U.S. and Canada. Puerto Rico's *plena* tradition similarly arrived in cities like New York, and joined the instrument's rich heritage. I humbly apologize for neglecting these and other areas.

☞ PART ONE ☜

THE DAWN

 *OF THE*

ACCORDION

REVOLUTION

THE STORY OF the accordion begins amidst some of the most drastic cultural transformations in history. Colonial empires and industrialization were spreading, slavery was officially ending, wars and famine swept through Europe and elsewhere. These and unprecedented intercontinental migration were the backdrop as musicians from all parts of the world stumbled upon this new instrument.

1

The Accordion
Conquers the World

THE ACCORDION EMERGED at the height of Europe's Industrial Revolution and quickly traveled across the planet. Everywhere the instrument came ashore, squeezeboxes transformed, trampled, and sometimes totally obliterated existing music. Folk cultures faced a musical virus with no immunity, and the accordion was generally unstoppable. As factories in Europe churned out instruments, they followed the colonizing empires everywhere, from the Arctic poles to Zanzibar off the coast of East Africa. Any place early steamships went, sailors dragged along the cheap, sturdy accordion, and its cousin, the concertina.

As the instrument developed and changed over time, the kinds of accordions that gained regional popularity left a chronological map of their arrival in each new culture. They changed names at every border while developing radically different shapes and sounds. Buttons were rearranged or transformed into piano keys as different instruments became associated with each region's styles.

By the early twentieth century, the most famous Irish accordion records were being made by a German American in New York City. Louisiana's Black Creole accordionists mixed with Cajun fiddlers to create separate but similar musical first-cousins. All across the U.S., a heady mix of recent European immigrants joined longtime Hispanic residents and Native peoples to share stories and music that enriched distinct traditions and created hybrids (often bridged by the ever-mutating polka and other European dance music).

Over and over, the accordion entered the musical arena through ethnic styles from various ends of the earth to compete with instruments like fiddles or bagpipes. It secured a place because it could be heard over audiences' cheering and dancers' stomping feet. It may not have made the world a better place, but the accordion, manifesting the industrial age, certainly made it a noisier one.

In North America, accordions eventually reached the height of their popularity in the 1950s. They were promoted as modern and even futuristic. Compared to family pianos they were portable, relatively cheap, and as stylish as the latest chrome-accented automobile. By the 1960s, the instrument's glory days were numbered, but how had they reached their height?

The fiddle was the most common instrument before the Civil War and was part of many traditions in the colonies and the new republic. Horns and brass bands rose after the Civil War, but pianos were the king of home instruments as people began to purchase the first "pop songs" as sheet music. By the 1920s, mail-order instruments like guitars began to dominate many folk traditions.

Things change, though, and vast numbers of outdated parlor pianos were eventually discarded. By the 1920s, record players were among the most significant "musical instruments" in peoples' homes. Live music began to wilt before the power of the household radio and the cheap jukebox. The home piano market crashed, but they provided cheap instruments to support blues, boogie-woogie, and jazz.

Though blues and jazz players largely rejected the accordion, it became incredibly popular in mainstream culture. One result today is that a glut of used accordions from the boom times of the '50s and '60s is fueling the rebirth of the instrument we're seeing today. What happens when the pool of old accordions are used up remains a topic of nervous debate amongst aficionados.

Uncovering the accordion's history is uniquely challenging, because for several decades most writers ignored it. Research into folk, blues, and rock music blossomed from the 1960s to the '80s, just as the accordion arrived at its lowest point of cultural cachet. One concrete result was that most historical accordionists died without being investigated.

The Pirate Accordion Anachronism

The notorious pirate concertina. *Art by Jeremy Wakefield for 16 Horsepower.*
Thanks, Sunja Park.

IT'S OFTEN ASSUMED that the smaller concertina must be an earlier design than its larger cousin, the accordion. "What about those little accordions pirates play?" In fact, concertinas and accordions are contemporaries and—shockingly—pirates never played either one.

The golden age of piracy ended in 1726 when captain William Fly was hanged in Boston Harbor after a violent three-year career. But the accordion didn't emerge in Europe until one hundred years later. Even the most long-lived pirate lass had no concertina lament at her funeral.

It wasn't until a century after pirates like Blackbeard and Edward Low made their names notorious that sailors had a chance to play concertinas and accordions. By the time Victorian writers such as Robert Louis Stevenson began mythologizing piracy in books like *Treasure Island* (1883), modern navies had banished pirates into the realm of literature.

In truth, pirates and other sailors of the seventeenth and eighteenth centuries probably played fiddles. Musicians were even mandated on naval vessels where crews were ordered to dance "The Sailor's Hornpipe." Exercise was believed to prevent scurvy, so musicians were at times listed as members of the medical sick bay. It wasn't until years later, in the mid-1800s, that cheap Anglo-German concertinas became a seafarer's commonplace. By then, steam was replacing sails, scurvy was treated with limes, and the squeezebox was for entertainment, rather than piracy.

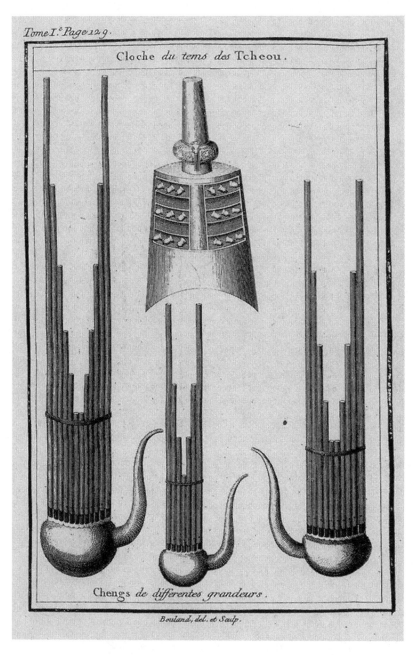

1780 French image of various sheng. *Courtesy of Pat Missin.*

We're missing the accordion's share of the tens of thousands of books that discuss Miles Davis, U2, or John Lennon's intent in "I Am the Walrus." Books on genres like western swing—where a quarter of the bands had accordionists—might name only a few players or even imply that accordions were not typical instruments. It is a frustrating challenge to research topics no one has worked on in fifty years. And it's deeply saddening that so much has been lost through neglect. At the same time, uncovering new characters and stories amidst otherwise well-trodden popular music is thrilling. The accordion offers this balance of joy and loss with every new artist and era.

The Accordion's Ancient Roots

The earliest relatives of the accordion appeared in Asia's Bronze Age. The most basic Asian free-reeds looked like precursors to Western jaw harps. These simplest free-reeds were made from natural materials like wood, palm, or bamboo, and eventually copper and bronze. When mouth harps like this are played—as they still are today in Southeast Asia—a plucked reed is amplified when air is blown through it. If the reed has close tolerances, blowing through it can sound a note with no plucking necessary. These are the seeds of all later accordions.

Resonating chambers of gourd or bamboo were added by early instrument makers, along with fingering holes to adjust the reed's pitch. Finally, reeds were tuned to individual pitches to improve the range and strength of the notes. Multiple reed instruments like the Chinese sheng—said to have been invented three thousand years ago when the emperor wanted to hear the sound of the mythical phoenix—or the Loatian khene eventually bore fruit in Europe.

Caravans like those described in the tales of Marco Polo carried Asian free-reed instruments to Europe, where they began to appear in illustrations during the 1600s. According to researcher Pat Missin, by the mid-1700s a Bavarian named Johann Wilde was performing on the sheng in St. Petersburg, Russia. At the same time a French Jesuit returned from China with detailed descriptions about how instruments like the sheng worked. Back in St. Petersburg, in 1780 Christian Gottlieb Kratzenstein won a prize for his "speaking machine." It was the first known original European free-reed, designed to imitate the human voice using unusual semi-circular reeds.

European wind instruments had already been using bellows to sound pipe organs, bagpipes, and smaller "portative" organs. The basic ingredients for the accordion and its relatives were thus present in Europe by the late 1700s. The non-musical ingredients that led to their dramatic success were at the same time quite literally picking up steam.

The Industrial Revolution

Aside from a few handmade metal parts, early accordions were made of wood and paper, which had been available to European craftspeople for centuries. Mass production of accordions, however, required new technology to make wire and screws. Most pressing was the need for sheet metal to produce accordion reeds and reed plates.

Very early reeds were individually hammered from silver or brass wire. Brass and steel reeds were later cut and tempered in small quantities using processes perfected for watch springs. Without technological advances, accordions would have remained an exotic luxury for the wealthy.

As early as 1700, crude metal sheets were made using flatting mills with water-powered hammers weighing as much as eight hundred pounds. Precisely gauged sheet metal would require the development of precision rollers. Making rollers in turn involved the casting of gigantic lathes. By 1829, mines and smelters, lathes, rollers and mills were all in place, and on cue the age of the accordion began.

In the 1780s, James Watt's steam engine began powering his partner Matthew Boulton's Birmingham factory and producing brass sheets for making toys. As materials became available, manufacturers began developing new musical instruments. Screws, fasteners, metal rods, levers, springs, and the reeds without which the instruments were silent: what began as toys inspired more advanced cousins that in the next half-century spread throughout the world.

Even today the accordion remains a hybrid of hand craftsmanship and industrial manufacturing. The most expensive handmade accordions use some pre-manufactured parts. At the same time, accordion factories never fully mechanized. Even as models grew more complicated, with hundreds of machined components, the factory-made reeds at the heart of the instruments were still finished by hand and tuned by ear.

SINGLE OCTAVE ÆOLIAN.

No. 9. THE TRUMPET ÆOLIAN.

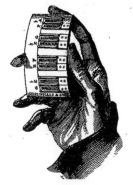

No.10. THE TWO-OCTAVE CHROMATIC ÆOLIAN.

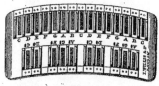

Scale ascending.

No. 11. THE PANDEAN ÆOLIAN.

No. 12. THREE-CHORD PANDEAN ÆOLIAN.

No. 13. CHROMATIC PANDEAN ÆOLIAN.

BACK.

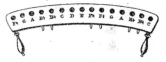

No. 14. EIGHT-CHORD PANDEAN ÆOLIAN.

FRONT.

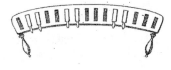

German Æolian Tutor, published in 1830. *Courtesy of Pat Missin.*

The Instrument Is Born

The accordion is one of the few instruments with a verifiable birth certificate—though one with its share of controversy. The first patent for something called an "accordion" was filed on May 6, 1829, by Cyrill Demian and his sons in Vienna, the center of European music at the time. Instruments similar to Demian's, with metal reeds, bellows, and keys or buttons, had been developed by a number of inventors in the second decade of the 1800s. By 1822, Christian Friedrich Ludwig Buschmann had invented his *Handaeoline/Handharmonika* (hand-harmonica) for use in tuning organs. It had bellows, but didn't play groups of notes together. Demian's innovation was to add chords and promote his instrument for use by amateurs.

Also in 1829, the British physicist Charles Wheatstone patented his symphonium, a hand-held metal box with buttons that triggered reeds when blown into. His patent includes a diagram of a bellows-driven version that presaged his English concertina, though he didn't get around to patenting that until 1844.

The accordion's mouth-blown cousins were progressing at the same time. Wheatstone had seen the German *Mundharmonika* mouthorgan and the simple æolina, which were the first commercially successful European free-reed instruments. These led directly to what we would recognize as the common pocket harmonica and an array of more elaborate designs.

As an aside, 1829 also saw an American, William Austin Burt, patent his "typographer" typewriter, which mechanized writing the way accordions mechanized music. Typewriters and accordions required similarly sophisticated machined parts enabled by the same engineering advances. As with the accordion, in a barrage of innovation, it is estimated the typewriter was "invented" more than fifty times by different people.

Accordion-related instruments developed quickly in Russia, Austria, Germany, France, England, and later Italy. There were constant innovations in workshops turning out a flurry of different designs. Given people's unprecedented mobility, immigrants then took the various concertinas, accordions, bandoneons, and others, and spread them around the world.

Accordions eventually arrived up and down the eastern coast of the Americas and along trade routes around the African continent toward Asia. By the 1840s they had reached missions in Canada and minstrel stages in the eastern U.S. The future of music had arrived in North America.

James Bazin: Yankee Tinkerer

THE FIRST KNOWN accordion-builder in North America was Yankee inventor James Bazin. His father immigrated from France where he'd been a watchmaker. During the rise of free-reed development predating Demian's accordion, the young Bazin began making pitch pipes and harmonicas. In 1824 he developed a horn-shaped mouth organ controlled by a large compass-like dial over a range of three chromatic octaves. Suffering from a cough in 1827, he added bellows to this unique instrument. Fifty years later he was still playing his Jules Verne-ian "reed trumpet" in his local church choir.

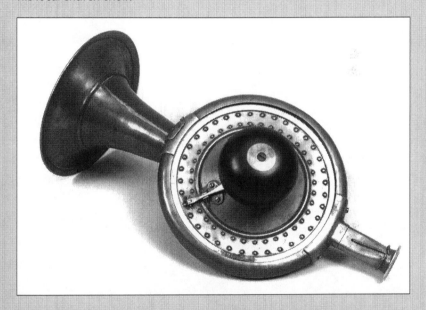

Bazin's reed trumpet, 1824. *From the collection of the Canton Historical Society, photo by Stephen Korbet, courtesy of Darcy Kuronen.*

After seeing early French and German instruments, by 1835 Bazin was designing and building accordions and selling them around Boston. Unfortunately, none of his innovative instruments were commercially successful or influential going forward, leaving him as little more than a footnote in a much larger story.

2

The Accordion's
Family Tree

HE ACCORDION'S MANY relatives include concertinas, pump organs, and mouth-blown harmonicas. They are all classified as "free-reed aerophones." In these instruments, air flows past reeds, which swing freely in frames to produce sound. This differs from saxophones or bassoons, where reeds vibrate against another surface.

The diversity of accordion-like instruments can seem either confusing or chaotically delightful. A virtuoso on one accordion may be unable to play the simplest tune on another. Similar diversity exist in other instrument families as well: guitar formats and fingering patterns may be roughly similar, but within the larger string family it's unlikely a banjo player could immediately play concert harp.

The lines between different squeezeboxes overlap but there are basically three or four major varieties in North America: piano accordions and diatonic button accordions are by far the most common. (It's rare to see European-style chromatic button accordions, but they're out there.) In folk circles you may find compact hexagonal concertinas, and some regional polka bands play the larger square-shaped Chemnitzer concertina. (If you're lucky enough to stumble on a tango orchestra you might also spot the Chemnitzer's lookalike cousin, the bandoneon.)

Free-Reed Relatives

Once European instrument makers got hold of the idea, they couldn't help themselves and quickly developed a whole family of instruments. The harmonica became the most common free-reed in the world after its invention in the 1800s. More complicated mouth-blown instruments included hand-held melodica keyboards, whose earliest ancestors included the psallmelodikon, which resembled a steam-punk oboe. Prior to harmonicas were simpler instruments like the æolina, a bare set of reeds held flat on an ivory plate. To make them easier to play, harmonica manufacturers added protective covers and rearranged the æolina's reeds into the familiar diatonic "in/out" blowing pattern. German companies like Hohner hired out-of-work clockmakers and sold millions of harmonicas by the turn of the century.

Even before they were miniaturized into harmonicas and accordions, harmonium pump organs were the original European free-reeds, with prototypes dating to the 1700s. Basically stationary keyboards with bellows pumped either by hands or feet, large models were marketed to churches that couldn't afford pipe organs. In the 1800s, ornate pump organs dominated upper-middle-class parlors. Chaplains later used collapsible pump organs on the front lines during both world wars. As the instruments spread around the world, Indian musicians so passionately embraced hand-pumped harmoniums that they are identified almost exclusively with South Asian music today.

Perhaps the most extraordinary historic free-reed was the melophone, invented in the 1830s using the same technology as early pump organs. The melophone's creators went beyond the exterior decorations of other early free-reeds and built the whole instrument into what looks very much like a small cello. It had a handle on the bottom, which pumped bellows hidden inside. The neck was encrusted with buttons where the fingerboard would be—one report said it was fairly easy for string players to pick up. A removable lid covered a veritable circuit board of wires and rods connected to mechanical valves to let air reach reeds mounted inside. The Paris Philharmonic's Museum of Music has several melophones, as well as a similar instrument called the cecilium. Shaped like a large lute, it was pumped by swinging a lever back and forth across the front as if you were bowing a string instrument.

Top row, L to R: Vaudeville-style Soprani piano accordion, ca. 1930s; simple German Meinel & Herold piano model, ca. 1920s; Tiger Combo 'Cordion, 1960s. Center: French flutina, mid-1800s. Bottom: Alfred & Arnold German Chemnitzer concertina, ca. 1910–30; Wheatstone English Concertina (#19489), 1876; mass-produced German Hohner button box, ca. 1915–20. *Photo by Laurel Dykstra; instruments from the author's collection; flutina courtesy of John Krieger; Tiger courtesy of Tempo Trend Music.*

Early French "Flutina" Accordions

Demian's 1829 patent finally named an instrument the "accordion" because it played five-note chords rather than individual notes. This was a fine innovation for simple accompaniment, but within a few years improved versions emerged (as his patent predicted they might) for playing single-line melodies along with chords. French instrument makers dominated the early market with what became known in the U.K. as "flutinas," after a particular brand that had a muted sound like a flute. These tall, narrow, and often ornately decorated instruments were the first accordions to gain success in the United States and Canada and can often be seen in daguerreotypes from the 1800s.

The French-style accordions were used in North America both for parlor entertainment and as curiosities on the early public stage. They

Alfred Mirek:
The Accordion Revolution in Russia

NOT MANY MUSIC historians can put on their curriculum vitae that they went to prison for their discipline. But researcher Alfred Mirek, founder of Moscow's Accordion Museum and author of the comprehensive *Book of Free-Reed Instruments: Scientific and Historical Commentaries on the Development and Classification Schemes of the Major Classes of Free-Reed Instruments*, is also known for his *Tiuremnyi Rekviem: Prison Requiem, Notes of an Inmate*.

Mirek was sent to prison in 1984 by Soviet prosecutors based on anonymous accusations. The fact that he had been internationally recognized by UNESCO in 1977 and was working on a PhD did not save him. His research and historical collection of 140 accordions (stored in his three-room apartment) were officially deemed worthless. Considering the popularity of the accordion in Russia, it seems particularly shocking that such a specialist was persecuted.

Thankfully, easier times came for accordion scholars, and his collection is now accessible as an offshoot of Moscow's State Historical Museum. They have hundreds of accordions and related music and photos. Mirek describes the history of the accordion with unprecedented detail, including a visual family tree of more than two hundred ancestors and varieties of free-reed instruments worldwide. Interestingly, his work supports the theory that the accordion had roots in Russia before the rest of Europe, beginning in St. Petersburg in the 1780s, a good fifty years before Cyrill Demian patented his instrument in Austria.

There are a number of historic accordion collections worth visiting around the world. The most impressive in North America is Helmi Strahl Harrington's A World of Accordions Museum in Superior, Wisconsin. Luckily, no one has been imprisoned there for preserving accordion history.

were portable, increasingly affordable, and not least they consistently played in tune. Flutinas were, however, relatively quiet and fragile compared to later, cheaper button boxes. More robust German designs advanced in the 1870s when the French accordion industry disappeared in the aftermath of the disastrous Franco-Prussian War. The newly united and rapidly industrializing Germany quickly swept the flutina from history.

Concertinas

Instruments we generalize as accordions also include the concertina family. Most concertinas are smaller, often hexagon-shaped squeeze-boxes that developed at the same time as accordions (ca. 1830-60). There were three somewhat common concertinas, the Anglo-German, the English, and larger Chemnitzer-types.

Concertinas play individual notes for each button, rather than the chords that gave the accordion its name. Anglo-German and English concertinas are smaller than accordions and require no shoulder straps. Concertina players' hands also face each other in playing position, in contrast to the keys of an accordion, which face the audience. The internal construction of most concertinas is also radically different from accordions, though some later designs incorporated elements like removable reed blocks.

Because of their high quality and durable construction, a remarkable number of concertinas are in regular use today that are more than a century old. If you are lucky enough to find a playable British-built concertina in your grandmother's closet or sea chest, it might be worth more than a thousand dollars. Comparably old accordions are much less frequently seen in working order and as a result are seldom worth half as much as their smaller, in-demand cousins.

English Concertina

Inventor Charles Wheatstone debuted the "English" concertina in about 1833, and was the first to give the instrument its distinctive hexagonal shape. His instrument played the same notes pushing and pulling, with a complete chromatic scale that was capable of playing complicated melody lines from written scores. Wheatstone's instrument was warmly received in upper-middle-class homes, salons, and stages until the rise of more affordable Anglo-German versions.

Gentlemen and ladies played classical music on Wheatstone's concertinas at a time when other squeezeboxes were still considered toys. The English concertina's chromatic layout was well ahead of other accordions of the time and its facility with single-note melody suited it to the counterpoint of chamber music. Artists like Giulio Regondi began as a child prodigy on the guitar, but took up the concertina to great acclaim.

Marie Lachenal was one of several early female concertina virtuosos. In the 1860s she performed solo, with her two younger sisters, and sometimes in a quintet of treble, tenor, and baritone concertinas. She stepped away from the stage in order to raise eight children, then returned in the 1880s. Lachenal proceeded to teach and perform for twenty more years. Her name remains familiar amongst concertinists because Marie's father, Louis, manufactured some of the finest instruments ever built.

Though highly regarded by many at the time, within a few decades the glow of the classical concertists faded as cheaper "Anglo" concertinas (confusingly developed in Germany, see below) grew popular with the working-class.

☞ Charles Wheatstone: Victorian Inventor

ENGLISHMAN CHARLES WHEATSTONE invented the concertina and significantly impacted modern life. Besides musical endeavors, in the 1840s he helped originate the telegraph (first used to prevent railway collisions). His "Wheatstone bridge" circuit tester is still a standard among electrical engineers. In his spare time Wheatstone experimented with optics, measured the speed of light, and invented the first 3-D glasses along with a "pseudoscope" that made objects appear to be inside-out. So if you use electricity, your ears, or your eyes today, you might give a tip to the next concertina player you encounter.

Anglo-German Concertina

From the Napoleonic Wars in the early 1800s to the Franco-Prussian War of 1870, dozens of German states were struggling to unite as a nation, and then after 1850, to industrialize. While Wheatstone's concertina premiered in England, a German designer in the city of Chemnitz (in Saxony, southeastern Germany) named Carl Friedrich Uhlig came up with a small square-shaped instrument that had a simple diatonic, push-pull scale. It required half as many reeds as Wheatstone's and cost ten to twenty times less than the English instrument. Marketed as "konzertinas," "concertinas," or more confusingly, "accordeons," they rapidly grew in popularity, forcing Wheatstone to distinguish his higher-quality instruments as "English concertinas."

By 1850, these affordable German instruments were available in England. British makers combined the accessible German button system with the English hexagon shape, and created "Anglo-German" or just "Anglo" concertinas. Distinct concertina traditions developed in Scotland, Ireland, Australia, and South Africa. In North America they were common from 1850 until 1900. Most concertinas in use around the world today are descendants of this diatonic (push-pull) "Anglo" system.

Chemnitzer Concertina

As the hexagonal Anglo concertina spread throughout the British Empire, the humble square-ended version continued to develop back in Germany. Accordions would eventually supplant almost all continental concertinas, but two German varieties became the icons of immigrant styles in South America and parts of Wisconsin.

The first German concertinas were developed in Chemnitz. The city gives its name to the large Chemnitzer concertina. Eschewing the multi-sided design of English-influenced instruments, the Chemnitzer concertina remained steadfastly box-shaped. It grew about five times as large as early German prototypes, requiring most players to sit resting it on their knees. German designers expanded its simple diatonic keyboard by adding dozens of buttons, from a limited ten or twenty notes to over a hundred, enabling a sweeping chromatic range. Buttons were arranged such that chords could easily be played, but no separate chord buttons were used. Multiple reeds for each note made them loud enough for one of their primary markets: churches that could not afford organs.

Words to Squeeze By:
Diatonic/Chromatic, Bisonoric/Unisonoric

A BIT OF mechanics, a few terms, and a touch of music theory will help you identify most accordions. (Feel free to skip this part if it is too boring.)

Bisonoric/Unisonoric: Accordions use paired reeds, one when the bellows press in, and one when they open out. Most accordions with buttons on the right-hand side (rather than piano keyboards) play one note going in and a different one on the way out. This division of labor is called *bisonoric* (two sounds). A small ten-button accordion can thus play up to twenty notes. The in/out format began as a space-saver on early accordions, but influences musical technique all over the world as the staccato sound of the rapidly shifting bellows drives the rhythm of Irish, Cajun, and Texas/Mexican border music.

Piano accordions, in contrast, play the same note as the bellows open and close. This is called *unisonoric* (one sound) and facilitates smoother melodic playing. English concertinas and chromatic button accordions (common in Europe) are also unisonoric.

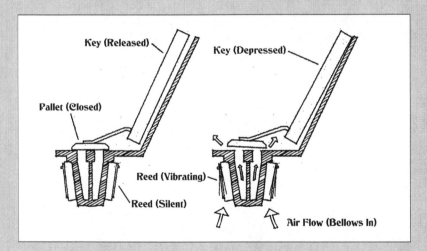

Accordion button mechanism. *Design by Lindsay Broadwell and Neczor, licensed under CC BY-SA 3.0.*

Chromatic/Diatonic: Almost all accordions are tuned to play Western music. Some, though, cannot play all the notes that are on an instrument like a piano. Due to the limited number of buttons on early machines, makers had to decide which tones to include. The results are chromatic or diatonic instruments.

Chromatic is Greek for "color," as in, "all the colors in the musical rainbow." In North America, what are known as chromatic accordions have all the tones in a Western octave arranged in logical order. On a piano keyboard this includes seven white keys and five black ones.

The term *diatonic* is tricky: it refers to the seven simple "do, re, mi" notes of a Western scale. Diatonic accordions have buttons arranged to make it very easy to play pre-set major scales by simply leaving out unneeded notes. (When playing a C scale on a piano the major scale shows up as "the white keys." For a C-tuned accordion the notes of the piano's black keys are left out.) This becomes limiting when musicians want to play outside these basic scales. The solution for accordions was to add additional "accidental" (black key) buttons and then more rows of buttons laid out in different keys.

Confusion arises in North America because "diatonic accordion" is commonly used to refer to all bisonoric (in/out) accordions even though many of these designs have enough buttons to play beyond the limited diatonic scales. Really, none of this matters if you're just listening to the music, it simply means each instrument challenges players in different ways.

The Chemnitzer concertina made its way across the Atlantic in the hands of Germans and Czechs when they immigrated to the Midwestern United States. They became a mainstay in some polka styles, exemplified most famously by Hans "Whoopee" John Wilfahrt and Walter "Li'l Wally" Jagiello. North American manufacturers developed ornate decorative inlays and flashy colors not seen on any other concertina. Today it remains linked to the Czech polka community of Wisconsin and the Upper Midwest. Interestingly, this relatively obscure ethnic instrument surfaced in the twenty-first-century's accordion revival on the knees of rock musicians like David Eugene Edwards in his powerful bands 16 Horsepower and Wovenhand.

Bandoneon

The most well-known box-ended German concertina is the bandoneon, named after an 1840s instrument distributor, Heinrich Band. The bandoneon was almost forgotten in North America outside of an occasional tango orchestra until, in the late twentieth century, Argentine Astor Piazzolla brought global attention to the instrument with his nuevo tango revival. Remarkably challenging to play (Piazzolla called it "diabolical"), it remains much rarer in North America than the many varieties of button and piano accordions. Besides various arcane button layouts, the main difference between a Chemnitzer concertina and a bandoneon is the deep divide between tango and polka style: Tango musicians do not play cheerful multi-colored instruments covered in rhinestones, and most polkas don't have titles like "Knife Fight."

Accordions

Piano and organ builders more or less settled on a standard keyboard four centuries ago at around the year 1600. Guitar makers sorted out a fretboard in the early 1700s. But even after two hundred years, accordion designers still haven't decided how we should play their instrument. This didn't hinder its global spread—it may have even helped. Like modern consumers of electronics, musicians lined up to pay for each new innovation.

While concertinas developed in several directions over the years, accordions splintered into more than two hundred different varieties.

FACING *Woman Holding an Accordion,* tintype, late 1860s. *Metropolitan Museum of Art.*

During the next century, dozens of styles were played in North America alone. Each ethnic group had their preference, and new innovations were rapidly added from Europe. Less than ten years after the premiere of Demian's Viennese instruments, high-class French models had arrived in North America. In the second half of the 1800s, German (and later Italian) instruments flooded North and South America and different forms dominated the Western accordion world for a hundred years.

The Industrial Revolution and Europe's age of imperialism broke down barriers of distance and trade. Early accordions spread as consumer goods to every corner of the globe. The instruments were adapted to local music in each place they landed, and local music changed to accommodate accordions. Fiddles, bagpipes, and earlier instruments were often marginalized by the indomitable intruder.

The two major accordion types are most visibly distinguished by the different combinations of buttons or keys that sound their notes and

☞ Stradella Bass: The Chords in "Accordion"

THE SYSTEM OF left-hand bass and chord buttons on most accordions developed over the course of a hundred years. It originated from Demian's original model, where a few buttons allowed air to flow through small clusters of reeds, making chords to accompany singing.

What came to be known as the "standard" or "Stradella" system (named after an Italian village that rivaled the accordion manufacturing hub of Castelfidardo) grew to include individual bass notes and major, minor, seventh, and diminished chords. Arranged in sequence based on the circle of fifths, this allowed most players to quickly learn to accompany basic tunes. For instance, the buttons for simple waltzes, polkas, and "Louie, Louie" are right next to each other. In the hands of a gifted player, the standard 120-button Stradella system can accommodate music of great complexity. An alternative to Stradella accordions developed in much less common "free bass" systems that played individual bass notes. Most often used for Western classical music, these never caught on with the general public.

chords. The broadest common forms are diatonic button boxes and chromatic instruments like piano accordions.

Diatonic Accordion

Diatonic button accordions of one kind or another became the most diverse and widespread instrument in the accordion family. More piano accordions probably exist in the world—millions were produced for the American market alone—but a huge assortment of button accordions took root in more of the world's musical cultures than any other squeezebox.

Early diatonic accordions were small. Instrument makers picked a likely starting pitch and filled up the available buttons in a row of bisonoric notes (one note in, another note out). Like Anglo concertinas, they were relatively simple to learn, and far easier than instruments like violins, which required training to produce even basic tones. These simple instruments that let people play music without years of training came to support diverse and often virtuosic styles.

Further chapters will show how one-row button accordions became the symbol of Cajun music in Louisiana. The same boxes (in different keys) were played by French Canadian musicians in Quebec and New Brunswick. Various two-row accordions are the norm in Irish, Irish American, and Canada's Newfoundland music.

In Texas and Northern Mexico they took up one- and two-row button accordions, then in the 1920s adopted three-row instruments, eventually developing a technique that transcended the diatonic limitations to achieve—in the hands of virtuosos like Esteban "Steve" Jordan—fully chromatic jazz harmonies.

Two- and three-row accordions were used by Black Creoles in Louisiana and Texas to mix French folk music with the blues to create zydeco. Zydeco players like Clifton Chenier then followed many North American ethnic musicians in adopting the piano accordion. All these varied instruments were played in drastically different ways for their different audiences.

Piano Accordion

By the end of the 1920s, a new kind of accordion held sway in North America. Experiments with adding piano keyboards to accordions began in the 1850s, but it didn't become common until the early twentieth century. Using a piano keyboard on the right hand had a number of advantages. Piano training, sheet music, and instruments were common by the turn of the 1900s and greatly expanded the customer base for accordions that used the standard keyboard. Customers dreaming of a full-size piano were more likely to choose an affordable piano accordion than a similarly priced button model.

For dealers, piano keyboards were a sensible response to the problem of immigrant musicians who played different instruments back home. Stocking different accordions for Italian, Jewish, German, Polish, Russian, Finnish, Swedish, French, Czech, and Basque accordionists tempted bankruptcy. By promoting the piano keyboard as modern and American, dealers united immigrants in one salesroom.

Both button and piano models benefited from technical advances that allowed register switches to extend the accordion's range. A forty-one-key piano accordion with low, middle, and high reed switches could have the respectable range of sixty piano keys. The various European chromatic button accordions with even wider ranges and other technical advantages fell rapidly from favor. The piano keyboard may not have been the best system objectively, but it clearly won out.

PART TWO

THE

GOLDEN

AGE

ETWEEN THE ADVENT of the variety stage and the age of television, the accordion became one of the most common musical instruments in North America. It's hard to imagine today, but in the 1920s accordion players were among the highest-paid entertainers in the country. Factories in Germany, Italy, and North America produced millions of these instruments. They were sold in catalogs and shops in even the smallest towns. The demand never stopped until the rise of rock 'n' roll.

U.S. audiences first encountered the accordion in the hands of nineteenth-century minstrels performing in blackface.

When attendance at minstrel shows dwindled in the 1870s, canny minstrels followed the money into vaudeville. And there, just before recordings, radio, and movies reshaped entertainment, the golden age of the accordion began.

The accordion's ascension brought together disparate groups unified by the desire for acceptance and success. European immigrants from Scandinavia, Italy, Germany, Ireland, and Eastern Europe folded their ethnic influences into vaudeville, Tin Pan Alley, and the long-running craze for dance bands. Classical enthusiasts added their voice to reform the plebeian reputation of the instrument. All these groups fed a growing accordion industry in North America. Manufacturers opened factories and workshops in San Francisco, Chicago, Seattle, New York, Vancouver, and Montreal to service a wide network of dealers, teachers, and schools. With chart-topping success by professional performers, the accordion had a successful multi-level, multi-angle marketing strategy that lasted for years.

3

Blackface Minstrelsy:
Roots in Racism

MINSTRELSY WAS BORN when Thomas Rice's 1828 "Jump Jim Crow" became one of America's first hit songs (and a lifelong meal ticket for Rice). The song launched a century and a half of blackface impersonators just as the accordion entered the world.

Dealers like Albany, New York's Obed Coleman advertised French accordions in 1837, and they became widely available, if still rather a luxury item. Some of the most influential early accordionists took to the American stage in blackface. Less than fifteen years after Demian's patent in Vienna, both Moody Stanwood and Charley White played French accordions as they helped invent the minstrel show while filling halls on both sides of the Atlantic.

By 1863, musician Charles Fox called blackface minstrels "our only original American institution." Along with early circuses and the seeds of Broadway and vaudeville, minstrels were the earliest "popular" musicians in the United States—the first original music that reached the majority of the American populace. Minstrels also helped birth Tin Pan Alley's sheet-music publishing empire (which was the seed of today's corporate music industry) and vaudeville's nationwide chains of variety theaters. Minstrelsy, founded two hundred years ago amidst the horrors of slavery, can thus make the disturbing claim of being America's most influential secular music.

The Blackface of Prejudice

Blackface minstrel shows, in which white performers dressed up as caricatures of black people, were first created by urban Northerners in Boston and New York in the pre–Civil War era. White men from the North, dressed as black men from the South, joked about slavery and denigrated free blacks. These blatant cartoon-like stereotypes inspire outrage today, but blackface was more than a disturbing historical novelty. Well into the twentieth century, minstrel radio performers Amos 'n' Andy were among the most popular entertainers in America. Finally removed from TV (after protests) in 1966, they encapsulated more than 140 years of racial stereotypes and dehumanizing propaganda.

After the Civil War, minstrels in blackface continued to play accordions and concertinas during racism's re-entrenchment following Reconstruction's retreat. Known as the nadir in African American history, the period from 1870–1940 saw a system of overt racism established and backed up by force. As often as once every three days, lynchings were committed to terrorize the black community. These political murders were sometimes celebrated as entertainment. Picnic lunches were eaten, concessions were sold, souvenir postcard photos were printed as crowds gathered to murder black people (and Latinos, Italians, and others). The distortions of blackface were part of this pervasive system of prejudice that allowed and encouraged decades of post-slavery violence.

Blackface caricature was however sometimes more complicated than it appears from a distance. Early minstrels were pretending to portray African Americans' lives at a time when Americans were concerned about issues of slavery and freedom but often had little contact with black culture. Prior to the Civil War and emancipation, minstrel performances ranged from at least mildly abolitionist to virulently pro-slavery. After emancipation, actual African Americans also performed in blackface as their entrée into the American entertainment industry. Minstrel stereotypes of wisecracking buffoons however limited black performers well into the twentieth century. Minstrel music, meanwhile, had become the bedrock on which later American popular music was built—influencing jazz, blues, country, show tunes, and pop across color lines.

Minstrel performers toured their pre-fabricated stereotypes to great acclaim from coast to coast and even internationally. Minstrel

Ethiopian Serenaders playbill (detail): 1845–49, Moody Stanwood, accordion.
American minstrel show collection, 1823–1947. MS Thr 556 (373). *Harvard Theatre
Collection, Houghton Library, Harvard University.*

accordionist C.C. Keene's tour of the Sandwich Islands (not yet known
as Hawaii) flopped in 1859 when the whaling season floundered. Minstrel tunes and styles reached port cities around the world where some
are remembered and played even today. American minstrels, for example, were surprisingly inspirational to South African audiences of various
races, as well as Irish traditional musicians.

American blacks in the North and South attended and presumably
enjoyed minstrel shows, though some recognized the danger that stereotypes represented for downtrodden people. In 1848, Frederick Douglass
unequivocally called minstrel performers "the filthy scum of white society, who have stolen from us the complexion denied to them by nature,
in which to make money, and pander to the corrupt taste of their white
fellow citizens."

Minstrel performances reinforced a racist system by acting out narratives of blacks as lazy, foolish, and sometimes violent, but mostly happy
and entertaining. It's not hard to see that minstrel-like stereotypes in
modern media continue to influence political opinion and reflect and
promote injustice. Minstrels' faces reflect our culture and the lasting
legacy of Jim Crow.

MELODEON.

Friday Evening, Sept. 10th

And Every Evening during the Week.

CHANGE OF PROGRAMME

Fifth Appearance of the Celebrated

ETHIOPIAN SERENADERS

Germon, Stanwood, Harrington, Pell, White & Howard

Since their return from EUROPE, where they had the distinguished honor of appearing before **Her Majesty the QUEEN, H. R. H. PRINCE ALBERT, the ROYAL FAMILY, the Nobility and Gentry of England.**

PROGRAMME.

PART I.

NEW QUICK STEP,	FULL BAND
SONG and CHORUS, "A Life by the Galley Fire,"	COMPANY.
SONG, "Dandy Broadway Swell,"	HARRINGTON
CHORUS, "The Darkies Bride," (from Bohemian Girl,)	COMPANY
SONG, "Lucy Neal,"	HARRINGTON
GLEE, "You'll see them on the Ohio,"	COMPANY.
SONG, "Lucy Long,"	WHITE.

PART II.

NEW POLKA,	FULL BAND
GLEE, "Merry is the Minstrels Life,'	COMPANY.
SONG, "Mary Blane," original music)	HARRINGTON
PHANTOM CHORUS, (from Somnambula)	COMPANY.
SONG, "Rosa Lee ; or, don't be foolish Joe,"	WHITE.
SONG, "Old Joe,"	PELL.
SONG, "Buffalo Gals,"	GERMON.

PART III.

GRAND MEDLEY OVERTURE,	FULL BAND
(Composed expressly for these Entertainments)	
SONG, "Going over the Mountains,"	GERMON.
DUET, "Get along home Yellow Gals,"	GERMON & WHITE
SONG, "Uncle Gabriel,"	HARRINGTON
DUET, [Accordion and Bones,]	STANWOOD & PELL
SONG, "Old Dan Tucker,"	WHITE.

FINALE.

The Celebrated Railroad Overture,   **Full Band,**

As originally performed by the Ethiopian Serenaders.

UNDER THE DIRECTION OF MR J. A. DUMBOLTON.

ADMISSION 25 CENTS.

Doors open at 7 1-2,   Concert to commence at 8 o'clock.

From the Daily Mail Leviathan Book and Job Office, Nos. 14 and 16 State Street—Boston

Blackface to Black Accordion

Among the less-damaging distortions that early white minstrel performers spread was the image of blacks with accordions. Minstrels promoted themselves as portraying authentic plantation life, but few blacks would have played the newly invented accordions prior to Northern minstrels' tours. At the time, the young instrument had been seen by very few Americans.

With the precedent of the minstrel shows, however, slave owners, who regularly assigned slaves to play music for their households, began to buy accordions and include them in the instruction of enslaved musicians. Eventually the accordion spread to whites and blacks nationwide. An African American accordion tradition developed in the South that has been almost forgotten today, but it survived, in parallel with the minstrel shows that presaged it, from before the end of slavery until the modern recording era.

As minstrels reached all parts of the country, affordable accordions followed. By the 1860s, one town in Germany was producing 214,500 accordions per year. By the time the minstrel shows proper were replaced by vaudeville and then radio and film, the accordion was firmly established in the United States, where it had spread into dozens of other ethnic and popular styles.

Minstrel Accordionists

Moody Stanwood: The First Pop Accordionist

Moody Stanwood was a concert musician, blackface minstrel, and probably the most important early accordionist in North America. He took up the curious new instrument in Boston in about 1838 and, in addition to formal concerts, accompanied giant moving dioramas that recreated historical spectacles like the volcanic eruption at Pompeii and Napoleon crossing the Alps. In 1840, he published one of the first American instruction books for the instrument, *The New and Complete Preceptor for the French Accordion.*

FACING Ethiopian Serenaders playbill: 1845–49, Moody Stanwood, accordion. *American minstrel show collection, 1823–1947.* MS *Thr 556 (373).* Harvard Theatre *Collection, Houghton Library, Harvard University.*

After seeing the earliest minstrel performers, in 1843 he joined the Boston Serenaders (later Ethiopian Serenaders) and toured widely in the U.S. and Europe. They played for U.S. President John Tyler and, with the help of the president's personal recommendation, for European aristocrats including the British royal family. Their English and Irish tours were notably promoted by the wealthy Duke of Cavendish, who was both a staunch abolitionist and, though a lover of music, mostly deaf.

Returning from Europe, the Serenaders' high-class minstrelsy had fallen from fashion, replaced by coarser, more energetic groups. The accordion became less central after Stanwood died of consumption in 1850 at age thirty. For years, his wife preserved his accordion, his memory, and the ring he received from Queen Victoria.

Stanwood and his flutina-style French instrument were featured on the cover of the group's 1843 songbook, *Boston Minstrels' Ethiopian Melodies*, as well as in posters and music books from their well-attended tours in 1845-46. These remain some of the earliest images of the accordion in North America.

Charley White: Most Useful and Popular Performer

In 1907, former minstrel Isaac Odell walked into the *New York Times* offices and recalled the minstrel performers of sixty years earlier: "Charley White was making a great hit playing an accordion in Thalia Hall on Grand Street. In those days accordions were the real attraction to the public."

Accordionist Charley White premiered his White's Serenaders in New York in 1846. His minstrel career then extended for more than forty years as a performer, theater owner, and promoter of "the minstrel art." A skillful businessman, he was deemed "one of the most useful and popular performers that ever put on burnt cork." White's several theaters in New York included one named the Melodeon, where the shows were decidedly "popular" with admissions starting at only 6¼ cents. During the final decades of his life, White regularly played the role of Uncle Tom, an elderly black caricature played by an elderly white man. He died in 1891.

Elias Howe: Minstrel Publisher

Following Stanwood and others' lead, music-publishing pioneer Elias Howe (who later assembled the traditional music "bible" *Howe's 1,000*

Jigs and Reels) produced his own *Complete Preceptor for the Accordeon* in 1843, and it reportedly sold 100,000 copies. With an ear to the latest trend, Howe released minstrel-themed banjo tutors and songbooks and, in 1850, *The Complete Ethiopian Accordeon Instructor* published under a minstrel pseudonym "Gumbo Chaff." All these innovative accordionists were laying the groundwork for the American music industry that survives to this day.

Carte de visite of the American melophonist John B. Donniker (blackface minstrel, ca. 1850s–60s). The melophone was a French free-reed with bellows pumped by a handle on the bottom. Held like a guitar, players fingered buttons arranged like a stringed-instrument's frets on the neck. *From the collection of Stephen Chambers.*

The Ghost Accordion
of Daniel Dunglas Home

Daniel Dunglas Home with his accordion apparatus. *Courtesy of the Internet Archive and the U.S. Library of Congress.*

OUTSIDE THE REGULAR history of the stage are stories of more unusual performers. In England and the U.S. during the 1870s, Daniel Home was a clairvoyant and member of the spiritualist movement, famous for knocking on tables and speaking with the dead. Arthur Conan Doyle supported Home, while Harry Houdini singled him out as a fraud, with a glancing reference to what Houdini referred to as Home's "accordion trick."

Home's supernatural performance included the playing of a phantom squeezebox. With one hand he held a small accordion in a basket under a table and it would play simple tunes (with the help of the spirits). There are no reports of what happened if the ghosts he was commissioned to contact did not play accordion.

It's not known exactly how Home (or the ghosts) played the instrument under the table. A hidden supporter may have played another accordion, or Home may have had a very small harmonica in his mouth to assist the ghosts. One can only hope that further investigation may lead to a timely revival of this extraordinary act.

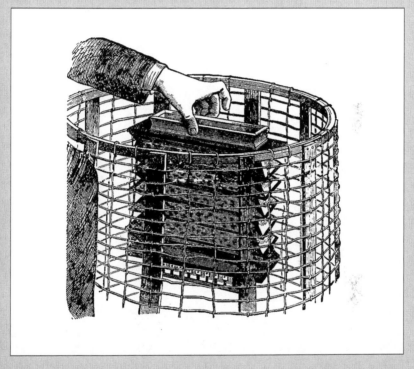

Daniel Dunglas Home with his accordion apparatus (detail). *Courtesy of the Internet Archive and the U.S. Library of Congress.*

4

Vaudeville Stars and the Dawn of the Golden Age

IN THE 1890s chains of theaters sprouted across the continent allowing performers to play in towns for a few days or weeks before moving on. It was the largest network of live entertainment that North America (and possibly the world) would ever see. Following in the footsteps of minstrelsy, the variety or "vaudeville" theater soon became the dominant theatrical entertainment. As minstrel shows shut down, competing circuits of these variety theaters sprang up all over the U.S. and Canada. The ambiguous French-sounding name let middle-class folks know it wasn't a drunken or immodest show (like some of the minstrels' had been). Whatever the term meant, vaudeville was tremendously popular. From its beginnings around 1880 until 1930, musicians, comedians, public speakers, and dancers shared stages with animal acts, magicians, acrobats, and accordionists. The Marx Brothers, W.C. Fields, and Mae West all had their start in vaudeville, and even after it was eclipsed by radio and film, the variety format lived on in shows like that of TV's Ed Sullivan.

Vaudeville produced the first great accordion stars. They criss-crossed the country on the new railroads to play shows in every city and a lot of small towns. Today a few enthusiasts remember big-name accordionists like the Deiro brothers; countless others left only photographs, newspaper clippings, or very rare recordings. Vaudeville faded with the rise of moving pictures and the burdens of the Great Depression. The luckiest acts went on to radio, record, or film careers, but many were never heard from again. The accordion, though, never stopped growing in popularity, carried from the stage into the future by vaudevillian survivors like Charles Magnante and his kin.

An Industry Takes Shape: Schools, Sales, and Accordion Picnics

On June 1, 1940, vaudeville star Guido Deiro directed a group of 1,500 accordionists, joined by 300 majorettes, a 1,000-person choir and thousands of other performers to entertain crowds at the 100,000-seat Los Angeles Coliseum. In parallel with professional performances, such gatherings regularly demonstrated the instrument's mass popularity.

Ronald Flynn's book *The Golden Age of the Accordion* includes dozens of pictures of school and student groups, full-scale accordion orchestras, and picnic-festivals with as many as ten thousand participants. All of these were promoted by the manufacturing and sales industry that had spread in the space of a few decades.

During the instrument's twentieth-century ascendancy, small accordion factories opened in urban centers across the continent. By the late 1930s, the American market was the biggest in the world. Immigrants with experience building instruments found Americans' hunger for accordions irresistible. Between the 1920s and the Second World War, accordion companies—most owned by Italian Americans—made more instruments domestically than they imported.

An industry sprang from these factories, each feeding dealers who relied on salesmen doubling as instructors, often with schools for students. Aspiring players, mostly young people, were offered cheap beginner's accordions with the idea that their hidden talent might be recognized. The more unscrupulous salespeople inevitably saw signs of genius. This was followed by encouragement to buy bigger, better, and more expensive instruments.

Accordions were designed and marketed the way automobiles and other consumer products were during the growing advertising age.

Millions of people were enticed to purchase bigger and fancier instruments by their teachers, who took a cut of the profits. One result is that most of today's used accordions are large 120-bass instruments. More portable models of good quality are much rarer and often command higher prices.

By the 1930s, accordion catalogs focused almost exclusively on piano accordions, "old-fashioned" button keyboards faded early in the 1920s. The industry could be cutthroat. Manufacturers touted their unique, often patented features and obliquely or overtly impugned the integrity and quality of lesser brands. A brochure from the Guerrini company divulged, "Not all accordion makers... are guided by a scrupulous honesty." Customers had to judge the value of touted features like "new invisible patent switches," "airflow interior (30% more volume)," and "deep fold bellows for quicker response." Competition did, however, produce many real advances in tone and quality that led to the smoother-sounding but heavier machines of the 1950s and '60s. Many of these are still solidly playable today.

In a photo of the 1931 Vancouver Accordion Band, forty students sit with instruments that are almost all Soprani accordions, obviously the chosen manufacturer for a local dealer. Each year, the whole group took a ferry out to a nearby island for a picnic, getting free fare by entertaining passengers on the way. This kind of musical outings were part of the accordion world until electronics eroded the need for people to make their own music.

Early Squeezebox Recordings

Accordion students could take inspiration from nationally known accordion stars. Recordings of these vaudeville heroes give us a chance at last to hear what early accordion fans were aspiring to. When the first audio recordings were made on wax cylinders in the 1870s, the accordion was only fifty years old. Those fragile cylinders document a young instrument still very much in development. What we think of today as traditional folk accordion styles were only a few years removed from the very first players who ever picked up the instrument.

The recordings we have are a mix of rudimentary players and those demonstrating a growing technical virtuosity in folk and professional music from the blossoming popular stage. Some of these recordings greatly influenced musicians who heard them, promoting the accordion while spreading new tunes and repertoire.

In retrospect, Thomas Edison and other early record company managers had no idea how to produce and market music. They didn't know what to record, and often simply guessed what would sell by trial and error. It didn't help that Edison himself was almost deaf while insisting on approving performers.

Jarringly, until mid-1908, each cylinder began with a loud announcement of the artist, title, and company name. *"Accordion Solo, 'Medley of Reels,' played by Mr. John J. Kimmel, Edison Records!"* This "Edison shout" at the beginning of every three-minute song was analogous to today's "digital rights management" to prevent piracy, but was discontinued after a few years, presumably after listeners complained.

Before the turn of the century, recordings were produced individually. Acoustic microphones similar to the horns on top of antique record players had to use a needle to cut directly into each cylinder. Musicians then had to perform songs over and over. Sometimes ten recording machines could be crowded in front of an artist at once, but musicians still had to perform a hundred times to make a thousand copies. These earliest recordings come down to us as personal messages created in the room with the long-dead artists.

This changed in 1902 with Edison's Gold-Molded process, which produced a metal mold from a musician's master recording. Wax blanks were then heated inside the tubular metal mold, and expanded to press the recording onto them. When they cooled, the copy popped out and was ready for sale.

Early squeezebox recordings remind us of both the surprising permanence and fragility of culture, art, and memory. Fewer than a hundred accordion cylinders are preserved in the U.C. Santa Barbara Cylinder Digitization archive. Some of the performers remain obscure; others like Scottish concertinist Alexander Prince were major figures either in vaudeville or European music halls. A few may have been well known within their ethnic communities or could have been local performers whose playing happened to be preserved. The pristine antiquity of these and future recordings dramatically changed the study of music going forward.

Accordionists in the Vaudeville Era

Madame Suzette Carsell: "Mother of the Accordion"

The earliest vaudeville accordionists played diatonic button boxes. Among these players, quite possibly the first professional female accordion player was Suzette Carsell. Her family immigrated from Italy to New Orleans in 1884 and she sang on riverboats while her brother played accordion. She got her own instrument in 1889 and was hired to play at the 1893 Chicago World's Fair. She hit the vaudeville circuit in 1900 and her career lasted another twenty-five years. She wasn't a main attraction though, and seldom topped the bill. In 1904 she performed at a dime museum in Illinois where she played five instruments at once, followed by a female snake charmer and an "elastic skin man."

In 1914, Carsell had an instrument built that looked like the piano models played by star vaudevillians. Interviewed years later she recalled, "I was still playing the old fashioned accordion—twenty-one buttons and twelve bass... I went to the Italo-American Accordion Company and asked them to build me a large box... It looked like a 120-bass accordion with forty-one keys, but only twelve basses played. The rest were dummies. I never let anyone pick up my accordion or let them try it, as I wanted to keep it a secret."

Known as the "Mother of the Accordion," she retired and opened the first accordion school in Arizona. Carsell returned to the stage at the start of World War II. Mortgaging her home, she moved to Long Beach, California, in 1941 to play for sailors on the Navy bases there. During the New Year's holiday in 1943 she gave twenty-eight USO shows (United Services Organizations, set up to entertain the troops) over six days for more than 27,000 Army and Navy troops. After the war, the "Sweetheart of the Navy" went home to Arizona, where she died in 1946 at age seventy-one.

Pietro Frosini: The Maestro

In 1905, Pietro Frosini, the first big vaudeville accordionist, immigrated from Sicily, where he had been scouted by a traveling American agent. Billed live as "the Wizard of the Accordion," Frosini became one of the earliest accordion recording stars, premiering on Edison cylinders in 1909. He used his full-size chromatic button accordion to perform

numbers that would have been impossible on previous instruments. In search of repertoire to match his skill, Frosini began composing his own light classical pieces. His 1915 "Panama Exposition" refers to the San Francisco world's fair celebrating the opening of the Panama Canal. Following the lead of his contemporaries the Deiro brothers, Frosini added marches and ragtime numbers to his program. His own "Frosini Symphonic March" crossed several of these threads.

Skillful and adaptable though he was, Frosini remained the most well-known hold-out against the rising wave of the piano accordion. In order to get jobs in the 1930s he had his "old-fashioned" button accordion refit to look like a modern piano instrument. Frosini's "finto-piano" (false piano) accordion also had a unique free-bass system years before they spread among classical accordionists. The year he died, 1951, one of these custom accordions was stolen, leaving him to lament, "Who can play this thing besides me?"

As live vaudeville was squeezed out by movies, Frosini played accordion for silent film showings, and when the silents faded, he did decades of studio work for WOR radio in New York (where it didn't matter what his keyboard looked like). In effect his first job (vaudeville) was killed off to make room for his second job (silent film accompanist) which was then partially replaced by his last job (radio).

The Deiro Brothers: Guido and Pietro

Italian immigrant Guido Deiro was the first accordion pop star. When Deiro arrived in North America in 1908, accordions had been on stage for sixty years. Deiro, however, brought a new innovation: an accordion with a miniature piano keyboard.

He had performed in various parts of Europe before coming to the U.S., and quickly targeted the huge crowds at Seattle's Alaska–Yukon–Pacific Exposition. There he was invited to join the elite Orpheum vaudeville circuit, and by 1910 Deiro was making $600 per week ($15,000 today), staking the claim that an accordionist was once the highest-paid instrumentalist in the American theater. By 1913 he had reached the biggest of the big time, the Palace Theater in New York.

FACING The Peerless Trio: Tom Savage "Tom Rosa," Bertha DeCroteau "Mazie Berto," and Suzette Carsell with her false-piano button accordion (1915–21). *Courtesy of Charles Patrick Behre.*

Deiro was a superlative showman, sporting expensive clothes, a flashing smile (especially for pretty women), and the novelty of his innovative instrument. He played so spectacularly that critics marveled and audiences refused to allow him off the stage. More than any single person, Deiro sparked North America's shift from button boxes to piano accordions. He is even said to have given the instrument its name at a bar in Seattle in 1909. He introduced "piano accordions" on most of the big vaudeville circuits in the U.S. and Canada, and later premiered them on recordings (1911), radio (1922), and sound film (1928). Millions saw and heard him across the world during his more than twenty-year career.

Like rock stars today, Deiro lived a celebrity lifestyle. In 1914, his entanglements reached a climax as he sought a divorce from his first wife in order to pursue his latest flame, the then-unknown actress Mae West. West left Deiro a few years later, and it remains unclear if they ever legally wed (West was at the time secretly married to another man). Nevertheless, one of the great female icons of the twentieth century was the lover of America's most important accordionist—and at the time, the accordionist was the bigger star.

Unfortunately, what Deiro didn't spend on extravagant cars, clothes, and women, he lost in the stock-market crash in 1929. Chronic money difficulties followed, and fame retreated. It was Deiro, however, who gave piano accordions the visibility and credibility to take off in North America. Audiences had never seen such a thing before his performances, and his legacy is sustained by every piano accordionist today.

Guido's brother, Pietro Deiro, never became the vaudeville star his brother was, but ended up being the more lasting success. Pietro preceded Guido to America in the early 1900s, doing manual labor as a miner in the mountains east of Seattle. When Guido arrived and demonstrated a showbiz alternative, Pietro left the mines and headed for the stage.

By agreement, Guido billed himself as "DEIRO," while Pietro settled on embossing "PIETRO" on his accordions. Guido remained the bigger stage draw, but Pietro's prolific cylinders and discs eclipsed his brother's. Guido made 111 recordings for Columbia, while rival Victor Records hired Pietro to make 152 recordings. Pietro continued with Victor until 1935, well into the Depression, while the recording industry

FACING Guido Deiro in his prime (1913). *Courtesy of Count Guido Deiro and the Graduate Center Library, CUNY, "Deiro Collection."*

The Accordion Novelty Company

THE ACCORDION NOVELTY Company introduced themselves with an antique art nouveau image of four unnamed female performers. The University of Iowa's digital archive on "Traveling Culture—Circuit Chautauqua in the Twentieth Century" includes a splendid three-fold booklet promoting this historical (ca. 1920s–30s) group of accordion-playing women.

The Chautauqua circuit provided entertainment similar to vaudeville, with performers traveling from town to town around the country, but it had more of a rural focus and an element of educational uplift and social change. As with vaudeville, all the documentation we have about many artists is promotional photos or pamphlets that were sold to audiences as commemoratives. The Novelty Company glowingly summarized their appeal:

> The irresistible spirit of youth rules the entertainment of The Accordion Novelty Company... In their bright, charming costumes they present a delightful bit of old-world color... The most interesting feature, from a musical standpoint, is the use of four accordions. Truly beautiful and novel music is attained with this combination. Cello, violin and piano are also used, and harmony singing adds attractive variety.

Accordions were impacting different ethnic groups in all parts of the country and every branch of the growing entertainment industry. Styles and venues like vaudeville and the Chautauquas grew and faded but the instrument and its players continued to spread.

The ladies of the Accordion Novelty Company. *Redpath Chautauqua Collection, University of Iowa Libraries, Iowa City, Iowa.*

collapsed around him and almost all artists, including his brother, went unrecorded.

Guido watched his career fade with the vaudeville era, but his younger brother built a small empire of accordion music publishing and instruction. Pietro released his *Complete Method for the Piano Accordion* in 1919, which sold sixty thousand copies and become the standard instruction for early piano accordionists.

As Pietro's network of students grew, he styled himself "the Daddy of the Accordion," and eventually usurped a number of his brother's historical accomplishments. Amongst others, he allowed claims to go unchallenged that he had been the first accordionist in vaudeville, slighting his brother.

Both Deiro brothers helped found the American Accordionists' Association in 1938, and Pietro initiated battles within the organization over acceptable sheet-music notation. Not surprisingly, he strongly preferred a format he was already selling. Pietro later joined the push for more "serious" music for the instrument, going so far as to have classical works ghostwritten for him to publish in his own name.

Galla-Rini: Vaudeville to Classical

The Deiros were not the only ones promoting the piano accordion. Anthony Galla-Rini was a professional accordionist for ninety-eight years. When he was seven, he took a train alone for 1,200 miles from Connecticut to Wyoming to join his family's vaudeville act. From his opening cornet solo with the Galla-Rini Four, he never stopped working until his death at age 102. As a child he learned to play flute, clarinet, trombone, and tuba, and gave headliner Harpo Marx lessons on saxophone. Galla-Rini eventually settled on accordion, and as moving pictures silenced vaudeville, he began his life's project of trying to bring classical legitimacy to the instrument.

Galla-Rini supported research into how accordions could be improved, and promoted the now common system of dots used to indicate which register switches control different reeds. He also advocated for standardizing the removal of the fifth note from the seventh and diminished chord buttons on the left hand. Advanced players like him used pliers to clip the wire tabs that triggered these fifths tabs inside their instruments. Simplifying the seventh chords let players combine buttons on the left hand to create harmonies that would have clashed on earlier Stradella systems.

With the Deiros, Frosini, and others, Galla-Rini was one of the founding members of the American Accordionists' Association, but he quit over an arcane, unresolved conflict about music notation: Galla-Rini wanted bass chords to be written out note-for-note as if they were played on a piano, while Pietro Deiro and others wanted chords to be notated with a simple indicator of which button should be pressed. Debating the benefits and compromises of various notation systems has become almost a tradition amongst American accordionists.

With the passing of vaudeville, Galla-Rini continued on to new venues. He played for radio and on soundtracks for Hollywood films like *High Noon*. His mission matched Andrés Segovia's concurrent one with the classical guitar—to overcome the accordion's reputation as a folk instrument. Over the years he composed or arranged hundreds of classical works for accordion, including two concertos of his own. When he died in 1986 he had rigorously trained seventy years' worth of accordion students, always with the goal that the accordion should succeed by earning its place in "serious" European concert music.

The Three Vagrants' Two Sisters

The Three Vagrants were one of many other acts who played accordions on the vaudeville stage but never made it into the history books (until now). The group featured John Oddone on clarinet, with Frank Lucanese on accordion, and John Bergamasco playing harp guitar—a sadly almost forgotten novelty instrument to go with the innovative piano accordion. A photo of them in New York from 1908 tantalizingly hints at a challenge to Guido Deiro's 1909 claim as first piano accordionist on stage in the U.S.

The trio had a two-decade vaudeville career that included early cylinder recordings for Thomas Edison. By 1920, the act included accordionist sisters Josephine and Lena Bergamasco, with Josephine staying until they folded in 1928. The Vagrants never became headline stars, but they like many others brought entertainment, and the accordion, to thousands of audiences in vaudeville's gilded theaters.

Charles Magnante: From Carnegie Hall to the Comics

As vaudeville faded, figurehead artists like Charles Magnante continued to promote the accordion. Magnante got his start playing on New York's Staten Island Ferry. Friends remember him using his breaks between routes relentlessly practicing. He moved on to New York studio work in the 1920s and did a tremendous number of recordings and especially radio broadcasts, which influenced accordionists across the country. He also appeared anonymously on early country records with Fred Hall's Missouri Mountaineers, a "city-billy" band that never left New York.

Breaking ground for the instrument, he and his quartet played the first accordion concert at Carnegie Hall in 1939. By the 1950s he became a fixture through endorsements for accordion companies, including a biographical comic book that finished with a pitch for Excelsior accordions: "So easy to play! Start now on your career in music"—a rather light-hearted recommendation from someone who dedicated a lifetime to mastering the instrument.

Josephine and Lena Bergamasco, who performed in vaudeville with their father John B. of the Three Vagrants (ca. 1920s). *Courtesy of Richard Harris (Josephine Bergamasco's son).*

5

Polka and "Ethnic" Music

POLKAS AND WALTZES were all the rage in the mid-century United States. Slovenian bands like Frankie Yankovic's were achieving widespread success in and outside their ethnic communities. But the era's polka hitmakers shouldn't distract us from the music's deeper history. Polka was American roots music decades before anyone played bluegrass, zydeco, or Chicago blues. For many immigrant Americans and their descendants, polkas are more richly traditional than jazz, blues, or country (though country music incorporated a lot of polkas).

When the polka boom faded in the 1960s however, the music followed the accordion into its long exile. The ridicule heaped on accordionists during much of the rock era was mirrored by a disdain for polka. Few writers gave a thought to why this particular genre became so curiously despised. Of course, a good-time party music like polka almost defies critics to take it seriously. Nevertheless, a defense of polka's cultural place is long overdue.

Polka's low pretentiousness reduced its defenses against cultural snobbery. I myself came to polka with all the resistance common among rock 'n' roll fans. I've come to believe that the prejudice against polka has left a significant gap in our culture. People's casual disregard for this music is built on ethnic prejudice and a painful rejection of simple pleasures. Polka should be embraced as one of American's core roots musics. We dismiss these riches at our peril.

The Original Polka Mania

Czech and Polish communities dispute the legendary origin of the polka. It developed in Europe in 1830 or so, possibly based on earlier folk styles, or as an offshoot of couples dances like the waltz. Regardless, it was quickly adopted by the upper classes, first in Prague and then in Paris. It became a transcontinental phenomenon when it hit the U.S. in 1844 (accompanied by unavoidable, humorous jabs at James K. Polk, then successfully running for president).

What would become the Polish American polka was probably not a traditional dance in Poland. They may have danced polkas to traditional Polish tunes during the original ballroom polka craze in the 1800s, but there's no definitive proof for the dance's folkloric origin before that.

L to R: Mickey Kling, Pete Sokach, Kenny Bass, Eddie Habat, Frankie Yankovic, John "Hokey" Hokavar, Jim Kozel, and Johnny Pecon. Yankovic Cafe, Cleveland, Ohio, 1946. *National Cleveland-Style Polka Hall of Fame.*

The polka's origins didn't matter, though, once immigrants brought the dance to the Americas.

That original polka fad became so intense that it spun off products like polka hats and polka pelisses, and eventually polka dots. London's *Punch* magazine reported in 1845's "History, Symptoms, and Progress, of the Polkamania" that it "resembles the Plague," and that there was no hope for a cure other than "vaccination, in the shape of some new jig ... or caper" which might be worse than the disease.

Almost a century later, in 1937 the Archdiocese of Quebec was still warning about the risks of "mortal sin" associated with lascivious dances and polka mania. But polkas were less threatening than the close-dancing waltz or the notorious tango, so they remained in fashion for years, drawing spite mostly for insipidness and "shabby" gentility.

What we think of now as "polka music" embraces other styles like waltzes and schottisches from the mid-1800s. Waves of nineteenth-century German, Polish, Scandinavian, Italian, Slovak, Czech, and other European immigrants clung to these dances. As musician/folklorist Richard March put it, "When these immigrants left Europe, the polka was all the rage in their homelands ... It would be as if a group of Americans migrated to a distant country in 1960 when the twist was the latest dance fad, and then preserved twisting as an important part of their American cultural legacy."

Breaking out from the boundaries of these ethnic immigrant communities, polkas became immensely popular during the 1930s and '40s. By the 1950s, this second wave of polka mania faded as aging enthusiasts either assimilated—with their children leaving the music behind—or retreated back to their separate ethnic strongholds. Meanwhile, outside of polka's dedicated immigrant communities, an aging echo of its mainstream success went into syndication on Lawrence Welk's TV show.

Based on these stereotypes, one might assume that all accordionists played polkas. During the instrument's rise though, a significant faction of the accordion industry shied away from ethnic-identified music in an attempt to target larger audiences. Early musicians like the Deiro brothers recorded many more waltzes, rags, marches, and even opera preludes than they did polkas. During the dark days of the early 1940s though, the polka joyfully skipped up the pop charts. One hundred years after they emerged separately in Europe, the polka and the accordion became inseparable in the public's ear.

Geography of the Polka: Loosening the Polka Belt

"The Polka Belt" describes territories where European ethnic music was historically popular. The area traditionally stretched from the Prairies of Canada down into Nebraska and the Dakotas, then east through the Upper Midwest of Minnesota, Wisconsin, and northern Illinois. It reached into Indiana and Iowa and then to southern New England and Pennsylvania, with large concentrations in urban areas like Cleveland, Chicago, New York, and New Jersey. Sometimes mentioned are rural East Texas Czech and German bands.

Different ethnic groups developed their own styles. Slavic polka includes Polish ("Eastern" and "Chicago style"), Slovenian (known as "Cleveland style"), Ukrainian (especially prominent in the Canadian Prairies), and Czech (reaching down into Texas). German American "Dutchman" bands were especially known for their "oom-pah" sound. Scandinavians and others played polkas too, often in crossover bands for mixed audiences in rural communities.

Mexican, Mexican American, and Native American polka musicians from the southern border region have often been excluded from discussion of the polka belt. This seems to have more to do with a history of prejudice than with musical distinctions. Given the number of competing language groups and styles within the European immigrant regions, polkas in Spanish should logically be included. Ethnic polka communities heatedly debate partisan preferences for local or cultural genres such as Cleveland or Chicago style, so there's no inherent obstacle to adding more to the discussion.

One distinction may be that immigration from much of Europe was greatly curtailed in the 1920s. Several generations of assimilated German, Scandinavian, and Eastern European descendants haven't experienced the discrimination their first-generation immigrant ancestors faced. Immigration from Mexico, meanwhile, continued through many shifts in policy and civil rights. One result has been the shifting of social prejudice onto more recent immigrants. Today, Mexican Americans whose ancestry may predate the founding of the United States experience more racism than Europeans whose families arrived later.

More recent immigrants from Mexico have kept the norteño branch of polka especially vibrant. Close contact with Mexico has also helped sustain the Spanish language within much of the U.S. Latino community.

This has reduced the erosion of the language base faced by European American polka styles several generations removed from migration.

More than just a marker of folk heritage, accordion music from the U.S./Mexico border region remains a cultural mainstay and is without doubt the most popular polka culture in North America. Norteño accordions, however, haven't crossed over to the pop charts the way European-immigrant polka did in the 1940s. For these reasons, the Texas/Mexico border accordion, while definitely part of the polka landscape, is discussed in Chapter 8.

The Other American Roots Music

The development of polka in North America has many similarities with American country music and the blues. Listeners even referred to polka as "old-time music," since it played a similar role in their communities as old-time country in the South. These were the familiar tunes people sang and danced and celebrated with. Ethnic bands traveled between regional dance halls just like country, blues, and jazz musicians. They got radio sponsors to promote their regional bands, and eventually some had hit records.

Despite its cultural impact, polka has been neglected by most books, documentaries, and anthologies about early popular music. As a result, outside their lively ethnic-music communities, modern artists and audiences have missed the chance to be inspired by this invisible-in-plain-sight party style.

The most obvious barrier faced by ethnic music has always been language. Blues and country songs were fairly accessible to English-language listeners outside their intended audience. Exotic sounding but understandable dialects could even grant an aura of authenticity for aficionados. Czech, Polish, or Finnish lyrics presented a much greater hurdle. Only occasionally, in passing flirtations like the mambo craze in the late 1950s, have songs incorporating other languages won over English audiences.

Purely musical flavors and rhythms have been less of an obstacle. Spanish and Hawaiian guitar, Italian mandolins, and Latin percussion can be heard in American music every day. In recent decades, French-speaking Cajun and zydeco players have shown that musicians can transcend and even find strength in their unique language.

In the 1940s, polka escaped its multilingual fragmentation and spent more than a decade in popular jukeboxes. What failed to follow in the decades since, is popular recognition that immigrants produced music that was as authentically American as Woody Guthrie or Howlin' Wolf. In fact, some ethnic musicians probably had more impact than their more famous Americana contemporaries.

If we honestly re-examine the musical landscape of the mid-twentieth century, the fickleness of history is clear. "Oom-pah" bands like the Six Fat Dutchmen from New Ulm, Minnesota (three hundred miles south of Bob Dylan's hometown), were in their day more influential on American music than were unknown bluesmen like the legendary Robert Johnson. The Dutchmen toured and recorded widely for crowds of thousands, while even most of Johnson's peers hardly remembered the mythologized "King of the Delta Blues Singers." History has distorted the historical consequence of obscure players like Johnson because their rare recordings were discovered decades later and touted by rock guitarists. If Keith Richards or Eric Clapton had collected reissues of "Whoopee" John instead of Robert Johnson, there might have been a British polka revival instead of a blues revival.

Somehow immigrant polka became separated from the American genres we think of as roots music. Mainstream country and pop musicians abandoned polkas when they joined with R&B to give birth rock 'n' roll. Rock and even folk groups seldom played waltzes, schottisches, or other social dances common to ethnic polka bands. The burgeoning field of pop criticism never questioned this. Decades later, with thousands of volumes written on the development of popular culture, it is not unusual for books on roots music to focus only on Appalachia or the blues. Even in modern overviews, French-language zydeco or Cajun music and an overdue awareness of Latin contributions may be the only non-English cultures mentioned. Listeners are thus not surprisingly confused when they hear about Czech western bands from Texas, or Slovenian polka hits on the top ten in the 1940s.

It is remarkably difficult to even access this historical music today. There is no annotated compilation of the hundreds of classic polkas that sold millions of records at the height of the polka craze. This notable segment of early popular music has been all but ignored in our otherwise obsessive assessment of American culture.

Immigrant Songs

What we think of as traditional ethnic folk music was usually recorded to make a buck. Alvin Sajewski worked at his father's Polish music store in Chicago starting in 1914. "The record companies... didn't care what language it was in or how it sounded... If you went to a record company and said you had somebody who was good... you'd have to be able to say you could sell five hundred."

The vast immigrant population in the U.S. opened new markets for the recording industry in the early years of the twentieth century. Eager companies began by simply guessing what would sell in a given ethnic community. Ethnic musicians were frequently documented in the United States years before recordings were made in their original homelands. No commercial recordings of folk fiddle tunes were made in Finland until the 1950s, but Victor had been recording them in the States since 1926. The recording industry aimed to sell familiar sounds to homesick audiences. Back in their countries of origin, people generally had less money to buy recordings (poverty was one inspiration for emigrating). They also had less need for reminders of home—since they hadn't left. For record companies, immigrant nostalgia was a business opportunity.

Interestingly, record labels discovered the market for immigrant music at a time when nativist street-thugs, established politicians, and even medical and social scientists were openly advocating racial intolerance. The recording industry, in contrast, saw cash value in immigrants' desire for music from their former homes. In 1915, the Eastern Talking Machine Company donated a Victor phonograph to the waiting area at the federal immigration receiving station in Boston. New immigrants were welcomed as a target market the moment they stepped onto American soil. Columbia Records alone released recordings for thirty-three different ethnic groups. Despite public vilification and marginalization, immigrant cultures were preserved in these historic recordings. The desire for a dollar saved music that is now culturally priceless.

During the Great Depression, though, much of the recording industry closed down. Many immigrants who could no longer afford record players followed their favorite bands on radio, in person, and nickel by nickel on jukeboxes. Bands survived—and some did well—by touring and appearing on radio stations that were opening around the country. Looking to maximize income, musicians also began to work outside their separate ethnic communities. Americanizing their ethnic names was one way to leave their origins behind. Instrumental tunes were another method for reaching pan-ethnic audiences. Many simply stepped into the mainstream. This could be confusing: Jazz drummer Gene Krupa was Polish but joined the Dorsey Brothers' jazz band to back up black-face singer Emmett Miller's pioneering country-yodeling records. Krupa's drumming style later found its way back into polka. Ethnic music wasn't traditional any more.

The Second World War boosted multi-ethnic polka as labor demands and military service mixed people together. Bands with different ethnic origins became wildly popular during and after the war. Musical battles between groups might feature Frankie Yankovic's Slovenian band versus the Six Fat Dutchman's German oom-pah and various other styles, all were struggling to carry on their tradition while appealing to the widest possible audience.

"Happiness" Is Polka's Blues

Unpacking the works of polka artist Li'l Wally, critic Michael Anton Parker described him as, "tormented by indestructible happiness . . . happiness taken to fantastical, transcendent extremes as the mirror image of the deepest blues." Happiness is polka's response to the difficulties of life.

Country music, blues, and immigrant American polka all developed at the beginning of the twentieth century, and each was based on folk music that had been uprooted and transplanted. African American blues and jazz listeners weren't interested in nostalgic looking back to a better life in the South. Country fans, in contrast, were comforted by a style that harkened to an imagined earlier time and place. The depth of the blues and the lonesome spirit of country music were mirrored in polka with a kind of boundless cheer, as if looking at the other genres in reverse.

Polka songs are about drinking, dancing, being in love, and laughing away troubles, but it can't be overstated that it is dance music. It succeeds or fails based on whether pairs of people move to it together. The deeper meaning of lyrics is secondary—in some cases the singers may not even speak the language they're singing. The songs, though, reflect both the musicians and audiences reaching for moments of joy.

Drinking, dancing, and romance bring their share of problems, of course. Polka may have fewer songs about infidelity and violence than some other American roots styles, but this doesn't reflect a difference in the situations where it was created. Minnesota writer Dale Holtz recalled, "Fights were quite common in the ballroom scene ... I remember fights in at least three of the corners of the ballroom at the end of the night."

Barroom brawls never made it onto *The Lawrence Welk Show,* but glimpses remain of the musical grit that was polished away in the search of mainstream acceptance. Li'l Wally released a series of winking "party" albums that responded to the facts of life with a bit of laughter and innuendo. Going back to "the old country," the Arhoolie roots label released a record with a parental advisory sticker for "explicit content." *Uncensored Folk Music of Austria* contained polkas and other songs that Arhoolie founder Chris Strachwitz had been collecting since the 1960s. These traditional tunes dealt with sex and violence, finding the ridiculous in what others might call crude. It was one of the label's bestsellers.

The often zany shtick of ethnic polka brings to mind the stereotypes of other genres. Torn clothes and mosh pits are expected parts of hardcore or heavy metal shows. Classical musicians and audiences wear formal dress. If there's an off-putting cliché that polka is goofy, it may spring from behavior that polka audiences understand, expect, and appreciate. Many genres have customs and costumes that appear strange to outsiders. The showmanship remains the same in each: attempting to reach people with something that will keep them coming back. It just happens that what people wanted from polka was to throw caution to the wind, smile, and dance.

Polka in the Shadow

When it ended, the twentieth-century polka craze just about took the accordion with it. All fads pass, but polka fell further than most, and never rebounded in the waves of nostalgia that periodically revive forgotten eras of pop music. Polka bands of various styles continued to play festivals and regional events, but most of the players needed day jobs. Today jazz has degree programs at universities, while Wynton Marsalis curates well-funded series at the Lincoln Center. Polka has nothing like this support amongst the intelligentsia.

Of course, a good beat can't be beat, so polka music continues in communities where it never faded. In the 1960s Eddie Blazonczyk's "Chicago push" style updated Li'l Wally's Polish "honky" polkas with electric bass and rock amplification. "Whoopee" John's Dutchman brass groups gave way to jazz-influenced concertina players like Karl Hartwich. As years went by Frankie Yankovic's protégé Joey Miskulin recorded with everyone from Johnny Cash to U2, and upstarts like Brave Combo presented polka to unsuspecting audiences with punk rock adventurousness.

Polka also slipped into pop music under other names. The norteño/Tejano music of Northern Mexico and the American Southwest frequently calls on polkas. Jamaica's enduring ska music is polka's two-beat cousin, and re-emerges in different subgenres every fifteen years or so. When a Mexican *rock en Español* band plays a song in a 2/4 beat to a stadium of tens of thousands of fans, they effortlessly mix trendy pop-ska with Mexican-country ranchera. The beat still makes people dance, and a savvy musician might one day roll it back up the charts like Will Glahé's "Beer Barrel" did in 1939.

Polka Pop Accordion

Beginning in the late 1930s, polka and its musical partner, the accordion, stole the heart of the American populace. As the Great Depression bled through war and eventual recovery, people wanted distraction from their troubles. Polkas landed on the newly established record charts and fueled this latest wave of the social dance craze that began after World War I and lasted until the 1960s. Young swing-era fans who'd been derided as "jitterbugs" a few years earlier picked up ethnic dances and evolved into "polka-bugs."

Upwardly mobile polka groups blended jazz instrumentation with ethnic styles to create mass-market polka acts that sold millions of records. Big-time pop stars like the Andrews Sisters made themselves bigger thanks to ethnic input—unexpectedly scoring with a Yiddish theater tune "Bei Mir Bist Du Schön," and topping that with the indelible lyrical version of the "The Beer Barrel Polka."

Many ethnic musics in North America used accordions of some sort, but none came close to the impact of the polka craze of the 1930s and 1940s. Scholar Pekka Gronow wrote, "For a while polka music showed promise of entering the mainstream of American popular music, just like Hawaiian music in the 1910s and swing in the 1930s."

Polka was unique for being one of the last musical fads prior to the largest generational musical revolution in history. Polka reached its peak just as technology and timing combined to electrify pop music. As polka faded, a musical generation gap developed as second- and third-generation immigrant Americans assimilated. When audiences shrank, polka continued to develop in its former ethnic strongholds, but it lost its place as king of the dance floor across the continent.

All Hail the "Beer Barrel Polka"

When asked to name an accordion tune, folks from my grandparent's generation would probably pick the "Beer Barrel Polka." They learned it as teenagers from the radio or the local jukebox when it surged across North America in 1939. Despite its universality, the tune didn't originate in folk music. Jaromír Vejvoda wrote it for his dad's brass band near Prague in 1927. It was published with Czech words as "Škoda Lásky" ("Wasted Love") and spread through Europe with different translations until bandleader Will Glahé laid down an instrumental recording with accordion, saxophone, and a Hawaiian-style slide-guitar solo. That version mounted a successful German invasion of the North American pop charts in 1936, and sold around a million records in the next five years.

Hastily crafted English lyrics with the chorus "Roll out the barrel" were handed to the up-and-coming Andrews Sisters, and their vocal-driven cover dominated the charts throughout the summer of 1939. The Andrews Sisters' version lacked accordions, but with close harmonies inspired by New Orleans' innovative Boswell Sisters, it lifted spirits (during the post-Prohibition era) as the Depression headed toward war.

With the "Beer Barrel Polka" came polka bands to play it. While some groups limited themselves to one ethnic community, "international-style" bands branched out to reach larger modern audiences. Some added polka to other styles like Adolph Hofner's Czech-language western swing. Music genres on the whole were still very much in flux; historian Elijah Wald noted that, "When the *Los Angeles Times* did a feature on the hillbilly music boom in 1940, it singled out 'The Beer Barrel Polka' as the biggest hit in the genre."

Record companies were in dire straits at the time because the Depression and the growth of radio had caused many of their customers to stop buying. The upbeat "Beer Barrel" recharged an ailing industry. Some reports have it that this one song did more to save the struggling trade than any other. A Spokane jukebox operator reported, "I have been using this platter more than a month and many times it collected as many nickels as all the other records on the machine together. I have had them wear out in two days."

Not all accordionists were happy with the success of their polka-playing brethren. Some, like Anthony Galla-Rini, protested against polkas as "inferior." He and others had pinned their hopes on lifting accordions up to the level of "serious" instruments. Their tastes, however, never translated to the jukeboxes.

Long after the polka boom faded, the "Beer Barrel Polka" remained the most enduring song in the American accordion repertoire. But it became a cliché without a history—the song people jokingly asked accordionists to play without knowing why.

Polka Accordionists: Missing Roots Legends

Viola Turpeinen: The Finnish American Accordion Princess

Viola Turpeinen was probably the most famous early female accordionist in America, and certainly among the first to record. Her parents had immigrated from Finland, and in the 1920s she started playing the Finnish dance circuit in the Upper Midwest: Michigan, Wisconsin, Minnesota. Eventually working out of New York, she toured widely and her traveling shows became a summer tradition for many. She played mostly Finnish halls, but other folks came to see her—an example of how ethnic "crossover" musicians gained larger audiences.

Growing up in Michigan, she learned to play piano accordion (rather than her Finnish mother's button model) from her music teacher, an Italian who lived across the street. While recording in New York, she studied at entrepreneur Pietro Deiro's accordion academy. Over her career she

FACING Viola Turpeinen, 1928. *Courtesy of Toivo Tamminen.*

made an impressive ninety records and was one of the rare ethnic artists who continued recording after the stock-market crash in 1929.

Researcher Carl Rahkonen described her solo and small group repertoire: "They performed a surprisingly wide variety of music, certainly Finnish and Finnish American tunes, but also classical music, standard American popular tunes, Scandinavian tunes, and other ethnic American tunes. They performed mostly dance genres: polkas, schottisches (jenkkas), waltzes, foxtrots (humppas) and tangos, but also concert pieces and songs."

Turpeinen moved to Florida with her husband in the 1950s to retire in what she called their "house that polka built." In 1958 she died of cancer at age forty-nine. Her place as a folk and ethnic-music pioneer is now nearly forgotten. Had she lived, she might have enjoyed the kind of revival that other folk artists experienced in the decades to come. I, for one, would happily pay money to see an *Accordion Princess* movie.

"Whoopee" John Wilfahrt: In Heaven There Is No Oom-pah

Hans "Whoopee" John Wilfahrt embodies several enduring accordion stereotypes. His millions of records forthrightly represent the jovial sound people think of when they call polka music "happy." His "Whoopee" stage name was an onomatopoeic reference to his enthusiastic vocal interjections. As polka historian Victor Greene put it, "His appearance was clownlike and ethnic, characterized by frequent vocal 'whoops' and pronounced corpulence." He also wore lederhosen and a Bavarian-style Tyrolean hat.

Cynically sophisticated audiences may feel squeamish faced with such out-front exhortations of base joy. Wilfahrt's exaggerated "ethnic" character also paralleled the Irish "Mick," the blackface minstrel, and rural "hillbilly" stereotypes of the early American stage. Sifting through our discomfort may reveal the hidden value within.

Wilfahrt and the equally influential Six Fat Dutchmen propagated the German/Bohemian sound we think of as oom-pah polka. These bands and their Midwest prairie audiences literally defined "corny." Entertainment-industry rag *Variety* popularized the term to denote "corn-fed" rural audiences who didn't require a lot of sophistication in their entertainment.

FACING "Whoopee" John Wilfahrt, playing Chemnitzer concertina. *Minnesota Historical Society.*

Apparently a lot of Americans were comfortable throwing off sophistication because "Whoopee" John was huge.

The origins of the Dutchman bands in "Oompah Town" New Ulm, Minnesota, are revealed in Victor Greene's *Passion for Polka: Old-Time Ethnic Music in America*. Greene relates how they built on brass, drums, and the large Chemnitzer concertina and were not conservative but rather modern, commercialized, and varied. In rural areas where Slovenians, Poles, Finns, Czechs, and Germans gathered together, non-traditional bands who saw them all as American audiences made more money.

Unlike many musicians of the era, "Whoopee" John's group made most of their income through record sales. Spurred by the jukebox's new popularity, they succeeded without touring outside the Upper Midwestern states. Starting in the 1930s and up into the '50s he recorded about three hundred records, including "In Heaven There Is No Beer," and is reported to have been the third-biggest seller for Decca Records, behind only Bing Crosby and the Andrews Sisters.

During World War II, Wilfahrt's German image became an issue as patriotic panic targeted the band. Greene reports, "Rumors spread that 'Whoopee' John and his musicians might be disloyal. It was even said that the bandleader's son, Pat Wilfahrt, was... pounding out Morse Code on his drums, revealing troop movements to Nazi agents dancing in the audience!" The group's popularity outlived the rumors, and their success hardly faltered, though they were prevented from appearing in films during the war.

Concertina player Wilfahrt might rightfully be included in the "roots" pantheon next to Bill Monroe and Muddy Waters. "Whoopee" John played immigrant folk music that crossed over into a truly American style that eventually adopted sophisticated big band arrangements. His career lasted for decades with a sales total of over three million records, but behind that success (and slightly absurd outfit) he brought folk music to modern audiences and a wider world.

Frankie Yankovic: Cleveland Polka King

Second only to TV pioneer Lawrence Welk (who we'll meet in Chapter 7: "The Closing Acts of the Golden Age"), Frankie Yankovic was the most important performer carrying polka to the mainstream of American pop music. As the big bands faded, Yankovic polished his group's sound down to twin accordions (lead and rhythm—like rock bands to follow), piano, banjo, and standup bass. In sectarian polka parlance they played fast "Cleveland style" Slovenian polkas. Augmented with vocals and keyboards including an early Solovox electric Hammond organ; late-1940s polka exemplified modern, even futuristic music.

Yankovic's career began before World War II. His band aligned itself in 1938 with the Joliet record label, calling themselves the "Jolly Jugo-slavs," and recorded "Joliet Illinois Waltz." Other recordings followed, but things remained uncertain; the band practiced in the basement of the bar Frankie ran in case the music business didn't pan out. The grand opening of the club was on December 6, 1941, the night before Pearl Harbor.

Frankie eventually joined the Army and on February 2, 1944, invited his bandmates to a legendary session in Cleveland where they got drunk and recorded thirty-two songs in one sitting before shipping out to Europe. In the bitter cold winter of 1944, Yankovic was on the front lines near Aachen, Germany, and suffered severe frostbite. As he told the story later, doctors wanted to amputate his fingers, fearing gangrene. He begged them not to, and eventually recovered after being dosed with antibiotics. He returned to duty as an entertainer, and after the war returned home to his greatest success.

He started to record with Columbia and had a monster hit in 1948 with a country song, "Just Because." The company refused to release the track until Frankie promised to buy the first ten thousand records himself. After selling more than a million copies, Yankovic's gamble paid off, proving that his sound was ready to cross ethnic boundaries.

By 1949 the polka craze was in full effect. Yankovic hit again with "Blue Skirt Waltz." This multi-ethnic breakthrough had a "Bohemian tune, Slovenian musicians, and Jewish vocalists." It is said to have been the second-biggest seller for Columbia after Gene Autry's "Rudolph the Red-Nosed Reindeer." Regional dealers reported that polkas were selling more records than big swing artists like Tommy Dorsey. Yankovic earned his title as "Polka King" in national competitions between ethnic bands, and in 1952 he even bested Duke Ellington's orchestra—after battling in front of a polka-inclined Milwaukee crowd.

Throughout the 1950s, Yankovic's group filled concert halls and casinos, between appearances in people's homes on their new TV sets. Even after polka left the charts, Yankovic kept his fans happy. Without national media exposure, he maintained a touring schedule unimaginable to most musicians, wearing out band members by playing more than three hundred dates a year. Until he died in 1998 he, and his thirty million records sold, remained a living reminder of polka artists who had paid their dues and earned their titles.

Li'l Wally: Chicago Style

In the 1950s, Li'l Wally (Walter E. Jagiello) took inspiration from older Chicago musicians like Chemnitzer concertina virtuoso Eddie Zima, to develop a distinctively modern Polish American polka. His band was small, amplified, and loud, with slowed-down tempos so it was easy to dance to. He passionately sang Polish and English songs improvised on Polish folk models. It was like a wild polka version of Chicago's electric blues, and people loved it.

Wally grew up in 1930s Chicago, familiar with poverty and tragedy. One sister died of influenza, while another was struck by a train and killed. With his parents sick or unable to earn enough, he never finished school, and worked from an early age. Nevertheless, he had a remarkable ability to remember songs and loved to listen to local musicians. As a small child he was hired to stand on tables and sing at weddings. He told author Charles Keil, "They're saving more than they pay me. The guy is gawking. The woman's gawking. That's wasting time and saving booze [the hosts don't have to pay for]." At ten years old Wally would bribe bartenders to let him sing in their taverns for tips. Soon he was performing with his mentor Eddie Zima and learning concertina—an instrument identified with poorer rural Polish immigrants.

He formed a band and purchased a half-hour of weekly radio time to promote his performances. People would send in a dollar with song dedications or requests. His response, "I'll be happy to play it if it is a polka." He collected all the mail to prove to sponsors that they should advertise. Eventually his show grew to three hours every morning. He built a live audience for this new style until they filled the largest ballroom in Chicago, the Aragon, with four thousand people. He remembered, "They had to call the bartenders' union for more help."

In contrast to previous Eastern style groups, Wally's band was small, with as few as three or four players: a trumpet or two, a clarinet/sax player, maybe an accordionist, and him switching off on drums and Chemnitzer. Sometimes he played kick-drum and concertina while singing at the same time. Thanks to electrical amplification, his small group could fill a dance hall and keep the payroll down.

In 1951, Wally started Jay Jay Records, which over the decades released more than 150 albums. He built a recording studio that included his own record press and put out every format: vinyl, cassettes, 8-track tapes, and eventually CDs. He sold them by mail or at shows and sometimes released dozens of records a year, creating a truly daunting task for later collectors.

"Wally has composed more than two thousand songs, all of them happy," wrote journalist Robert Powell. The process for the most prolific polka songwriters echoed other commercialized folk traditions. They relied liberally on public domain music for composing and copywriting new works. Many a blues tune had interchangeable fragments of lyrics, while Woody Guthrie and A.P. Carter famously borrowed tunes or whole songs that now bear their names. Similarly, musician/researcher Gary Sredzienski relates that American polka tunes, including Wally's, can often be traced to Polish originals.

Most of his records were in Polish, but he had English-language hits like "I Wish I Was Single Again," which went to number twenty-two on the pop charts in 1954. In addition to his own polkas, Wally's label released topical and novelty tunes like "Let's Go, Go-Go White Sox," (1959) which had a comeback when it led Chicago into a sweep of the 2005 World Series.

Other oddities from the Jay Jay catalog include surf-rock band the Venturas (separated by only one letter from the hundred-million-selling Ventures of Tacoma, Washington). Another instance of striving for a modern audience was Wally's lo-fi 1964 polka, "We Love You Beatles." It had him on drums singing over the Venturas' electric guitar, "Take this polka-hop, and dance around / it has your instruments, it has your sound." Not exactly the sound Beatles fans were after, and it was not a hit.

Wally also released mildly racy records like *Polish Dance Party—Adults Only* with risqué lyrics in Polish. His *Suggestive and Hot* LP for the English market included the tune, "She Hugs Me Very Nice" which got as rough as, "I like it once, but prefer it twice." The quaint earthiness of these "party" records corresponded to under-the-counter R&B and country "hokum" music and added spice to polka's relentlessly "happy" image.

In 1954, Wally was twenty-four years old and had ulcers from stressing over his business. A doctor recommended surgery, but instead Wally slowed down and moved to Florida. Despite his early "retirement" he kept producing records and performing. Independent business models like Wally's eventually became the standard for polka artists as they were forced out of the mainstream, and prefigured the indie-rock labels of later decades. By the late 1950s, Wally's Chicago style totally dominated Polish polka, and in 1969 he and Frankie Yankovic were the first inductees into the Polka Hall of Fame.

Wally had escaped poverty and knew that his audience wanted a good time, so he gave it to them and they loved him. He also did that rare thing: he almost single-handedly created a new strain of American roots music, all this while surrounded by ecstatic dancers as he played concertina above his head. That's happiness.

6

Jazzing the Accordion

HISTORICAL PHOTOS SUGGEST that accordions may have been featured in one out of ten dance bands of the Jazz Age. Nevertheless, they haven't made it into most histories of jazz. Even the somewhat marginalized study of polka has fared better than jazz accordion. Many players never recorded and aren't remembered at all.

The accordion became an important instrument in North America just as jazz was developing. Why isn't it a bigger part of jazz history? One reason is that accordions seem to have been prevalent in more "pop"-oriented dance bands. Jazz writers and fans have been up front about favoring improvisational "hot" jazz over the "sweet" (i.e., less adventurous) dance bands. Almost all of jazz history has been written with the assumption that these sweet bands weren't worthy of much attention. If we look back to the Jazz Age though, there was much more sweet dance music than hot jazz. Writing sweet musicians out eliminates an awful lot of what people heard at the time, and coincidentally a significant number of accordion players.

Another problem jazz accordionists still face today is the left-hand bass system. A young musician friend related that as a student, jazz was difficult to learn on the accordion because it's not set up to play jazz chords. The Stradella bass system was designed for European folk music. Simple I–IV–V chords are easily reachable on the left hand. More complex harmonies require a more advanced accordion player or more advanced accordions.

A final barrier for jazz accordionists was the delay in finding a pleasing jazz accordion tone. Up until about 1940, most accordion recordings sound brash or "reedy." In order to achieve a smoother timbre, accordionists had to wait for internal mutes and other advances in the instrument. Even then, accordions may not have been loud enough to be heard over more aggressive brass instruments. The upshot of all these difficulties is that when Fletcher Henderson and others standardized swing band instrumentation, accordions weren't included.

By the 1940s and later, improved accordions shone in smaller combos. The instrument could finally be heard without the din of the horn sections. By the time Art Van Damme and others formed small accordion-led groups, big bands had faded. But the audiences shrank with them. The accordion found a place in jazz, only to see the music increasingly isolated. Nevertheless, accordionists had participated in the entire history of the music, starting in places like New Orleans with the very first jazz players.

Early Jazz Accordionists: 1890s–1930s

A few pioneer accordionists brought the relatively new instrument into the first years of jazz. They were part of the New Orleans scene in the late 1800s but then faded, probably due to the mechanical and musical limitations of early accordions compared to the soon-pervasive piano. Black pianists especially seem to have only occasionally chosen to play accordions.

African American musicians had taken up the instrument before the American Civil War. They kept playing them while the twentieth century dawned and jazz began to manifest in Southern urban centers. But only a few African Americans played piano accordions after button accordions and pre-jazz instruments like violin and banjo fell from fashion. Art Tatum (born 1909), picked up the instrument for at least one nightclub gig as a youngster, but quickly returned to his dominion on the piano. Despite enticing cameos from big names like Tatum, there were few other examples of black accordionists. It's challenging for even knowledgeable jazz scholars to recall others besides Kansas City's Ira "Buster" Moten.

The earliest jazz accordionists of might have seen the old blackface minstrels playing French flutinas. Later they could have encountered African Americans and others playing button box accordions in Southern string bands. Even after more restrictive segregation laws were enacted in New Orleans in the 1890s, locals interacted with Italian immigrant musicians and others who were promoting the fashionable instrument.

Jazz developed in these back-and-forth interactions between artists of different ethnicities. Jews and Sicilian Italians lived in the same New Orleans neighborhoods as African Americans and Black Creoles. As accordions of different designs arrived from France, Germany, and Italy, early jazz players would have had the chance to try all of them.

The accordion, however, never became a standard jazz instrument. Perhaps the first reason for this was the advent of the blues. When early jazz players like Buddy Bolden began improvising on blues scales, their new style went beyond the capabilities of early diatonic accordions. By the time Guido Deiro introduced the piano accordion in 1909, Bolden's career was already over. (He was committed to the Louisiana State Asylum in 1907.) The piano keyboard came too late for the instrument to be embraced in blues-inspired jazz.

William Henry Peyton and His Accordiana Dance Band: The Earliest Players

Louis Armstrong is probably the most famous jazz trumpet player. Armstrong came up in New Orleans where he learned from Joe "King" Oliver, who gave Armstrong his first big break in Chicago. In his own youth in the early 1900s, Oliver learned from the original "King of Jazz," cornetist Buddy Bolden. Before taking up cornet, Buddy Bolden in turn had played with one William Henry Peyton, who in 1894 led the most important accordion band in New Orleans.

Henry Peyton was among the earliest remembered bandleaders in New Orleans. Bassist Papa John Joseph recalled Peyton playing "windjammer" accordion in his Accordiana Dance Band in the late 1800s, before what we'd recognize as "jazz" came together. The group played European-style dance music, quadrilles, polkas, marches, and waltzes, but with a syncopated flavor unique to New Orleans. They enriched the formal dances by adding the influence of ragtime and the Spanish and

French Caribbean. Bands like theirs led the way toward more improvisational formats to come.

Few descriptions of Peyton survive. We know he was heavyset because he was once ticketed for gambling and, when asked why he didn't run from the police, he said he "was too fat and couldn't cover ground as fast as the bluecoat." In addition to being a bandleader, he owned a music shop and built violins and other instruments. Clarinet player Louis "Big Eye" Nelson remembered, "He wasn't no humbug musician. He come from Alabama, made and played all the string instruments." Peyton wasn't the first or only dealer of accordions in New Orleans, but he may have been the first African American luthier with his own shop anywhere in nineteenth-century America.

Peyton's group was what was known as a "string band." This differentiated them from brass bands, which became the standard later. New Orleans string groups were slightly different from the white and African American string band tradition that gave birth to modern country music. Peyton's band typically centered on guitar, bass, and his lead accordion (a large two-row model). For volume, they added clarinet, trombone, or cornet. Piano and drums weren't generally attached to New Orleans groups before about 1905.

Trombonist Kid Ory remembers seeing Peyton play to the north of the city in Parish St. John during what was called "grinding season." Bands would perform as the sugarcane was brought in for refining. For several weeks the harvest called for music and celebration every Friday after the workers got paid. Growing up across the road from a sugar mill, Ory remembered Peyton playing his button accordion backed with guitar, mandolin, violin, and other strings.

Peyton's band was a training camp for later groundbreakers. "Big Eye" Nelson remembered how Bolden took up accordion in Peyton's band: "I was playing at Club 28 with Buddy Bolden, and at that time he didn't even have his own orchestra. He was just a young apprentice playing the accordion and making his first attempts on the trumpet."

In an interview with pioneering jazz writer Robert Goffin, Nelson remembered that he and Bolden were playing with Henry Peyton the night the Robert Charles riots started. Charles was a black man who shot and killed a police officer in July 1900. A white mob gathered, and over five days murdered dozens of African Americans. Peyton ignored reports that trouble was coming, saying, "Aah, we never had nothing like that in New Orleans yet, and it won't happen tonight." Nelson remembered

Peyton simply "stomped off the next tune," but an hour later shooting was heard and the doors broken down. The band escaped in a panic. When Nelson returned home, he found that his father was among those who had been killed: "I've wished many times I had gone home to warn my people."

Peyton's band was one of the last to include accordion in New Orleans. When he died at age fifty-one in 1905, the limitations of the instrument for playing ragtime and the blues had pushed younger musicians to take up other instruments. Besides Bolden, young Freddie "King" Keppard, who was in the Original Creole Jazz Band, also dropped the accordion in favor of the cornet.

Keppard sprang from New Orleans' middle-class, interracial Creole community. He was trained on a variety of instruments including violin, mandolin, and accordion, but following Bolden's example he started on the cornet in about 1905. Without recordings, we can't tell how close the New Orleans black and Creole string bands were to what eventually became early New Orleans jazz. But these early figures either started on accordion or were taught by players and bandleaders who used accordions as a prominent part of their music.

Bolden, Peyton, and the other New Orleans accordion players predated recording by a generation or more, so we know them only through a few fragmented recollections. Bolden's epochal cornet was also never recorded, and he became the most famous unheard player in jazz. The mystery surrounding him hints at even earlier sounds like Peyton's Accordiana band. Their "windjammer" accordions had set the stage for jazz to come.

Creole Musical Three: Covered in Glory

The spread of jazz outside New Orleans can be traced through papers like the *Chicago Defender*, the largest "colored" newspaper in the country. In July 1926, the *Defender* previewed a vaudeville performance at the Koppin Theater in Detroit. The Creole Musical Three appeared, made up of Fred Jennings, Anita Ried, and Hazel Whitman with "an array of musical instruments, using banjos, sax, guitar, Italian accordion, jazz cornet and piano." The *Defender* particularly lauded Jennings's performances, saying, "He covers himself in glory with his numbers."

The Musical Three's "Italian" instrument may mark the earliest promotion of an African American group playing piano accordion. By 1926, Italians like Guido Deiro were playing new piano keyboard instruments and filling vaudeville theaters across the country. The Creole trio

may have used "Italian" to differentiate their act from the older African American accordion style played on German button accordions.
Assuming theirs had piano keys, the Creole Three finally demonstrated
an accordion built to handle jazz and blues scales. The Creole Three
were promoting modern music on modern instruments for their Northern urban audiences.

From this distance, it's unclear what the Creole Three were trying
to say with their "Italian" instrument. In the end the accordion never
attracted much attention in African American jazz. We have only fragments like the *Defender's* review, which warranted half a paragraph and
closed with, "The act is classy and well dressed up."

Cornell Smelser: "Accordion Joe"

As jazz moved north it was adopted by varied audiences and players. In
late 1920s New York City, Cornell Smelser became perhaps the most
in-demand session accordionist playing the new music. In the early days
of radio he sometimes performed thirty-seven live shows a week. He
recorded with orchestras and singers, but side musicians often went
uncredited and his playing remains scattered and uncollected today. His
rising accordion career only lasted from the late 1920s until about 1931,
when he was stricken with tuberculosis and dropped out of music. Until
recently it's been assumed that he had died. For a few short years though,
he recorded with Jean Goldkette's hot band, studio aces Jack Teagarden
and Jimmy Dorsey, and he was one of the first white musicians to record
with Duke Ellington (and the only known accordionist).

Billed simply as "Cornell," but also "Joe Cornell," "Jack Cornell," or
rarely, his full name, he was a songwriter, organist, and pianist in addition
to playing accordion. Most information on him has been confined to his
few available recordings and one nostalgic article by Hilding Bergquist
published in a 1950 issue of *Accordion World Magazine.* I was able to contact his daughters in 2013 and cleared up many questions about his life.

Cornell grew up in Hungary and was a piano prodigy at the conservatory in Budapest. There he picked up the accordion. His parents divorced
and his stepmother didn't care for him, so at fourteen he ran away with
the circus, lying about his age to play accordion and piano. Somebody
found out how young he was and sent him home. In 1902, his mother

FACING Cornell Smelser (later Charles S. Cornell), ca. 1920s. *Courtesy of
the Cornell family.*

"Cornell"
RADIO AND RECORDING
ARTIST

brought him and his sisters to New York City, but when he was sixteen she took the girls back to Hungary, leaving him with an aunt and uncle.

Because he knew so little English, the only work he could get was playing organ in silent-movie houses. His children remember him saying that because there was no musicians' union, "They wouldn't even let me go to the bathroom, they gave me a bottle." He started to get jobs playing around New York and formed his own small orchestra to play for wealthy families like the Vanderbilts and the Astors. His youngest daughter remembers him saying he toured Europe with Cole Porter. Cornell especially loved Venice and Italy, and recalled that Porter was gay—"he swung the other way"—a real bon vivant, and brilliant. One of the drummers in Cornell's band was African American. His skin wasn't very dark and they lightened his hair so he could pass as white in the places they were staying.

Cornell (along with many others) played for Sam Lanin's many bands, which together probably recorded more sweet dance music (and a few hot numbers) than any other artists in the early jazz era. Lanin used so many aliases with different labels that no one has collected all his records, much less those of his sidemen. Between 1920 and 1931 they easily exceeded a thousand sides—an unknown number including accordions.

Irving Mills' Hotsy Totsy Gang was another outfit in which Cornell played with the Dorsey Brothers, with Gene Krupa on drums. Jean Goldkette's late-1920s hot band also had Cornell (or sometimes Harold Stokes) on accordion. After one gig a gangster-type demanded, "I want you to come and play at a party." Cornell replied, "I'm too tired, I've been playing for hours." But the guy said, "I'm giving you a thing you can't refuse here." So he went.

In those days, songwriters personally demonstrated songs by playing them for sheet-music publishers. Cornell's daughter Melody recalled his story about plugging a song he composed and being turned away, but then seeing it published by Irving Berlin, who had been in the next room writing it down: "My father was furious about it. He was so upset because he wrote it and it was good. And so my father said, 'I'm gonna sue that son of a bitch!' All the musicians said, 'Forget it, he's a gangster. It's not worth it, you'll be dead.'"

Cornell's most famous composition is the snappy anthem "Accordion Joe," which he recorded with his own group and later with Duke Ellington. Joan Crawford would dance to the tune in her racy film *Dance,*

Fools, Dance (1931). Cornell did more soundtrack work for Max Fleischer cartoons, and "Accordion Joe" became the titular song in a long unseen 1930 Betty Boop cartoon. A copy survives in the UCLA Film Library, where obsessives can view it with care. It's been described as, "A flimsily put together story with an accordion-playing Bimbo [a dog] flying a plane (miraculously playing while not controlling the plane), then flirting with Betty and being captured by a native tribe."

Cornell's greatest claim to musical fame was probably his appointment as one of very few radio musicians (not just accordionists, but *any* musician) approved by George Gershwin to broadcast his composition "Rhapsody in Blue." After they met in an elevator, Gershwin gave his blessing and Cornell played "Rhapsody" in its entirety with the Arden-Ohman Orchestra on NBC's *Gold Medal Fast Freight Hour* in 1931. The only other musicians allowed to play the piece at that time were Paul Whiteman, who had commissioned it for his orchestra, and Gershwin's organist friend Jesse Crawford. Sadly, Cornell's unrecorded "Rhapsody" performance was never heard after its live broadcast eighty years ago.

Cornell related that he also played "Rhapsody in Blue" at the opening of the Empire State Building in 1931, reportedly while sitting with his legs dangling over the side. In addition he told of playing organ at the opening of Radio City Music Hall in 1932, an event that was a spectacular disaster and seen as the death-knell of vaudeville. One hopes his playing wasn't too much of a contributor.

Tuberculosis then ended Cornell's accordion career. With no labor law protections, musicians worked terrible hours, and the conditions made his illness worse. When his accordions became too heavy to play he had to sell them. The finest went to his friend Fred Astaire. Prior to his illness, the Dorsey Brothers had convinced him to purchase insurance because there was no security for musicians. Unable to play and with no income except for the insurance money, he quit New York and returned to his native Hungary to be with family for his final days—but then he failed to die.

He went to a sanatorium in Switzerland and survived the TB. Eventually he returned to the States and lived in Arizona and then California to benefit from the dry weather. Meanwhile, the insurance company was still paying benefits and awaiting his death. He eventually cut a deal for a lump sum and used it to start up a construction business in Los Angeles—all thanks to the Dorsey Brothers' prudent advice.

When World War II drove up the cost of materials, he went back to playing organ on radio programs like the *Boston Blackie* detective show (where he was credited as Charles Cornell), and formed a group called the Hollywood Rhythm-Aires. He also recorded song demos at home on his own disc-cutting machine, including the topical "The Axis Trio: Hitler, Tojo, Mussolini."

He played USO shows locally during the war and recalled, "Some of the pianos were really funny, the keys wouldn't work and all. You just took what you could get." His children remember two fine grand pianos and an organ in their own living room. Famous guests from Cornell's music days would play them together. The children also saw Léon Theremin's electronic instrument, and Harry Partch's homemade ones.

In the mid-1980s an as-yet unidentified jazz researcher mentioned Cornell's accordion career while talking on NPR, repeating the story that he had died young. A friend called and corrected the man who then interviewed Cornell. The family never heard more from him or saw anything in print. If it can be found, that writer's interview might be a fascinating document of early jazz accordion history.

Cornell's final impeccably timed farewell came in 1993 when he died at five minutes after eight o'clock, echoing his own song, "South on the 8:05." His accordions were long gone, sold in the 1930s after he got sick. All that remains with his family are the glittering personalized nameplates taken from the instrument that had played with Ellington in the Jazz Age. The final reminder of the short but extraordinary career of Accordion Joe.

Mario Perry: "The Old Accordion Man," with Paul Whiteman and Rudy Wiedoeft

Jazz accordionist Mario Perry worked with some of the most influential musicians of the Roaring Twenties. That's him on Ruth Etting's Tin Pan Alley classic "Sam, the Old Accordion Man," recorded in 1927 during the time he filled the accordion seat in Paul Whiteman's famous orchestra. Earlier he also played with the less well remembered but remarkably influential saxophonist Rudy Wiedoeft.

Perry was an Italian American born in 1900, and, like Cornell, his career was cut short. He died on August 2, 1929, at the Queen of Angels hospital in Los Angeles, killed by his friend, jazz violinist Joe Venuti, who had been driving while drunk.

Years later, powerhouse accordionist Charles Magnante called Perry's work with saxophone pioneer Rudy Wiedoeft key in the development of jazz accordion. When not dressed up as a cowboy and touring London on horseback, Wiedoeft made at least three hundred early saxophone recordings with every major record company. His Palace Trio recordings (named after New York's famous vaudeville theater, the Palace) included the young, doomed accordionist. By the time Wiedoeft's popularity faded with the advent of jazz (and the increase of his alcohol intake), Perry had moved on to play violin and accordion with Paul Whiteman's tremendously popular orchestra.

Whiteman is remembered today for his oft-dismissed self-billing as "the King of Jazz." He's associated with mostly sweet non-improvised dance music, which has earned few enthusiasts among modern historians and critics. Whiteman nevertheless was one of the key innovators of the big band era. Most of the classic leaders like Ellington were very interested in Whiteman's arrangements and voicing (and of course his popularity and the size of his bank account). The exposure that Perry and his accordion got with Whiteman must have been extraordinary.

Given that Cornell Smelser and Mario Perry's careers both ended just as jazz was accelerating, it's impossible to know how influential they might have been in the new music had they lived. Wiedoeft's saxophone career shows how one artist could introduce an instrument to the nation or even the world. Though other accordionists like Ira "Buster" Moten recorded later, losing Perry and Cornell cost two trailblazing proponents of the instrument and set back its chances of finding a place in jazz. Their few scattered cylinders and 78-rpm records echo a time when the accordion's future in jazz was still uncharted.

The Cellar Boys and the Mysterious Charles Melrose

Early jazz players from the 1920s and '30s have slipped from all but the faintest living memory. Some are recalled for association with known artists, in this case the ill-fated but well-known clarinet player Frank Teschemacher, who recorded a series of brash, forward-looking solos in Chicago around 1930, before dying in a car wreck. "Tesch" famously played and recorded with Bix Beiderbecke, but he also made one record with a small group known as the Cellar Boys (named after a place they played), which included a certain Charles Melrose on accordion.

In an interview, Ida Melrose Shoufler (daughter of the Cellar Boys' pianist Frank Melrose) claimed that there was no "Charles Melrose." This gave rise to speculation that the player might be "Buster" Moten (see later in this chapter) under an assumed name, integrating the all-white

Cellar Boys. There are similarities between the Cellar Boys' recordings and those "Buster" Moten made with his uncle Bennie Moten's pre-Count Basie band. But based on the very short solos it's difficult to judge. The two Cellar Boys recordings seem to feature more use of the left-hand bass for accompanying, and the longest solo on their "Wailing Blues" is a nice rough ride. Ida Melrose recalled that her Uncle Lee did play accordion, but did not record with her father. If there was no "Charlie Melrose," it remains a mystery whose music was cut into these fragile discs.

It's easiest to jump to the conclusion that an early accordionist might be a name known from other records: "Buster" Moten, Cornell Smelser, Charles Magnante, or even an unlikely Charlie Creath (also appearing later in this chapter). But the few known jazz accordionists did not fill all the accordion chairs in bands around the country. Whoever Charlie Melrose was, he (or she) was one among many. There is next to no information about these players because nobody ever thought to ask. As Ida Melrose put it, "We are left with a 'musical mystery.' I wonder if there is anyone on the planet who would know."

J.C. Woodard: Lonely Minstrel of the Circus/ The Greatest Jazz Accordionist in the South

Beginning in the early 1930s, accordionist J.C. Woodard was looking for bigger things. Today we can follow his professional path in scattered clippings he left behind. The trail begins with an undated photograph of Joe White's Harmony Kings in Jackson, Mississippi. Eight members of the band are dressed in white, standing by their leader's trap drum kit. Joe White's bass drum is painted with text and a butterfly-winged fairy. It reads hopefully, "On The Air Regular," with the band's name, phone number, and address. On the ground in front of the group are numerous horns, various saxes, and a clarinet. One member holds a megaphone for pre-electricity vocals. In the center, in a contrasting dark suit, White holds what must be sheet music while the other members of the band, including piano player J.C. Woodard, look on attentively as if to say, "This is a high-class band that reads music."

According to the *Chicago Defender*, in 1931 Woodard was still in Jackson, but playing accordion with the Southern Troubadours. He'd vacated his piano bench in favor of "Little Brother" Montgomery. Montgomery was a local star because he had been to Chicago and made some early piano jazz recordings. As the "race" record industry fell into the Depression he returned to Mississippi. One piano player must have been enough, so Woodard took the somewhat unusual route of switching to accordion.

There is no clear evidence of what type of instrument Woodard played, but "Little Brother" Montgomery's blues and boogie-woogie would presumably have required a chromatic instrument. Since Woodard had been a pianist, it seems likely he would take up piano accordion.

Woodard's career continues through the pages of the *Defender*. In 1933 he wrote from Natchez, Mississippi, "looking to join some hot orchestra," and billed himself as "the greatest of all jazz accordionists and pianists in the South." The Chicago-based paper aimed to serve the black community nationwide, and in February 1933, Woodard garnered a small headline by thanking the *Defender* for assisting him in finding a "big job." His new employer was Arthur A. Wright, music supervisor for Ringling Brothers and Barnum and Bailey. Woodard was joining the circus.

The possibly self-penned notice lauds him again as "America's greatest jazz accordion player," and adds "composer of over one hundred songs, some of which are now being brought to the public by Famous Music Publishers" (a company founded in 1928 to publish music for talking pictures). Woodard ends by saying he's on his way from New Orleans to New York to join Ringling Brothers and "a letter from friends would be appreciated."

At the end of the circus season in the fall, Woodard was back in Mississippi looking for work. In December 1933 he wrote Meridian, Mississippi, "Star accordionist (squeeze box) of Ringling Brothers circus, promises to answer all letters." He must have struggled in the heart of the Depression but in 1936 he got back with Ringling Brothers.

The circus's sideshow in 1936 included: "Prof. Disco" (Punch and Judy puppets and magic); "Melvin Burkhart, the anatomical marvel"; "Singales, the man with the fireproof skin"; a performer billed as "Alfred Langevin, the man who smokes through his eyes!"; and a troupe of South Sea Islanders and hula dancers.

Below the hula dancers, and just above "ticket sellers," was the sideshow band's brass and drum sections, and finally: "Minstrels: Roland Canada, comedian; Dusty Cunningham, comedian; W.H. Bowman, singer; J.C. Woodards, accordionist." He was the last performer on the bill.

The only other mention we have of Woodard has him again with Ringling Brothers' small minstrel troupe in 1943. Almost 1,500 other

Surplus Pianos Outplay the Accordion

IN THE EARLY 1900s there were no piano players yet in most New Orleans dance bands. One reason this changed was a sudden prevalence of pianos for musicians to play. While blues and jazz were developing around the turn of the last century, pianos' cost and portability were (counterintuitively) quite competitive with the accordion. Expensive new accordions were something to dream about, but pianos were everywhere.

Millions of middle-class households in North America had purchased mass-produced pianos by 1920. Mostly female musicians played them in family parlors as both entertainment and status symbol. Combined with store-bought sheet music, they were the home-entertainment system of the day. Then came "pianola"—player pianos. These technical marvels were marketed as replacements for what were disparagingly called "silent pianos" (those requiring music lessons). More than a million "self-playing" instruments were sold in the years prior to the Great Depression. These new passive music-makers greatly concerned musicians, instructors, and sheet-music publishers. Little did they know the technological upheaval to come with the rise of recording and radio.

By the time jazz recording began, millions of serviceable pianos were facing early retirement in the United States. They became common in all but the most impoverished bars and clubs, and widely available for young and aspiring musicians. Ray Charles for instance, famously learned to play on a beat-up upright in a local café in the early 1930s. This abundance of pianos made them an easy choice for jazz musicians over other accompanying instruments like accordions.

"The Passing of the Silent Piano." New player piano leaves a traditional instrument out on the curb. Aeolian Company advertisement, September 1911. *Pianola Institute, London.*

circus folks were with the show at the time, and even though wartime gas-rationing cut into their travel they still did 370 performances in 188 days. Officials claimed that more than four million people saw the circus that year.

It's not known if Woodard had worked the circus through the Depression or if he found better situations. Circus bands tend to be tightly choreographed to follow a show's action, leaving little room for jazz. The sideshow band wouldn't have had to coordinate with trapeze artists, but it probably wasn't the "hot orchestra" Woodard had advertised for in 1933. We're left with a fading glimpse of the "best jazz accordionist in the South," performing in a sideshow, presumably in blackface, remembering life in Mississippi and hoping for letters from friends.

Accordionists Take Jazz to the Territories

As jazz grew in urban centers in the 1920s, "territory bands" formed and toured to less populated areas—pretty much anywhere where people wanted to dance. The 1920s to the '50s represented the largest communal dance craze in history, so there was a lot of work for musicians. Traveling hundreds of miles between shows, each group would stake out a territory, often promoted from a central radio station that featured the band as entertainment and advertised upcoming dances.

Hundreds of these bands played in different regions. Accordions would not have been unusual, especially in areas with ethnic populations. The territory system also worked for distinctly ethnic ensembles and western swing bands, which often featured accordions.

To be heard, bands included as many instruments as they could afford, especially in rural areas before electrical amplification. The accordion had the necessary volume and could hold chords and sustain notes to fill more space than a piano. The reedy sound of early accordions also cut through (for good or ill) the din of other instruments. As accordions grew more sophisticated they could shift tones to add color like a synthesizer might today. A squeezebox was also, of course, more portable than a piano, and you could stand up to do a solo.

Many traveling bands didn't record and aren't widely remembered. Without many recordings of well-known and admired players, accordions fell out of the jazz narrative.

Hollis Peavey's band at the Roseland Ballroom in Winnipeg. Includes (L to R): Eddie Condon, banjo; Doris Peavey, accordion; Hollis Peavey, center, saxophone; Harold Cranford, drums; Tal Sexton, trombone. *University of Winnipeg Archives, Western Canada Pictorial Index, Miscellaneous Collection (A0268-8598).*

Doris Peavey and Peavey's Jazz Bandits

Jazz guitarist Eddie Condon played banjo as a teenager in accordionist Doris Peavey's territory group Peavey's Jazz Bandits. Lead by Doris's husband, Hollis Peavey, the band played improvised jazz and pop tunes in Iowa, Wisconsin, and Minnesota, wintering in Winnipeg, Manitoba (music promoters called the whole region "the Near Northwest").

Beginning after World War I, Doris began playing piano for silent-movie houses and joined her future husband in a band that gradually began to play the new jazz style. The young Condon joined them after they formed the Jazz Bandits in 1922. Years later he remembered Doris as "beautiful and a fine musician. She spent a lot of time teaching me chords and modulations." She could sing, too, but the band was so loud it drowned out vocalists in the days before PA systems.

The Bandits brought jazz to new audiences in the pre-Depression 1920s. Condon recalled their small-town shows: "On dance nights the cows and the dead men stayed home; everyone else got to the pavilion by foot, horse or wheel. A Model T Ford normally carried twelve." They broadcast widely on radio to promote their shows, but unfortunately the group never recorded, sticking with playing dance halls far from the music-industry centers of New York or Chicago.

The Peaveys eventually moved out to California and kept a band together all the way up to 1960. Hollis was elected Republican mayor of Huntington Park, California, in the 1940s, and Doris continued to play mostly piano and organ at home and church. She died in 1973, the first known female jazz accordionist.

Charlie Creath: Jazz-o-Mania on the Mississippi

Another artist from a different territory was Charlie Creath, an African American bandleader and trumpet player who operated on steamboats up and down the Mississippi in the 1920s and '30s. He was from Missouri, and was recalled as the most famous St. Louis bandleader of the time. Jazz researcher Garvin Bushell reports that Creath was one of the only players outside of Louisiana to play blues as well as or better than players from New Orleans.

Creath's group, the Jazz-O-Maniacs, recorded in St. Louis several times between 1924 and 1927. Band members included guitarist Lonnie Johnson playing violin and singing some of the first male vocal blues on record. Creath was so successful regionally that, like Paul Whiteman's orchestras, he had several bands working different steamboats under his name.

He stopped playing trumpet after a two-year illness from 1928–30 (reportedly tuberculosis). Afterwards he played saxophone and also picked up accordion, but unfortunately he never recorded with either. Creath was in ill health for years and dropped out of music in the 1940s. He worked as a saloon keeper and bouncer in Chicago, then in an airplane factory. Meanwhile, he was said to have had a serious gambling problem and he died by suicide in 1951. The coroner's report read, "Shot self while temporarily insane due to ill health."

Unless some unknown recordings are discovered, Creath's jazz accordion remains undocumented. But he was there, playing squeezebox on the riverboats of the Mississippi in the 1930s, spreading jazz everywhere the river went.

Ira "Buster" Moten: Squeezin' with Basie

The two most famous black big bandleaders were Count Basie and Duke Ellington. Anyone associated with them had a chance to make history.

Both leaders had passing associations with accordion players. Cornell Smelser recorded a few sides with Ellington, and a young Count Basie played with Bennie Moten's accordionist nephew Ira ("Buster" or "Bus") Moten. Basie recalled, "And then there was Bus. He knew what was happening, and he could really swing on that accordion."

Little is known about "Bus" Moten, though he is the most well-known black jazz accordionist. He was born in about 1903 and his birth name seems to have been Ira Alexander Smith. He changed his name to Moten after joining his famous uncle Bennie's Kansas City Orchestra in about 1929. Reports that they were brothers or cousins appear to be inaccurate.

"Bus" was a good-looking guy who acted as front man and conductor for the orchestra, and sat in on piano when Bennie was off-stage managing the band's business. Bus added accordion to his showmanship after Bennie hired the talented young William Basie as second piano. Picking up the instrument with little training, Moten remembered, "I had no job... My job was sitting there on the bandstand looking at my watch... I drove everyone out of the rooming house trying to learn it...

The Bennie Moten Band: Jimmy Rushing, vocalist at left; Count Basie, piano L; "Buster" Moten, accordion; Bennie Moten, piano R. *Courtesy of the American Jazz Museum.*

I got five tunes down and played choruses only on those." People then told his uncle, "Who is this kid, better keep him in, he's forty percent of the band."

Basie remembered his days with Moten's orchestra: "The audience also loved the way Bus riffed on that accordion." Moten wasn't the best player, and reportedly had a challenging personality and was difficult to work with. But he was the only accordionist who played with Count Basie—until Basie walked off with the band. Basie's famous orchestra sprang from the breakup of Bennie Moten's group after Bennie died in 1935 from a botched tonsillectomy. Moten's nephew took over the group for a time, but Basie soon split, taking many of the other players to join the fledgling jazz aristocracy.

Prior to Moten's death the band had recorded more than two dozen sides with Buster playing accordion between 1929 and 1930. Many of the tracks are uneven; Buster's short solos are often rather loud and jarring. But "Moten Blues" may be the greatest representation of Kansas

Christine Chatman and band at the Rose Room in Dallas, 1943.
Courtesy of Dan Kochakian.

City jazz squeezebox. You can imagine Bus on the bandstand with his comping accordion chords while others soloed. The sound would have carried over a crowded ballroom full of dancers, and still rings fine today.

After Basie left, Moten led the remaining Moten big band and as the 1940s turned into the '50s, took up electric organ and recorded as Bus Moten and His Men. The accordion had fallen away—and Moten died in 1965 at age sixty-two. If he'd been a better bandleader or a better player, Bus Moten might have kept his uncle's group together and brought the accordion more friends in jazz. As it was, the instrument didn't carry on into the swing bands and only a few jazz accordionists continued into the small groups of the 1950s and later.

More Black Jazz and R&B Accordionists

A persistent trickle of lesser-known black jazz accordionists showed up from the 1920s through the '40s. The most widely remembered was probably Alphonso Trent, who, in the late 1920s, led the most popular and influential territory band out of Texas. They played extensively in Dallas and up into the Midwest, filling ballrooms for weeks and months on end as well as broadcasting on major radio stations. Trent played piano on their few recordings but doubled on accordion live. Publicity photos show the instrument up front as a colorful part of his act as leader.

The fabulously named Texas Blues Destroyers were a power duo who, in 1924, recorded the same two songs for three different New York record labels in one week—a fine way to stretch your repertoire if you can make the deals before being found out. The records feature Arthur Ray on harmonium/pump organ and Bubber Miley on trumpet. Advertisements for the records, however, include an image of an accordionist, suggesting that Ray might have also played squeezebox. It's equally possible that the designers for Ajax Records (company slogan: "The Quality Race Record") didn't listen carefully enough to their recordings to draw the correct instrument.

Madame Dewey was a less widely publicized black accordionist. In 1931 she broadcast on WLTH in Brooklyn, New York, with the May-Mil Trio on a show called *Plantation Sketches*. A review from *Negro World* billed her as a "noted contralto" and "the only known woman of our race who has mastered [piano accordion] technique."

The Sepia Syncopators were John Smith's band based in Washington, D.C., in the 1930s. They are preserved in a damaged photograph featuring an unknown black piano accordion player.

The famous all-women International Sweethearts of Rhythm orchestra was led by an accordionist. Researcher Antoinette Handy reports that Sweethearts' musical director and arranger Edna Armstead Williams was "fully capable of filling in on any instrument in the band." Usually she sang, played trumpet, or accordion. Williams later had her own sextet in Los Angeles where she recorded an album (on trumpet), but apparently died young before it was released in 1946.

While World War II raged, Christine Chatman rocked the African American chitlin' circuit as the "Boogie Woogie Piano and Accordion Queen." In 1943 the *Pittsburgh Courier* hyped her orchestra's performances to benefit the Tuskegee Airmen. The "highly resourceful" Miss Chatman "distinguished herself on the piano, accordion, trumpet, and saxophone, while her 'torch blues chirping' added color and radiance to her winning charm." The show featured lessons in a new dance "that may soon have jitterbugging on the downgrade," provocatively called the "Rubbin." More reasons to remember Chatman; her opening act was future blues icon Big Maybelle.

Atypical as they were for taking up the accordion, these artists are undeniably intriguing. Ironically, one of the reasons their stories are compelling today is because so few recorded, and so little is known about them. Beyond a few other notables like Julie Gardner, not until the 1980s rise of zydeco and African players like Tony Cedras would black accordionists return to popular stages.

Julie Gardner: The Accordionist behind Charlie Parker

"Hail the Queen of the Squeezebox," declared the *Chicago Defender* in 1941. Raised in Augusta, Georgia, Julie Gardner (born 1925) not only toured to remote parts of the world, but joined Earl Hines's stateside band while Charlie Parker and Dizzy Gillespie were working out the advances of bebop.

Before her brush with modern jazz, Gardner performed solo as a singer and accordionist in Chicago and then in Boston with Sabby Lewis's band, eventually appearing with Louis Jordan and Charlie Barnet as well. In 1942, *Billboard* magazine described her as "a buxom lass with plenty of vim and a fair enough delivery." The following year she was famously photographed with Charlie Parker and Dizzy Gillespie in Earl Hines's big band.

Gardner left Hines, and by December 1943 was returning from her first trip abroad performing for the U.S. military with Willie Bryant. She was part of the global USO wartime entertainment project. For the first time, "Negro talent" was included, organized throughout the world by Harlem Renaissance theater producer Dick Campbell.

Gardner's group first played for military outfits in the Caribbean. Fellow performer Kenneth Spencer hoped that, "Our appearances before those men, almost all of whom were white, brought back to them an awareness of the Negro back home whose problems they may have thought were left behind." At one point in their ten-nation Caribbean tour, they were flown to an unmarked, unnamed supply ship on the open sea. They were treated "like visiting royalty," did their show, and were flown to base. They never knew what secret mission their sailor audiences were bound for.

Earl Hines's big band, Apollo Theater, 1943: Dizzy Gillespie, far left; Billy Eckstine, at microphone; Sarah Vaughan, piano; Charlie Parker, far right; Julie Gardner, accordion (detail, above). *Photo by Austin Hansen, Photographs and Prints Division, Schomburg Center for Research in Black Culture, New York Public Library.*

By July 1944, Gardner was with the first small group of black USO performers that played, "to the delight of soldiers," in the South Pacific. Uncommon though it may have been in jazz, her accordion was practical for small mobile groups playing for audiences from fifty people to five thousand under small tents or outdoors. Servicemen called the well-built Gardner their "Pistol Packin' Mama," after her jump-blues version of Al Dexter's well-armed country-accordion hit.

Vincent Tubbs was one of very few African American war correspondents in World War II. (Prior to the war, his reporting had focused on lynchings in the U.S.) He saw Gardner open a USO show in the South Pacific in May 1944:

> The hot midday sun beamed down mercilessly on the backs of the audience... Julie Gardner crept unobtrusively across the stage with her accordion. She was the first female of the troupe the boys saw. They did not greet her appearance with applause. A strong hum swept the audience as she crossed the stage, the men were dubious.
>
> But when she grabbed her squeeze box and began to sing, "that locked it up." She was the star of the show... To the boys she's a whole constellation... they had to join in, and the whole hillside jumped.
>
> [Slipping some street references to her audience, Gardner sang a Nat Cole song:]
>
> "Hit that jive, Jack / Put it in your pocket 'til I get back / Goin' downtown to see a man / I ain't got time to shake your hand."
>
> Julie worked hard on her first number and the sun worked hard on her. She perspired profusely; but for all her effort and discomfort she was richly repaid... the soldiers howled and applauded so loudly she dared not step more than two feet away from the microphone.*

After the war ended in August 1945, Gardner continued to perform for the USO. In November she finally returned from playing for service men and women in Alaska who had yet to make it home. Tracing her travels during the war, it seems likely she appeared on civilian or Armed Forces' radio, but no recordings have come to light. Much of her career

---

* Reprinted with permission from the *Baltimore Afro-American*, May 6, 1944.

was during the time of the 1942–44 Musicians' Union recording strike. Once she returned from her travels, she disappeared from the public eye.

Almost thirty years later, in November 1973, "accordionist and vocalist Julie Gardner" was acknowledged during a "Women's All-Star Jam Session" at the New York Jazz Museum. Gardner played with pioneers from the big band era including Norma Carson and Carline Ray of the International Sweethearts of Rhythm, and with drummer Dottie Dodgion who played with Benny Goodman. The show achieved "the largest attendance to date" for the museum, and served as a reminder of the thousands of women whose music meant so much to a country at war.

Today, photos of Earl Hines's 1943 band appear frequently with comments about Diz and Parker's challenge to the expectations of swing bands and audiences. No one seems to have noticed Gardner seated directly behind Parker playing through three challenges: as a woman, as a woman playing jazz, and as a woman playing jazz accordion. Every fan knows Charlie Parker. It may be time to look just behind him to check out Gardner's challenge to the expectations of what it meant to play jazz.

Jazz Accordionists at the Pinnacle: 1940s–60s

By the postwar 1950s and 1960s, the social dancing craze had settled down as fans started families and stayed home with their new TVs. Jazz shifted away from the massively popular dance bands of the 1930s and 1940s. Instead, many listeners followed small-group R&B or studio-produced pop and mood music. Modern jazz spun into an era of splintered subgenres. The wilder reaches of bebop and Ornette Coleman's free jazz never sold a lot of records, and forward-looking jazz became outsiders' music. The public amicably ignored it and moved on.

The accordion, meanwhile, was at the absolute peak of its popularity, with millions of students emulating their favorite accordion idols. Most 1950s and '60s accordion records served this market. Some of the easy-listening sort were so tasteful they lost any flavor. Others exploited the dynamics of the new "hi-fi" craze for exotic effects. A few jazz accordionists advanced the instrument, but not all of them left recordings from their journey. Almost all the records that did come out have entirely escaped the reissue frenzy of the CD and digital eras. This has made appreciating the masters of accordion jazz nearly impossible for modern audiences. Their music deserves better.

Tito Guidotti's Swingtette: Organize Your Own Ensemble

Despite the efforts of jazz accordionists in the 1920s and '30s, famous swing bands we think of today—Glenn Miller, Count Basie, Benny Goodman, and Duke Ellington—rarely if ever featured the instrument. Other big dance bands did hire accordionists, but they haven't stuck in the public's memory.

Some skillful accordionists had a style unsuited for working with bands. Vincent Pirro told of tracking down "a strictly accordion player who was supposed to be a topnotcher" to fill in for him one night. He returned to an outraged orchestra after the replacement hogged the spotlight, demanded solos, and played too loud. Pirro warned, "Desire to show off is one of the greatest drawbacks to keeping a steady job [at least in a 1936 society band]." Regardless, from the 1930s on, the most famous swing bands had settled into Fletcher Henderson's standard sans-squeezebox instrumentation. Accordionists who wanted to play out had to make their own way.

"In your own community you have probably encountered the difficulty where other musicians have refused to permit the accordion into their swing bands." Jazz accordionist Tito Guidotti shared his enterprising response in a 1948 article: "There are undoubtedly two or three more persons in your locality with similar experiences ... Instead of fretting ... contact the other accordionists and organize your own ensemble."

At age eighteen in 1928, Guidotti was on the paid staff at WLS radio in Chicago. He moved to New York and played for the Ziegfeld Follies on Broadway in the early 1930s, then went into vaudeville. He'd toured the U.K., and did some movies in Hollywood. Frustrated by the resistance to jazz accordion, in 1938 he formed his Swingtette (three accordions, bass, and guitar). They got noticed by Paul Whiteman, who boosted the band with appearances on his Chesterfield radio show. Guidotti became one of the first jazz accordionists to play as an equal to the others in the band—the accordion felt like a real jazz instrument rather than a colorful interloper.

Interrupted by the war, Guidotti did USO tours with a four-man "foxhole" group on the front lines in the Pacific. He returned as the big bands folded or split up at the end of the Depression. Smaller jazz groups came into their own, and accordion jazz, following Guidotti's example, spread amidst the great accordion boom of the 1950s.

During the Musicians' Union strike in 1948, Guidotti was said to be "preparing new material to record when and if the recording ban is lifted." He released his only LP, *Accordion Magic*, around 1950, collecting tracks like, "Accordion Boogie," "High Tension," Opus for Squeezebox," and the evocative "Nightmare of a Termite." He continued composing, with several classical pieces emerging in the 1960s and '70s, but no further recordings are known. He spent his time teaching, handing down what he had learned in his career, and died in Los Angeles in 1982.

Cleveland Nickerson's Music Masters

One last black jazz accordionist known to have played in the 1940s was Cleveland Nickerson. What little we know about him is that he played piano accordion during World War II and a few years after, and he never had a big break. He kept small groups together under different names in Chicago and then out west, but left only scant evidence.

"Three boys who really are masters of the art of jive." Cleveland Nickerson's band the Music Masters left a trade-paper trail starting in mid-1940s Chicago. Throughout the war, Nickerson's trio played clubs there and in "some of the nation's outstanding spots." *Billboard* commended their scat singing and "solid swing." Another reviewer said the "trio punches out all the way" on guitar, bass, and Nickerson's accordion, calling it an "unusual instrument for a colored lad."

By 1945 all the members of the trio had moved to Los Angeles and were performing at the upscale Zanzibar Room. They were billed as the Ali Baba Trio, complete with fezzes and turbans. The Ali Babas made two short "soundie" films with the remarkable singer Valaida Snow. Snow was a multi-instrumentalist trumpeter/singer/dancer/bandleader at a time when women were allowed to dance or sing and maybe play piano, but few led bands with a horn. Unfortunately we can't watch Snow play her trumpet with Cleveland and the Ali Babas. The trio made a total of four short films in 1946: two with Snow on vocals. All feature laid-back West Coast jazz, fezzes, and Nickerson on accordion.

Unfortunately, Nickerson's trio never succeeded in their climb toward fame. After they left the Zanzibar Room in 1945, they seemingly disappeared from the entertainment press. Finally, less than ten years after their start in the business, the trio (still called the Ali Babas), received a *Billboard* magazine farewell in 1948 noting that they and other "semi-name bands" were playing up in Oregon at "Salem's newest night club," the Club Combo. The Ali Baba Trio had come "from Hollywood" for one week only. As far as we know, they may never have made it back.

Art Van Damme: The Hippest

Art Van Damme was by far the most well-known and influential American jazz accordionist. When he died in 2010 he was held in the highest esteem by old-school accordion fans. Classic jazz listeners as well would certainly mention his name if they were asked to name a jazz accordionist.

Writers introducing Van Damme use colorful phrases like "the hippest cat to ever swing an accordion." Art earned that title in the 1950s with records like *Cocktail Capers* and *Martini Time*, almost always combining his smooth accordion tone with guitar and hovering vibes. Van Damme ushered the accordion into the hi-fi era, and the dramatic improvements in recording technology and in accordions themselves make these much better recordings than earlier ones.

Van Damme was undeniably a virtuoso, but today's casual listener is tempted to classify his style as "lounge music." One hipster historian described it as "just a little more jazzy than easy listening, and a little more light than the bebop of his jazz contemporaries." It fits Brian Eno's definition of the greatest background music, being easily ignorable if you didn't want to be distracted, but interesting if you stop to listen. In the 1950s and '60s a lot of listeners were interested in Van Damme. He made dozens of records over a sixty-year career, and won the *Downbeat* readers' poll for "Best Jazz Accordionist" ten years running—back when *Downbeat* had such a category.

Would modern audiences react similarly? Like most recordings in the 1950s and early '60s, before the shift to youth-oriented rock music, his were adult-oriented, especially the newly developed, upscale LPs. But Van Damme's five-hour retrospective compilation *Swingin' the Accordion* wouldn't be my first choice to convince modern listeners to listen to the instrument. "Up-to-date" and "modern" perfectly encapsulated the Van Damme sound, but it's the cool of another era.

It takes uncommon ears to appreciate such impeccable unobtrusiveness. For shallower listeners, an amusing entrée to set the mood for Van

Damme's music is to imagine the early 1960s bachelor's pad for which his LPs were marketed. Cocktail jazz like this had romance built into it, alongside a territorial chance to demonstrate expensive hi-fi equipment. The new extended format (fifteen minutes per side!) lent itself to amorous endeavors, so you could stack your record-changer with *Cocktail Capers* (1950), *More Cocktail Capers* (1952), *Martini Time* (1953), and *Music for Lovers* (1967), all in hopes of making it to *Ecstasy* (1967).

Besides campy titles and sleeve designs that practically define "retro," Van Damme's music is definitely worthwhile. His *Accordion à la Mode* and *A Perfect Match*, from 1961 and 1963 respectively, hold their own as cool jazz with a bit of grit. And if you are throwing a *House Party* (1956), Van Damme may be the perfect *Invitation* (1974).

Alice Hall: Queen of the Jazz Accordion

Though he remains by far the most well-known modern jazz accordionist, Van Damme was by no means the first or the most adventurous. When you want to put on someone with a bit more traction, Alice Hall is the jazz accordion star you've probably never heard but should. It would be easier if the accordion was more acceptable in jazz, and if being a female jazz musician didn't already offer plenty of obstacles, and if she'd recorded more.

Alice Hall was born Alice Marie Laquiere in 1917 in Brussels, Belgium. Her family immigrated to the U.S. and she grew up in Detroit. Her father played accordion and started her on drums when she was five so she could accompany him. At eleven she followed in her dad's footsteps and began playing European-style chromatic button accordion. She carried on playing this instrument, rare in the U.S., adopting the finto-piano keyboard that Pietro Frosini and other vaudevillians used to hide their old-country backgrounds.

Hall ended up being one of the hottest jazz accordionists in history. She got her first professional jobs at age thirteen on Detroit radio. As her age made it hard to find club dates, her dad opened his own bar, the Blue Star, where he could watch over her. There she started a group with her sister Rae (Rachel) on drums and second accordion. They got significant attention during the war, when men were away and women musicians had more opportunities. In *Billboard* magazine's *Music Year Book* of 1943, her quartet was advertised simply as "2 Boys, 2 Girls, Sax, Piano, Accordion, drums."

E. Reed

She admitted later that she wasn't that interested in recording: "I was too busy gigging to record much." In a 1997 NPR interview she told how Benny Goodman invited her to join him on tour, but the club owner where she was on contract wouldn't release her. She then turned down Jack Teagarden when he asked her to join his band. She later said, "Playing with a big band, you know how many chances you get to play sixteen bars of something or eight bars of something and that's it? You know, there's nothing there... I wanted to prove that something can be done on this instrument, other than playing just the ordinary, 'Jolly Caballero' stuff, you know? So I proved it."

Sticking with her small group where she controlled what she wanted to play, Hall made only one known commercial recording, a single 78-rpm disc released by Capitol Records in 1949. The two sides of this record—the standards "Caravan" and "Pennies from Heaven"—reveal a scorching soloist joyfully scatting in harmony with herself over bop improvisations. Capitol had signed her to a year-long contract, but the 1948 recording strike was in effect; after it finally ended she never recorded beyond those two sides. When she died in June 2000, her lone recording had been out of print for fifty years.

Her only other known recordings are from a self-released cassette tape made in the 1950s or '60s. They feature her trio and quartets and the quality is live and raw. I hunted for this tape for six years in archives and online auctions, and though imperfect, it does not disappoint. Hall is a force of joyous energy. There may still be other surprises out there: Hall appeared on the barrier-breaking *Nat King Cole Show* during its short run challenging TV's racial segregation from 1956–57. She had the same manager as Cole and may have been one of the artists who worked the show for low or no pay to support Cole's challenge to all-white TV programming.

Hall worked and played with Benny Goodman, Lena Horne, Dizzy Gillespie, Peggy Lee, and Duke Ellington. Louis Armstrong said about her style, "Nobody teaches you to play that kind of music, you gotta feel it." Jazz virtuoso Leon Sash and his wife, bassist Lee Morgan (not the well-known trumpet player), were great friends of Hall's and told a story about when she was about sixty years old. She had a broken arm in a sling and was attacked by a mugger, but she knocked the guy unconscious with her cast. Alice Hall was not to be trifled with.

FACING Alice Hall. *Author's collection.*

In the 1970s though, she disappeared from the music scene entirely. Talking with Dean Olsher on NPR in 1997, Hall told how she'd fallen into a deep depression when she found out her husband was cheating on her. She eventually checked herself into an institution where she did not speak for almost ten years. In 1985 she returned to a changed world for the accordion. At perhaps its lowest ebb of public support, she became an energetic booster of the instrument, publishing the *Friends of the Accordion* newsletter in Los Angeles and counseling players who came to her for support. She lived until June 2000, long enough to watch the beginning of the revival of her instrument, but no one has come close to replacing her.

Leon Sash: The Master

He was called "Leon the Lion" or simply "the Master" and is spoken of as the Art Tatum or Oscar Peterson of jazz accordion. Sadly, since his early death in 1979, Leon Sash has remained unheralded outside of a small circle of his students and other old-school accordionists. Of his five albums only one was ever reissued on CD. In this age of supposed digital liberation it is nearly impossible to hear his crucial music.

Born into the Polish community of Chicago in 1922, Sash lost his sight when he was twelve. His uncle Charlie gave him a chromatic accordion to take his mind off the loss of his vision. Without taking lessons he could imitate music he heard coming from the apartment upstairs. He then studied with various teachers, including Lou Klatt and Andy Rizzo, and played guitar, vibes, and violin semi-professionally before finally resolving to focus solely on accordion.

Like Alice Hall and the vaudeville maestro Pietro Frosini, Sash played a finto-piano button accordion with false piano keys. His technique was so daunting that his posthumous LP *The Master* suggested slowing down the record in order to hear him playing two time signatures with different fingers on the same hand. Curiously, Sash encouraged students to stick with the piano accordion, saying that the three-row chromatic he played was "not a musical keyboard."

Sash's accordions were custom-made by the Giulietti company with a mic system to amplify their acoustic sound. Giulietti also designed an early electronic rig in a small external box as a response to the Cordovox accordion-organs, but it didn't win Sash's favor. Sash did support the innovative free-bass system, which he studied for only three months

Leon Sash, Jerry Cigler, and Jerry Brown who played as part of the Leon Sash Quintet, Chicago, 1962. *Courtesy of Paul Betken.*

before premiering it in the United States with a performance of Bach's organ music. Sash's last accordion was a lightweight model paid for by his students after he'd had a heart attack, but he seldom played it before his death.

Sash's first recordings were released as singles for Mercury in the 1950s, and were finally collected in 1983 on a posthumous LP, *Leon Sash: The Master*. These early records featured Leon with six singers, the Meadowlarks, who arranged a vocal blend imitating a band of horns and reeds a decade before groups like Manhattan Transfer. Sash released four LPs during his life. Two with his quartet, which included the great Ted Robinson on sax. One of these was Sash's performance in 1957 as the first accordionist invited to play the Newport Jazz Festival. His later two LPs and posthumously released tapes featured a slimmed-down trio or a quintet with two students playing specially tuned accordions in place of reed and brass sections.

When he died, Sash had not released any records in five years. Like Alice Hall, he claimed to be too busy playing to record much. He also gave up traveling almost entirely and focused on teaching and playing around Chicago. Listeners of the time had little to go on when comparing more prolific accordionists, but Sash's technique and style in existing recordings from the time demand his inclusion next to the top jazz accordionists.

Those lucky enough to study with Sash were first grilled with questions to discern whether they were serious enough to be worth teaching. If they passed the interview, they joined a select group who became Sash's friends and often his backup musicians. His unorthodox lessons were called "sittings," where he would demonstrate (without written music) how he thought the music should be played. Students would devise their own piano-key fingerings and go home to practice and repeat what they learned. Three highly regarded instructional transcriptions of his playing were published, *Leon Sash 'n' Jazz (Parts 1 & 2)* and 1963's *Rockin' Blues for Accordion*.

Sash died suddenly of a heart attack at age fifty-seven in 1979, he left friends and fans bereft, and an irreparable gap in the world of jazz accordion. His innovations remain as surprising as they were when he first played, and they demand to be heard.

Gordon "Gordie" Fleming: Sparkling Arpeggios

Some of the best North American accordion jazz came out of Winnipeg, Manitoba, in the Canadian Prairies. If scintillating cocktail jazz isn't your thing, this is the place. Gordon Fleming's flowing bebop solos earned support from the harshest critics. The posthumous CD *According to Gordie* bears proof. Compiled by his daughter after his death, it's a wonderful tribute and covers Fleming's whole career, from his early 78-rpm records to radio broadcast tapes that might otherwise have been lost.

Fleming (1931–2002) started touring the Manitoba vaudeville circuit at age five. As a youngster he entertained at army camps during World War

II and started a lifetime of radio appearances. For the next four decades he did radio, TV, movie soundtracks, pop recordings, and jazz festivals, while fitting in after-hours jams and recordings with his various combos.

He also added his piano or accordion talents to pop and folk recordings and played with noted figures including Cat Stevens and Édith Piaf. Journalist Len Dobbin noted, "He made more money recording country tunes with artists like Hank Snow and Willie Lamothe [legendary French Canadian western singer] than he ever did playing jazz." He recorded folk music, orchestral pieces, and world music. He also produced a fake book of tunes from a hundred different countries, everything from Greek bouzouki and Yiddish horas to "gypsy" waltzes, but also Irish, Scottish, and Québécois jigs and reels.

The 1955 *Metronome* jazz accordion poll held him second only to Art Van Damme. Musicological listeners left reviews like, "Fleming's sparkling solos are full of bitonal arpeggios." Unlike some virtuoso performers, his work sounds relaxed and creative even when blazing along. If the accordion gets its due in jazz history and criticism, Fleming will be one of the ones who make it worthy of inclusion.

The most inspiring part of Fleming's story may be that it doesn't end in regrets but instead in familial dedication and tribute. It's encouraging to encounter an alternative to the tediously tragic stories of artists' struggles with drugs and failure. He lived a long life, and even after he suffered a stroke in 2000, he continued to play a keyboard with one hand until he died two years later. Thanks to his daughter Heidi compiling his recordings, we're able to appreciate him again. Nicely done, Gordie.

West Coast Accordionists: Cool Jazz and Polytones

Besides Van Damme, a small group of pro accordionists in California kept pushing jazz accordion. The first were what we might call "cool" jazz players like Joe Mooney, Ernie Felice, and Pete Jolly. All of them had diverse careers notable for stylish recordings in the late 1940s to '60s. Less orthodox were Tommy Gumina's experiments with clarinetist Buddy DeFranco.

Pete Jolly, for one, took the route of a behind-the-scenes session player in Los Angeles. For forty years he played mostly piano professionally, but after work he would bring out the accordion for club dates where he'd wow audiences. His style is borne out in the few surviving recordings of his sharply improvising accordion. He's probably indicative of many accordionists who found it hard to get work with the instrument they loved, despite the lack of the public's and record companies' attention. A few others are worth talking about in detail.

Joe Mooney: You Don't Need a Million

Joe Mooney said, "I haven't got a voice, just a delivery," but Frank Sinatra called him "the best." Mooney was a master of cool vocal jive, but also had a marvelous touch on accordion. LPs like 1946's *On the Rocks* arrived early in the "cocktail" era with a splash of wry lyrical humor. Unfortunately, he was a little too hip for most rooms, and broader audiences eluded him.

Mooney's career had begun in the 1920s when he sang in a crooning trio, the Sunshine Boys, with his brother and a young Tommy Dorsey. Later Mooney played for Paul Whiteman and did arrangements by dictation (Mooney was blind since childhood). Whiteman sponsored a visit to the Mayo Clinic to see if they could improve his sight, but no cure was possible. Mooney was grateful for the bandleader's gesture, but the disability never dented his good humor.

He formed a quartet in the late 1940s and sang laid-back jive like a natty Nat King Cole. He further developed his style with accordion and organ on a pair of records in the early 1960s. Heartbreakingly, despite bands and record deals in three different decades, audiences turned away each time in favor of brasher voices and, eventually, louder guitars.

Mooney maintained his cool and was greatly admired by musicians, regardless of the wider public's indifference. His up-tempo tune "You Don't Need a Million" is a sly charmer, and may have been a comment on the fortune he never quite garnered. As a posthumous consolation, unlike many groundbreaking accordionists, Mooney was so fondly remembered by people like Terry Teachout of the *New York Times* that reissues of most of his records made it to digital by the end of the CD era. Mooney's hip squeezebox is thankfully still available for discovery by that elusive wider audience.

Ernie Felice: The Sound

Before rock 'n' roll ensnared record companies with the allure of adolescents' wallets, music was for grown-ups. Postwar accordionist Ernie Felice spun sophisticated adult-oriented pop-jazz with a Sinatra feel.

When he had been a teenager himself in the 1930s, Felice was captivated by swing bands. In the audience at a Benny Goodman concert he told his friends, "I'm going to play with that man." Eventually he did. Without knowing of any other jazz accordionists, Felice formulated a unique style adapted from big band arrangements. While still in high school he began using sophisticated chords as if he was playing all four lines of a Glenn Miller or Benny Goodman sax section.

He was invited to join Goodman's sextet in 1946 after an audition where he outplayed the bandleader on pieces intended to test the limits of the accordion. Goodman used Felice in place of vibes (displacing one uncommon instrument with another). He later switched Felice out to bring the vibraphone back, but Felice had a Capitol Records contract by then and was off and running.

Felice and his quintet recorded while appearing on TV and film. His many records feature Felice singing along with stars like Bing Crosby and female harmonies reminiscent of the then-current "sisters" groups. They mostly showcase his smooth accordion and vocal tones with occasional showpieces demonstrating well-practiced fingering fireworks.

Felice's most lasting influence for jazz accordion was his sound. He developed a custom mute system, patented in the 1950s, with which he got a tone similar to a flute, layered with chiming accordion reeds. His sponsor, the Sonola accordion company, advertised his "tone chamber accordion designed especially for amplification. This means the accordion gives a pure, Felice-like chamber sound of its own." His subtle tone blended expertly with smooth jazz vocalists or mellow clarinets provided by Goodman or the Felice quintet. His "Felice-like" tone became the sound of jazz accordion.

When pop music bowed to its new youth market, artists like Felice could look back on their classy work with pride. They'd be forgiven for dismay at what was replacing them. Buddy DeFranco, who played with master accordionist Tommy Gumina, remembered, "When the Beatles came from England and played, a true musician couldn't believe it. It was impossible to fathom how that music was so popular and why it was putting so many great musicians out of work."

Tommy Gumina and Buddy DeFranco's Polytones

One can make a pretty good case that a particular apex of jazz accordion was reached by Tommy Gumina in his experiments with modern jazz clarinetist Buddy DeFranco. Gumina was a prodigy. As a kid he wanted to play so badly that his father, who'd been unemployed due to pneumonia, bought him an accordion on credit. Gumina spent five years studying under Andy Rizzo (Leon Sash's teacher), and in the early 1950s joined Harry James's big band. Gumina made a name for himself with a series of jazz and classical records and performances, joining the push to earn respect for the accordion in "serious" music circles.

Having made the move to the West Coast, the charmingly handsome Gumina was on contract with Columbia Pictures and in the running for the role of Angelo Maggio, the doomed Italian American soldier in 1953's *From Here to Eternity*. Frank Sinatra got the part, which resuscitated his career, after the most famous campaign for a role in Hollywood history. Gumina stuck with jazz and added electronics to create his own unique sound.

Gumina met Buddy DeFranco at the end of the 1950s. DeFranco had been looking for a keyboard player to sit in with his quartet but hesitated to consider a jazz accordionist. He later recalled, "An accordionist in 1960 was the kiss of death. It was a fast way to sound like a lounge act." DeFranco reluctantly hired Gumina for the date, and they stayed together for five years and as many LPs. Between 1960 and 1964 the partnership took them places few jazz players have explored since.

They were part of the jazz experimentation of the 1950s but not by playing cutting-edge free jazz. Instead, their small group used a structural technique that simultaneously balanced improvisation with the chordal and harmonic variations of a set tune. DeFranco would improvise with his clarinet, while Gumina backed him with a blaze of notes and contrasting chords from each hand on his accordion, as if they were playing the same song but in several different changing keys at once. Their carefully crafted pieces followed logically from the orchestral leanings of Ellington's and Charles Mingus's big bands, and resulted in dissonant oppositions that could have come from American composers like Charles Ives.

The effect was related to techniques pianist Art Tatum was known for. Rather than improvising melody over a set chord structure, Tatum endlessly switched the chords, harmony, and key of a melody, turning jazz on its head and revealing the richness of standard tunes in new ways. DeFranco had recorded with Tatum and appreciated the challenge this kind of playing required. With Gumina, he found a partner with whom he could explore this new approach. To a non-musician, the technicalities slip by and the music suggests a sense of a slightly off-kilter prowess. Unfortunately, by the end of the 1960s, audiences did not give Gumina and DeFranco (or challenging jazz in general) the time they deserved. DeFranco mused, "Maybe 10 years earlier, what we were doing would have been more accepted. Instead, we were a bit too complex to catch on commercially."

The Buddy DeFranco/Tommy Gumina Quintet's *Kaleidoscope* (1962) and *Pol-y-tones* (1963) records are desperately in need of a reissue. Five decades later, these pivotal recordings maintain their position as groundbreaking inspirations. Unfortunately their quintet foundered for lack of work. DeFranco went on to play with the New Glenn Miller Orchestra. Gumina carried on with accordion design and electronics. The Polychord electronic accordion he developed used a unique bass system and custom amplification. Based on his experiments, he founded the Polytone amplifier company and became a sort of Les Paul of jazz amplification, supplying superstars like George Benson with guitar and bass amps.

When he died in 2013, Gumina's pioneering efforts on the part of amplifying the accordion and other acoustic instruments carried his unique sonic vision forward as the standard for jazz amplification. We're left, though, with the fact that accordions only began to gain acceptance in jazz as the whole genre was sidelined by alternatives like rock 'n' roll. Gumina didn't go quietly. Buddy DeFranco remembered, "Sometimes they'd ask for a Lawrence Welk song. Tommy had a little temper. Plenty of times I had to talk him out of throwing his accordion at them."

7

The Closing Acts
of the Golden Age

TODAY EVEN MOST accordionists can't fathom how popular their instrument once was. The pinnacle came in the post–World War II era when baby boomers were in elementary school. This was a 1950s before Elvis or leather jackets or rebels without causes. It's easy to forget that much of the decade paid little heed to rock 'n' roll and showed no sign of the changes to come.

A few rockers eventually had hits, but early rock 'n' roll was surprisingly ephemeral. The standard telling is that rock lost its way when Little Richard found religion, Buddy Holly died, Elvis got drafted, and Chuck Berry was railroaded into prison. Record companies meanwhile were putting out millions of Frank Sinatra albums targeted at adults grateful to survive the Depression and World War II. Accessible, family-oriented tastes were satisfied by the updated vaudeville of Ed Sullivan's and Milton Berle's TV programs.

Before rock made it onto television, *Lucky Strike Presents Your Hit Parade* kept a staff of professional vocalists who sang the hit songs every week on live TV, dispensing with original artists because "the song was more important than the singer." At the same time, the most in-demand live performers included crowd-pleasing pianist Liberace, whose two hundred fan clubs sent him between six and ten thousand letters a week.

When it came, it certainly wasn't obvious that the 1950s flirtation with rock 'n' roll was more than a fad, and it was this non-rock 1950s that gave the accordion its greatest taste of fame. To grasp how fashionable the instrument was it's worth recalling how they introduced accordionist Lorna Andersson in her finalist spot for the 1957 Miss America pageant: "Miss California, Lorna M. Andersson, is going to perform a solo on an instrument that is probably most desired by most youngsters in the United States of America. Ask any child what instrument he'd like to play the most, chances are he would say, 'an accordion.'"

Squeezebox at the Movies

As the accordion entered its prime, film and then television came to define pop culture. The first appearance of an accordion in a motion picture actually happened within the first eight seconds of film history. There was no sound, but it could be considered the first movie musical. Louis Aimé Augustin Le Prince made the earliest moving pictures in 1888, in Leeds, England. There, the subject of his fourth surviving film is his son, Adolphe Le Prince, dancing and playing a button accordion in front of his grandfather's house. Prince's films only captured about two seconds at a time, so the accordion made the cut for the seventh and eighth seconds of movie history.

Skipping ahead about four decades, a number of famous accordionists played accompaniment in silent-movie houses. In Hollywood itself, Syl Prior (born 1894) and others played accordion on set while silents were being filmed. Their portable instruments provided live accompaniment during shooting, setting the emotional tone for actors like Gloria Swanson and Rudolph Valentino.

Talkies opened the way for a number of golden age accordionists to feature on film soundtracks. When he wasn't pushing classical accordion music, Anthony Galla-Rini played for *High Noon, Rhapsody in Blue, The Gunfighter, Shine on Harvest Moon, Laura,* and *The Razor's Edge.*

Ernie Felice was perhaps the hippest accordionist in the movies. His Felice Quintet shared the screen with Doris Day and Rita Hayworth in films like *The Big Clock* and *Tea for Two.* Felice also found himself dubbed in for Bob Hope's concertina in the distressingly racist *Paleface.*

Chances are that if you heard an accordion in a Hollywood movie or on television between 1950 and 2010 it was probably one of two guys: Carl

Louis Le Prince's son, Adolphe, playing a diatonic button accordion, 1888. *Science and Society Picture Library (U.K.).*

Fortina or Frank Marocco. Between the pair of them they played accordion on at least eight hundred film soundtracks, plus countless TV and advertising gigs and pop recordings. They even played together at times, as they did on Brian Wilson's Beach Boys classic "Wouldn't It Be Nice."

A few highlights from Fortina's roughly five hundred soundtrack credits include *Love Me Tender, Breakfast at Tiffany's, The Godfather, How the West Was Won, Witness for the Prosecution* (working with Marlene Dietrich), and Jimmy Stewart's accordion parts in the western *Night Passage* (Stewart knew how to play, just not so well). Fortina played TV squeezebox on *Star Trek* and *The Brady Bunch* and was adaptable enough to work with Elvis, Bob Dylan, Ringo Starr, Diana Ross, and Luciano Pavarotti.

Marocco's three hundred films included *The Blues Brothers, Heartbreak Hotel, Edward Scissorhands, Finding Nemo* (animated features seem bound to hire an accordionist), *Pirates of the Caribbean, Schindler's List, The Muppet Movie,* and *Revenge of the Nerds.* Marocco died in 2012 and Fortina in 2014; the longest gigs of the golden age of the accordion left some big session chairs to fill.

Closing the Golden Age

Dick Contino: Pre-rock Rock Star of the Accordion

Young Dick Contino, the "Rudolph Valentino of the accordion," burst into stardom on radio in 1947 when he played Horace Heidt's *Original Youth Opportunity Program*. Contino beat out ten thousand contestants in the 1940s *American Idol*–style talent series and won $6,000 ($60,000 in today's dollars), which the eighteen-year-old took home to his working-class parents. His showpiece number was "Lady of Spain," which whipped his bobby-soxer audience into a frenzy as an "electric applause meter" declared his victory night after night.

Heidt's contest expanded from radio to television in 1948, when only one in ten Americans had seen a TV set. By then Contino's confident grin and flashy playing were attracting record numbers of young people to accordion classes across the country. The instrument was sexy in his hands, and he was hot. In 1950 he was making $4,000 a night ($35,000 per gig today). The Soprani accordion company named an instrument after him, and he released his first album on RCA (future home of Elvis's biggest hits). Contino also began his long association with Ed Sullivan, which eventually netted him more than thirty-five guest spots on Sullivan's show.

In 1950, Contino was a twenty-year-old accordionist with twenty thousand young girls swooning for him at the Hollywood Bowl. Then he got drafted. The Army in 1951 wasn't the same one that Elvis joined a few years later; it was the middle of the Korean War. Millions of civilians and soldiers were dying during two and a half years of unimaginable suffering. Contino panicked the night before his induction and went AWOL. The disappearance of the rising young accordion star was front-page news for months. He eventually turned himself in and was sentenced to six months in prison and a $10,000 fine. After his release he served in Korea for two years, but his music career never recovered.

Contino was honorably discharged after the war but he spent years playing small clubs and occasional private parties for movie stars or even mobsters. Interestingly, Ed Sullivan stuck by Contino and emphasized his service record when introducing him on the show as, "the Michelangelo of the accordion, Staff Sergeant Dick Contino." But his late 1950s and early '60s TV appearances couldn't compete with the likes of Elvis or the Beatles. Young listeners compared "Lady of Spain" to the Beatles' "Love Me Do," and abandoned their accordion lessons in droves.

Over the next few decades Contino managed a quiet comeback, supported by Italian American festivals and a community of loyal fans. He emphasized his repentance for his draft conviction with spectacular patriotic medleys and Fourth of July fireworks. Contino even surfaced in the 1990s as a minor cult figure, when his less-than-stellar appearances in 1950s beatnik exploitation flicks were rediscovered. These led hard-boiled crime writer James Ellroy to produce the novella *Dick Contino's Blues*, starring a fictionalized Contino as a hard-luck character trying to recover from his demons. Ellroy convinced the accordionist to approve the story after he summed up Contino's life as being about "redemption." When Contino died in 2017, he had given it his best shot.

"Lady of Spain," the Free Bird of the Accordion

When accordionists put on their instrument, people of a certain age invariably call for "Lady of Spain." This can mostly be laid at the feet of Dick Contino, who played his pyrotechnic version dozens of times on TV and is remembered by the era's youngsters as "the guy who played accordion on *Ed Sullivan*."

"Lady of Spain" was originally written in the 1920s by two English songwriters to make their act more exotic. It sounds vaguely Spanish but is basically a four-beat quick step. Big bands and accordionists brought it to America in the 1930s, and it was a favorite of middle-of-the-road bandleader Guy Lombardo. A young Lawrence Welk had his band dress up in stereotypical Spanish costumes to play it. The song became a standard for accordion students and pros, sealed by Contino's rush to stardom. Lawrence Welk's Myron Floren finally enshrined it as the square accordion anthem.

Today most young accordionists have never heard "Lady of Spain" and no longer get the joke. The stereotype has faded as fewer people remember Contino or Floren. The song's last big TV appearance may have been the sketch on *The Muppet Show* starring Marvin Suggs and his Muppaphone. It is harder for young listeners to recall the tune after hearing it hammered on puppet-heads: "Ow! Oww! Ow! Ow! Owww!" Hot accordionists like Contino may have played the song in a blur that imprinted the flourishes more than the melody, but at least they weren't accused of cruelty to their instrument.

The Three Suns: Your Grandparents' Electronica

One of the few golden age outfits who've garnered attention from modern fans is the Three Suns. They were a prolific and long-lived act who, thirty years after their demise, caught the ear of hipsters during the irony-laced lounge-music revival of the 1990s.

Starting as a trio in 1939, the Three Suns played authentic lounges and recorded in different lineups from the 1940s until the '60s. They struggled until they landed a two-week stint at New York's Hotel Picadilly that stretched for seven years. A series of "soundie" film clips made in the 1940s showcase their unorthodox instrumentation of organ, accordion, electric guitar, and occasional vocals. They finally took off in 1944 when their tune "Twilight Time" sold a million copies.

By the 1950s they had slowly replaced their original members and split into a Hollywood recording unit and a separate live act that continued to play clubs. Their recording arm capitalized on the new LP format with experiments in "exotic" instruments and electronic effects. "Stereo Action: The Sound Your Eyes Can Follow" meant marimbas and bongos ping-ponging back and forth amidst organs and accordions, punctuated with jaw harp and whatever else lay at hand. From the mid-1950s until the death of guitarist/producer Al Nevins in 1965, their records epitomized the space-age pop sounds that not only carpeted postwar bachelor pads, but apparently counted First Lady Mamie Eisenhower as a fan.

The Three Suns' ricocheting Latin percussion and sweeping accordion laid the groundwork for the music revolutions of psychedelic rock just a few years later. Their records seem like a zany twist on the accordion's golden age, unknowingly standing on the precipice before pop music retooled and the accordion was relegated to obscurity aside from the isolated empire of Lawrence Welk.

A Modern Accordionist's Guide to Lawrence Welk

As other artists and most of the public gave up on the instrument, one man came to symbolize the accordion in the age of television: Lawrence Welk. Even some accordion lovers would rather forget the most well-known accordionist in North America. Welk was an imperishable American entertainer who aged with his fans over a fifty-year career.

FACING Lawrence Welk, ca. 1940s. *NDSU Archives.*

He premiered as an accordionist in the 1920s and led a commercial dance band notable for annoying critics with its innocuousness. Welk was one of many regional polka artists who shed most ethnic attributes. He developed a common-denominator style that prolonged his career decades after the polka craze and the big bands of the 1930s and '40s had passed on.

Welk was raised by German/Russian immigrants in rural North Dakota and didn't speak English until he entered school. He was obsessed with music, and in 1920 agreed to work for four years on his dad's farm in order to buy a piano accordion. Welk performed at local halls called "opera houses," where he stood on a chair in the corner and played until his bellows-wrist bled. He paid off his debt to his father by bringing home three months' worth of farm income in one night.

In spite of his heavy German accent, Welk didn't limit his market to a single dispersed ethnic population. His hope was to succeed like "King of Jazz" Paul Whiteman. Welk's band wore suits, not lederhosen, and they didn't record any polkas until ten years after their first discs. Only after it became a pop music fad in 1939 did he start recording the music that would become his band's trademark.

Known for charming mixed metaphors like, "Don't count your chickens until they cross the street," Welk methodically built his audience base on the promise of accessible dancing. You didn't have to jitterbug to know you'd have a pleasant time at his show. With himself and Myron Floren on accordion, his Novelty Orchestra followed the territorial band formula of playing live dances to make payroll while performing on radio for promotion. During World War II he added appearances at military bases and hospitals, where he recruited fans who remained loyal while his musical business grew.

Welk led his band for two decades before appearing on television, but his thirty-year run on the small screen secured his place in our cultural memory. The road to *The Lawrence Welk Show* started in 1945 when he landed a gig in San Francisco after the war. Despite fears that audiences wouldn't be familiar with his band, thousands of demobilized GIs and their dates filled his dance floor. Welk's six-week engagement stretched to six months, after which he headed south to Los Angeles to entertain equally enthusiastic crowds.

Once in LA, Welk caught the lens of the burgeoning television industry. His show landed on ABC's national TV network in 1956, the same year Elvis appeared on *Ed Sullivan*. The Welk act, though, was everything but "shook up." They codified their band as the Champagne Music Makers, and could be counted on for well-known, easily danceable, "bouncy" tunes and a few mildly ethnic polkas and waltzes. Overall there were no musical surprises, and on every episode Welk would step from his bandstand to dance among the audience with his latest "champagne lady." An always-smiling cast sang and played while the studio audience danced and Welk's famous bubble machine bubbled. His conservative audience was remarkably faithful to Welk's wholesome televised values, and the show eventually brought him a salary of $2 million a year.

The band's biggest record, "Calcutta," went to number one on the pop charts in 1961, but stranger still it also hit number ten on the black-oriented R&B chart. Welk's business model worked. His show was aggressively nostalgic and one of the last un-ironic appearances of the accordion in mainstream American culture for several decades. He made millions of dollars every year by ignoring the advice of critics who called his music dull and insipid. *Look* magazine summed up the result: "Nobody likes him but the people."

His amazingly successful "champagne music" was the butt of jealous hipsters' jokes for much of his career. Welk's show only occasionally reflected up-to-date styles, including 1969's bizarre fifteenth-season opener, in which the maestro emerged dressed in a Sonny Bono wig and furry vest fronting a funk-rock version of his group. Before things went too far, Welk's Lennon Sisters ripped off his hippie outfit, revealing a conservative suit. He reassured his audience, "Of course, by now you folks know we were only kidding. We're not going to change our style, folks, and that's a promise. We wouldn't do that to you nice people." Given his pledge, we can only ponder what was going on behind Welk's back during the legendary (but preserved on tape) 1971 episode when the uncommonly straight singers "Dale and Gayle" performed Brewer and Shipley's dope anthem "One Toke over the Line," seemingly without inhaling.

The Lawrence Welk Show was canceled in 1971 as part of the "rural purge," when the entertainment industry gave him and his aging audience up for dead. In response, he pioneered TV syndication to hundreds of individual local stations and stayed on the air, producing new episodes for another eleven years. His great success—from child of immigrant parents to media mogul—took ethnic music to an audience of millions. As Welk himself said in 1939 when *Billboard* magazine asked his formula for success, "Primarily we try to please all customers."

Squeeze Burgers: Lawrence Welk Opened a Diner

Welk didn't mess with his musical recipe. He never strayed from meeting audience's expectations without pushing their boundaries. Off-stage, though, he constantly experimented, especially with promotion and merchandising. There were Welk-themed ashtrays, silverware, glasses, jewelry, ties, games, letter-openers, dancing puppets, champagne-bottle radios, and of course, toy bubble machines. If his fans hadn't worn button-downs, he would have invented the concert T-shirt.

Way back in 1951, before he started his TV show, Welk even tried opening a hamburger stand. The Lawrence Welk Diner served Squeeze Burgers on Rhythm Rolls with Piccolo Pickles and Fiddlestring Fries packaged in patented accordion-pleated boxes. He picked a location where his band stopped regularly, near the interchange of highways 65 and 18 in Mason City, Iowa. It was supposed to be the first in a chain of theme restaurants, but Welk sold it after only a few years. He had to choose between the band and the diner, but without the band the restaurant had no theme. So he left the hamburger business and headed for California, with a Lawrence Welk-branded "Drive Carefully" bumpersticker on the bus.

Myron Floren: Happy Norwegian and Lawrence Welk's Second Accordion

Lawrence Welk was billed as "America's Greatest Accordionist" early in his career. Reportedly, he was honestly amazed that lying was allowed in show business. When Myron Floren joined Welk's band to play lead squeezebox he became America's greater-than-greatest accordionist. Content to stay on payroll in Welk's shadow, the self-effacing Floren became one of the most widely seen accordion player ever. Even as memory of the *The Lawrence Welk Show* fades, fifty million viewers a week was a hard record to beat.

Floren grew up the son of Norwegian immigrants, saying later that sixteen years milking cows prepared his fingers for the rigors of the accordion, and that performing was "even more fun than farming." They didn't have much entertainment aside from friends and families rolling up the carpets to dance. At age four, he saw a farmer playing a button box accordion at one of these house parties, and after two years of pleading, his father ordered him one from the Sears–Roebuck catalog. The next county fair was his first paying gig: $10 for two shows per day over two days.

As a kid he bartered eggs for piano lessons, and hoped to major in music at Augustana College. But the director of the classical orchestra told him they didn't need an accordion, and he couldn't afford $50 a year to rent a piano. So Floren studied on his own and eventually got on local radio in 1939. In the 1940s, he joined a western swing group called the Buckeye Four. He later remembered, "We'd play things like 'San Antonio Rose' and 'Letter Edged in Black.' We'd always play a tear-jerker."

Floren was classified 4F in World War II; he couldn't be drafted because childhood rheumatic fever had damaged his heart. He volunteered instead to serve as an entertainer on the front, armed only with his accordion. Floren's biography recalls his arrival in Europe along with ships full of soldiers, weapons, and medical supplies, knowing full well where each were headed. In an air-raid shelter beneath the streets of London he learned "Lili Marlene" when a thousand people sang it for him together, while the bombs dropped over their heads.

After the start of the Battle of the Bulge, he noticed soldiers at one show were weighted down with extra ammunition and hand grenades, so he cautioned them to sit down very carefully. A lieutenant asked him quietly to play the best he could because they were going into battle that night and many wouldn't be coming back. The next day they crossed the Ruhr River into Germany.

At one point his touring group got lost behind German lines. "As we neared our destination, we noticed GIs in trenches. Suddenly a sergeant called out, 'What in the world are you doing here? There are Germans all over the place!' There I was, hanging on to my accordion with one hand and a side of the truck with the other... the only thought I remember clearly: Where would I get another accordion if the Germans shot a hole in this one?"

Floren survived and returned to the States. He got married and took his accordion on the honeymoon. Arriving at the hotel lobby with forty people looking on, he blushed and explained that he brought it because he "might want to practice in [his] spare time."

In 1950, Floren and his wife attended a show where Welk's band was playing. He was invited to play and given a piece of sheet music to try out. Floren blazed through a couple of numbers and then looked around and couldn't find Welk. Legend has it the bandleader emerged from under the piano, waving a white flag. He hired Floren that night and the gig lasted thirty-two years. When Welk's manager found out, he yelled, "You can't do that, Lawrence. The patrons say that this new fellow is better than you are. You'll have to get rid of him—quick." Welk's reply was, "Of course he's better than I am, that's why I hired him."

As their national popularity grew, the band played the inaugural ball for President Eisenhower, and if anybody needed proof of Floren and the boys' loyalty in those McCarthyite times, Mary Coakley's pleasantly conservative Welk biography, *Mister Music Maker* (1958) noted that "Lawrence carries his idea of investment and savings so far that he has encouraged an investment club, started and managed by accordionist Myron Floren. The plan is that each member invest a set sum each week, the total to be used for the purchase of securities listed on the New York Stock Exchange... Lawrence Welk's boys like being capitalists." The coming world of rock 'n' roll rebellion hardly seems like the same planet.

Myron arrived in the Welk family just before their first local black-and-white television broadcast. This led to their 1955 national network broadcast, then into self-distributed syndication. His description of Welk's Midwestern mix of sweet dance tunes and reminders of ethnic music was, "I guess we did one [polka] practically every week. I even remember an instance where we were saluting Duke Ellington and Lawrence added a polka just in case." Like Dick Contino, Floren adopted "Lady of Spain" as a showpiece, shaking his bellows in concentration to impress TV audiences. It laid the foundation for accordion stereotypes for years to come.

Despite cementing his instrument's link with the categorically unadventurous Lawrence Welk, Floren was a skillful accordionist and the backbone of Welk's group. He was known as "the Happy Norwegian," and seemed to genuinely enjoy playing the part. One night at Madison Square Garden before twenty thousand people, Welk said to Floren, "Isn't it wonderful what can happen to a couple of farmers from the Dakotas?" Their lives were so American Dreamy it hardly seems real. When Floren died in 2005, he'd played accordion for eighty years. Welk's show had ended in 1982, but Floren had continued to tour, saying, "I'm going to keep squeezing this thing, until nobody calls anymore."

Lenny Bruce Digs Lawrence Welk

Welk was never a hit with critics, but succeeded by ignoring their advice. He drew the line, though, at comedian Lenny Bruce. Welk apparently couldn't take a joke at his expense when it was about drug-using musicians and the bubble machine. Albert Goldman relates in his book *Ladies and Gentlemen, Lenny Bruce* that in 1959 Welk threatened a $100,000 lawsuit if Fantasy Records didn't bleep his name off Bruce's records. The bit that got censored was part of an extended narrative about a young musician, with Bruce occasionally demonstrating the kid's radical "new sound" by blasting on a trumpet he borrowed from the backing band. Climactically, the hero ends up looking for a gig with Welk.

Bruce's hipster musician nods off during the interview and his slang and drug references go way over Welk's head. With Bruce doing all the voices, Welk sounds like a Jewish Bela Lugosi, and he hires the new guy because: "I'm a good judge of character!" Finally the jazzer admits, "I gotta tell you up front baby, I've got a monkey on my back." To which Bruce's Welk replies, "That's all right, we like animals on the band. Rocky's got a duck, they can play together."

Jo Ann Castle: *Accordion in Hi-Fi*

No one knew the golden age of the accordion had reached its peak when Jo Ann Castle released her space-age *Accordion in Hi-Fi* album in 1959. Filled with show-stoppers, the record had a little mambo, a funky hint of jazz (the version of "Cherokee" is jammin'), as well as slower cocktail numbers. A totally worthwhile jaunt. Her intense "Bumble Boogie" arrangement exemplified the flashy workouts that "Flight of the Bumble Bee" got in the mid-century accordion world.

Castle's *Hi-Fi* record caught the eye of Lawrence Welk's team and the maestro invited her on the show as a guest. At the time she asked him not to publicly reveal she was only nineteen, since she didn't want to jeopardize her Vegas club dates. He spilled the beans on the air, though, with a piano-shaped birthday cake and an offer of a steady contract.

Years before she joined the Champagne Music Makers, Castle (born Jo Ann Zering) had taken her stage name from the Castle brand accordions she played. She started performing on Tex Williams's radio program when she was fifteen, then worked with Spade Cooley, Spike Jones, and Ina Ray Hutton's Emmy award–winning All-Girl Orchestra.

Castle became the only regular female instrumentalist on the Welk show. Originally she traded accordion choruses with Myron Floren, making a case that she might have filled his shoes if given the chance. But rather than occupying a "third accordion" chair behind Floren and Welk, she took over the piano spot from Big Tiny Little—a tough name to follow. She picked up his saloon-style ragtime and pounded it out for ten years.

She recorded several mostly piano records during her "champagne" decade, closing her time in the Welk organization with 1968's curious *Hawaiian Ragtime* album. A decade and a half later she rejoined the Welk family on piano at the Lawrence Welk Resort Theater in Branson, Missouri, but by that point there was no returning to the golden age of the eighteen-year-old *Hi-Fi* accordionist.

PART THREE

ROOTS MUSIC:

AN OUTSIDERS'

CANON

EUROPE'S CLASSICAL MUSIC canon amassed its status and prestige over centuries. In the modern era, folkloric traditions have also been recognized as worth preserving. Colloquial and even popular music gained standing in the world of scholarship, and a canon of roots music developed.

For years, most portrayals of North American traditional music focused almost exclusively on the American South. But the true roots of folk music could easily incorporate Jewish klezmer, Irish immigrant dance tunes, the cross-border Mexican American repertoire, and many other English and non-English-language musicians spread across North America.

As often as not, these styles can be connected by the sounds of the accordion. A history of American music that doesn't include the squeezebox is suspect.

In the last few decades, a few ethnic accordion styles like Cajun, zydeco, and klezmer have gained followings and inroads into the roots pantheon. Canada's Irish-inspired and French Canadian music opened another squeezebox-shaped gateway into folk music's deeper history. Besides missing out on polkas in general (see Chapter 5), English speakers' most glaring accordion oversight has been the vital conjunto/norteño style that has nevertheless grown from folkloric to full-on pop music status.

Today, accordion-centered genres are helping build a more inclusive canon while drawing modern listeners back to the squeezebox. It wasn't jazz or classical music or the repertoire of the golden age that sparked today's accordion revival. Most modern accordion fans were inspired by roots traditions that maintained their vitality despite being marginalized for years.

8

Acordeón: Mexican and American Roots

THE MUSIC OF the U.S./Mexico border region provides by far the most popular accordion style in North America. No other music consistently sells out arenas full of accordion fans. At the same time, for years major labels and institutions like the Grammy Awards snubbed the music and blocked it from mainstream media attention.

The shared cross-border roots of Texan conjunto and Mexican norteño music are indisputable. Both styles use button accordion (almost exclusively three-row diatonics) and the twelve-string bajo sexto guitar (often augmented with electric bass and other instruments). Both play European-derived dance music (polkas, waltzes, etc.) with distinctive Mexican folk contributions.

Texas's regional conjunto style relates to the wider norteño world something like the way bluegrass does to commercial country music. It's tended to be more instrumentally driven and less focused on lyrics. Most Texas conjunto musicians are also far less financially successful than the big stars of the cross-border norteño phenomenon. A few conjunto musicians have nonetheless had noticeable success. Flaco Jiménez especially has connected with musicians all over the world—crossing over to Anglo listeners more successfully than his norteño counterparts. Conjunto and norteño are branches on the same tree, but they faced different environments and succeeded in different ways.

Most obviously, the twin styles share the accordion. The instrument's arrival in the region hovers on the edge of historical memory, just distant enough to be contested. Though most listeners may not care whether the accordion appeared first in the United States or in Mexico, it can be a heated debate, charged with national and regional pride.

Accordions may well have appeared both in Mexico and Texas at around the same time (ca. 1850–60). By the turn of the century, the instrument was certainly in widespread use by multi-ethnic musicians all over the region. Bohemian Czech and German immigrants may have brought accordions to Texas, but there was (and still is) a significant German presence in Mexico itself. Manuel Peña makes a strong case for the northern Mexican city of Monterrey as a likely epicenter of the earliest European accordion arrival.

In the upheaval of the Mexican Revolution (1910–20) people of many ethnic groups fled north. From then until recently, many accordions likely came through dealers in Texas. Cathy Ragland, in her book *Música Norteña*, relates how accordions became a portable, affordable sign of success that Mexican workers brought back from their jobs in the north. Related accordion styles took shape on both sides of the border, influenced by the barrier's shifting permeability over the years.

Women in Conjunto/Norteña

Historically, professional musicians in the border region (and most other accordion traditions) have most often been men. When the styles that eventually became conjunto and norteño were taking shape in the Rio Grande Valley, respectable society forbade women to even enter most places where accordions were played. Cantinas and *bailes de negocios* where women were paid to dance with men were considered physically and morally dangerous for women (and occasionally for men, too). A female musician being hired in such a place was unlikely.

There were, however, venues where women did play in public. Lucia Alderete remembers her mother playing accordion in the 1930s at *bodes de ranchos* (country weddings) and *bailes caseros* (house dances), where families would gather in great numbers. *Músicos caseros* (house musicians) made up of family and friends would play for dancers, but strict courtship rituals prevailed. No dating was allowed outside these public

☞ *¿Cual Nombre?* What's in a Name?

WHAT TO CALL the accordion music from the border region remains something of a dilemma. *Música norteña* originated in Northern Mexico and has become the most fashionable accordion style on both sides of the border. Conjunto (literally a "group" of musicians) is a roots music that developed simultaneously in Texas. Some tunes appear in both styles including ranchera country songs like those heard in classic Mexican movies. Corrido storytelling ballads are at the heart of the norteño style and have been part of the border music since before the Mexican Revolution.

Tex-Mex was the title of a 1979 record by Freddy Fender, and the term became a Texas-centered way to market the region's roots music. In Texas, *Tejano* was used for various "sophisticated" relatives of the conjunto, but more recently signifies "Texas music" more generally. *Billboard* magazine eventually decided on "regional Mexican" to refer to this radio-friendly combination that included: "Tejano, norteño, conjunto, grupo, mariachi, trio, tropical/cumbia, vallenato, and banda." Like "Celtic," these terms may be useful for promoting radio formats and record sales, but not so helpful in understanding the music itself.

gatherings, and if couples weren't dancing, even hand-holding or private conversations were forbidden. Nevertheless, while the accordions played, couples passed secret notes and, with a nod from their elders, initiated the next round of weddings. These were very different circumstances from the rougher crowds that male musicians often faced.

Aside from the work of pioneering piano accordionist Ventura Martínez Alonzo, it wasn't until the 1970s and '80s that a slow acknowledgment of women accordionists began within the region. In these years Eva Ybarra started her own group, as did Isabel Ortiz Hernández, who was known as "Chavela" before her life was tragically cut short. Another accordionist, Lupita Rodela (born around 1949 in San Antonio), taught herself to play as a child by imitating records after an uncle gave her an old instrument. She grew up to be one of the earliest women to front their own conjunto and toured the region during the 1980s and '90s.

These three, Ybarra, Chavela, and Rodela made way for more women to take up the instrument, and were the first female accordionists to play San Antonio's Tejano Conjunto Festival.

As the twenty-first century begins, women continue to make their way within the world of conjunto and norteño. A growing number of young people have studied with Eva Ybarra and others at the Guadalupe Cultural Arts Center in San Antonio, which hosts the Tejano Conjunto Festival every year. Artists like Susan Torres, who performs with vocalist Clemencia Zapata in the group Conjunto Clamencia, and Berna Rodriguez of the group Las Fenix are carrying on the tradition of female accordionists that leads back to the earliest days of border accordion.

Border Accordionists

Narciso Martínez: The Hurricane

In the mid-1930s, Narciso Martínez, "El Huracán del Valle," became the most influential early accordionist on the Texas side of the border. Martínez was known to play with musicians from different ethnic groups and learned styles and tunes from all of them. He later pioneered cross-ethnic marketing by releasing polka records under pseudonyms like "Louisiana Pete" and "Polish Joe." His instrumental compositions became standards and, though based on European forms, were adapted to create their own unique style.

In search of more chromatic variety, Martínez led the move to newer two-row accordions, and most radically he dropped the use of his instrument's limited left-hand bass buttons. This let him engage the full potential of the available treble buttons and allowed his virtuosic bajo sexto player, Santiago Almeida, to extend his role for more flexible bass possibilities. Martinez's records are more prized and remembered north of the border than south, but in the 1930s they were among the most important accordion recordings in the region.

Antonio Tanguma: "King of the Accordion"

Antonio Tanguma is "King of the Accordion" in his native Nuevo León (northeastern Mexico) and is considered by many the "Father of Norteño Music." He purchased his first accordion across the border in Texas in

Ventura Martínez Alonzo with Alonzo y Sus Rancheros: Frank Alonzo plays guitar beside Ventura, Houston, 1950s. *Gregorio Torres Valerio Collection,* MSS0101-0002, *Houston Public Library,* HMRC.

1927, but spent his life in the Mexican industrial city of Monterrey. Like his contemporaries in the U.S., Tanguma mostly played instrumentals, but he often performed without bajo sexto accompaniment and used the bass buttons of his accordion. Frustrated by the limited left-hand system of most diatonic instruments he sometimes played a three-row diatonic accordion with a forty-eight-button Stradella bass. Tanguma recorded countless records (nearly fifty LPs), many of which are so well known on both sides of the border that people mistake them for traditional folk songs.

Ventura Martínez Alonzo: The First Queen of the Accordion

Ventura Martínez Alonzo may have been the first professional female accordionist in Texas. Born in Matamoros, Mexico, in 1904, her family fled the revolution when she was five, settling in Brownsville, Texas, in 1914. Her father died soon after, leaving her family struggling; she left school after the tenth grade to work. Ventura took piano lessons, but mostly learned to play by ear. She later taught herself piano accordion because of its portability.

She divorced her first husband because he didn't want her to be a musician, and then married the more amenable Francisco Alonzo. In 1938 they formed Alonzo y Sus Rancheros and began playing around the Houston area and on radio. In 1947 they made their first recordings, featuring Ventura on lead vocals and accordion.

After World War II they became Alonzo y Su Orquesta, a bigger *jaitón* (high-tone) orchestra that played big band swing arrangements and romantic rancheras (Mexican country songs). This stylistic shift may have helped them reach more affluent audiences, but it definitely gave Alonzo, as a woman, more respectable places to play. She knew conjunto's founding fathers like Santiago Jiménez and Valerio Longoria, but at that time their button accordion music was still associated with cantina bars and other places of ill repute.

In 1956 Alonzo and her husband opened their own club, La Terraza, in Houston and featured many of the biggest touring artists of the day. Among them they welcomed some conjunto artists who had begun to enter the middle-class market. (Paulino Bernal's was the first group to play there.) Alonzo and the Rancheros were the house band.

Pioneering researcher Deborah Vargas interviewed Alonzo, who related that she was also responsible for six children, sometimes traveling with the youngest. "I would hide him under the piano," she explained, "and he would fall asleep." She later described her workload at the club: "I would be the ticket taker at the door, play in the band, manage the accounting of the business, and even after a long set of playing onstage, I would return home and wash and starch all of the band members' shirts for the next day."

Perhaps because she didn't play button accordion in working-class cantinas, Alonzo remains mostly unsung in the conjunto narrative. Her piano accordion and her orquesta style puts her more in the realm of the region's society dance bands than the small groups that spawned today's conjunto style. Smooth orquestas like hers faded away when upwardly mobile Tejanas assimilated and left "Mexican" music behind. Conjuntos, meanwhile, became recognized as folkloric, lifting the button accordion to its current place of prominence in Tejano music.

Ventura nevertheless remains a musician and businesswoman who not only paved the way for female accordionists, but managed the top club where classic conjunto accordionists played in Houston. Before she died, Ventura told her daughter she wanted to be remembered for a photo of her playing with the band: "All male musicians and just me, the only woman."

Valerio Longoria: *Nueva Generación*

As the 1940s rolled into the 1950s, the first of the postwar *nueva generación* (new generation) conjunto players was Valerio Longoria. While earlier artists played almost all instrumentals, Longoria mastered his accordion while singing at the same time. Settling in San Antonio after he got out of the Army in 1947, he was one of the first local musicians to bring drums on stage, drastically modernizing the conjunto sound. He also tuned his accordion reeds with a cleaner, brighter tone, in contrast to the rich tuning preferred by many norteño artists. Longoria's final innovation was exploiting his diatonic instrument's light weight by being the first accordionist in the region to play standing up. His simple act of showmanship has been emulated by almost every player on both sides of the border ever since.

Prior to Longoria's modernized style, conjunto was thought of as drunken cantina music. His use of vocals, especially for higher-class *jaitón* Mexican-movie rancheras and romantic boleros, helped bring conjunto accordions to a wider audience in the Tejano community. Longoria revitalized the conjunto genre and opened the door for changes to come. Accordion wizard Esteban "Steve" Jordan later reported that hearing Longoria play at migrant labor camps as a child was his inspiration to learn accordion, thus setting off another generation of border accordion experimentation. From 1980 until his death in 2000, Longoria continued to share his influence by teaching accordion classes for beginners and masters at the Guadalupe Cultural Arts Center in San Antonio.

Los Alegres de Terán: Los Padres

Los Alegres de Terán, with accordionist Eugenio Ábrego, formed in Nuevo León, Mexico, in the late 1940s and are considered (along with Antonio Tanguma) "the fathers of norteño music." "They were like the Mexican Beatles," explained an elderly fan from rural Mexico. Influenced by local vocal duet traditions, they, like Valerio Longoria in Texas, cemented the connection between accordion and vocals.

They wrote hundreds of songs that focused on the narrative content of rancheras and especially corrido ballads. This solidified the early split between classic norteño's corrido story-song emphasis and conjunto's

ALEGRES DE TERAN
(Ortiz y Abrego)
Exclusivos en Falcon

Los Alegres de Terán. *Arhoolie Foundation, AFIA22.*

attention to instrumentalists. Conjunto musicians were much more likely to play accordion behind vocal parts, for instance, rather than just between verses.

Los Alegres spread their norteño sound via radio and recordings from the border region all the way to Mexico City and remain by far the most well-known early group for most Mexicans. The example they left in songs and corridos about working people and their struggles and lives continues in every norteño group since.

Tony de la Rosa y Su Conjunto

Tony de la Rosa solidified the modern conjunto sound and was the most influential conjunto accordionist in the 1950s. He grew up poor, traveling with his farm-worker family on routes he would repeat for years, playing music for migrant laborers. His father bought him his first accordion for $7 from the Montgomery Ward catalog, and he taught himself to play by listening to Narciso Martínez on the radio.

He also listened to Texas's western swing trailblazers Bob Wills and Adolph Hofner. Inspired by them, de la Rosa boosted his own band with amplification, a full drum kit, electric bass, and an electrified bajo sexto guitar. He also slowed down the beat compared to earlier players and developed a distinctive staccato accordion style that became a standard part of the conjunto sound.

People probably started calling the style "conjunto" after the well-traveled Tony de la Rosa y Su Conjunto band. He released at least seventy-five albums over thirty-five years, even after he and other artists from Texas began to have trouble distributing music and touring in Mexico. This division signaled the beginning of a split between the conjunto dance halls and the more lyric-driven (but of course still danceable) norteño style.

El Conjunto Bernal and Oscar Hernández

From the 1950s into the 1960s, El Conjunto Bernal was led by accordionist Paulino Bernal with his brother (and fantastic bajo sexto player), Eloy. Together they developed the Texas conjunto into a never-before-heard richness and complexity. Balancing innovation and tradition they maintained a base in the working-class conjunto market but expanded their audience into the middle class, where fans of big band style *orquestas Tejanas* appreciated their use of smooth three-part vocal harmonies. Bernal hired the masterful Oscar Hernández as a second accordionist, who encouraged Bernal to adopt the larger chromatic button accordion. This resulted in an unprecedented instrumental duo. No other group in the border region ever approached their level of technical fluency.

Conjunto music in general was becoming more conservative in the early 1960s, but that's when Bernal's group engaged in their greatest experiments and had their biggest hits. As Manuel Peña and other critics have stated, Conjunto Bernal took the music "to the limits of public acceptance" but instead of rejection, audiences rewarded them.

In January of 1968 Conjunto Bernal were among the first Latino artists to perform in Vietnam. As writer Agustín Gurza relates, "During the 21-day tour, organized by the USO, they crisscrossed Vietnam in three helicopters, one for the musicians, the second for the instruments and the third for soldiers protecting the performers." For the high proportion of Chicano soldiers on the front lines they were a welcome reminder of home. (Singer Cha Cha Jiménez himself was drafted and served in combat in Vietnam.)

But by the 1970s Paulino Bernal had left his band to escape the temptations of the road and join the ministry. He worked to bring accordions to Christian radio, and after overcoming conservative resistance gained yet another audience there. Oscar Hernández continued with the secular group and later formed his own Tuff Band, continuing to produce exemplary music but never with the success of the original Conjunto Bernal. Hernández remained an honored figure, teaching and performing as one of the greatest accordionists ever to play border music.

Ramón Ayala y Los Relámpagos del Norte

In the early 1960s, Paulino Bernal was scouting talent for his record label. On the streets of Reynosa in northeastern Mexico (across the border from McAllen, Texas) he discovered Ramón Ayala playing accordion with singer/bajo sexto player Cornelio Reyna. They became norteño music's breakout group, Los Relámpagos del Norte ("Lightning Bolts of the North"). Los Relámpagos built a cross-border following based on Reyna's corrido ballads and a willingness to play hundreds of shows a year, sometimes for little pay (endearing them to a hard-working audience). They standardized the cowboy-hat northern "charro" look that film idol El Piporro had brought to the movies, and stuck to their roots, using lyrics written by fans to create songs that related to their base. When the group split after eight years of success, Ayala launched Los Bravos del Norte who continued as a major force in the norteño world.

By 2013, when Ayala celebrated his fiftieth-anniversary tour, he had released more than one hundred albums—twenty with Los Relámpagos alone. His fans called him "the King of the Accordion." He and various singers had firmly established the corrido story song as the central norteño form, while modernizing the sound with the drums and electric bass already in use by conjuntos in Texas.

Ayala's long career with Los Relámpagos and Los Bravos had gone almost totally unnoticed outside the norteño world. He'd sold more records to more fans than most pop stars, but it took forty years before an English-language magazine did their first story on him. Without much support from the recording industry, artists like Ayala continued to sing about working people and the hard times of migrant labor, economic inequality, and the trauma of the border. On both sides of the frontier, he helped create the biggest accordion fan-base in North America.

El Conjunto Bernal: (L to R, top) Armondo Peña, Eloy Bernal (bajo sexto, voc), Cha Cha Jiménez (voc), Juan Sifuentes (voc), Manuel Solís (voc). Acordeón: Oscar Hernández (L), Paulino Bernal (R). *Arhoolie Foundation, AFIA52.*

The Jiménez Accordion Dynasty

The most well-known conjunto musicians outside of Texas represent a family that's played accordions for almost a hundred years. Patricio Jiménez played one-row button accordion in the early years of the twentieth century, sharing tunes with European immigrants in Texas's Rio Grande Valley while the upheaval of the Mexican Revolution raged south of the border.

Don Patricio's son, Santiago Jiménez Sr., took up the instrument in 1923. When the opportunity presented itself in the 1930s he became an early radio and recording artist. Along with Narciso Martínez, he helped invent the classic conjunto sound. Jiménez switched to a two-row accordion in 1935, but stayed truer to the old-fashioned style, more conservative than Martínez's extended right-hand improvisations. Outside the region, Jiménez's records were never as well known as Martínez's, and today he's quite unknown to most norteño fans. Without achieving marketable renown though, Jiménez left a rich legacy of recordings, and two sons who inherited his talent.

Santiago Jiménez's sons aren't household names in Mexico's norteño world either, but they are mainstays in Texas conjunto. Flaco Jiménez and his younger brother, Santiago Jr., took up their family instrument and carried the music of the Lower Rio Grande valley well beyond Texas. In the 1970s and '80s they were "discovered" by Anglo folk and rock musicians and became (along with David Hidalgo from Los Lobos) the most well-known conjunto/norteño accordionists to audiences outside the traditions.

Flaco Jiménez in particular opened people's ears to the border accordion as part of American roots music. In 1973, Texas roots-rocker Doug Sahm invited Flaco to play with Bob Dylan and Dr. John on his *Doug Sahm and Band* LP. Since then, in addition to many recordings of his own, Flaco has played with Santana, the Rolling Stones, Tish Hinojosa, Lila Downs, *rock en Español* groups Los Fabulosos Cadillacs and Café Tacuba; and country performers Chet Atkins, Tanya Tucker, and Buck Owens, as well as polka's Grammy Award mainstay Jimmy Sturr.

Flaco's 1992 album *Partners* features appearances by Dwight Yoakam, Emmylou Harris, Ry Cooder, John Hiatt, Linda Ronstadt, and Los Lobos. In the 1990s he played with Doug Sahm again in the supergroup the Texas Tornados with Freddy Fender, continuing to represent the ethnic mixture that helped make Texas one of the deepest musical sources for American music.

Santiago Jiménez Jr., meanwhile, stayed closer to home and to the traditional sound and memory of his father and grandfather. Researcher Cathy Ragland writes, "It is the San Antonio players who remain more dedicated to the traditional European rhythms such as the polka, waltz, redova (a Mexican folk dance with a rapidly alternating rhythmic pattern), and schottische, while players further south and along the border favor Latin and Mexican rhythms such as the cumbia and huapango."

Together, the three generations of the Jiménez family represent nearly the entire history of the border accordion. For more than a century, they've played with bajo sexto accompaniment and created and preserved one of the great accordion traditions in American music.

Esteban "Steve" Jordan: "Squeeze Box Man"

The first song that conjunto accordion genius Esteban "Steve" Jordan learned to play as a child was "Steel Guitar Rag," by western swing star Bob Wills and His Texas Playboys. Jordan embodied the ethnic richness inherited by native Texans and brought it to the accordion. He picked up the instrument from Valerio Longoria and other conjunto innovators, and proceeded to take it further than perhaps anyone on earth up to that point. Self-taught on dozens of instruments, he became a world-class master of the three-row button accordion used by most conjunto and norteño musicians. Not content with his lauded virtuosity on the instrument, he layered his sound with rock 'n' roll effects like phasers and the Echoplex.

He was the only conjunto accordionist to exceed Paulino Bernal and Oscar Hernández's urge for exploration. Jordan's performances and recordings slid seamlessly from rancheros and corridos to eclectic jazz experiments. His amplified and custom-tuned instruments (extra dry to clarify extended chords) eventually inspired a specially designed series of hot-rod "Rockordians" from the German Hohner company.

Jordan's playing was radically different from his forebears in the region, and showed how the conjunto accordion had developed differently than European polka groups. Jordan elaborated on Narciso Martínez's innovative use of the right hand. Ignoring the limited bass buttons, he played chromatically across the rows of his supposedly limited diatonic instrument. Jordan extended the virtuosic advances of Bernal and Hernández, without relying on the help of their larger accordions. His style ended up ranging from polkas through 1960s soul, and from reverb-heavy jazz ballads to Latin salsa workouts, all driven by some of the finest button accordion work ever played.

Sadly, many of Jordan's most adventurous recordings have remained out of print in North America for decades. His late-1960s psychedelic rock album *La Bamba* included James Brown-style funk and R&B alongside what may be the most satisfyingly exploration of the accordion warhorse "Lady of Spain" ever played. Done in a conjunto jazz style with a dizzying array of improvised chords and runs, it musically outshines anything seen on TV during the accordion's golden age.

In the 1980s, Jordan seemed on the verge of breaking through to the trendy Anglo market. He appeared in movies like David Byrne's *True Stories*, and his 1986 album *Turn Me Loose* was nominated for a Grammy. His music and appearance (rock accordion with wild hair and an eye-patch) were enough to attract attention, and his sound and the fact that he sang in English as well as Spanish had crossover appeal.

But Jordan never got the success his prodigious talent could have earned. As John Burnett said in an obituary for NPR in 2010, "He had grown bitter... after a lifetime making music but not attending to the business end of his career." Jordan ended up hoarding his music in the last ten years of his life, not trusting record companies he felt had ripped him off. In interviews before he died he said he had nine albums of material recorded, but only one limited-release appeared after his death.

If Jordan had written himself into one of the corridos he sang, his braggadocio would obviously have cast him as the hero. His combination of history, transcendence, transgression, brilliance, and life on the uglier side of the music industry leave us wishing he could sing one more number, so we could listen to him play on into the night.

Eva Ybarra: "I Always Wanted to Play the Accordion"

Eva Ybarra's father gave her an accordion when she was four years old. She remembers first performing in public at age six. Her family had music in the house all the time, but "there were no little girls that played the accordion." Her father especially encouraged her, thinking she might do something better than working in the fields. Her grandmother, however, strongly objected and asked for Eva to live with her. Ybarra had to beg her mother not to send her away so she could keep playing music.

Her mother feared that pushing and pulling on the bellows was somehow bad for girls, and the young Eva was given more proper piano lessons. They didn't lead her to quit the accordion, but did give her a grounding in music theory that some boys missed as they learned from older relatives. In the 1950s, Ybarra didn't know of any female accordionists to model herself after. She practiced mostly with the radio, standing on a stool to listen to Narciso Martínez and Tony de la Rosa, slowly repeating what she heard. The jazzy sounds of Oscar Hernández and Conjunto Bernal were among the influences she absorbed. In person, she watched and listened to local accordionists like her brother Pedro and his friend Flaco Jiménez Jr., but mostly she learned by herself.

While her father was alive he acted as her manager. She and her brother became breadwinners for the family, playing in local dance halls, restaurants, ice houses, and eventually even the cantina circuit that Ventura Alonzo had avoided. When she was fifteen, Ybarra quit playing after getting bullied in school. In Deborah Vargas's book on Chicana musicians Ybarra said, "I remember this one time an older girl started a fight with me in the girl's bathroom. She was saying all kinds of things about me and about playing the accordion." Ybarra dropped out of school in the seventh grade because of the harassment.

FACING Eva Ybarra: radio, theater, and television artist. *Courtesy of Eva Ybarra.*

Being a female performer was no easy feat. Beyond the taboos against girls playing accordions, the young Ybarra confronted professional challenges few of her male peers faced. Years later, she remembered a promoter tried to force himself on her after a show. She later told author Kathleen Hudson, "I want to mention this because I don't want something to happen to other young ladies out there. Every lady he made a contract with, they had to sleep with him." Nevertheless, she continued, and in the 1980s she founded her own group and has led it ever since. She made several now rare regional albums, and released two records with Boston-based folk label Rounder in the 1990s. Unlike many conjunto players, she wrote most of her own songs along with vocalist Gloria Garcia. Her *Romance Inolvidable* ("Unforgettable Romance," Rounder, 1996) features all songs by women, including several composed by Ybarra's mother.

For years Ybarra heard, "You play really good for a woman." It was a uniquely meaningless comment because there were almost no other women to compare her to. She struggled as a child for the simple right to learn to play, and continues working today to overcome barriers women face in her tradition. Now considered a master of what was once thought a man's instrument, her extended chords and unique ornamentations put her amongst the best accordionists—of any style—in North America. Her perseverance has created a role model for young women (and men), unlike any she had when she first picked up an instrument as a child.

Los Tigres del Norte: From Sinaloa to Stardom

Los Tigres del Norte are the culmination of the journey from regional folk music to transnational popular phenomena. They symbolize the accordion-based border music's adaptability and its greatest success in the modern world. Based in San Jose, California, for much of their career, Los Tigres were originally from Sinaloa, a region known for Mexican *banda* brass bands, not for accordion-based norteño.

The small agricultural village where Jorge Hernández and his brothers and cousins grew up in the 1960s had no radio or record players. They had little contact with the world of modern music, but learned corrido ballads orally—the way people had for generations. When their grandmother eventually bought a radio, the only station it would pick up was one broadcasting accordion music from Texas. Their grandfather's cousin had an accordion and the boys learned to play. They performed to make money for the family, and eventually moved to Mexicali on the border to reach more people. When they first arranged to tour in the United States, a border guard asked the name of the band and they let him put down whatever he wanted. On their immigration documents that day, he named what would become the biggest band in the history of the Mexican border accordion.

Los Tigres eventually had two accordionists, Jorge Hernández and younger brother Eduardo. They didn't make a big stir until they released the corrido "Contrabando y Traición" (Smuggling and Betrayal) in 1973. Their songs were rooted in the tradition of storytelling they grew up in, and helped establish the corrido ballad as the heart of modern norteño music. At the same time their records initiated the *narco-corrido* genre of songs about the often violent drug-smuggling industry. Over the years the majority of Los Tigres's corridos have been about other issues, though, with a consistent social commentary on the lives of immigrants.

Corrido-focused norteño bands like Los Tigres have become far more popular than any Mexican American conjunto group. The band catapulted to fame after appearances in popular movies based on their songs. Their fourteen films promoted the sale of more than thirty-two million records over forty years, and their concerts have attracted hundreds of thousands of fans.

With their fantastic success, the members of Los Tigres have offered a unique gift back to their musical community. Led by their desire to know more about the roots of their cultural inheritance, they gave $500,000 to set up the Strachwitz Frontera Collection of Mexican and Mexican American Recordings at UCLA. "We wanted to know more and we wanted the real history of the corrido," said Tigres leader Jorge Hernández. The collection is based on more than 100,000 recordings collected by Chris Strachwitz, the founder of Arhoolie Records. As Agustín Gurza relates in his guide to the collection, "This humble band of brothers from Rosa Morada, Sinaloa, helped establish the largest archive of Mexican and Mexican American music in the world." Together the corrido, the ranchera, the conjunto, and norteño border accordion live on.

Chavela: Acordeón Express

In the 1970s and '80s, "Chavela" (Isabel Ortiz Hernández) became the most successful female conjunto accordionist until her life was cut short.

Frustratingly, years later, almost none of her recordings are legally available, though songs are shared online by fans.

Raised in a musical family in Fresno, California, her mother gave her an accordion when she was nine so she could join her sisters in the family band. Las Incomparables Hermanas Ortiz (the Incomparable Ortiz Sisters) featured her sister Stella on drums, her mother on bajo sexto, and her grandfather on Fender bass. The family played clubs and community events from 1964–68, then broke up when Ortiz was sixteen.

In 1976 Ortiz joined the group Brown Express as lead singer and accordionist. Based out of Fresno, they were trendsetters in expanding the conjunto sound beyond the Texas border region. They followed music of the day by layering early monophonic synthesizers with accordion, and using electric guitar effects like the wah-wah pedal on the intro to their otherwise traditionally structured "Maquina 501." Chavela and the guys also sported super-snazzy unisex polyester outfits and trendy hairstyles.

Most of the band officially became Chavela y Su Grupo Express in 1980. (Chavela's husband, Eduardo Hernández, played keyboards in Grupo Express before joining his brothers in Los Tigres del Norte.) Chavela led her bands on accordion and vocals and recorded fifteen albums over the life of both groups. Her LP *Rey del Barrio* ("King of the Barrio") was nominated for a Grammy in 1987.

Then, when she was only thirty-six, Chavela was thrown from a horse while on a photo shoot. She struck her head and lapsed into a coma, and died on October 7, 1992. She was inducted into the Tejano Roots Hall of Fame in 2008, but her music deserves a revival today.

Waila: "Chicken Scratch" Polka

Along with its conjunto and norteño cousins, and the polka music of European immigrants, the other accordion style of the Southwest is the Waila music of the Tohono O'odham nation. Waila takes its name from the Spanish *baile*, for dance. It's also been colorfully but slightly derogatorily called "chicken scratch," because of the shuffling dance that developed to go with it.

Waila bands played polkas and waltzes on violins and guitars as early as the 1860s. During the 1950s, some Tohono O'odham who had been in military-style bands in government boarding schools began including saxophones and accordions into their dance music. Another obvious influence was the neighboring styles of conjunto and orquesta Tejana bands, which used accordions and other instruments.

For the last hundred years, Tohono O'odham land has been officially restricted to four reservations in what is now southern Arizona and reserves across the imposed border in Northern Mexico. European missionaries, who began arriving in the 1600s, brought musical instruments that were played at festivals. Today, the local religion, a kind of folk-Catholicism, includes feasts on saint days with processions, prayer, and dancing to European-style music.

Like the Tohono O'odham religion, waila music is a syncretic mixture of European forms repurposed by local communities. It is used for dancing polkas ("waila" also means polka in O'odham) and other European folk and salon dances like schottisches, along with more recent cumbias from the neighboring norteño style. The instrumentation is distinct for using saxophones paired with the accordion, along with electric bass, guitar, and drums.

A modern waila band may have all their instruments amplified, but no microphones on stage. Besides the influence of early conjunto artists like Narciso Martínez, who mostly played instrumentals, University of Arizona professor Janet Sturman has studied the reasons for waila's lack of vocals. Singing in O'odham may be reserved for traditional and spiritual songs that don't fit waila's European-influenced secular rhythms. This has led some to worry that waila may discourage the passing on of the language. If so, this would sadly echo the boarding school punishments for speaking Native tongues which, as Sturman notes, "may have also played a role in establishing the practice of not singing O'odham lyrics in mixed [Native/European] settings."

Despite the fact that it is European-influenced, waila has been embraced for much of the last hundred years and became a significant part of the O'odham culture. Most waila musicians learn from older members of their families, with those players having learned from their parents. The style, however, isn't static. John Manuel from the group the American Indians learned to play by transferring fiddle tunes to accordion, and by 1976 was plugging into a wah-wah pedal.

Most waila accordionists don't use the bass side of the instrument; some take those reeds out entirely. Frank Valenzuela of the Joaquin Brothers and Valenzuela and Company preferred to lighten his accordion because others were "too heavy for a ten-hour gig." With feasts often lasting from dusk to dawn, the father of accordionist Damon Enriquez from the Cisco Band taught him to take out the bass reeds "because it makes it easier to play loudly for a long time."

The O'odham pattern of adaptation continues in what some would call a flouting of modern copyright. Waila musicians regularly borrow songs and melodies so that old-time dance tunes absorb fragments of modern pop songs with or without attribution. If waila musicians can't recall the name of a tune, they may make one up, or change a known title to indicate memorable occasions or people. (Researcher Jim Griffith found that a song he often requested—the Mexican tune "Las Nubes"— became known as "Jim's Waltz.")

Waila groups of note have included the Joaquin Brothers band, who played from 1957–93; the Cisco Band, which did include singing sometimes; and Southern Scratch (founded by descendants of the Joaquin Brothers). Gertie Lopez of Gertie and the T.O. Boyz is one of the only female waila accordionists to have her own band, though there have been other women who've played with family members. Longtime Native American music label Canyon Records has released as many as fifty waila recordings since the 1970s, but not all are still available. Even award-winning recordings by Gertie Lopez and others can be very difficult to find outside the region.

Since 1988, the best way to encounter the music was at the annual Waila Festival in Tucson. The music is also heard at local bars, rodeos, and at all-night festivals in villages on the reservations. As it has for most of the last century, waila continues to adapt and change for its people. As Janet Sturman found, "Tohono O'odham accordion players do not think of the accordion as modern or old. For [waila musician] Frank Valenzuela, 'it's somewhere in between.'"

9

Creoles, Cajuns, and Zydeco: French Music in the American South

F ASKED TO name an accordion genre besides polka, many people mention Cajun music or zydeco. By the end of the twentieth
century these Louisiana-based styles had risen from almost total
obscurity to unimaginable global prominence. This chapter cannot
hope to do justice to the work that's been done to document Black Creole
and Cajun music. The region has a richer bibliography than any other
in accordion history. For those looking for more, recommended works
include the *Fiddles, Accordions, Two-Step & Swing* anthology and Michael
Tisserand's *Kingdom of Zydeco*.

Louisiana, with its Native, French, African, and Spanish influences—
as well as significant Italian, German, and other immigrant populations—
may have the most complex racial, legal, and cultural history in the
United States. Under French and Spanish law, multiple castes—black, free
people of color, and European (plus Native and immigrant populations)—
created racial nuances that echoed on after Americans took control
in 1803.

Statehood was granted in 1812, before accordions appeared in the
United States, but the Cajuns and Black Creoles who eventually took up

the instrument had already been making music in the region for many years. Black Creoles—French-speaking mixed-race free blacks—were present in Louisiana since the 1700s. They included a significant number of musically educated people of color who played in New Orleans and surrounding rural areas. Around 1760, French colonists known as Acadians were interred and exiled from Canada. Many initially sought refuge in France, but over the following decades a few thousand migrated to Louisiana and became known (and looked down on) as Cajuns. These various French-speaking populations, African and European, created distinctive—primarily fiddle-based—music in Louisiana for half a century before their descendants encountered accordions.

☞ Acadians and Cajuns

AS ACCORDIONS SPREAD across the world they arrived with no clear instructions, so every culture came up with new ways to play the instrument. For example Louisiana's Cajuns and their Acadian relations in Canada share some old songs, but their accordion styles developed totally separately. The new instrument was introduced to northern Acadian and southern Cajun musicians as much as a hundred years after their division, and the differences between their musics reflect the century they spent apart. Most significantly, French Canadians were impacted by the many Irish immigrants who came to Eastern Canada. Down south, the Cajuns were deeply influenced by Black Creoles—their musical partners in Louisiana French music. Even though they played similar folk accordions, the northern and southern traditions had no way to coordinate their adoption of the instrument, so each developed in its own direction.

Cajun Fiddle and Accordion: Dancing Back and Forth

After Cajuns took up the accordion, a competitive partnership with the fiddle commenced. Four-stop (four reeds playing each note) accordions were so loud that the traditional lead fiddle was pushed to play only backing rhythms. In the 1930s though, inspired by Bob Wills and other western swing groups, "Cajun swing" acts like the Hackberry Ramblers amplified their fiddles. Ramblers' fiddle player Luderin Darbone told Ann Savoy years later, "When we played in these dance halls, we'd get big crowds, and a fiddle with two guitars and no amplifiers; you can imagine how it sounded if you had a hundred couples dancing. They couldn't hear us on the other end... The amplifier came in and we played a dance with it at the Evangeline oilfield. And man, the people couldn't understand that. Even the fiddle and guitars were carrying." As the fiddles got louder, the distinctive accordion fell from fashion.

After World War II, accordionist Iry LeJeune and others led a nostalgic revival that pushed the country fiddles back and returned the accordion to the center of most Cajun bands. When LeJeune was killed in 1955, his legend helped lift the accordion's stature within the tradition even further, just before Cajun music cracked into wider consciousness during the 1960s folk revival.

The battle between fiddles and accordions had musical consequences: one-row diatonic accordions were incapable of playing the full repertoire of fiddle tunes, especially those with complex structures and key changes. Musicians adapted to this limitation by dropping songs that had been part of the music since the Acadians were forced from Canada. Today we have the happy compromise of both accordions and fiddles (amplified when they need to be), combined to carry forward the whole French-speaking history of Louisiana.

Accordions Arrive in Creole and Then Cajun Hands

Louisiana's French Creole free people of color long walked a precarious path. They struggled to maintain a higher status than most African Americans, including the legal privileges granted by French law, which fell away under American rule. Their French language and identification as a separate group let them hold on to unique traditions, including their music.

More than likely, minstrel performers or upper-class parlor players brought the very first French "flutina" accordions to Louisiana by 1845. In cities like New Orleans, Black Creoles quickly took to the modern,

European instrument. By the 1880s, German button accordions were being played by urban Creole musicians like Henry Peyton and were likely trickling out to rural Creoles and eventually their Cajun neighbors in Southwest Louisiana's bayous and prairies.

Canray Fontenot, the great Black Creole fiddler born in 1922, recalled how his father, mother, and grandfather all played accordion; he was told that during the times of slavery, blacks had been taught to play the instrument. By the turn of the nineteenth century, accordions had become widely available at local stores or through catalogs. "Accordions were cheap then," recalled Black Creole Éraste Carrière (born 1901), whose father bought him his first accordion as a child for only $1.50 (cheaper than a violin and the equivalent of about $36 today).

Cajun musicians seem to have resisted taking up the accordion for some time. Reports from the 1880s about communities of hundreds of families of Cajuns in the prairies of Louisiana mention "no less than sixty fiddlers," but no accordion at all. Though Creole players likely brought the accordion into rural Louisiana, the instrument only endured with the Cajuns' help, anchored by both French cultures together. The French dance repertoire was crucial to the survival of the accordion. Every French speaker, no matter what color, added to a cultural critical mass that sustained the music.

Cajun culture survived by being both conservative and adaptive. Since their arrival in Louisiana in the 1700s, Cajuns stubbornly held on to their Catholic faith and French language while also learning from their new surroundings. They were never truly isolated from the outside world; their food took on the spices of the Caribbean, their language was influenced by two centuries of contact with other dialects. Their music blended the sounds of Anglo country music with the Afro-Creole French styles that eventually incorporated the blues. Ultimately the Cajuns adopted the accordion and made it their own. During the latter half of the twentieth century, when Anglo culture abandoned the instrument, Louisiana's French-speaking communities nurtured some of the most exciting accordion music in the world.

It is difficult to say exactly what the "French music" of rural Louisiana sounded like before the first recordings were made in the 1920s, or how Cajun and Creole music may have differed from each other in the past. Language and cultural similarities seem to have produced a shared music based on fiddle tunes—and eventually the accordion—backed with rhythm instruments like the *'tit fer* ("little iron") triangle or washboard. European social dances like the waltz, the mazurka, and contradances laced together the Cajun and Creole shared musical heritage.

Prior to World War II, *bals de maison* house dances were the primary venue in rural Louisiana for both Cajun and Creole music. People moved furniture out of their homes and dancers took over the largest room or spilled outside. Musicians usually featured small groups of as little as two instruments: one fiddle or accordion and percussion.

Descriptions of house dances and later dance halls speak of singers crying out to packed rooms in Louisiana's summer heat. To be heard over the noisy crowds, Cajun fiddlers began to play together in pairs and developed a distinctive double-stop technique that increased the volume of their instruments by sounding multiple strings at once. The region's accordionists followed suit, playing notes paired in octaves, intensifying their already powerful German accordions. By the early 1930s, the volume of the accordions was threatening to overwhelm the fiddle's role in the music entirely.

"English Only" in French Louisiana

It's reported that when Columbia engineers recorded Cajun accordionist Dewey Segura in New Orleans in 1929 they told him, "We don't know what you're singing, we ask you just one thing: don't sing anything dirty." Cajuns' and Creoles' French language separated their music from the increasingly homogenized culture surrounding them. Outsiders' intolerance in fact threatened to wash away their distinctive culture, starting with their language. Louisiana's French population had been in conflict with English-speakers (called "Americans") for generations, and official policy—beginning with mandatory English-language education in 1916—seemed bent on destroying the region's French cultures. America's turn-of-the-century "melting pot" ideology emphasized assimilation, not admiration. Immigrants were discriminated against when they maintained Old World customs and language. Children in Louisiana were punished for speaking French in schools (one result being that many remained illiterate). Along with the language, French music was looked down on as old-fashioned, uncultured, and backward.

This marginalization coincided with the increasing influence of country music and R&B on Cajun and Creole musicians. As their regional culture was inundated with commercial radio and recordings, local musicians changed their sound and began to sing in English. The Cajun accordion nearly disappeared before World War II, and by the time Clifton Chenier started making records in the early 1950s, he mostly played R&B and didn't believe anyone wanted to hear him sing in French.

In that postwar era though, artists like Iry LeJeune helped bring the accordion back to the center of the music. French culture began to take a stand for its own identity and value. Being Cajun or Creole slowly became a source of pride, rather than shame. The 1960s helped unite the French-speaking population of Louisiana to support dramatic policy reversals to accommodate and support French in public schools. Music became an instrument for French language preservation, as artists like Dewey Balfa (Cajun) and Rockin' Dopsie (Creole) visited schools together to share the value of their cultures. The shift would have been unimaginable decades before, but over the latter half of the twentieth century, French music and specifically the accordion became central and even profitable symbols of cultural renaissance.

The Louisiana Accordion over Time

After the accordion was introduced, Louisiana accordionists resisted further technological developments that the instrument experienced outside the region. Their increasingly archaic one-row diatonic instruments and the reliance on French repertoire and oral tradition separated them almost entirely from North America's commercialized accordion industry. Even though Cajun musicians took in the sounds of western groups that used them, larger piano accordions made only a few appearances. "Bill from Ohio" remains an unusual and mysterious exception in old photos, playing his piano accordion upside-down with Leo Soileau in the 1930s or '40s.

The choice of instruments certainly had an element of economics. Today, a handmade "Cajun accordion" costs thousands of dollars, but in 1915 a ten-button accordion cost as little as $3.50. Compared to those cheap button boxes, a vaudeville-style piano accordion remained an unthinkable luxury. Outside of Louisiana the "accordion arms race" for fancier and more expensive instruments raged, but those were well out of reach for most rural Cajun and Creole musicians.

When instruments became hard to come by during the Allied embargo of Germany and Italy in the Second World War, Cajuns resorted to making and repairing their own accordions. This tradition continues today with several Louisiana-based accordion makers (most famously Marc Savoy). These Cajun master-builders stubbornly keep alive the simple ten-button style imported from Europe a century ago.

The first recordings of Louisiana's French accordion in the 1920s are the earliest clear impression of what their music sounded like. Cajuns and Creoles were playing similar ten-button accordions in more or less a single style. Black and white musicians sometimes played together, but audiences were usually segregated. Trouble could arise when cultural color lines were crossed, and most dance halls and house parties served either the Creole or the Cajun community, but not both. An outside listener might have trouble telling an old-fashioned Creole fiddler or accordionist from a Cajun player, but probably wouldn't confuse either for music from Ireland, Kentucky, or the Cajuns' ancestral Acadia. The combination of emotional waltzes with energetic instrumental embellishments, all pushed out powerfully in noisy dance halls, was unique to its milieu.

In the 1920s, Dennis McGee, a Cajun fiddler, famously played and recorded with Creole accordionist Amédé Ardoin, who was unquestionably the most highly regarded early Louisiana accordionist. Together the two set the standard for the combined accordion/fiddle style the region became known for.

Ardoin had a bluesy flavor in his playing, and even called several of his tunes blues, but many of his blues elements were suggested by his singing voice rather than his accordion. He could play some blues notes using a "cross position" technique by playing in the key of A on a box tuned to play in D, but deeper blues awaited more advanced accordions.

Outside the Creole community, most African Americans dropped the accordion in the early 1900s because the instruments struggled to play the newly popular blues. But one-row button accordions continued to be practical for the pre-blues French dance repertoire that Creoles shared with Cajuns. As a result, Cajun and Creole French folk musicians retained the accordion as they preserved this non-blues repertoire together.

Modern Creole and Cajun musicians have sustained their musical relationship despite racial and cultural divisions. When Rockin' Dopsie recorded his *French Style* album in 1981, producer Samuel Charters suggested bringing in Cajun players like Dewey Balfa. "By the time they'd gotten through half a chorus it was obvious how closely they had all grown up with each other's music ... the traditions had never really lost touch with each other."

Creole fiddler and accordionist Cedric Watson's partnership with the Cajun band the Pine Leaf Boys is probably the best-known recent example of the ongoing interplay between Cajun and Creole music. The two cultures linked by geography and language worked in parallel to build the musical foundations that inspire people still.

Cajun and Creole Music as a Folk Tradition

In the 1940s and '50s French accordion music was widely dismissed in Louisiana as old-fashioned "chank-a-chank." Things changed as modern audiences began to find value in regional sounds. Harry Smith's groundbreaking 1952 *Anthology of American Folk Music* entirely excluded accordions except for a few Cajun songs. Smith erased Northern and urban accordions, but perhaps because Cajuns were from the South, they were the first folk accordionists to receive the attention of the folk revival, paving the way for Irish, conjunto/norteño, klezmer, and zydeco in years to come.

Cajun folk accordionists gained their first exposure outside the region in the early 1960s. Ironically, this was precisely when popular music was abandoning accordions. Cajun and Creole musicians were invited to the Newport Folk Festival starting in 1964. Dewey Balfa remembers being told not to go to, that people would only laugh at Cajun music. Instead he was received with adulation.

The unexpected acclaim from folk revivalists helped spark a revival of its own back in Louisiana. It was not, however, met with universal support. Burton Grindstaff of the *Opelousas Daily World* opined in 1965, "Some say they can't understand Cajun music because it is in French. Others say they can't understand it because it isn't music." Cajun musicians, folklorists, and regular folks responded by making the music Grindstaff had satirized central to what became known as the Cajun renaissance.

Players like the Balfa family bands, along with researchers (often also musicians) like Barry Jean Ancelet, Ann Savoy, and many others led the musical arm of a movement to gain acceptance for French language and culture. In 1974 the first "Tribute to Cajun Music/Hommage à la Musique Acadienne" took place in Lafayette. (It took on its current, more inclusive title "Festivals Acadiens et Créoles" in 2008.) It became an annual event and a model for support and preservation that saw Louisiana's French culture become not only globally recognized, but even trendy.

It's worth recalling that a good number of the artists at even the earliest "Cajun" events were Black Creoles. Clifton Chenier and Alphonse "Bois Sec" Ardoin both played 1974's premier Musique Acadienne tribute. Negotiating the distinctions between the closely related Creole and Cajun styles and the cultural uniqueness of each has been a touchy issue. Changing festivals from "Cajun" to "Cajun and Creole," or the rejection of the term "Black Cajun" have been steps toward historical clarity in the musical mix that gave birth to what most rural Louisianans used to just call "French music."

Black Creole Accordion

From the 1930s to the '60s Cajun musicians embraced country music and western swing, then returned to their distinctive accordion in time to be "discovered" by the folk revival. Louisiana's Black Creoles followed their own path in connection with other African American musicians. Anglo blacks had overwhelmingly dropped the accordion even before the "race record" boom of the 1920s–30s. French-speaking Creoles like Amédé Ardoin were unique for prominently including the instrument in landmark recordings that influenced every later Cajun and Creole accordionist.

Ardoin and other Creoles played accordion for both Creole and Cajun audiences. Blacks and whites would not dance together, but their shared French language and the fact that the musicians often performed together (for segregated audiences) was enough to create and sustain a coherent musical culture between them. Insulated somewhat from the surrounding Anglo culture by language and the unique French repertoire, the accordion maintained its place as a central instrument in Creole music.

At the same time as the first commercial Cajun and Creole records were being made, fragments of Creole styles that may have predated the accordion were preserved in a handful of short field recordings made by Alan and John Lomax in 1934. The Lomaxes collected extremely rare examples of old syncopated Creole *juré* a cappella singing. The young Alan Lomax called it the "the most African sound I found in America." Musicians like Clifton Chenier later claimed juré as the rhythmic forebear of zydeco. These recordings also contain the first recorded use of the term "zydeco," in Wilfred Charles's juré shout, "Dégo/Zydeco." Years later, Lomax regretted not recording more in the region in the 1930s, when Amédé Ardoin and many other professional Creole musicians were still alive and in their prime.

Almost everything we know about the largely unrecorded early Creole music comes from the recollections and playing styles of older musicians interviewed and recorded years later after zydeco had gained global attention. Some, like fiddler Canray Fontenot, insisted the earlier style was "Creole," or just "French music," to differentiate it from the modern R&B-influenced zydeco players.

By the time anybody bothered to ask, the players who remembered early Creole styles were in their sixth decade as musicians. Amédé Ardoin exists today only as a legendary voice on scratchy old records. But the music of Creoles like him lived and breathed when he was a young man. Unknown numbers of Creoles played music in their communities, but record companies and folklorists never knocked on their doors.

Creole Music and Zydeco after the Depression

When the record industry faced ruin in the Great Depression, Black Creole recording ended almost completely. By the 1950s when recordings were being made again, Creole accordionists were adapting to dramatic innovations in African American music. Drums, saxophones, electric guitars, and bass augmented the traditional accordion and washboard. They gave rise to a hybrid between African American R&B and older French styles that echoed the Creoles' rich African rhythm and heritage. This was the birth of what they called "la-la," or eventually zydeco.

Under the influence of blues and R&B, Creole accordion music slowly diverged from its Cajun neighbors. Early blues arrangements required players like Amédé Ardoin to reach beyond the capabilities of their single-row button accordions. To continue incorporating blues elements, Creole players—unlike their Cajun neighbors—began to adopt two- and three-row button accordions. As Creoles encountered western swing and other dance bands using piano accordions, they experimented with them as well and created zydeco.

The Great Migration that drew Southern blacks to Northern cities also stretched west, and many French-speaking Creoles relocated to Texas and California. They maintained family ties and cultural elements, as younger musicians picked up and modernized old styles and maintained a connection with their roots. Cajuns also migrated west, and in the San Francisco Bay Area smaller communities of Creole and Cajun musicians often played together, uniting their "French music" once again.

Historic creole and zydeco music stretches back to before the Civil War, when the Creole people of Louisiana first took up the accordion. Years later, "new traditionalists" like Cedric Watson resurrected old styles going all the way back to the pre-accordion Creole fiddle. More than a century and a half later, Creole and zydeco music still keeps the people dancing.

Louisiana French Accordionists

Amédé Ardoin: Thirty-Four Historic Recordings

Amédé Ardoin, born March 11, 1898, cut his first disc in 1929 and his last just before Christmas in 1934. These thirty-four recordings endure at the heart of Creole and Cajun accordion. Ardoin's parents had been enslaved, but after emancipation they owned and farmed their own land. His father died when he was small and his mother when he was about twenty; by then he was playing accordion and singing for a living, making more than he ever could working in the fields.

Ardoin played house parties and was renowned for the emotion of his singing and the passion he pulled from his accordion. Women would cry as his high, wailing voice improvised lyrics about lost love, often inspired by the personal lives of the dancers in front of him. When fights broke out— as they did when his songs cut too close to a jealous heart—he'd play a religious tune to calm down rowdy crowds. If that didn't work, he might have to flee the stage and come back later for his accordion. When the

music finally stopped he'd walk home or hitch a ride with his instrument in a sack over his shoulder.

When he wasn't playing professionally, Ardoin sometimes entertained friends and family. Vincent Lejeune, who knew Ardoin, told *Kingdom of Zydeco* author Michael Tisserand, "He played at the church gathering, for the black people. On Wednesday nights, there would be a religious meeting, maybe the whole neighborhood would get in one house, and Amédé would go play for them." One account has him playing for kids, laughing as he made his accordion bark like a dog. Another remembered him singing for friends without using the accordion at all, improvising lyrics while pounding on the porch like a drum.

A combination of factors led to the making of Ardoin's shellac records. In the late 1920s music companies were targeting rural populations that didn't yet have radios. Cajun accordionist Joe Falcon and his guitarist wife, Cléoma, made the first Louisiana accordion recording in 1928. They had a hit and proved the viability of Cajun and Creole "French music." These regional recordings, sold to play on wind-up gramophones, made artists like Ardoin and his white fiddle partner, Dennis McGee, briefly marketable in that pre-radio era.

Mystery surrounds Ardoin's later days, but his career was cut short and ended tragically. It is rumored that a racist attack in the late 1930s left him unable to play; he fell into dementia and died in 1942. He was buried in an unmarked grave at the mental asylum in Pineville, Louisiana, where he spent his last days. He left his recordings and the memories of family and fellow musicians like the long-lived McGee, who continued to share tunes he and Ardoin played in their youth.

In 2018, a carved metal statue of Ardoin was unveiled in St. Landry Parish. It is based on his only known photo, taken a hundred years earlier in about 1915. In the picture, Ardoin is holding a cane over his shoulder—for the statue, the artist Russell Whiting replaced the cane with a golden lemon, representing Ardoin's habit of carrying one to soothe his throat to ease his voice, as if he's preparing for the chance to sing one more song.

Alphonse "Bois Sec" Ardoin & Canray Fontenot: Creole French Music

The recordings of "Bois Sec" Ardoin (born 1915, Amédé Ardoin's younger cousin) and Creole fiddler Canray Fontenot (born 1922), evoke Louisiana's

FACING Amédé Ardoin statue, 2018. *Artist: Russell Whiting, St. Landry Parish Tourist Commission.*

pre-R&B black country dances. Their music, made with acoustic one-row diatonic accordion, fiddle, and rubboard or triangle sounds similar to early Cajun recordings. The links between the two musical cultures are clear.

Both "Bois Sec" and Fontenot started out playing triangle with Amédé Ardoin in the 1930s. Fontenot had been set to join the accordionist on his 1934 trip to New York to make his last recordings, but Fontenot's mother forbid him to go, saying he was too young. The fiddler would not have another chance to record for thirty years.

In 1966, Ardoin and Fontenot were among the performers invited to the Newport Folk Festival, where they were recognized as among the last stewards of the older Creole tradition. They played at the first 1974 Tribute to Cajun Music in Lafayette and returned many times, passing on their fiddle and accordion repertoire to modern Creole and Cajun players like Terrance Simien, Marc Savoy, and others lucky enough to spend time with them.

"Bois Sec" Ardoin died in 2007 at age 92, the oldest link to generations of Creole French accordionists. Along with his records with Fontenot, the old Creole style was also preserved on record by the Carrière Brothers in the 1970s. Together with early commercial records and Alan Lomax's home-music recordings from the 1930s, they remain vibrant reminders of how Creole music sounded in the years before the addition of R&B instruments led to zydeco.

Iry LeJeune

Before World War II, the amplified fiddles of western swing invaded Cajun territory. Accordions dropped from prominence until one player, Iry LeJeune, brought it back in the postwar 1940s and '50s. Long after he was killed by a speeding automobile in 1955, he is still regarded as one of the best and most influential players in the region.

Without a lot of store-bought entertainment options, the LeJeunes were a musical family: Iry's father, grandmother, aunt and uncles all played fiddles or accordions at house dances. Born in 1928, the young LeJeune's first paid gig was playing harmonica for coins at an election rally while riding on a politician's shoulders. He started on accordion at age six when he could only play while opening the bellows, since his arms

FACING Iry LeJeune (date unknown). *The Iry LeJeune Collection—Ervin LeJeune/ Ron Yule.*

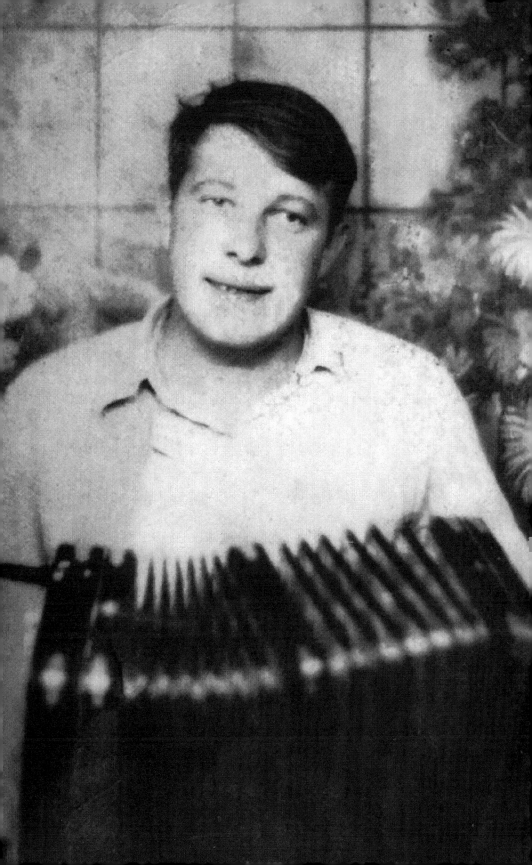

weren't strong enough to close them. His father stayed up all night teaching him tunes, much to the annoyance of family members wanting to sleep.

LeJeune also learned by listening to records from pre-Depression artists Amédé Ardoin, Joe Falcon, and LeJeune's own uncle Angelas (who shared old records with the young player). By the time he was grown LeJeune was playing with his band the Lacassine Playboys, mostly at dance halls, since big, organized house parties were a thing of the past. He made his first record in Houston in 1947. Returning to Louisiana, he continued to record and play on local radio. He also made a series of records at his house with the recorder on the kitchen table. The engineer would make him take his shoes off, so his stamping foot wouldn't make the needle skip.

LeJeune's short life was a struggle with poverty compounded by the challenges of his near blindness. He'd hitch rides to shows, sometimes playing music wherever someone was headed. Like Amédé Ardoin, he'd carry his beat-up accordion in a sack rather than a heavy case. After his death at age twenty-seven, his family faced dire need, with the loss of his disability income and no help from those who profited off his records. Despite these hardships, his children and grandchildren survived to carry on his musical legacy.

He didn't live long enough to see the revival his music would inspire. There are fewer than thirty of LeJeune's pathbreaking but deeply rooted recordings. With them, he restored the accordion to Cajun music.

Nathan Abshire, the Balfa Brothers, and the Cajun Revival

"I had no idea what a festival was," Cajun accordionist Nathan Abshire told Barry Jean Ancelet. "I had played in house dances, family gatherings, maybe a dance hall where you might have seen as many as two hundred people at once. In fact, I doubt that I had ever seen two hundred people at once. And in Newport, there were seventeen thousand. Seventeen thousand people who wouldn't let us get off stage."

The story of the 1970s revival of Cajun accordion ironically begins with a fiddler, Dewey Balfa. In 1964, Balfa filled in on guitar as a last-minute replacement at the Newport Folk Festival along with fellow Cajuns Gladius Thibodeaux (accordion) and Louis "Vinesse" LeJeune (fiddle). When Balfa returned from Newport, he took up the work of saving his culture.

Nathan Abshire (1913–81) often played with the Balfa Brothers' band as the Cajun renaissance began in the 1960s. He became one of the most highly regarded Cajun accordionists. His career began decades earlier and he remembered playing with Amédé Ardoin as a young man in the 1920s. Abshire was a contemporary of Iry LeJeune and continued the work of returning accordions to their place in Cajun music.

Then, as now, few Cajun musicians were able to survive on music alone; Abshire worked at the town dump while Dewey Balfa drove a school bus. Extending his connection with school-age youth, Balfa brought Cajun and Creole musicians (with Rockin' Dopsie and others) to classrooms all over Louisiana as a way to share the roots and value of French music.

Abshire once said he was uncomfortable with musicians' recordings being played after their deaths: "When I die, I wish they would break all my records... and bury my music with me." His wish has not been granted, as his records and films of his performances still inspire modern players. All of Abshire's and the Balfas' performances are worthwhile. Those from their early days are a thrilling reminder of when they were just beginning the fight to preserve their music. The Balfa family band lives on as Balfa Toujours (Balfa Forever). Led by Dewey's daughter Christine, Balfa's children and grandchildren carry on the effort that Abshire and the Balfas started to awaken their unique culture.

Clifton Chenier: King of the Zydeco

Few musicians launch an entire musical genre. Bill Monroe saw bluegrass become "traditional" and pretty much ageless within his lifetime. Clifton Chenier similarly helped build zydeco from personal vision into global phenomena. As a child near Opelousas, Louisiana, Chenier probably played button box like his father had, but started playing piano accordion as a teen in the early 1940s. The piano keyboard opened up new possibilities for Creole blues accordion. Chenier mastered the left-hand buttons to accompany his brother Cleveland, who played a custom *frottoir* rubboard that Chenier designed. When he saw another player trying to steal his licks, Chenier would drop his right hand entirely and intimidate copyists with his left-hand technique alone.

One story had a young Chenier "borrowing" his first piano accordion from a player named Isaie Blasa and leaving town with it for Texas. Living in Houston, Chenier later found junk accordions in garage sales and had them repaired and tuned by John Gabbanelli (founder of the Gabbanelli Accordions). Speaking to Michael Tisserand, one friend remembered the impression Chenier made with his modern

"Big La-La Dance," advertisement for "King of the Zydeco, Clifton Chenier."
Courtesy of Johnny Nicholas, Hilltop Cafe, Fredericksburg, TX. Photo by Jack Garton.

instruments: "Before that we had only seen the old French accordion, that these people had in the sack. They had no color to it, no chrome or nothing. But his accordion, it had glow into the color, man. And we'd go home and tell people what we had seen."

Chenier and a few others began to record the new style in the 1950s. His Creole French "Ay-Tete Fee" ("Eh, Petite Fille," or "Hey, Little Girl") even became a national R&B hit in 1955. Fats Domino and other English-speaking R&B artists were breaking into the white pop market, and Chenier was eager to follow. He electrified his accordion the way Little Walter had the blues harmonica, so Chicago style urban blues met Louisiana–Texas proto-zydeco. (More on Chenier's R&B side later.)

Chenier's jarringly unfamiliar accordion failed to catch nationally and he retreated back to his Creole audience. His wider career didn't reignite until 1964, when Lightnin' Hopkins (Chenier's cousin by marriage) introduced him to Chris Strachwitz of Arhoolie Records. Chenier came prepared to record in the style of Ray Charles, but Strachwitz urged Chenier to focus on his unique French material. They compromised and the resulting Creole/R&B mix set the mold for zydeco. Chenier became Arhoolie's bestselling artist, while remaining an icon within the French Creole communities stretching from Louisiana out to the West Coast. Years of touring, recordings, and recognition ensued until diabetes slowed Chenier and finally killed him in 1987. Throughout, he remained the undisputed King of the Zydeco he helped create.

Boozoo Chavis: Country and Zydeco

As a young man, Boozoo Chavis won a calf in a horserace and sold it to buy an accordion. He began his recording career in 1954, around the same time as Clifton Chenier, but Chavis stopped playing professionally after being burned by the music industry. He raised a family and had a successful career training quarter horses, then came out of musical retirement in the 1980s when he heard a local player making money impersonating him.

Chavis's music and image were less polished than Chenier's and largely unchanged from when he had played in the 1950s. His lyrics and tunes were raw and often repetitive, but consistently entertaining and danceable. He was known for wearing a cowboy hat and a barbecue apron to keep the sweat off his accordion bellows. Musically, his style harkened back to rural Creole sounds with him playing one- and three-row button accordion. He was known for his unpredictable time shifting and added beats that sounded like John Lee Hooker and other country blues players. He told musicians in his band (often members of his family), "If it's wrong, do it wrong, with me!"

In 2001, at the crest of his second career in music, Chavis died from a heart attack at age seventy. Since his death, his cowboy aesthetic and its acknowledgment of Creole music's rural roots have been tremendously influential. The majority of young zydeco musicians today play button accordions like his. Without Chavis's inspiration, many of these young people might not be playing accordion at all.

Marc Savoy: Accordion Artisan

In the 1960s, a new generation of Cajuns saw value in the music promoted by Dewey Balfa and older players. Joining the "Cajun renaissance" was Marc Savoy, who became perhaps the most famous accordion maker in North America. Growing up near Eunice, Louisiana, Savoy never identified with his peers as a youngster, preferring to spend time with their grandparents (preeminent Cajun fiddler Dennis McGee, for instance, was a tenant farmer for Savoy's grandfather). Inspired by the music he heard from his relatives and older neighbors, he taught himself accordion at age twelve.

Savoy eventually joined a growing number of young educated Cajuns (he had an engineering degree) who championed their culture by preserving the repertoire of older players. Savoy played with the Balfa Brothers and with Michael Doucet, as well as in his own family band, but his greatest fame came from his hand-crafted accordions.

Not satisfied with the broken-down instruments available to him, Savoy taught himself accordion repair. In 1966, at age twenty-five, he opened a music store and took up building instruments full time. His Acadian brand accordions set a high standard, and professional Cajun players soon flocked to "Joel Savoy's son" to have their instruments fixed or replaced.

There had been Cajun accordion repairers and even builders before. During both world wars, new instruments had been scarce because trade with Germany and Italy was embargoed. Later, most accordion makers focused on piano accordions, with diatonic styles treated as passé. Specialized operations like Savoy's filled this gap with instruments of unprecedented craftsmanship. Savoy explained, "I'm a firm believer—in fact it's what I've based my success business-wise in the last thirty-five years—that there's always going to be a market for quality... Your clientele depends exactly upon what you're selling. If you sell crap, you're going to get... people who want to buy crap."

Savoy was challenged anew after hearing Québécois accordionist Philippe Bruneau. Though French Canadians played similar instruments to those in Louisiana, Bruneau's technique demanded an accordion that no Cajun had ever contemplated. Wanting to share his inspiration locally, Savoy refused to ship a custom accordion to Canada until Bruneau came to Louisiana to expose Cajun audiences to his music.

Today, in the Savoy Family Band, Marc and his wife, author and guitarist Ann Savoy, continue to promote Cajun culture. Their son, Wilson Savoy, carries the vision of Louisiana French music in the Pine Leaf Boys, and their daughter, Sarah, leads a band in France. Savoy is still making accordions that take the sound and culture of Louisiana to discerning customers around the world.

"Queen" Ida and Louisiana's Accordion Women

"Queen" Ida Guillory came to represent zydeco's second home on the West Coast. Born in Louisiana in 1929, she grew up in the Creole community in East Texas. When she was eighteen, her parents moved to the San Francisco Bay Area. As she traveled, she picked up the three-row button accordion with distinctive influences from her acordeón playing neighbors in California's Latino clubs.

She learned accordion by playing with her brother to entertain family. Their mother had played in private, but Ida was among the first women in Creole or Cajun music to play accordion in public. She kept at it while raising her children; at one point working as a school bus driver and practicing on the bus while waiting for her students. When she was around forty years old, she went public. "I didn't know how the men... would accept a middle-aged woman on the stage with an accordion," she told author Michael Tisserand. Playing in front of Clifton Chenier at the New Orleans Jazz Fest she thought, "Oh God, is he just going to think that this little lady should be home with her kids?"

Her initiation at festivals coincided with the 1980s zydeco boom, and quickly led to international tours and media exposure in film, advertising, and TV, including appearances on both *Saturday Night Live* and *Mister Rogers' Neighborhood*. Ida's debut album came out in 1976, and in 1982 she won the first Grammy Award for a zydeco artist (a year before

Clifton Chenier won his) for her *Queen Ida & Bon Temps Zydeco Band on Tour, featuring Al Rapone.*

Early field recordings of Cécile Audebert, Amélie Alexandre, and Inez Catalan all indicate a wealth of home-based music shared by women. Scholar Lisa Richardson relates that Louisiana dance halls and house dances were seen as places where "respectable" women might attend but not perform. Women's "home" songs were often the basis for "public" music, but only men got paid to play them.

By performing in public, "Queen" Ida, along with women who came after her like Ann Goodly and Rosie Ledet, founded a tradition of female-led zydeco groups. Together, they brought Creole women's perspectives from the home to the stage and the world. Cajun accordionists like Sheryl Cormier and scholar/musician Ann Savoy (of the Magnolia Sisters and the Savoy Family Band), along with younger players like Kristi Guillory, Sarah Savoy, and others continue to extend the influence of female musicians into the future.

Louisiana Accordionists Go Global

In the 1980s, zydeco and Cajun music turned up in dozens of movies and TV advertisements. Awards and record deals were handed out and the world got an earful of Louisiana French accordion. Many new artists appeared along with modern trends and developments.

Buckwheat Zydeco (Stanley Dural Jr.) learned piano accordion while playing organ in Clifton Chenier's band. When the opportunity presented itself, he went solo and promoted the music in advertising, movies, and international venues like the 1996 Olympic games in Atlanta. His name and sound made room for others to follow. He is notable for carrying on Chenier's piano accordion style and for emphasizing the uniqueness of the cultures by refusing to perform if promoters called him and his Creole music "Cajun."

Rockin' Dopsie exemplified the self-taught nature of many zydeco musicians by playing his three-row button accordion left-handed and upside down. He and his band performed the old song "Josephine c'est pas ma femme" on the *Graceland* LP. Paul Simon added words to the music and claimed credit for the song that became "That Was Your Mother." Dopsie wasn't happy, but neither was he angling for fame and profit (he once turned down a chance to appear on *Saturday Night Live* because he was scheduled to play a church dance that night). In 1993

Dopsie died at age sixty-one, with his mantle carried on by his son, remarkably skilled accordionist, Dwayne Dopsie.

Singer-songwriter, activist, and author Zachary Richard took Cajun music in new directions in the 1970s. He split much of his career between his home in Louisiana and supportive Francophone audiences in Quebec. Working to support the French language and culture, he bridged national and generational boundaries. Along with Steve Riley and many other young Cajuns from the 1970s and '80s, Richard's accordion made the culture sing.

New generations of musicians continue from the rich cultural mix of Louisiana. Cajun rockers the Lost Bayou Ramblers won a Grammy Award in 2017 for their noisy, electrified album *Kalenda*. Cedric Watson and others brought Creole fiddle and accordion back to prominence. Watson reached out to global Creole accordion traditions as far afield as the Dominican Republic and Cape Verde off the coast of West Africa. Their accordions connect musicians and cultures across the world with the vitality of Louisiana's once disparaged French music.

10

Irish and Scottish Accordion: Immigration, Transition, and Tradition

FREE-REED INSTRUMENTS BECAME popular in Scotland and Ireland during the later 1800s. It was time of upheaval marked by poverty, famine, and unprecedented global migration. Irish immigrants especially were often despised by racists and nationalists. Traditional musics were imperiled if immigrant cultures succumbed to the pressure to homogenize into new homelands. As Irish and Scottish musicians spread throughout the world, many refused to abandon their cultures. They brought some of the most powerful "roots" accordion styles to North America. But how did the instrument become such an important part of these traditions?

Irish and Scottish music survived not just because it was popular. It endures in part thanks to more than a hundred years of preservationists' efforts. Accordions, however, were not always on their agenda. During times when the Irish were often disparaged by anti-immigrant nativists, the accordion was frequently targeted by advocates of traditional music. It was seen as an interloper and a musical impurity that threatened the place of pipers, fiddlers, and the memory of the already vanished harpers.

Modern accordions and concertinas gained popularity despite folklorists' efforts as Irish and Scottish musicians adapted and updated their traditions. The instruments flourished because music history is told in changes, not in purity.

"Celtic Music" before the Accordion

Fifteen-hundred years before the first accordion, iron-working Celts inhabited much of what is now central Europe. The rise and fall of the Roman Empire left Celtic populations in Brittany (northwest France), Ireland, Wales, and Scotland, but no one knows what their music sounded like. Ancient Celts certainly did not step dance to jigs, hornpipes, or reels. Bagpipes were played in Ireland and Scotland by the 1500s, but even they may have originated elsewhere because pipes have been documented all across Europe since the Dark Ages (1000 AD or so).

What some call "Celtic" music today almost always reflects Irish or Scottish traditions, but has less acknowledged influences from England and elsewhere. In fact, Irish and Scottish dance music, along with French Canadian, Appalachian, and English folk traditions—and even Inuit square dances—are all part of a larger family that came over from Europe and influenced traditional fiddle tunes throughout North America.

The catch-all term "Celtic music" came into use in the 1960s and '70s to describe bands like Planxty and the Bothy Band, who played both Scottish and Irish (and sometimes English) tunes. It was such a successful marketing tool that by the 1980s both the Irish rock band U2 and rural field recordings from Brittany were branded as "Celtic music." Heated discussions on the issue can easily be elicited amongst traditional music fans, most often rejecting the "Celtic" moniker as worthless, if not offensive.

At any rate, any musical descendants of the ancient Celts had to wait 1,500 years for the Industrial Revolution to bring accordions and concertinas to Scotland and Ireland in the mid-1800s. By then, folk preservationists were distressed because urbanization threatened older music. As early as 1792, Edward Bunting was hired to notate tunes at the Belfast Harp Festival, and his *Ancient Irish Music* (1796) documented some of the last harpists in a dying tradition.

Nineteenth-century publications like *Ryan's Mammoth Collection* (1883) and Francis O'Neill's *Music of Ireland* (1903) set out to document and preserve pipe and fiddle tunes that existed before the accordion, and they became the foundation for much of the Irish and Scottish traditional repertoires today. These writers often carried a hearty antipathy for the invasive squeezebox, but that didn't prevent accordionists from using their books as they infiltrated the tradition.

Scottish Accordion: Pioneers and Critics

When accordions finally arrived on the scene, they came to Scotland a few years before Ireland. Compared with Irish accordionists though, the influence of Scottish players has been less pervasive in North America. Areas like Canada's Nova Scotia ("New Scotland") were heavily Scots-influenced but most settlers had arrived before the accordion was invented. Thus the Scottish fiddling tradition of Nova Scotia's Cape Breton Island dates to the 1700s, and includes relatively few accordions.

In Scotland, the playing of pipes, fiddles, songs, and dance music goes back centuries. The industrial age, though, wrought drastic changes in Scottish culture. Many saw the modern Victorian era as one of "impoverishment and musical corruption" and they laid the blame on newcomer instruments.

French and English accordions and concertinas were imported into Scotland as soon as they appeared in the 1830s. Marketed to noble and bourgeois men and women, these were finely crafted instruments, far out of reach of the working class. The closest they initially came to playing folk music were "improved" transcriptions of Scottish airs, interspersed with English and Italian music, almost all published in London. In the later 1800s, cheaper German accordions and concertinas became available, and bourgeois enthusiasts quickly dropped the instrument. The affordable Anglo concertina was extremely popular in Scotland between 1850 and 1875, as were louder German button accordions in the late 1800s.

Urban musicians played all styles of concertinas and accordions for Scottish music halls and variety stages, and less commonly in concertina bands inspired by the popular brass-band movement. But these popular entertainments never gained status as "folk music" among cultural critics and academics, and their memory faded in the late twentieth century while other accordion traditions were revived.

Diatonic accordions (sometimes called melodeons) were at one time promoted as an alternative to "more expensive dangerous amusement," which primarily implied the use of alcohol. The temperance movement used accordions and concertinas extensively at public events—as did the Salvation Army—and sacred songs remained a significant part of the home repertoire.

By 1903, Peter Wyper of Lanarkshire made the first wax cylinder recordings of Scottish accordion and one of the earliest recordings of an accordion anywhere. Wyper pioneered the two-row accordion tuned to the keys of B and C, which became a standard in Irish music in the 1950s. The Wyper recordings, by Peter and his brother Daniel, were extremely influential both in Scotland and Ireland. Columbia Records declared the Wypers, along with the Deiro brothers and John Kimmel, "the five greatest accordion players in the world."

By the turn of the twentieth century, melodeons dominated working-class social dances as Scottish players slowly expanded the capability of their instruments, especially the accordion's bass side. Champion early recording star James Brown was one who played three-row button accordion with an innovative Stradella left hand. Brown's career was cut short when he was killed by a poison gas attack in World War I. After the war, the global social dancing craze carried on, and larger, louder accordions grew in popularity. In Scotland, these included piano accordions that were easier to incorporate into typical dance bands.

The advent of radio was a double-edged sword for accordions. Imported dance music began to take up space once occupied by local styles. In the 1940s, the Royal Scottish Country Dance Society campaigned against the "threat" of jazz and other popular music on the radio. Some musicians took advantage of the new medium, and after Scottish bandleader Jimmy Shand began broadcasting in 1943, he defined Scottish accordion music for decades to come.

Jimmy Shand's Scottish country dance style, often using two or more accordions playing in unison to fill pre-amplification dance halls, was wildly popular in Scotland and much of the British Commonwealth from the 1920s–70s. Many dismiss Shand's famously predictable "strict tempo" and lack of improvisation as tedious, but they seldom acknowledge that his music was never meant for armchair listening. Country dance bands developed specifically to compete with modern popular dance orchestras, and without them traditional music would have suffered even greater erosion.

Shand's popular style grew from earlier forms but was derided by many Scottish folk revivalists in the 1960s. Their movement to rediscover Scotland's music found itself curiously at odds with a living tradition that did not need to be revived. Critics dismissed country dance bands or even despised them as symbols of the establishment or "musical mediocrity." At the same time, revivalists laying claim to authenticity were reshaping their music for contemporary audiences just as Jimmy Shand had.

Some detractors traced their dissatisfaction with the state of Scottish music all the way back to the advent of the accordion in the Victorian era. Fiddles and pipes were held up as archetypes while accordions were tuned out. The instrument became in effect a scapegoat for the decline of traditional music in Scotland. The most famous exception to this anti-accordion reaction was Scottish group Silly Wizard, which included accordionists Phil Cunningham and Freeland Barbour. They helped push the accordion, particularly the piano keyboard version, back to the forefront of Scottish traditional music. Despite their success in Scotland, the popular influence of Scottish accordion has never been as great in North America as that of the Irish. Still, it's helpful to know the background of this tradition as we look at the huge impact of the Irish.

Irish Accordion: The Arrival

The accordion appeared in Ireland at the same time as the first railroads broke the isolation of rural communities. The Industrial Revolution was on a collision course with Irish society. As in Scotland and elsewhere, prior to about 1850 concertinas and accordions had only been available to the wealthy. When the instruments became more affordable, their status fell and they were adopted by the middle class, and then spread through the temperance movement and other "self-improvement" causes as an alternative to vice. Workers earning cash wages for the first time were suddenly able to afford luxuries like these small musical instruments. Concertinas and accordions spread to this new mass market of amateurs.

Most of the Irish accordion repertoire, meanwhile, had developed on pipes and fiddles during the 1700s to 1800s. Until the Irish Parliament shifted to London around 1800, Dublin had been a cultural center with great support for music. The gentry had sponsored what would become the three foundations of broader traditional music: musicians, dances, and (often forgotten) a corps of traveling professional dancing masters who taught the latest steps, often accompanied by a piper or other musician. These musical traditions faced extinction, however, when Ireland faced the shattering of its culture and language in the second half of the 1800s.

The Famine and Mass Migration

Irish economist and historian Cormac Ó Gráda relates, "On the eve of the Famine, the poverty of Irish smallholding and laboring families... was legendary." Two-thirds of the Irish population lived in poverty, totaling two and a half million people. The failure of the potato crop in 1845 triggered catastrophic suffering that was then inflamed by the conservative British government's refusal to offer aid. Crop failures in Scotland and elsewhere were successfully addressed with social programs, but the "free market" was left to devastate Ireland. Needed food was exported to England for profit while more than a million people starved to death and a million and a half fled the country as refugees. For the Irish people, it was a political crime in the guise of a natural disaster.

It was only after the upheaval of the Great Famine that accordions and concertinas took hold in Irish music. The change began when professional bagpipers could find no work amidst the turmoil and (if they survived) were forced to emigrate. The pipers' place in Ireland was filled by newly affordable concertinas and melodeons, as many as half of which were played by women in their homes. Preservationists cried that the new instruments caused the decline of piping, but in the homes and kitchens of Ireland a generation of amateurs used these industrial intruders to preserve traditional music. Without them there might well have been no Irish music in Ireland.

Emigration influenced Irish music more than any other force after the Famine. Musicians, including the very first generation of accordion and concertina players, joined the flood of economic refugees out of Ireland. Of course they weren't the first Irish emigrants. Irish Gaelic speakers had already been working Canada's Newfoundland fisheries for two hundred years. More than a million had emigrated to North America in the thirty years before the Famine crisis.

Beginning in the time of the Famine, between 1845 and 1900, four million more Irish people emigrated just to the United States. There, they faced new challenges. The American magazine *Puck* reflected their new home's harsh welcome in 1892: "The raw Irishman in America is a nuisance, his son a curse. They never assimilate; the second generation shows an intensification of all the bad qualities of the first . . . they are a burden and a misery to this country."

Irish immigrants faced prejudice on many fronts, dramatized by the "stage Irish" caricature of a lying, vulgar, violence-prone drunk. Unable to find non-stereotyped parts, many Irish actors found work mocking African Americans as some of the first blackface minstrels. In this environment of prejudice and upheaval, the Irish found solace in music and dance. Additions like the accordion were introduced, and formerly isolated regional styles met and mixed for the first time. Preservationists, meanwhile, focused on saving the tradition's riches before they disappeared amidst the volatile modern world.

An Affordable Instrument for Dancing

Concertina and accordion historian Dan Worrall wrote that, "Excepting mouth harmonicas and jew's harps, these little boxes were . . . the first inexpensive, mass-produced consumer musical items, pre-dating future public love affairs with guitars, ukuleles, and mass-produced pianos." The Industrial Revolution changed some of the most personal aspects of life across the globe. In Ireland, laborers were scarce following the death and emigration of the Famine. This drove up wages and increased disposable income for Irish workers. At the same time, concertina and accordion prices had dropped. Instrument quality had also improved enough that they could play fast dance tunes. This set the stage for the squeezebox's entrance into the tradition.

Dancing was foremost among rural entertainments in the days before radio and television, and dance music was central to the adoption and development of Irish accordions. Beginning at rural house and crossroads dances and later at dedicated dance halls, the new instruments provided much of the accompaniment in the years after the Famine.

The dances themselves changed over time for both solo dancers and couples. Irish solo "step" dancing had been popular since the 1700s. In the 1800s, Ireland's traveling dance-masters added new group dances, based on continental quadrilles, that came to be called "set" dances. Together these proved ideal for the entry of the melodeon into Irish music. The new instrument was loud enough to be heard over the dancers' feet, and the music was simple enough to suit the young instrument. By the time the Gaelic League began promoting its own system of céilí dances in the early 1900s, the accordion was backing up Irish dancers around the world.

While the melodeon was first establishing itself, 1870–1930 was the heyday of the Irish concertina. These were almost exclusively Anglo-German models and were played at home or for small dances all across Ireland. Concertinas faded, though, after house dances were banned by the Public Dance Halls Act of 1935. The concertina tradition hung on in regions like County Clare in relatively isolated western Ireland. A remarkable number of women played, including Elizabeth Crotty (1885–1960) and others, who later passed their music on to modern revivalists like Mary McNamara and Noel Hill.

During the capstone years of concertina use in Ireland, they were scarcely mentioned by preservationists, who blamed them for the fading of pipers. Years later, laments about the state of Irish culture would ironically include the fading of concertinas as well: "When the Concertina and the Bag Pipes left the Cottage, the heart left the Country," said Brian O'Nolan in 1949. The instrument only gained admittance to the tradition when it had largely disappeared. By the 1920s, concertinas that could liven a house dance were unable to carry in the larger public halls and céilís. Accordions took their place.

An Irish dance hall melodeon could feature up to six reeds for each note, impossible to achieve in smaller concertinas. Melodeons were probably cheaper as well. As German and Italian accordion manufacturing grew, expensive English concertina makers were squeezed out.

Only County Clare maintained many concertinas after 1930. In other areas, recordings and radio arrived as early as the 1920s, and home instruments like concertinas fell from use. Clare, however, did not get electricity until decades after places like Dublin. At the same time, players in County Clare benefited from the decline of the concertina elsewhere. Travelers to London and other urban centers returned with once prohibitively expensive Wheatstone and Jeffries instruments found in pawnshops. Rural players had access to the finest concertinas ever made. Decades later, they would share their tradition with an appreciative folk revival in the 1960s and '70s.

The Gaelic League

The Gaelic League (Conradh na Gaeilge, est. 1893) was formed to fight against the decline in spoken Irish. It also took action to preserve traditional music, but not always accordions. Dan Worrall's history of the concertina reprints a lament from 1908, where League organizer "Mr. McNestor" opined that the Irish "were at one time the most musical nation when a harp hung in every house, but now they had got down to the concertina and melodeon, and even to the mouth organ. They had thrown away the music of their great composers for the abortions and abominations of the English music halls." Despite their opposition, by 1900 the accordion had become one of the most common instruments not only in Ireland but in Irish dance halls in North America as well.

"Un-Irish" modern dances were vocally despised by League representatives. For them, this included quadrille-based set dancing (square dances) which had been popular since the Napoleonic Wars. Expatriate League members in London developed and promoted new céilí dances as an Irish alternative. The League's influence became so strong that when set dancing was revived in the 1960s, some people avoided workshops for fear of being barred from Gaelic League–approved céilís.

The League and other nationalist groups were responsible for a remarkably successful program of cultural appreciation and preservation, a project that eventually served the accordion and all of Irish music, but their work changed the tradition as well as supporting it. In the 1930s and '40s, céilí bands playing in larger dance halls added accordions, but also began performing in unison rather than as soloists. Playing in groups added volume, but céilí bands by necessity reduced or eliminated improvisation and personal ornamentation, one of the hallmarks of the music previously.

Capt. Francis O'Neill and the Beginning of Recording

Originally from County Cork, Ireland, Francis O'Neill led a colorful life as a shepherd, schoolteacher, and a shipwrecked sailor before he was sworn in as Chicago's chief of police in 1901. He was also an extremely important Irish music collector. (O'Neill was not above hiring out-of-work musicians as police officers while documenting their music.) His first collection of almost two thousand tunes and songs, *Music of Ireland*, was published in 1903 and became known as "the Book" of standard tunes for generations of musicians. Throughout his writings, though, O'Neill hardly ever mentioned accordions or concertinas. (He didn't care for the pennywhistle either.) One of his only references to the instrument, and perhaps the first mention of the accordion's use in Irish traditional music, has O'Neill despairing, "Too true! The old must give way to the new; but what blessings has the change brought to Ireland? Mainly monotony, and melodeons made in Germany."

This rejection seems odd, since accordions are so much a part of the music today—they were in fact already widespread in O'Neill's time. But collectors like him were driven with preserving bagpipe traditions, which they feared were disappearing. Thus O'Neill's collection of early audio recordings consists entirely of expatriate pipers living in America.

One of O'Neill's concerns was that until higher-quality concertinas and two-row button accordions were popularized, many of the tunes documented in his book could not be played on lesser instruments. Knowing the historic fate of the Irish harp and seeing the decline of his beloved pipers, it is understandable that O'Neill opposed or ignored interlopers he saw taking their place.

Despite neglecting the squeezebox, O'Neill and scholars like him preserved thousands of tunes that might otherwise have been lost. Within a few short years of O'Neill's lament about the "waning" of Irish music, Irish accordionists captured on record were performing tunes from his book.

In 1902, O'Neill purchased his own Edison cylinder recorder to preserve his beloved pipers. Despite his efforts, fiddles and accordions became the most common traditional instruments in the recording era. One year after O'Neill got his machine, Scottish accordionist Peter Wyper released the first of his commercial accordion cylinders. Recording was still very much in its infancy. In the August 1903 issue of *Talking Machine News*, Wyper begged for a way to avoid performing tunes hundreds of times, making cylinders one by one: "I should take it as a favor if you could enlighten me as to how to take one record from another. It is so monotonous playing the same tune time after time."

As the century progressed, improved recordings became more and more important both for uniting immigrant audiences, and for spreading local and individual styles far beyond their original communities.

Amongst fiddlers, famous 1920s recordings that Michael Coleman made in New York not only intimidated and inspired, but unfortunately homogenized fiddling across the Irish diaspora. For the first time, local players compared themselves with distant virtuosos they would never meet. Prior to these recordings, there weren't "competing" regional styles, because it had never been a competition.

Ellen O'Byrne DeWitt and the First Irish Recording Artists

Susan Gedutis, with poetic simplification, suggests that a shopkeeper, Ellen O'Byrne DeWitt, "may be credited with single-handedly founding the Irish recording industry." O'Byrne DeWitt's was the first shop of its kind in New York, selling sheet music, instruments, and, as soon as she could procure them, recordings. Shops like hers became community centers where musicians and the public met and socialized. Along with the Irish dance halls, they were the financial and cultural foundation for music in the new land.

Accordionist Eddie Herborn was the first Irish musician to record (in 1916 with James Wheeler on banjo, for New York's Columbia Records). Recording in Ireland itself had to wait until 1929. Herborn was recruited from a park in Long Island by Ellen's son Justus. O'Byrne DeWitt guaranteed Columbia Records that her store would sell hundreds of copies if they had records of Irish dance music. At the time, the major labels were testing the ethnic music market during and after World War I, and the Irish audience did not disappoint.

With the help of immigrant insiders like O'Byrne DeWitt, record companies were able to connect artists with audiences who bought millions of records through the 1920s. As we saw in our polka chapter, the ethnic music industry became an island of multicultural capitalism that broke ranks with racist ideologies in America. Without intending to, they safeguarded the treasury of ethnic music as it came ashore with America's immigrants.

After Ellen died in 1926, her son opened a shop that became the hub of Boston's Irish music scene, branching out from records and instruments into radio and even travel tickets back and forth to Ireland. Their All Ireland Records label proudly recalled her pioneering role: "Produced by E. O'Byrne DeWitt's Sons." Ellen's legacy grew from recording a few displaced musicians to facilitating the international preservation of a people's culture.

North American Irish Dance Halls

Individual musicians traditionally played for local Irish house dances. This changed drastically between the 1920s and the 1950s first in London and later in America. In New York and Boston, hundreds of Irish and Irish American dancers would fill halls from Wednesday to Sunday for three decades.

In the days before amplification, as some Americans were stepping into the Jazz Age of trumpets and saxophones, immigrants brought their own flavors to social dancing. Accordions were well equipped to play the large halls. They were louder than fiddles, and stayed in tune for hours (unlike finicky pipes). Baldoni accordions were prized, but F. H. Walters in New York sold ten-button diatonic instruments with as many as eight sets of reeds, twice as powerful as any accordion before. Often two or more of these accordions were synchronized with up to ten other musicians in unprecedented Irish bands. They featured traditional music mixed with waltzes, foxtrots, and popular tunes, but the flavor was always Irish, and the accordion led the way.

The Impact of Radio

The "world's first broadcast of Irish music" took place on St. Patrick's Day, 1924, in Philadelphia. The advent of radio and recording dramatically changed the way traditional music was heard and learned. Radio let far-off listeners hear players and styles they might never have encountered. Records allowed repeated listening that helped tunes and styles spread. Together they opened up the music to cross-fertilization unimaginable a few years before.

In Ireland, the Aughrim Slopes Trio auditioned for Raidió Éireann (Radio Ireland) in 1927. The group included accordion player Joe Mills, who continued to make records and use radio to get gigs until the 1940s. In the 1950s, Radio Ireland sent remote broadcast teams across the country to capture musicians who couldn't travel to Dublin. This brought different musical styles to light from all over the country (especially more remote areas).

Accordions weren't recorded in Ireland until 1929, when among the first commercial 78s was concertina player Billy Roberts and accordionist Sam Madden. Madden played sets and couples dances that would have been familiar in rural homes, suggesting that the instrument had penetrated into the countryside. Unfortunately for Irish music, house dances and community music faced difficult times.

The Public Dance Halls Act of 1935

While Irish dance halls were packed five nights a week in Boston and other American cities, traditional music in Ireland was nearly exterminated by a campaign to save Irish culture. Since at least the time of the Famine, much of the clergy had been antagonistic to secular music and dancing. On Sundays, priests regularly railed against those who had spent the night before dancing, publicly shaming them with sometimes serious social consequences. The conflict became a national issue when bolstered by the Gaelic League's efforts to protect Irish language and culture. The League's intended targets were urban dance halls and imported jazz music. The clear intent was to eliminate "foreign" culture, while maintaining and promoting Irish dance and music.

The unfortunate result of this vociferous crusade was the Public Dance Halls Act of 1935. The Act made it illegal to hold a dance in a public place without a license, but it did not define which activities were "public" and made no distinction between modern and traditional dancing. Complaints poured in as crossroads, ceílí and house dances were targeted. Government officials ordered that traditional dances should be exempt, but many police and local clergy ignored the limitations and enforced the rules against all unlicensed dances. The law effectively silenced traditional music in much of the country. Fiddler and concertina player Junior Crehan (born in County Clare, 1908) called it "the greatest crime ever committed against our culture."

1940s and '50s: New Traditions Take Shape

Ireland remained neutral during World War II but was not immune to its global trauma. Postwar Ireland was extremely economically depressed, and migration from rural areas to cities or abroad greatly increased. Traditional music was shattered by the combined calamities of emigration, the rise of competing entertainments, the Dance Halls Act, and the emerging prejudice against rural "backward" customs. In scholar Máire Ní Chaoimh's words, between 1940 and 1965 Ireland "witnessed the almost total extinction of traditional music as a community-oriented activity."

The Dance Halls Act had forced dancing into large, purpose-built halls—ironically often owned by local Catholic parishes. There, ceílí bands with as many as twelve musicians and bigger, sturdier, and louder Italian accordions played in unison for officially approved dances. Steadily though, imported popular music was silencing even these new traditions.

While many in Ireland abandoned their music, Irish American dance halls kept bustling until the 1960s. One factor was the American halls' inclusiveness. They welcomed céilí dances and sets and sometimes had separate bands on different floors for polkas, waltzes, and swing dances. During the 1950s, however, Irish American accordions began to decline as Irish immigrants abandoned their urban communities.

In Ireland, the growing marginalization of traditional music inspired supporters to organize the Comhaltas Ceoltóirí Éireann (CCÉ; Association of Irish Musicians) in 1951. From the beginning, the CCÉ's annual *Fleadh* festival included accordions—a significant shift from earlier generations, when the instrument was viewed with suspicion. Competitions for the CCÉ's "All Ireland Championship" would have a huge impact on the shape of the music in the next half-century and beyond.

Outside of sanctioned events, by the 1950s the upheavals in pop music had uncoupled traditional musicians from the dance. This lack of dancing audiences led to the creation of new styles intended specifically for listeners. As early as the 1930s, Irish American players had organized "music clubs" where solo musicians played for seated audiences. Irish expatriates formed the first "sessions" in London in the late 1940s, where musicians could play together for their own and listeners' enjoyment. What they gave up in quantity (large, paying dance hall audiences), they gained in attentive listeners and the quality of the music in the new context. Session players were freed from the steady tempo and unison restrictions of the céilí bands and developed improvisation and ornamentation techniques that had never been heard in the music before. Experimentation and variation became the personal projects of individual artists. Building on the repertoire of the past, they were creating a new music for the future.

Seán Ó Riada's Inconsistent Loathing for the Accordion

The growing dominance of the accordion in Irish music was not without its critics. Most famously, composer Seán Ó Riada, a major figure in developing what came be called "contemporary traditional music," spoke out strongly against accordions. Lambasting the instrument in 1963 on his influential radio program, *Our Musical Heritage*:

> Most accordion players are so hampered by their choice of instrument as to be unable to produce anything but a faint, wheezy

imitation of what Irish music should be. And the most unfortunate part of it is, that this instrument, designed by foreigners, for the use of peasants, who had neither the time, inclination or application to learn a more worthy instrument [is] gaining vast popularity throughout the country... nothing could be farther from the spirit of Irish Traditional Music.

Curiously, on the same radio program, Ó Riada offered praise for the equally modern and mechanical concertina. This kind of erratic umbrage about violations of tradition didn't prevent him from almost single-handedly introducing the now-pervasive bodhrán drum into modern Irish music by including it in his band Ceoltóirí Chualann. Formed in the 1960s, this unprecedented Irish ensemble was intended for listeners, not dancers, and eventually evolved into the world-famous Chieftains. Contradicting Ó Riada's former pronouncements, Ceoltóirí Chualann itself included two accordionists, one of whom, Sonny Brogan, was among the oldest and most respected players in the band. Ó Riada granted him an exemption as "one of the very few players who can make their music sound like Irish music."

"Modern Traditional" Irish Music

This book mostly closes its account of the accordion in North America with the advent of the 1960s and rock 'n' roll, but Irish accordion music in particular passed through a few more stages before it entered its own "modern" era. In the 1950s, two-row accordions tuned to the keys B and C dominated dances and competitions, while smaller sessions increased in number. The 1960s then introduced extraordinarily popular balladeers like the Clancy Brothers and Tommy Makem, whose accordion was a rarity in the American folk revival.

Despite Seán Ó Riada's notorious sentiments, the accordions he permitted in his prototype Irish folk group Ceoltóirí Chualann carried on into the Chieftains. The Chieftains and other 1970s groups like the Bothy Band further developed a new Irish music for listening. Groups like Planxty, Altan, and De Dannan electrically amplified their traditional (and non-traditional) instruments: bouzuki, guitar, etcetera. They also had access to modern production to polish their recordings. Freed from playing only for dancers, they developed complex arrangements of songs and tunes as well as new material. To varying degrees, these groups incorporated the aesthetics of both virtuosic chamber music and rock concerts.

Non-professional players benefited from modern technology as well—recording had a particular impact. Since its appearance in the 1920s, Irish players on both sides of the Atlantic had been greatly influenced by the styles of players they could listen to over and over. Cassette

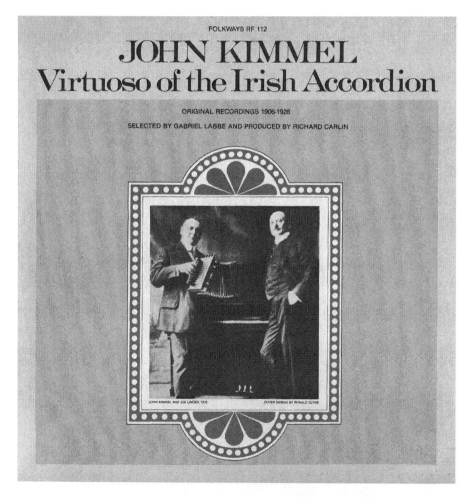

John Kimmel—Virtuoso of the Irish Accordion album. FWRF112, courtesy of Smithsonian Folkways Recordings, 1980. Used with permission.

recording revolutionized the process of spreading songs and styles after its introduction in the late 1960s. Individual musicians began avidly trading session tapes internationally. As a result, modern players have access to far more music, and have much larger repertoires from more regional styles than ever before.

After the 1970s "Celtic" revival, the floodgates were open. Irish and Scottish folk groups introduced fantastic accordionists and concertina players. Women like Josephine Marsh challenged prejudices against female instrumentalists, and Sharon Shannon became one of the most well-known traditional accordionists in the world. Scotland's Phil Cunningham and Ireland's Alan Kelly and Karen Tweed even stood up for the piano accordion in traditional music. These players also worked for the future of the music through schools and students.

Accordionists in Ireland and America

John J. Kimmel: Accordion Solo!

The original "Celtic" accordion star was born to a German immigrant family in Brooklyn, New York, in 1866. John J. Kimmel was known as "the Irish Dutchman," and exemplified the American melting pot by playing everything from marches and polkas to influential medleys of jigs, reels, and hornpipes. It's not known how he learned Irish music, so it's difficult to judge how his style related to earlier unrecorded players. Also unclear is whether his records were heard much in Ireland when they came out, but he greatly influenced players in North America, where they sold well for years.

Kimmel developed remarkable one-row accordion technique, overcoming their limited ten buttons and lack of chromatic notes. When a melody reached beyond his range, he skillfully leapt up or down octaves as needed. If a chromatic note was missing from his instrument's designated key of D, he embellished the tune with linking ornaments that made the gaps unnoticeable. Québécois virtuoso Philippe Bruneau performed some of Kimmel's tunes, and claimed they would take a dedicated student twenty or thirty years to learn. For years, Irish melodeon players expanded on variations of Kimmel's one-row style, even after they adopted two-row accordions.

Outside of his recorded work, Kimmel played in vaudeville and accompanied silent films. He also owned a series of saloons where he hired performers, including a young Brooklyn singer named Mae West. His last bar was in Queens, at the corner of Myrtle and Madison, and was called "The Accordion." When Prohibition was declared, Kimmel refused to bootleg alcohol and closed the place down.

His recording career lasted from 1903 until the crash of 1929, and he probably produced more cylinder recordings than any other accordionist. Kimmel never shifted to the larger button or piano accordions, and made no more recordings after the Depression. He died in 1942.

"P.J." and Mary Ellen Conlon: 1920s New York

Peter "P.J." Conlon was among the wave of Irish accordionists in the 1920s whose American-made recordings influenced players on both sides of the Atlantic. He played a one-row Baldoni accordion with eight reeds per button, giving him incredible volume in the growing dance halls. Some people criticized him for playing too fast and "ragging the accordion" as he adapted American Jazz Age tunes to his instrument. His many records made his style a benchmark for the early Irish accordion.

Conlon's sister Mary Ellen had arrived in Brooklyn earlier and paid for her brother Peter's passage to America. Theirs was a musical family, and she played accordion as well. Her style was lively like her brother's, suggesting that either the Conlons' high energy was typical of their native County Galway, or that Irish musicians were changing the tradition once they arrived in New York. It's also possible they picked up the pace to fit within the limits of the new recording technology.

In 1923, Mary recorded one 78-rpm record. She played two tunes on the A side, with a Mrs. Redie Johnston on the flip. This may well be the first recording of female accordionists in the world. Even though women represented a significant number of players of what was sometimes even called a "women's instrument," this is the only recording we have of these women. It is clear, though, that every player who came after them was influenced by recordings they and others made in New York.

The Famous McNulty Family

The bestselling artists at the O'Byrne DeWitt music store in Boston were the Irishman Bing Crosby and the now almost-forgotten McNulty Family. Ann McNulty was born in 1887 in Kilteevan, Ireland. She was the

America's Greatest
Irish Radio Entertainers

The Famous
McNulty Family

Ann McNulty and her children, Eileen and Peter, ca. 1930s. *Courtesy of Ted McGraw.*

youngest of nine sisters, which may have inclined her for the stage. Her husband died after she emigrated to the States in her twenties, and this left her a single mother. In response, she created an Irish song-and-dance act with her children, and billed it from the start as the "First Family of Irish Music." "Ma" McNulty produced the show, taught comedy bits, songs, and dances to the kids, and kept the family fed. They ended up a hit from New York to Newfoundland and all the way back in Ireland.

The McNultys' act combined vaudeville-style variety with Irish songs and humor, and an innovative mix of step dance and American tap-dancing. Rising above negative "stage Irish" stereotypes, their upbeat Irish-American blend won the heartfelt loyalty of their immigrant community during the trying years of the Depression.

Ann was the accordionist in the show, and played one-row melodeons decorated with rhinestones and Irish and American flags. She used five accordions, each tuned to appropriate keys for different songs. Despite this clever workaround, when she tried to join the Musicians' Union in 1928 they refused her, saying the button accordion wasn't a "real instrument." Her granddaughter suspects they were simply looking for an excuse to keep a woman out of the union.

Ann played her accordions twice weekly on the family's radio show and on most of their 155 recordings. After the Depression, major labels dropped most ethnic musicians, so the McNultys shifted to Copley Records, a specialty label owned by O'Byrne DeWitt that continued releasing records into the 1950s. The family band toured regularly between New York, Chicago, and Boston, and in 1953 won the fierce loyalty of Newfoundlanders by visiting the isolated Irish stronghold where people saved up batteries to listen to them on the radio. On returning, the family brought back songs from Newfoundland like "Star of Logy Bay" which joined the Irish repertoire through their recordings.

For decades the McNultys were billed as the "Little Irish Showboat" that carried listeners across the ocean for a nostalgic look at the land most of their audience had never visited or would not see again. Ann herself never returned to Ireland, but on the hundredth anniversary of her first concert there, her daughter Pat traveled back to Kilteevan for the presentation of the Annie McNulty Award named for the town's most famous (ninth) daughter.

Ann died in 1970, and her collection of memorabilia is the center of the McNulty Family Collection at New York University. Remarkably,

Ann saved every press clipping from her family's entire career, starting with a ticket from that first performance in Ireland in 1907, all the way until the family appeared on TV in 1956. Playbills, posters, sheet music, hand-sewn costumes, scripts she had written—her historical hoard offers a unique view into the lives of twentieth-century performers.

The McNultys may not have been typical Irish musicians, but they contributed to the tradition. For forty years, "Ma" McNulty kept Irish accordion in front of audiences who were hungry for reminders of home. Musicians today may have little time for their sentimental nostalgic material, and the McNultys' more than 150 recordings have never been officially reissued in the digital era. Nevertheless, entertainers like the McNultys sustained the Irish immigrant community through truly difficult times, and they remain one of the foundations on which today's traditional music was built.

Joe Derrane and the Boston Dance Halls

Irish dance halls flourished in Boston from World War II until the mid-1960s as young, unmarried immigrants arrived by the thousands seeking success in postwar America. A significant part of their quest seems to have involved dancing. Among the musicians who played for them was a young Joe Derrane. Born in Boston in 1930, he played the dance halls from the 1940s through the 1950s, sometimes joining more than a dozen musicians in order to be heard over as many as a thousand dancers.

As a child growing up in Boston, Derrane had heard accordionist Jerry O'Brien on radio. He recalled, "[I] just stood in front of the radio and stared at it and jumped up and down." When Derrane was nine, his parents arranged for O'Brien to give him lessons. Playing a two-row accordion (with the rows tuned to C#/D) he eventually developed what's been called an "extended melodeon" style. He played the main melody on the outside row (closer to the hand), and added notes he needed from the inside row (closer to the bellows). Combining the rows he could play all of the traditional Irish repertoire, avoiding some of the troubles faced by one-row players like Kimmel.

Boston dance hall crowds were probably sixty percent Irish or more, with the rest Irish American. They generally preferred polkas and waltzes to céilí or set dances, not in defiance of nationalist ideology, but because they were less complicated so everybody could join in. These couples dances also needed less room in the crowded dance halls.

Amplification was still minimal, so the need for volume shaped the music. Before electrical pickups arrived in the 1950s, unamplified fiddles were overshadowed by even a single melodeon. As multiple accordions became the standard, quieter instruments simply lost their place. Flute player Gene Frain took up saxophone to be heard over the accordions: "No one's going to hear a goddamned flute. You get one accordion, and forget it ... With the sax, I could drown out two or three with no trouble."

Horns like Frain's became a regular part of Irish American music. When the swing bands broke up in the 1940s, out-of-work jazz players found themselves sight-reading horn lines from O'Neill's *Music of Ireland*. Bands that played at least a few Irish tunes were the biggest draw, and Joe Derrane remembered that accordions led Irish tunes but sat out some modern numbers. "We were smart enough to know that three Irish button accordions just weren't going to fit that."

Radio was a big part of Irish American music between the 1920s and the 1950s, as stations catered to ethnic populations in most cities. Derrane played on several programs, and in 1946 or so he recorded a series of 78s for Copley Records while still in high school. These records astounded musicians on both sides of the Atlantic, and preserved his memory for decades.

By the end of the 1950s, though, the Irish music scene in America had gone bust. Immigration restrictions and "white flight" out of American cities cut off the crowds, and almost overnight the dance halls closed. Boston's halls lasted longer than Chicago's or New York's, but by the end of the 1960s they had all shut down. Derrane sold his instrument and did not play button accordion for three decades.

Over the years Derrane worked a day job and played piano accordion and keyboards in jazz, pop and wedding bands. Then, in 1993, his 1940s solo recordings were reissued and they attracted a great deal of attention almost fifty years after they were recorded. Many assumed Derrane had died, but a friend gave him a button box, and after a regimen of focused practice he emerged at the Wolftrap Irish Folk Festival in Virginia with probably the most dramatic comeback in Irish music history. He planned simply to play a few nostalgic tunes, but the audience's response was enormous. His grown children had never seen him play button accordion and they embraced him in tears when he stepped off the stage. As he recalled, "Outside of the day I got married and outside of the days that my son and my daughter were born, it was probably the biggest single day of my life."

In the following years, Derrane recorded numerous albums and toured widely, continuing to play the virtuosic two-row style he had developed in the 1940s. He was welcomed with acclaim in 1995 when he traveled to Ireland for the first time, and found that his Irish American style was part of bringing the music back. His death in 2016 finally brought to a close the glory days of Irish American dance hall accordion.

Joe Cooley: Persevering and Preserving

Amongst the accordionists who had cleared a path for modern instrumentalists was the legendary Joe Cooley. He and artists like him were the bridge between earlier innovators like Joe Derrane and later generations.

When Ireland's dance halls dried up in the 1950s, few if any traditional musicians like Cooley could make a living. Instead, over the years he worked construction and did heavy labor hanging billboards and signs. He traveled widely and (like many of his generation) left Ireland for the U.S. in 1954. He spent years in Chicago and then San Francisco, where he got along famously amidst the long-haired 1960s counterculture.

Cooley's vibrant playing was rooted in childhood memories of his parents' house dances. His style was not as fast and polished as some but was extremely expressive and rhythmic. It was his generation that kept the tradition alive in céilí bands and sessions, and were able to pass the music on when attention returned in the 1960s and '70s.

Great excitement met Cooley's return to Ireland in 1971, and his music achieved hallowed status when he died from cancer the following year. A lone album of his playing, simply called *Cooley* (1973), was released after his death and is widely considered essential.

Paddy O'Brien's New Style

Before leaving for America, Joe Cooley took second place in the 1953 "All Ireland" accordion competition at the Fleadh Cheoil na hÉireann; the winner was Paddy O'Brien. O'Brien was born in 1922 to a family of fiddlers. He learned to play accordion using an instrument kept at his parents' home, because the owner (a police officer) didn't want to carry it to parties on his bicycle. According to contemporary player Joe Burke, by the time O'Brien was fourteen he'd already been on radio all over Ireland and was developing a "mighty technique."

O'Brien was driven to emulate the fiddle styles he'd learned as a child, especially the virtuosic American recordings of Michael Coleman. Instead of the earlier melodeon-style based on the pumping bellows of the limited ten-button system, O'Brien developed a new technique on a two-row accordion tuned to the keys of B and C. His style was smoother and steadier, and allowed for more faithful imitation of the melodies and ornamentations played by fiddles and flutes. His B/C tuning became the standard Irish accordion, imitated by others, for years to come.

O'Brien's instrumental progression was not unique and wasn't inspired by any one player. Hohner began producing its "Black Dot" B/C accordion in 1934, and Peter Wyper played a B/C system as early as 1915. In the words of one scholar, all the innovators within the tradition, from Kimmel through Derrane and O'Brien, "enriched the experience of the instrument." Each played in ways the accordion had never been used before. New instrument designs gave musicians the challenge of incorporating them into the tradition while maintaining connections to older styles, and each player passed the challenge on to the next generation.

Jackie Daly/De Dannan: Reviving Traditions

The Irish music revival reached critical mass in the 1970s, after which accordionists of all stripes blossomed. Younger players studied with their elders at programs like the Willie Clancy Summer School, and the best then recorded albums that set the bar for decades to come. Jackie Daly was one of many who remembered as a youngster hearing Joe Cooley, Joe Burke, and others on recordings brought back from America.

Daly himself shifted the tradition significantly by departing from O'Brien's B/C accordion in favor of an older more rhythmic melodeon style. He also "dry" tuned his reeds to reduce the tremolo of the B/C era. This greatly improved the accordion's suitability for soloing and for playing in harmony with other instruments.

Daly's recordings with fiddler Séamus Creagh and the solo album *Music from Sliabh Luachra* (1977), as well as his work with the group De Dannan, made him a prime figure in the development of modern Irish accordion. For De Dannan's 1981 album *Star Spangled Molly*, a warm tribute to New York's 1920s Irish immigrant musicians, Daly built a John Kimmel-style melodeon and taught himself to play it. After repeatedly crisscrossing the ocean, the Irish accordion had come home.

11

Canadian Accordion: Northern Traditions (Squeezebox North)

CANADIAN ACCORDIONS CAME to echo the history of immigration in Canada. But the story opened well before the first accordion arrived. Beginning in the 1600s and rapidly intensifying into the twentieth century, the original First Nations and Inuit populations faced waves of French, Irish, English, and Scottish immigrants. These were joined by Loyalists fleeing the American Revolution, African Americans fleeing slavery, and a vast diversity of people from the rest of Europe.

The accordion took root in Canada in the late 1800s. At the time the settler population focused on timber, fur, and fishing extraction in exchange for imports—which included the newfangled instruments. The first accordions were purchased and played by French Canadians in Quebec. They were followed by Irish, Scottish, and Acadian musicians in Nova Scotia, New Brunswick, and Newfoundland and by whalers who brought accordions to the Inuit, who still play them in the North. As urban centers expanded in the east, the portable instruments were carried across the Prairies where the famous Louis Riel himself was among the mixed-ancestry Métis who owned one. Traditional accordionists in early Canada played mostly instrumental dance music. Aside from a few tune books and scattered field recordings, these instrumental tunes were long neglected by scholars. The study of Canadian folk music instead focused on lyrical ballads. Researcher Helen Creighton alone collected some four thousand of these songs in her lifetime. Only recently have musicians and scholars begun to catalog and acknowledge the once-commonplace music of folk dancers and their accordionists.

In the 1970s, a few younger folk musicians in Newfoundland and Quebec began to seek out older players. Modern artists like Figgy Duff (est. 1975) and Québécois accordionist Philippe Bruneau (1934-2011) used earlier recordings and the guidance of surviving elders to revitalize traditions of the past. New songs were crafted by combining words with dance tunes or by backing old ballads with group arrangements that would never have been heard before.

The music persists at Canadian festivals like the Carrefour Mondiale de l'Accordéon in Montmagny, Quebec, and the Acadian Georges LeBlanc Accordion Festival in Moncton, New Brunswick. The twenty-ninth annual Newfoundland and Labrador Folk Festival in 2005 broke the world's record for most accordionists gathered in one place. Today a new generation of singer-songwriter accordionists take up where guitar-playing folksingers of the 1960s left off. The accordion's portability, volume, and many flavors continue a unique journey in Canada.

The Melodeon's Irish Roots in Canada

Much of the folk accordion in Eastern Canada sounds surprisingly "Celtic" to newcomers. But for hundreds of years before accordions existed, Irish and Scottish immigrants in northern North America lived alongside French and English settlers, and the Indigenous peoples who preceded them all. Opportunities for cultural mixing were so plentiful that Irish and Scottish music wove themselves throughout early Canadian culture.

Two centuries before the first accordions arrived, the English had settled in Newfoundland, and the French founded today's Quebec. By 1700, the Irish began establishing their own communities in Newfoundland, and exiled highland Scots brought Gaelic culture to Cape Breton Island and the area the French called Acadia—which eventually became Nova Scotia (New Scotland) and New Brunswick. Between 1800 and

1900, a huge number of Irish immigrants came to Lower Canada (now Quebec). By the middle of the 1800s, the Irish were the largest ethnic group in so-called English Canada.

In the nineteenth century, most Irish immigrants came through either Saint John in New Brunswick (formerly French Acadian territory), or the port of Montreal. In the Famine years of 1846–47, ninety thousand Irish people passed through Montreal, which had a prior population of only fifty thousand.

For some, Canada was a destination of necessity before traveling on to the United States. The cheapest transportation from Europe was on rough freighters that carried timber from Canada and then passengers when returning across the Atlantic. Arriving north of the border, travelers handily bypassed U.S. immigration laws, and great numbers headed south to Boston, New York, and other U.S. cities. Music historian Máire Ní Chaoimh summarizes, "Thousands of Irish traditional musicians were among the 1.8 million people who left Irish shores for America between 1844 and 1855, with an estimated 350,000 of these believed to have come through Canadian ports."

There are few known "Famine songs," about the era's great suffering. Most Irish musicians had no reason to be sentimental for the gruesome reality of disease, poverty, and neglect they had fled. Privation followed some to the Grosse Île Quarantine Station in Quebec. At this camp in the Gulf of St. Lawrence, conditions were so bad that, during the worst of the Famine, bodies were piled like firewood and dragged from the holds of disease-ridden ships with boat hooks. Thousands of refugees died between 1847 and 1848 awaiting entry in Pointe Sainte Charles, Montreal. After the horrors, it is perhaps a wonder that music survived at all.

Of those who endured the crossing and stayed in Canada, most Irish immigrants spread throughout Quebec, where they became the second-largest population alongside the French. The Irish often intermarried with fellow Catholics, and many immigrant orphans were adopted into French Canadian families, leaving them indistinguishable from their neighbors except for their Irish names. Other Irish immigrants moved south to Upper Canada (which later became the province of Ontario), and a smaller number settled in the Maritimes and Newfoundland among earlier Irish settlers.

As the trauma of immigration faded, Irish music—formerly played on pipes and fiddles—became a key component of Canada's accordion traditions. The first accordions arrived in the 1840s at precisely the time Irish refugees flooded Canada during the Famine. At that time, the instrument was a middle-class novelty and probably as unfamiliar to the impoverished Irish immigrants as it was to Canadians. The fiddle was still the most popular instrument in European-influenced folk music (and continues as the main instrument in areas like Scots-influenced Cape Breton Island). Folk players finally took to the accordion in the late 1800s. By then, Irish influence had spread, and accordions followed the immigrants into all corners of the country.

Québec: l'Arrivée de l'Accordéon

If you listen to a modern folk group from Quebec like La Bottine Souriante, you'll hear a combination of musical styles. The oldest might be ballads and work songs with call-and-response French vocals in the style of the early fur traders. Originally, these were almost exclusively performed without instruments. Equally influential in the repertoire are French Canadian dance tunes. This is where the accordion comes in.

The French Canadian instrumental repertoire is deeply entwined with its Scottish, Irish, and English Canadian neighbors. Instrumental tunes crossed language barriers, and Irish tunes and fiddle styles were adopted in early French Canada, then adapted to the accordion as it was introduced in the nineteenth century.

An Ursuline convent school may have purchased the very first accordion in Canada in 1843. We know this because the nuns kept the receipts, and several of these delicate instruments survive in the convent museum. The Ursulines also had various accordions repaired in Quebec City at the head of the St. Lawrence River, source for European imports in Canada. These French-style instruments would have featured in bourgeois and upper-class parlors in Quebec, but were out of reach of most people.

In the later 1800s, more affordable German-style accordions and Anglo-German concertinas became available through the Eaton and Montgomery Ward catalogs. Then, in 1895, Odilon Gagné began producing the first Canadian-built German-style ten-button accordions in Quebec. He crafted every part himself, from the reeds to the bellows and buttons. His sons carried on the business and passed on the skills to their nephew, Paul-André Gagné. When André's son Richard took over in 1980, Gagné accordions had been crafted in Canada for more than one hundred years without interruption.

After the turn of the twentieth century, Québécois accordion players became ever more common and were among the first preserved in Canadian audio recordings. Artists like Alfred Montmarquette recorded scores of instrumentals as well as supporting singers like La Bolduc.

There were still obstacles for musicians in Quebec, including broad ecclesiastic condemnation: "Under pain of mortal sin," wrote the newspaper *Catholic Action* in the Archdiocese of Quebec in 1937, "it is forbidden to the faithful to dance or let their children or servants dance dances that are either themselves lascivious, like the tango, foxtrot, and others, or in the way they are performed as commonly happens today for the waltz, polka and other old dances."

As the century progressed, though, the accordion in Quebec remained popular and followed musical trends. Country and western accordions spread to Quebec in the 1940s and '50s on the trail of Hollywood cowboys. Accordion-heavy ethnic polka was also common. Vital French Canadian folk styles survived as well.

Quebec's Modern Folkoric Revival

With the rise of political and cultural nationalism in Quebec in the 1960s and '70s, folkloric music acquired new weight and passion. Musicians took up folk instruments in unprecedented numbers, reclaiming the accordion in particular as Québécois. Instrument makers like Marcel Messervier began building accordions to match the growing number of skilled players. Messervier and accordionist Philippe Bruneau cooperated with Marc Savoy in Louisiana to greatly improve the quality of folk accordions. As Savoy said about Bruneau, "Not only did I realize that I was in the presence of musical genius, I also realized that my Acadian accordions were not good enough for a musician of such talent."

One of the most important accordion events in Canada is the annual Carrefour Mondial de L'Accordéon in Montmagny, Quebec (east of Quebec City on the St. Lawrence River). Since 1989 it has welcomed Canadian artists along with internationally famous accordionists. Montmagny also houses the Musée de l'Accordéon, where scholars like Raynald Ouellet preserve not only French Canadian accordion history, but its connection to other influential traditions. In 2010, for instance,

Ouellet and three other artists re-recorded much of John Kimmel's challenging repertoire.

From the 1970s on, Québécois accordionists like Yves Lambert stretched the boundaries of old-time dance music, making a place for virtuosic playing in much the same way the Irish Bothy Band had. Today the music evokes the past without duplicating it. Bands like Le Vent du Nord and Les Tireux d'Roches add rock and jazz elements to create some of the most "modern" folk styles in Canada. The new century's RéVeillons! carry on Quebec's mixture of Francophone ballads and songs, combined with traditional dances and rhythms. Amidst this musical renewal, the humble button accordion carries tunes from player to audience and from old to young as it has since the first accordion arrived in Quebec 150 years ago.

☞ Gabriel Labbé and the Virtual Gramophone of the Library and Archives Canada

A REMARKABLE MODERN resource for Canadian folk music is the Library and Archives Canada's Virtual Gramophone website, which digitized and made available hundreds of historic accordion recordings (more than sixty by Alfred Montmarquette alone). The collection is founded on the donation of thousands of 78-rpm records by French Canadian music historian, writer, researcher, and harmonica player Gabriel Labbé (1938–2008).

This kind of digital resource is an invaluable tool for researchers, but also remarkably fragile. Funding for the Gramophone project was frozen in 2006, and though the incomplete collection remained available online as of 2018, it could evaporate in an instant without institutional support. Collectors like Labbé spent lifetimes preserving these old recordings. Public archives like this demonstrate how the past can be protected and shared with the future.

FACING Alfred Montmarquette. *Library and Archives Canada, Gabriel Labbé collection*, NLC-2559.

Accordéonistes Québécois

When not collecting records, Gabriel Labbé also authored the milestone works *Les Pionniers du Disque Folklorique Québécois 1920-1950,* and its 1995 update, *Musiciens Traditionnels du Québec (1920-1993),* which cover most of the important Québécois artists in this section and dozens more.

Alfred Montmarquette: The First Generation

Traditional Québécois accordion was once contemporary pop music. Early recording star Alfred Montmarquette sought to reach the broadest audience by recording marches, reels, clogging tunes, waltzes, "gigues" (jigs), and even a "menuet Canadien" (Canadian minuet). In the 1920s and '30s he appeared wearing lumberjack costumes that paralleled the "hillbilly" or cowboy outfits of American country music. His repertoire incorporated French and Irish numbers alongside John Philip Sousa marches he may have picked up from John Kimmel's recordings. The accordion was such a new instrument that the only boundary on repertoire was the single row of ten buttons.

Montmarquette learned accordion as a child in the 1880s, so he was one of the first generation of players after the popularization of the instrument. Most of his life he worked in Montreal as a bricklayer and only started playing professionally at age fifty. In 1923 he was invited onto the radio program *Veillés du bon vieux temps* (Good Old-Time Evenings) and kept at it until 1932.

He could not read or write and played entirely by ear. Overcoming any limitations he used his instrument's volume and a bright tone to compete with traditional fiddlers. Montmarquette made more than one hundred records. Almost all were dance tunes or accompaniment for his friend La Bolduc on her comic folk songs. Unfortunately, he was never able to make a decent living from his music, and having trouble with drink, died in poverty in 1944.

La Bolduc (Madame Édouard Bolduc): Queen of Canadian Folksingers

Most English-speaking Canadians have never heard of the woman known as "La Bolduc." She remains the forebear of Joni Mitchell, Jacqueline Lemay, Gordon Lightfoot, Félix Leclerc, and Raffi. Born Mary Rose Anne Travers, her music freely borrowed from both her French

Mary Bolduc (harmonica) and colleagues (accordion and fiddle), 1928. *Library and Archives Canada, Gabriel Labbé collection,* NLC-2618.

Canadian mother and her Irish father. Travers played accordion at her father's knee in the early 1900s, and her first childhood performances were playing for workers at the logging camp where her father worked and she was a cook.

In 1908, at age thirteen, she moved from Newport, a coastal town of one thousand people, to Montreal, a city of three hundred thousand. She worked there as a servant for $15 per month and later worked eleven-hour days in a garment factory for $15 per week. After marrying, she was pregnant more than ten times, but only four of her children survived their working-class poverty to adulthood.

Though poor, her family welcomed friends and guests for house parties filled with traditional tunes. In the 1920s, Mary stood in for a fiddler on folklorist Conrad Gauthier's *Veillées du Bon Vieux Temps* program, and quickly became a popular part of the influential troupe. Her family welcomed the added income at a time when show business was a rare field that paid women as much or more than men. Money was not the only consideration in conservative Catholic Quebec, and to belie complaints that female performers weren't respectable, Madame Édouard Bolduc always used her formal married name.

Her act combined vaudeville and folk music with humorous and topical songs she would compose based on instrumental tunes. She filled her original lyrics with colloquial expressions and slang. Working-class Francophone Canadians embraced her and her song's wry characters.

She composed with her fiddle and played jaw harp, harmonica, and nonsense "turlutage" mouth music ("deddle-dee-dum-dee-dum...") a common feature in Irish, French and other folk traditions. Her collaborators were the top regional instrumentalists, including her friend, accordionist Alfred Montmarquette.

La Bolduc signed a deal in 1929 to make records for $25 per side. When her recording "La Cuisinière" sold twelve thousand copies, she brought $450 home for her family. Breaking ground as the Francophone equivalent of a "hillbilly" country singer-songwriter, for several years she recorded more than one record a month, for a total of more than eighty discs. Tours took her throughout Quebec, French-speaking Ontario, and south into New England, where French-language culture reached as far as Boston.

Her folksy style lost ground to pop music and jazz in the later 1930s, but she continued to perform even as the recording industry went bankrupt around her. In 1937, good luck deserted her when she was in a head-on automobile crash. At the hospital, doctors discovered that she had cancer, and in early 1941, weakened by radiation treatment, she died at age forty-six. Her professional musical career had lasted only ten years.

Though her recordings don't emphasize her accordion skills, La Bolduc's childhood performances on the instrument heralded the huge influence her too-short adult career would have on Canadian culture. When modern Québécois groups like Bette & Wallet sing in French and English about street punks in Montreal, their rapid call-and-response lyrics, supported by accordions and guitars, echo back seventy years to the witty colloquial records of the queen of Canadian folk singers.

Mlle. Émilia Heyman: "La Reine de l'Accordéon"

The July 1943 issue of *Accordion World* magazine included an accordion "catechism" quiz with the question, "What Canadian girl accordionist was famous at the age of nine and still is? Every accordion fan should know. Do you?"

Émilia Heyman had been billed as the "Canadian Queen of the Accordion" in 1938, but she, along with thousands of other once highly regarded professional accordionists, has slipped from our societal memory. We are left with fragments: Heyman was an accordion student at Patsy Marrazza's school in Montreal, performing local engagements in 1932. Six years later she released records on the Ontario-based Starr label with her "Reine de l'Accordéon" title. She was involved at the start of the long-running *Les Joyeux Troubadours* CBC radio program in the 1940s. The show lasted thirty-six years, but at some point Heyman gave up her spot to accordionist Saturno Gentiletti.

Her few recordings are, as of this writing, not available online, and there are few mentions of her in news stories of the time. Only the faintest echo of this Canadian Queen of the Accordion remains.

The Greater Québécois Accordion Tradition

When Alfred Montmarquette drank too much, the skillful Arthur Pigeon filled in for him. For his sobriety, Pigeon lived a happier life recording dance tunes with a trio including his son-in-law on fiddle. Pigeon's twin grandsons carried his legacy into the Québécois folk-revival when they took up their grandfather's instrument as Les Frères Pigeon in the 1980s.

Other historical players included the wonderfully rhythmic Joseph Guillemette, and the highly regarded Théodore Duguay. Another friend of Montmarquette, Joseph Plante, made a string of lively recordings in the 1930s when he was sixty years old. In the 1930s–50s, players like Tommy Duchesne and his Cavaliers kept the folkloric accordion alive, touring to every corner of the continent as a sort of Jimmy Shand for Francophone Canada.

Universally lauded accordionist Philippe Bruneau headed up a revival of the instrument in the 1960s. He took inspiration from Alfred Montmarquette and John Kimmel and created intricate technical masterpieces on the one-row button accordion. Performing solo or with pianist Dorothy Hogan, he mastered hundreds of traditional and personal compositions. Always an iconoclast, Bruneau never tapped his feet in accompaniment like many Québécois musicians do. Apparently he once had noise-sensitive neighbors and learned not to tread on his housing.

Before he died in 2011, Bruneau emigrated to France in protest against government cuts to music and cultural programs. He turned down $30,000 when he refused to return to Quebec to receive the Prix Gérard-Morisset in 2001. A man of consummate skill, conviction, and dedication to French Canadian culture, he inspired many to carry the accordion forward.

The Maritimes

Canada's Maritime provinces—New Brunswick, Prince Edward Island, and Nova Scotia—exemplify the shifting cultural confluence that awaited the accordion in Canada. French, English, Scottish and other settlers struggled over land and language while sharing music and many commonalities of frontier and colonial life.

The accordion didn't arrive until almost a hundred years after the English forcibly removed long-established French settlers from the region they called Acadia. English and Irish immigrant music mixed with surviving and returning French Canadian culture. When accordions arrived, they took hold in some areas and were ignored in others. The region's musical styles reflect this history of conflicts, differences, and collaboration.

Acadia: Nova Scotia and New Brunswick

A century before the accordion came to Canada, thirteen-thousand French-speaking Acadians were deported from their homes in Nova Scotia and Prince Edward Island by the British government. Acadian families lost everything in what became known as the Grand Dérangement (Great Upheaval) of 1755-64. Thousands died while interred often in unsafe, disease-ridden ships or prisons.

Behind the deportation was the Seven Years' War between Britain and France, during which many Acadians refused to sign unconditional loyalty oaths. It didn't help that the British were eager to transfer Acadian farms to their own settlers. For the next two hundred years, many of the Acadians who remained in Canada survived on the poorer lands in New Brunswick. It wasn't until 1810 that they even achieved the right to vote. But Acadians survived and made New Brunswick Canada's only officially bilingual province in 1969. Today, descendants of the Acadians are concentrated in Prince Edward Island, New Brunswick, parts of Nova Scotia, the Port au Port Peninsula in western Newfoundland, and across the border in northern Maine.

Of the Acadian refugees who were forced to leave the region, most were first scattered amongst Britain's American colonies. A second wave were deported to France from whence many were resettled in Caribbean colonies. About 2,500 of these Acadian deportees made their way to Louisiana and became known as Cajuns. It bears repeating that the northern Acadians and their southern Cajun cousins each took up the accordion separately at least a hundred years after the expulsion. Their musics diverged, with many different influences, and would not be reunited until the 1960s folk revival a century later.

The exiled Acadians carried a storehouse of French folk songs, and their fiddle repertoire was in constant development. Centuries later, a modern reflection of the efforts of the Acadians to maintain and recover the dignity of their culture came together at the Georges LeBlanc Accordion Festival in Moncton, New Brunswick.

According to Joel Cormier, whose doctoral thesis was dedicated to the music of southeastern New Brunswick, many researchers have studied the Acadian a cappella songs and *complaintes* (ballad/dirges) that originated in France; hardly any work exists on equally traditional dance music. The research has focused almost exclusively on the region's fiddle styles. The Acadians play mostly jigs, reels, and waltzes; their style tends to be unembellished, with few ornamentals or improvisations. It was music for dancing, with listening only an afterthought. Though the Moncton Festival encouraged this unique local tradition, it also revealed New Brunswick players practicing more flamboyant styles, inspired by guest artists from Quebec and elsewhere.

Cormier points out unique differences between Acadian French Canadian accordionists and those from Quebec. He singles out the distinctive "long bellows" used in New Brunswick. Where Québécois accordionists (similar to early Irish players) play with quick, staccato push/pulls of the bellows, the Acadian tradition uses the whole bellows, playing a series of notes in one direction before "smoothly" returning.

To a great degree the acoustic music revival that erupted in Quebec, Cape Breton, and Newfoundland in the 1970s and '80s bypassed New Brunswick's Acadians. Few young groups took up the accordion to carry it to the next generation. In 2007, all the players and most of the audiences at the first Moncton festival were older. For lack of enough locals, players from Quebec filled out the schedule. Their hope was that an ongoing event would inspire young people to appreciate and take up the music.

Modern Acadian accordion crosses traditional boundaries. Elly Kelly (1952–2014) combined barn dance reels and jigs with slow country numbers for couples dancing, all with rough grace and few unnecessary flourishes. Edith Butler's 1992 album *Ça Swingue* leaned toward western swing and country. More recently, the trio Vishtèn has combined atmospheric old-time dance music and French Canadian foot percussion with gorgeous instrumental arrangements and harmonies. Their success at festivals across Canada and internationally bodes well for the future as Acadians carry on despite all obstacles.

English-Speaking Nova Scotia and New Brunswick (and Gaelic Cape Breton)

English-speaking New Brunswick and Nova Scotia were heavily influenced by Scottish, Irish, and English folk music. Scots especially were one of the largest ethnic groups in Nova Scotia after tens of thousands were forced to emigrate by the Highland Clearances of the 1770s–1820s.

Cape Breton Island (the northernmost part of Nova Scotia) has surviving speakers of Scots-Gaelic whose fiddle tradition retained stylistic elements that hadn't been played in Scotland itself in generations. If we want to imagine a "pre-accordion" fiddle style, we might find it here. Accordions and concertinas arrived hundreds of years after fiddles and pipes had been established. In Cape Breton especially, the fiddle never ceded prominence as the most common instrument.

The accordion was present, though, and remains part of local dances. By 1900 it had certainly spread to the industrial, mining, and maritime industries in the region, but a deeper understanding of the instrument's role in the English- and Gaelic-speaking Maritimes awaits exploration.

Métis "Accordion"

The Métis are a distinct aboriginal group in Canada descended from the historical mixing between First Nations peoples and European settlers. In the Métis language Michif, which combines many Native Cree verbs and archaic French nouns, the word for accordion is simply "accordion."

Métis music incorporated rich French *chanson* ballads (usually without instruments) and instrumental music for dancing. The primary Métis instrument was always the portable and affordable fiddle. It had come to North America from France in the 1600s, traveling along the fur-trade routes. Fiddles were compact, affordable, and could even be handmade when otherwise unavailable.

The centers of musical life were community and house dances, where almost everyone participated either as dancers or musicians. Accordions spread after they became available from the east in the mid-1800s. They were relatively cheap, durable, and well suited for the French and Scottish/English/Irish dance music of the time.

Louis Riel, the most famous Métis leader in the rebellions of the 1880s, reportedly owned a mid-size two-stop accordion at some point before his execution in 1884. The instrument, carved with his initials, found its way to Peterborough, Ontario, in 1899 and is now displayed by the Historical Society as a musical heirloom from Canada's past.

Modern entertainment (radio, movies, and eventually TV) led to the fading of Métis house dances. Accordions, never as common as the fiddle, were heard less and less. Today there is a revival of the Métis fiddle, but the accordion remains a rarity, seen mostly in historical depictions of traditional instruments. It's remembered, though, as part of the unique Métis culture that spread from Maine to the Northwest Territories and helped create what eventually became the Canadian nation.

Newfoundland: The Squeezebox Rock

"The Oldest Store, on the Oldest Street, in the Oldest City in North America," reads the sign at O'Brien's accordion shop in St. John's, Newfoundland. The accordion had of course been entrenched on the Island long before Roy O'Brien opened his music store in 1939. Newfoundland was settled by Europeans in the 1500s, drawn by the rich fisheries of the Atlantic. Four centuries later, its isolated towns and outposts had become home to so many accordionists that it was called the national instrument. Before that, music had mostly been played on fiddles by Irish, Scots, French, and English sailors and settlers.

The first known accordion arrived in St. John's when music teacher J.F. Myers gave a lecture in 1850 playing a French-style flutina. It wasn't until about 1900 that working-class fiddlers began to take up cheap German-style accordions, likely purchased from mail-order catalogs. Even as these replaced the less sturdy violin, musicians were sometimes still called "fiddlers," no matter what instrument they played.

Historically, accordion music was mainly for dancing. They were played over long winters in kitchen parties called "times," and for summer step dancing on the planks of local docks or bridges. Singing was saved for a cappella ballads, work songs, or religious music. When fiddles and accordions weren't available, dance tunes were sung with nonsense "mouth music," sometimes known as "gob music" or "chin-music." (Called "lilting" in Ireland, this "fiddle-dee-dee" technique began as an aid for learning and remembering tunes. It spread under many names including "turlutte/turlutage" in Quebec. In Newfoundland it was performed most often by women, who played fewer instruments.)

By 1900, local performances were held at community halls, and songbooks like O'Neill's *Music of Ireland* and Gerald S. Doyle's 1927 *Old-Time Songs and Poetry of Newfoundland* became influential fixtures in many musicians' homes. Newfoundland's well-established Irish connection was reaffirmed in the early twentieth century with the arrival of recordings by Irish-style accordionists like John Kimmel. The Irish American McNulty Family also garnered a huge following in Newfoundland when they followed their radio and recording fame north to tour there in the 1950s.

Records and radio became important ways for people to learn and pass on songs and tunes alongside the oral tradition. In the 1920s, radio also broke the isolation of outport villages and gave locals a chance to connect with each other through shows like *The Big Six*. "God had Newfoundland particularly and specifically in mind when he brought about the invention of the radio," said radio host Joseph R. Smallwood in the 1930s and '40s about his *Barrelman* show, dedicated to "making Newfoundland better known to Newfoundlanders." (In 1949, Smallwood became the first premier of Newfoundland.)

During World War II, U.S. and Canadian soldiers introduced swing jazz and other popular music to the region; these at times threatened to overwhelm local Newfoundland traditions. Longer-range radio also brought outside influences like American country music that lifted up the guitar at the expense of fiddles and accordions. In order to compete, homegrown accordionist Wilf Doyle formed an orchestra similar to that of Scotland's Jimmy Shand and the Irish dance hall bands. Doyle's invariable rhythms brought older tunes to large dance floors across

Newfoundland, and he became so literally iconic that a statue of him and his accordion stands now in St. John's.

As western music saddled up for the U.S. pop market, Harold Skanes founded a country band in the 1950s called the Buchaneers (from the mining town of Buchans) and by popular demand added Don Bursey on accordion. Skanes wanted to play country songs, but knew he needed to provide Newfoundland jigs and reels for dancing. This mix of accordion waltzes and country ballads represented the early stage of what for many became Newfoundland's own unique music.

Due to its remoteness and thinly spread population, no commercial recordings were made by Newfoundlanders until 1943, a generation later than in most of North America. It wasn't until 1956 that the first Newfoundland accordionist was recorded, when folksinger Omar Blondahl invited Wilf Doyle to join him on "The Kelligrews Soiree" and "The Wild Colonial Boy." Doyle thus opened the way for Newfoundland accordionists to accompany guitars and singers rather than simply playing on dance tunes.

In the 1950s and '60s, radio shifted away from live musicians and Newfoundland's music faded from the airwaves. The 1970s saw a renewal of local music, as broadcast regulations began requiring Canadian content on the air. Filling this need were artists like accordionist Harry Hibbs, who represented Newfoundland's version of working-class country music crossed with commercial folk singing.

In the late 1970s, young musicians who sometimes spurned Hibbs as embarrassing began rediscovering the roots of his music. Young musicians took on the role of musicologists and sought out songs from local artists who might otherwise have been forgotten. Bands like Figgy Duff helped draw attention to many older, non-professional, or only locally known musicians like Minnie White, and brought them to national audiences.

Revival bands did not, however, carry forward their tradition unchanged. A cappella ballads were augmented with musical arrangements, and new words were applied to instrumental tunes. The modernizers played mostly for listening audiences rather than dancers, and their music tended toward polished professionalism. Without a strong dance tradition to match their new musical accomplishments, more complicated traditional dances began to be simplified or even lost.

Newfoundland's cultural renaissance crested in the 1970s and '80s. Since then the fisheries that were the basis of life for centuries were mostly shut down, and many Newfoundlanders left the island seasonally or permanently. Despite the difficulties, musicians, often enough with accordions, continue to combine storytelling ballads, old-time instrumentals, and modern sounds. When a singer-songwriter or a band pulls down an accordion in Newfoundland it still brings echoes of cold nights in warm kitchens filled with family and friends.

Newfoundland: Vanguard of the Accordion Revolution

Decades before twenty-first-century pop songs dabbled in accordions, Newfoundlanders reveled in them. When the Newfoundland and Labrador Folk Festival set a world record for the "largest accordion ensemble" in 2005, almost a thousand Newfoundlanders showed up with their own accordions or ones borrowed from friends and family. Many players wore "Accordion Revolution" shirts bearing faux-socialist accordionists beneath Newfoundland's legendary (and historically ambiguous) pink, white, and green flag of independence.

Newfoundlander musicians continue to cement the instrument's role as a cultural symbol. Great Big Sea is perhaps most famous for successfully mixing Celtic rock with five-part harmony vocals that recall Newfoundland's work-songs and shanties. One of their instrumental tunes, "Dancing with Mrs. White," is dedicated to Minnie White, the island's First Lady of the Accordion. Younger bands like the Dardanelles carry the legacy of White's acoustic tunes and ballads into the new century with skilled, session-honed musicianship.

Newfoundland country music, meanwhile, still resonates with locals in the sometimes unromantic bars of St. John's and the outports. Where else would a homegrown band like Shanneyganock consciously reach seventy years into the past for a series of tribute shows recalling the influence of the Irish American McNulty Family? Even pop acts like Hey Rosetta! have genetic links to traditional music: bassist Josh Ward's mother and grandmother both played accordion. Others, like the formidable singer-songwriter Amelia Curran and the haunting folk trio the Once, are ready at need to haul out the instrument and remind listeners that Newfoundland hasn't forgotten the accordion after 150 years.

Memorial University and the Power of Folklore

IF YOU GO to the Memorial University Library in St. John's, and look up "accordion" in the *Discography of Newfoundland and Labrador,* you find almost a thousand entries. Since 1968, the folklore department at Memorial has had a huge impact on the preservation and appreciation of the culture of Newfoundland. Working musicians, scholars, and other revivalists were able to consult recordings and, more significantly, borrow tape recorders to collect and learn local folk songs. Much of Newfoundland's music hasn't just passed directly from artist to artist and within families and communities now, but spreads from the work at Memorial.

Band members from Figgy Duff, Great Big Sea, and others have worked with the university to travel the region in search of the songs and connections that were the basis of their careers. Hundreds of papers, recordings, and publications have not only archived tunes, but made songs and music available that might otherwise have been lost or known only to a few. While facing class and cultural divisions, Memorial has tried to make their academic work relevant to real Newfoundlanders. They have particularly wrestled with the importance of Newfoundland's centuries-old way of life as it rapidly, even catastrophically changed.

Newfoundland's isolated outport fishing culture has, over the last forty years, had its economic base virtually eliminated. When neighbors move away to find work, old accordion tunes played at community "times" take on new value. But how do people maintain a culture if it can't feed them? Tourism has increased in importance, but leans toward idealized versions of the past. How does reliance on visiting outsiders change traditions once based on communities hauling in fish?

Memorial has uniquely charted the specific story of how Newfoundland accordions became a regional symbol while they faded in other places. The efforts of countless community members have made the university a vital part of the culture it documents. That Newfoundland and Labrador's music survives shows the value of deeply committed public institutions.

Newfoundland Accordionists

Minnie White: First Lady of the Accordion

Billboard magazine once listed typical shows on George Street in St. John's, Newfoundland ("home of thirty pubs"). They ranged from the heavy metal band Sheavy, to alternative rock and blues acts. Holding her own amongst them was eighty-three-year-old accordion player Minnie White.

Born in 1916 in St. Alban's, on Newfoundland's south coast, at age eight White started playing her dad's accordion in secret. Her grandmother complained to her father about the racket, but he helped her keep on. As a teen, she accompanied dances on piano while inhaling Irish, English, Scots, and French tunes. Half a century later young people sought out her wellspring of knowledge about all the musics of Newfoundland.

After marrying in 1937, White put down her accordion for almost four decades. She raised six children and none of them knew she played anything but the family's old pump organ, stomping out tunes when they had fiddlers over for "times." Then, in 1971, a friend heard she'd played accordion as a child and gifted her one. White recalled, "Time was coming where I was going to have to sit in a rocking chair and knit all the time, or get up and do what I wanted to do. What I wanted to do was get into music, and that's what I did."

At a rebellious fifty-five years old, she formed a band and began booking shows. White established a reputation that influenced a generation of traditional musicians. Deflecting criticism about women taking the stage, she dressed in gowns and jewels and presented herself with "the epitome of dignity." Her producer Jim Payne recalled, "She once said that somebody referred to her as a lady playing the accordion, so she said she was going to dress and look like a *lady* playing an accordion." She released four independent records, starting with 1974's *Newfoundland Accordian* [sic] *and Mandolin Favorites.*

Her band worked a thirteen-year gig playing the local Starlite Motel, until it burned to the ground. In the meantime, Minnie was "discovered" by revivalists and invited to play festivals around Newfoundland and

FACING Minnie White at the Newfoundland and Labrador Folk Festival in 1995. *Photo by Shane Kelly.*

beyond. Young people came to learn tunes she'd kept alive for years, direct from somebody who remembered when radio and records had just begun to have an impact.

She appeared on TV and radio many times, including a spot as a musical passenger on the nostalgic *Newfie Bullet* radio show, where musicians joined hosts on a fictional trip on the one-time rail line that transported soldiers during World War II. When she died in 2001 at age eighty-five, the *Globe and Mail* reported: "Mrs. White didn't learn songs from records or the radio, she learned them from other musicians in her communities, communities that happened to be settled by the four most prominent cultures that flowed into Newfoundland music: the Irish and English on the Southern Shore, the Scottish in the Codroy Valley and the French on the nearby Port au Port Peninsula."

White was awarded the Order of Canada in 1993 in recognition of her role in preserving and reviving the unique culture of Newfoundland. Not bad for a lady who decided she'd rather play accordion than sit in a rocking chair and knit.

Harry Hibbs and Newfie Country

Within cultural revivals, some people who open a path for others are later derided for watering down traditions or just for being "unhip." America's Kingston Trio have been widely dismissed, even though luminaries like Joan Baez and Bob Dylan admitted their influence. In Canada, Harry Hibbs was a bit like a one-man Kingston Trio playing Newfoundland accordion. In his case, it's rather ironic that he's criticized as inauthentic, because unlike Dylan, Baez, or the Kingston Trio, Hibbs grew up amidst the folk music he would bring to the world.

Like many before and since, Hibbs left his economically estranged island to find work in Toronto. Unfortunately, his legs were crushed in a factory, and to make do Hibbs hobbled onstage with his accordion in 1968. His first audiences were Toronto's displaced working-class Newfoundlanders, who liked American country music as much as traditional tunes. Hibbs's unpretentious style mixed traditional and original tunes backed with guitar, bass, drums, and accordion. Today that's called "country music" in Newfoundland.

Hibbs was almost unprecedented amongst English-speaking North American singer-songwriters in the 1960s and '70s for hanging on to his squeezebox. His Newfoundland roots gave him the instrument, but playing it while singing was groundbreaking. Wilf Doyle had backed singers, as had the McNultys and other Irish balladeers, but Hibbs's singing solo with his own accordion was new. Meanwhile, some of Newfoundland's early 1970s trad-rock revivalists purposely avoided the accordion, partially to distance themselves from Hibbs.

For some young middle-class Newfoundlanders, Hibbs embodied the stigma of "Newfie" music. He was seen as either humorous or, at best, a second-rate Irish musician. Hibbs's demeanor was certainly not highbrow, and his Newfoundland country style eliminated subtle chord changes and complexities. In his favor, while looked down on by purists, Hibbs loved traditional players and progressive groups like Figgy Duff.

He eventually opened a nightclub in Toronto, where future superstar Shania Twain sang as a child while her mom worked in the kitchen. Over the next decade, Hibbs recorded twenty-six albums and sold millions of records. He even had his own TV show, but the good times didn't last. Trouble with alcohol didn't help, and in the 1980s he returned to work in a warehouse. Hibbs never had a chance for a comeback, as he died of cancer at age forty-six in 1989. If he had survived, he might well have benefited from a critical re-evaluation and been lauded as an elder statesman of Canadian folk music by former critics.

Tensions between tradition and innovation, class and elitism are close to the surface where the accordion is played and heard in Newfoundland. Hibbs unquestionably brought Newfoundland's music of to a much wider audience than anyone before. He also laid the foundation for revivalist bands that came after, whether they appreciated his style or not.

If you had asked an educated folk fan in the 1980s about the best Newfoundland music, they wouldn't likely have praised Hibbs. But if you asked your average Newfoundlander what they listened to, Hibbs and "country" bands like Simani that followed him would probably be high on the list. Simani (the duo of Sim Savory and Bud Davidge) produced bare-bones Newfoundland country with vocals, accordion, guitar, and a drum machine. Their huge hit "The Mummers Song" (1983), revived interest in the seasonal practice, and led to TV specials and a bestselling children's book.

For years, country musicians like Hibbs and Simani were the most popular accordion sounds in Newfoundland. Even if his stardom fades away entirely, at least one unusual memorial remains. At the peak of his career, Hibbs gained the remarkable distinction of being the only known accordionist to have a geological phenomenon named after him. The "Harry Hibbs Effect" causes "distinct concertina-like ridges" across the middle of Newfoundland. So even if accordions were to disappear entirely, Harry Hibbs would survive in the heart of the Rock.

Figgy Duff: Reclaiming Our Electric Heritage

Despite their isolation, and in some ways because of it, Newfoundlanders have frequently adopted and enjoyed new musical technologies, whether by picking up accordions in the 1890s or plugging in radios in the 1920s. People even used telephone "party lines" to play live music in pre-wireless electric kitchen parties. Newfoundland's country and western players mixed accordions with electrified steel guitars as early as the 1940s. In the 1960s, though, rock 'n' roll came to Newfoundland and traditional music felt old-fashioned.

A transplanted Irish trio called Ryan's Fancy (and several influential radio shows that featured Irish music) inspired a few young rock players to reconsider traditional music. Noel Dinn played drums in a psychedelic group called the Land of Mordor which, in 1967, was the first electric band to try to incorporate older Newfoundland songs. Dinn's next group was Figgy Duff, a successful revivalist band with an ornate sound akin to British folk rockers Steeleye Span or Fairport Convention.

There were really two pop-influenced folk revivals in Newfoundland. Harry Hibbs revived elements like the accordion, but his "Newfie music" was stigmatized as simplistic and banal. Figgy Duff were known to perform accordion versions of "All Along the Watchtower," but rejected Newfoundland's country style as "an imported substitute" for traditional music.

Figgy Duff were acclaimed outside Newfoundland for reviving old songs, but on occasion weren't successful at connecting with audiences in Newfoundland itself. Some listeners found their traditional songs unfamiliar or highbrow. They were trying to increase appreciation for Newfoundlanders' musical heritage, but were told at least once, "That's not fucking Newfoundland music."

Stylistically, Figgy Duff promoted elements of Newfoundland tradition while introducing things from outside. They used rock drums, keyboards, and guitars, with their flute, mandolin, and accordion. Even the accordion was not always played in a traditional manner.

Original accordionist Art Stoyles was a virtuosic player who expanded his technique with an uncommon three-row diatonic instrument (most Newfoundlanders play Irish-style two-row). He had played traditional tunes since childhood, but built a repertoire of popular and country songs and notably claimed inspiration from visiting Portuguese sailors well outside the standard Newfoundlander style.

The musicians of Figgy Duff often played songs and dance tunes they'd collected while touring to remote outports. Their sound, however, was influenced by highly skilled ensembles like Ireland's Bothy Band. They also incorporated atmospheric tunes to support what traditionally would have been a cappella ballads. The band repeatedly stressed their goal of freeing old tunes from the "embarrassing" Newfie style by creating richer, more complex arrangements. Singer Pamela Morgan summarized, "You can't cram a delicate and beautiful modal melody into a three-chord country format."

The Duff's technically advanced performances didn't always mesh easily with the island's house parties or country music, but even remote audiences welcomed Figgy Duff's mission of collecting and sharing songs. Despite any awkwardness, they helped inspire a generation of musicians to take Newfoundland's musical heritage seriously. They also significantly increased outsiders' awareness that Newfoundland's traditions transcended stereotype, and that truly "Newfie music" was something to be proud of.

Inuit Accordion in Canada's Arctic

Even the most remote Inuit musicians in the Northern Arctic were not immune to the accordion invasion. Whaling ships from England, Scotland, and New England had long carried musicians into the region. By the late 1800s, accordions and concertinas were popular items at Hudson's Bay trading posts.

Over a stormy hundred years, European-influenced music, first on fiddles and then accordions, replaced all but a remnant of traditional Inuit music. In the 1970s, ethnomusicologist Maija Lutz reported that in the Baffin Island area, "Inuit dancing" referred to "jigs and reels, rather than to earlier and almost lost traditions of Inuit dancing accompanied by the frame drum." The dancing she saw was accompanied by accordions.

Napachie Pootoogook, *My New Accordion*, 1989. Originally 112 × 80 cm color litho-
graph. *Reproduced with the permission of Dorset Fine Arts*

British and American whalers first wintered in the Arctic in the 1850s, after whales neared extinction in warmer southern waters. The Europeans relied on the Inuit's skills to survive, and ships eventually employed many Inuit rather than transporting entire crews from the south. It was while waiting out harsh winters together that Inuit musicians and dancers began incorporating European music and instruments. Whole families would stay aboard ships during the whaling season, and by the time whalers established year-round, on-shore stations in the late nineteenth century, fiddle-based music was standard entertainment among the Inuit.

In Dorothy Harley Eber's book *When the Whalers Were Up North*, Mary Ipeelie recalled the whaling station of Singaijaq (Cape Haven) in the 1920s at the close of the whaling era:

> We used to hold dances in one of the cabins. There were accordions stored there that belonged to the Inuit. They'd been left in the cabin to keep them safe, so they'd last longer. There were thirty or more, perhaps thirty-seven or thirty-eight. The people who owned them didn't dare take them in case they'd get wrecked. We danced by the light of oil lanterns... There we so many accordions—some more elaborate than others—and the Inuit were so happy to dance. Everyone took turns playing, my mother included... We kept dancing in those cabins for years. Every summer when we went caribou hunting we passed by the cabins and danced... Around 1930 they realized the whalers were not coming back... Finally my mother also took her accordions away. There were two—one remained good, but we children wrecked the other by taking out the different parts... I remember those cabins so well... No one touched them for years, thinking the *qallunaat* [white whalers] would come back.*

Christian missionaries had arrived in the middle of the nineteenth century and preached against alcohol and immorality in the whaling fleet, but also against Indigenous spirituality and music. They encouraged permanent settlements where hymns replaced drum songs and European dances were promoted over old traditions. Composer Jim Hiscott later reported, "Dances often take place around Christmas, when it's

---

* Eber, Dorothy Harley. "Final Curtain." *When the Whalers Were Up North*. Montreal: McGill-Queen's University Press, 1996.

night most if not all of the time. Andrew Atagotaaluk (Atagutaaluk) told me they used to build a big igloo especially for the Christmas dance—you'd have fifty or so people dancing with accordion music in one big igloo. They would tear it down afterwards. There was no heating—he said people there got used to the cold, and actually had to go outside to cool off between dances. This was on the Boothia Peninsula, above the Arctic Circle."

At dances, women often took turns playing accordion. Maija Lutz reported she "rarely saw a man play the instrument, but many women in the community seem able to play it." A Scottish zoologist in the 1950s remembered, "[A woman] brought an accordion and played the tunes. It was far better than the gramophone. Although a small woman, she swung the accordion mightily, banged a foot on the wooden floor in time with the beat, and smiled and laughed infectiously. She and other Inuit gave gay shouts. When I closed my eyes a moment and listened, I could have been in a dance hall in northeast Scotland where I had been raised as a child."

Today Inuit accordionists play "square dances" related to Irish and Newfoundlander polkas, jigs, reels, and slides. Hiscott explains, "The dance steps are variants of the square dances that you find in various forms across Canada." But in most kindred traditions, individual dance tunes seldom last more than a few minutes before switching to new ones. Inuit dances are different: "Each dance may be very long ... Andrew Atagota-aluk told me he once played for two hours nonstop—just one dance!"

Dances resembled the "reel, the country dance, and the square dance" with figures similar to hornpipes (sometimes called "jigging"). Maija Lutz remembered, "It appeared to me that most people had their own versions of the steps and were not concerned with doing them 'correctly' or 'accurately.'"

The fact that the "Inuit dancing" was adopted from European models has often confused observers. Lutz put it: "The prevailing idea has been that ... music which has been introduced to the Inuit by whites is not worthy of much consideration." But after more than one hundred years, the adopted music has become a symbol of Inuit culture. "By disregarding all music which has been borrowed, one leaves the ... Inuit with virtually no music at all." In reality, the Inuit accordion tradition is older than much of the music that receives significantly more attention and veneration by folklorists. For instance, Arctic square dances have been held since before the invention of the blues or most American country music styles.

The last whaling ship left the North in the 1930s, but the music the Inuit had embraced survived. In 1996, players from Northern Canada gathered for the CBC's 60th Anniversary Inuit Button Accordion Festival produced by Jim Hiscott in Iqaluit. Demonstrating the cultural importance of the instrument, Elisapi Kasarnak traveled twelve hours by Ski-Doo (snowmobile) and then four hours by plane to share her music at the festival.

Young people in Nunavut are still picking up accordions like the ones their ancestors played when the instrument was young and first traveling the world. Nancy Mike of modern rock band the Jerry Cans sings in the Inuktitut language and teaches Inuit history, throat singing, and accordion for youth summer music camps. Early in the twenty-first century, young people from Pangnirtung traveled to Peterhead, Scotland, for an exchange of cultures across the sea of history. Three hundred years after the Inuit first taught survival skills to Scottish whalers, their descendants were sharing accordion tunes and square dances together.

Matthew Henson: April 6, 1909– Concertina Player Reaches the North Pole

Joining the Inuit accordionists, African American sailor Matthew Henson played concertina while traveling north through Greenland in 1909. He is more often remembered, though, as the first person to visit the North Pole. His role in that journey is remarkable, not least because it was hidden for years due to professional jealousy, paranoia, and the color of his skin.

Orphaned in Washington, D.C., Henson ran away to sea at age twelve. Beginning as a cabin boy, he sailed around the world and eventually met explorer Robert Peary, who was then beginning his quest to reach the North Pole. They headed to the Arctic in 1891 for the first of many attempts, and a minor incident occurred in an igloo on the edge of the Arctic Ocean. Henson joined an "evening of Inuit entertainment," where he took his "battered concertina" out of his bag and sang hymns he had learned as a child aboard ship. It is impossible to know what kind of concertina or accordion it was, because they were often confused at the time. But it's reasonable to guess that Henson played a common Anglo concertina due to their durability and portability at sea.

After almost twenty years of attempts and preparations, on April 6, 1909, Henson and four Inuit named Egingwah, Ootah, Ooqueah, and

Seegloo reached the farthest North accompanied by Peary. Henson wrote that he realized he reached the Pole first and this angered Peary enough to break their long partnership. Henson remembered it as the beginning of a long disappointment with his employer.

Peary kept Henson's achievement secret and claimed full credit himself, writing that he relied on Henson as a servant, but not an equal. Peary may simply have been jealous, but he also may have sidelined Henson in order to avoid questions about whether the group had in fact reached the Pole, which some competitors doubted.

Peary nevertheless won his campaign to be declared conqueror of the Pole. Henson, who had spent nearly two decades with Peary and saved his life at least once, was denied recognition for his part in the expeditions. He received none of the medals or government pension Peary did. Instead, Henson worked as a clerk for the U.S. Customs office in New York. He was finally acknowledged near the end of his life, and may be as well known as Peary now that their story is retold together.

Henson led a remarkable life, of which the concertina is a lovely but minor part. When he played his childhood hymns to European and Inuit listeners in the Far North, the squeezebox once again served to connect people separated by vast cultural oceans.

Matthew Henson playing his concertina in an igloo at an Inuit village during the Peary group's first attempt to reach the North Pole, Greenland, 1891. *Original artwork by Ivan Montoya, 2019.*

12

Klezmer: A Restoration
with Accordion

K LEZMER IS FESTIVAL and dance music rooted in the Yiddish-
speaking culture of Eastern Europe. In the movies, it's what
they play at Jewish weddings. It turns out to be one of the
most well-documented non-English language folk musics
of North America. This is the result of researcher-players who were
significantly responsible for the continued existence of the style. One
unfortunate effect of their voluminous documentation is the impossi-
bility of summarizing the available history in this short account.

Klezmer's Origins

The music now known as klezmer reaches back centuries. Under Czarist
rule, from the 1700s to World War I, Russian Jews were restricted to the
boundaries of the "Pale of Settlement." This region included much of what
is now Poland (with the greatest number of Jews), Lithuania, and Ukraine.
By the 1800s, millions of Jews were fleeing the region during periods of
harsh repression. Many others were simply seeking economic opportunity.
Jews who remained in the segregated area sustained a rich Yiddish-
language culture that included musicians. For centuries the Jews blended
their music with neighboring Romanian, Greek, and Romani ("Gypsy")
elements into a vibrant, multicultural, but distinctly Jewish tradition.

☞ "Klezmer": Musician, Accusation, Tradition

IN YIDDISH, THE term *klezmer* originally referred to musicians themselves, rather than the musical style. It was sometimes used derogatorily, since traveling musicians, even if they were respected for virtuosity and their role in community life, were thought of as unreliable and suspect. The musicians were called *klezmorim*, and a band was a *kapelye*. When emigration to America threatened to shatter the music's community context, some musicians remember that "klezmer" became an insult. The style was seen as backward and unprofessional, similar to the stereotypes attached to "hillbilly music." The name "klezmer" didn't generally become attached to the music itself until the revival of the 1970s and '80s.

Klezmer music developed over generations within often dynastic bands. These groups traveled from place to place and faced strict and occasionally absurd rules about where, when, and even what instruments they could play. Their primary venues were multi-day wedding festivals where they provided scripted music for each portion of the event. Besides the officiating rabbi's spiritual role, the secular celebration depended on the *badkhn*, a singing wedding organizer who led participants while commenting and improvising with the support of the musicians.

Along with the communal, spiritual, and ceremonial aspects of the wedding, music was integral to the multi-day affair. Unfortunately it wasn't until decades after the old-style rituals were lost that Joshua Horowitz's modern band Budowitz led a project to reconstruct a village wedding as it would have been heard prior to the 1940s. Horowitz related, "We had no idea how beautiful and complete... the musical elements of the old style wedding [were]. It's as though we discovered a huge symphonic form." Aside from the Jews who emigrated, most of the artists who played this music in their homelands were silenced in the Holocaust.

Across the ocean in America, the number of immigrants is difficult to imagine. According to collector/scholar Sherry Mayrent, "Thirty-three percent of the Jewish population left Eastern Europe between 1880 and 1920 [for America]." Unlike some immigrant groups such as Italians, Jews seldom returned to their former homes. They crossed the Atlantic to stay, and they brought their music and culture with them.

Many of the Jewish musicians who came to North America assimilated. But the pressure to give up customs was balanced by a constant influx of new immigrants who sustained and extended the unassimilated "first generation" culture. Until the U.S. closed its doors with restrictive immigration quotas in 1924, there were always newcomers who relied on the Yiddish community, the Yiddish press, and Yiddish entertainment. This resulted in a relatively stable base for music that slowly adapted to its new home while maintaining its own flavor.

Eventually, world events shattered the musicians' relationships with their birthplaces. Whereas Irish musicians were able to travel back and forth between North America and Ireland, after World War II there was no old country for Jews to return to. By the 1960s, assimilation for third-generation American Jews in North America was well established. When their grandparents' Yiddish language and culture fell from favor, the distinctive Jewish music that took centuries to create nearly disappeared.

Jewish Music beyond Klezmer

To understand the place of the accordion in klezmer, one must understand that instrumental "klezmer" music was only part of Yiddish/Jewish culture. In the late nineteenth century, Jews in the modernizing cities of Eastern Europe, along with those who immigrated to industrial America, produced a wealth of other musical and cultural institutions.

Russian and European Yiddish immigrants sustained a host of religious, secular, and political organizations and widely read Yiddish newspapers. The three musical cornerstones were cantorial religious music, secular ballads and songs (many associated with the thriving Yiddish theater), and traditional klezmer bands.

After recording began around 1900, the majority of performances were sacred cantorial selections; most of the rest were Yiddish theater pieces and ballads, and only a minority were the instrumental pieces we might call klezmer. As collector and archivist Sherry Mayrent remarked on this little-known history, "Although cantorial selections and folk/theater songs vastly outnumber instrumental recordings, the latter have attracted the most attention over the past 30 years and accordingly comprise the vast majority of the reissued material."

Heard as a whole, the immigrant Jews' festive klezmer tunes—by whatever name—were only part of the music of the day, though genres influenced each other and even mixed. Compilations such as Mayrent's *Cantors, Klezmorim and Crooners 1905–1953* strive for a fuller picture of Yiddish musical life at the beginning of the twentieth century. Co-producer Henry Sapoznik commented, "You get a chance to hear klezmer elements in cantorial singing, or cantorial phrasings in Yiddish theater songs."

Klezmer's focus on early instrumental recordings also tends to bypass the historical role of women. In Eastern Europe there had been women in some bands, and even all-women klezmer groups, but few if any were recorded in the early twentieth century. Women were, however, well-known artists in a whole genre of romance songs and as singers and writers of ballads and topical and political songs.

Women eventually did claim a significant place in the klezmer revival, but their driving role in historical Yiddish vocal music is often forgotten. Their songs and songwriting strongly influence modern singers (not all women) who are reclaiming space alongside instrumental klezmer. Today's post-revivalists incorporate portions of the broader forms from secular theater and ballads into singer-songwriter styles often backed with klezmer accordions.

Klezmer Instrumentation Old and New

Until the mid-nineteenth century, klezmer groups (*kapelyes*) were usually small, limited to three to five members, and at times were legally restricted to what were called "soft" instruments like flutes, fiddle, and a hammered dulcimer called (in Yiddish) a *tsimbl*. No brass or drums were permitted at all in many places, and Czar Alexander II was considered liberal for allowing Ukrainian Jews to start playing clarinet in 1855. The earliest klezmer accordionists appeared in these small ensembles, and solo accordions or duets with tsimblists appear on the first klezmer accordion recordings.

Poldek Kostowski with accordion, ca. 1940. Poldek's younger brother, Dolko Klein-man Brandwein, is seated to Poldek's right. Dolko, a klezmer violin virtuoso, was murdered by Ukrainian nationalists. *Courtesy of Joshua Horowitz.*

As with many folk styles, the accordion was gradually incorporated into European and American klezmer between the 1890s and 1900. Like the players of other instruments, accordionists sought to imitate Yiddish vocal styles. Fiddle players had developed ornamental techniques over hundreds of years, based on singing from the synagogue. In the 1800s, these fiddle ornaments were adapted to new instruments like the clarinet and then the accordion.

One could make the case that klezmer's longest historical period predated both clarinets and accordions and that authentic klezmer should only be played on fiddles, flutes, and the tsimbl. Traditions change, though, and fiddles were mostly sidelined as the clarinet became klezmer's most prominent solo instrument. At the same time, accordions often took space previously filled by the rhythmic second violin (which had already been silenced by louder brass instruments).

Decades later, revivalists based their work on recordings and the memories of surviving players. These sources reached back only to the beginning of the twentieth century, and emphasized more recent trends from the 1930s–40s. Only slowly did research uncover the wealth of sheet music and other documentation for a wider range of unrecorded klezmer authenticity.

Klezmer Accordion?

Oddly enough, some klezmer revivalists questioned whether the accordion was part of klezmer's history at all. By comparison, while a few Irish preservationists had been suspicious of the instrument, it was (generally) accepted and celebrated after it had been played in Ireland for a hundred years. If nothing else, a history of complaints proved it had been present. In contrast, a century after the introduction of accordions, some klezmer revivalists retroactively questioned whether the instrument had earned its place in the music.

One 1999 book stated, "The inclusion of the accordion as a historical instrument of the East European klezmer tradition belongs to [a] 'newly fabricated tradition'; in fact it was first used in klezmer ensembles in the 1930s." Belying this, even the minimal selection of historical photos then available included klezmer accordionists playing in earlier groups. Music historian Joshua Horowitz rejected such talk: "The accordion has been present at every stage of klezmer music in both the Old and New Worlds for at least the last hundred years. History shows that there has never been a decisive break in the tradition of klezmer music or in the use of the accordion since its appearance on the scene."

This debate may seem puzzling, since accordions eventually became part of the iconography of modern klezmer, but players had to work for that recognition. Eventually, klezmer accordionists would become a major influence within the instrument's post-1960s struggle for respect in North America.

Revivalist Henry Sapoznik admitted that, as he recruited for the band Kapelye, he was uncomfortable with the out-of-fashion instrument, perhaps seeing no way it would help spread the music beyond its aging Yiddish audience. Reportedly, he only acquiesced to the accordion when he couldn't find a cello player: "No big fan of accordion music, I was initially unenthused at the prospect of adding it to the band. But [Lauren] Brody's pronounced musicality won me over to the instrument."

Klezmer Comes to America: The Recording Era

Second-generation Jews were among the immigrants who most rapidly abandoned their language and customs, and Jewish musicians were certainly impacted. For some, a significant part of their income still came from traditional weddings, but many broadened their skills to play other music. Most abandoned the term "klezmer." Living predominantly in urban areas, Jewish musicians would have a huge influence beyond klezmer via figures like George Gershwin and countless jazz and swing musicians. Larger klezmer orchestras eventually became the norm in the new land, but the earliest recordings were still mostly smaller groups, often including accordion.

Ten years before the earliest clarinet recordings, America's first klezmer accordion record was made by A. Greenberg for the United Hebrew Disk and Cylinder Record Company in 1906. Accordionists eventually produced more solo recordings than any klezmer instrument except the ascendant clarinet.

Among the earliest recorded Jewish accordionists were some who didn't play klezmer at all, and they played concertinas, not accordions. Several Russian Jews made their living in late 1800s playing concert music on the English concertina. Isaac Piroshnikoff and Grigori Matuse-witch entertained bourgeois drawing rooms before eventually crossing the sea and recording in America. Matusewitch led a colorful career, which began when he traded a bottle of vodka to a drunk Russian for his first concertina, and from those temperate beginnings eventually played for the Czar's family. Matusewitch's repertoire was mainly classical violin pieces, but in 1929 he recorded three Yiddish folk tunes he had included in his performances. Matusewitch played vaudeville, clubs, and radio up into the Depression, and performed in support of labor causes, including striking members of the International Ladies' Garment Workers' Union (ILGWU).

The first truly influential klezmer accordionist was Max Yankowitz, who recorded from 1913-37. All of his records were duos interweaving accordion with piano or a tsimblist credited simply as "Goldberg." Yankowitz only sparingly used the bass side of his limited nineteenth-century instrument—producing a notably mellower sound than later accordions. Paired with the relatively quiet tsimbl, his expressive and subtle playing remains haunting more than a century later. Several of Yankowitz's pieces have been included in recent reissues; they demonstrate a beautiful sound, almost like the clarinet that soon took hold in America.

Klezmer accordion reminds us that throughout the development of Yiddish music there were rich interactions with other ethnic groups. In the 1920s and '30s, the Greek accordionist Andónios "Papadzis" Amirá-lis represented several overlapping cultures from regions once part of the Ottoman Empire (Greece, the Balkans, southeastern Europe, Turkey). With his distinctive ornaments echoing the *krekhts* "crying" style associated with klezmer, Papadzis's recordings particularly show klezmer's relationship with Greece's urban rembetika folk music.

Another non-Jew was Mishka Tsiganoff (or "Ziganoff") who became known as "the Gypsy Accordionist." He was born in Odessa, Russia, before moving to New York; he was a Christian but spoke Yiddish and moved in klezmer circles. Tsiganoff recorded from 1919 to the Depression, which put an end to most ethnic recording. After that he continued using his "Gypsy" moniker on Philadelphia radio. Besides instrumental klezmer, Tiganoff backed up Yiddish singers like David Medoff. Tsiganoff and others, like the singing Pincus Sisters, also played accordions for Yiddish orchestral and theater shows.

Max Yankowitz, from a 1934 Hebrew Actors' Union souvenir booklet.
Courtesy of Henry Sapoznik.

Between immigration's cut-off in the 1920s and the effects of assimilation in the postwar era, klezmer's high-water mark in the U.S. coincided with the accordion's peak popularity. During this period, clarinetist Dave Tarras may have been the most famous figure in American klezmer. His early recordings with the Abe Ellstein Orchestra had Tarras trading solos with a talented but now sadly anonymous accordionist. By the 1940s Tarras added the instrument to his own projects and Sam Musiker's klezmer big band. In the 1950s Harry Harden was the accordionist with Tarras in Musiker's orchestra. After klezmer's mid-century retreat from popularity, longtime accordion accompanist Sammy Beckerman played with Tarras in his triumphal reunion concert in 1978.

Exactly how many accordionists were active in the klezmer scene of the 1920s, '30s, and '40s is difficult to say because of the lack of documentation of band members in orchestras and klezmer groups. Often only the leader is known (usually a clarinet or violin player). We do know there were dozens of accordionists with typical Jewish surnames on registries of musicians in cities like New York over the last one hundred years; many of them likely sprang from klezmer roots.

Klezmer Rejection and Rediscovery

The Jewish traditional music that became known as klezmer was generally excluded from America's folk revival of the 1940s–60s. That resurgence focused on English-language Appalachian and African American music, repurposed for (mostly) white, middle-class audiences. The young musicians and fans, however, included a remarkable number of more or less assimilated Jews.

By the 1950s, accordions were associated with mainstream pop and Lawrence Welk-style "Americanized" ethnic music. Most second- and third-generation children of immigrants who embraced the folk revival rejected accordions. This didn't change until the late 1970s, when young Jewish folk fans finally began to seek out traditional Jewish music. Despite widespread cultural neglect of the instrument by then, klezmer revivalists could not escape the accordion, and it became a distinctive part of most of their ensembles.

Klezmer Record Collectors

As much as they could, klezmer revivalists sought to learn from elder musicians who had played during the music's glory days in the 1930s–50s. But most klezmer students relied on recordings. Henry Sapoznik said, "Of every traditional music scene, whether it's Balkan or Greek or blues or early jazz, the only one that relied completely on using 78s as a style and repertoire model was the klezmer scene." A few young players on the East Coast were able to study with masters like Dave Tarras and accordionist Sam Beckerman, but out west, new klezmer musicians didn't learn from living players like Tarras; they sought out enthusiastic Yiddish-speaking record collector Martin Schwartz.

Without Schwartz's and others' compulsive collecting, the aural history of klezmer would simply have been lost. Along with discographers like Richard Spottswood, it was collectors and the musicians themselves who gathered and organized the echoes of a century of Yiddish culture. Records languished for years in the YIVO Institute for Jewish Research until Henry Sapoznik helped organize them and produced the first klezmer compilation in 1981. Since then, dozens of anthologies of historic Yiddish music have fueled modern klezmer.

The reissues that were so inspirational had their limitations. The original record company's commercial decisions meant that many things were never recorded (like the lack of a complete recording of a Jewish wedding). Of the thousands of records that survive, only a tiny fraction were then chosen for reissue during the revival, so the majority of Yiddish music remained unavailable to the public.

Collector Sherry Mayrent estimates there were about ten thousand Yiddish performances recorded (one per "side" of each 78-rpm record). Of these, fewer than five hundred have been reissued for modern listeners—four percent of the original recordings. And the historic record-ings don't favor the virtuosic instrumental music people think of as "klezmer" today.

Space constraints and personal taste led reissue producers to disregard the religious cantorial recordings, which far outnumbered other styles. The revival reissues reflect what amounts to the "hot jazz" portion of Yiddish immigrant culture, while leaving out the other genres that made up the majority of recordings. Only recently has attention begun to focus on the Yiddish theater repertoire and other untapped depths of Yiddish culture still trapped on archival recordings.

None of the producers who compiled the first reissues of old klezmer recordings were accordionists. Perhaps partially as a result, though the instrument may predate the better known clarinet on klezmer records, from a total of almost seventy existing accordion recordings, only about five accordion "sides" were reissued. One early reviewer of the first two klezmer reissue LPs objected to accordions being included at all, opining in 1987 that the accordion "was not a klezmer instrument." Decades later, a complete discography of early klezmer accordion is still lacking, much less a comprehensive anthology that adequately represents klezmer accordion through time.

With the coming of digital media however, many historical recordings are becoming available from organizations like the Judaica Sound Archives. Collectors like Mayrent are also partnering with academic institutions to make their collections of old recordings available en masse. Today's archivists are only held back by copyright laws that restrain historical recordings that probably belong in the public domain. When access is finally granted to what are basically abandoned works, listeners may have unprecedented, unfiltered entry into the world of Yiddish culture from the turn of the last century, including all the accordions on record.

Revival Accordion Players

Joshua Horowitz remembers, "The first accordionist of the early years of the 'klezmer revival' was ... Lauren Brody, leading a discipleless crusade at that time, armed only with a Bell piano model and an impressive background of experience in Bulgarian music." With very few primary recordings to go on, klezmer revival accordionists had to recreate a tradition that was unavailable for consultation. As a member of the early revival group Kapelye, Brody transferred her experience with Bulgarian music to reimagine the accordion's role within klezmer ensembles. Similarly, Lorin Sklamberg joined the New York–based Klezmatics after co-founder Frank London saw him playing accordion in a Balkan brass band.

Coming from yet another angle, Alan Bern of Brave Old World drew on his classical and jazz training. His goal was to seek out a klezmer accordion technique as it might have developed over the twentieth century if that progression had not been suppressed by the Holocaust: "I approached the accordion as a wind instrument that accidentally happens to have buttons and keys. In Yiddish and all other musics I play on the accordion, I listen to what wind instruments and the voice do and model my playing on them." All of these players were, intentionally or not, "reverse engineering" ways to play klezmer on accordion.

Klezmer Restored

By the early 1990s, klezmer's revival had largely succeeded. Yiddish culture, music, and language study was more popular than they had been in several previous lifetimes. It was, of course, impossible to restore the *klezmorim*'s role within once-vibrant communities in Poland and Russia. Assimilated children of immigrants in the United States were never able to apprentice themselves with klezmer musicians who were killed amongst millions in the Holocaust. But klezmer, and the movement that grew around it, proved that roots musics can survive even horrific histories and still connect people to a cultural past.

While enlivening their fading tradition, the revival did change the music that inspired it. Some revival bands took the sounds of village celebrations and created "art" music for concert halls. Other groups inspired rock audiences to dance without knowing historical steps. Every generation creates anew while losing nuances and details earlier artists took for granted. Valuable history can vanish for lack of someone asking an elder musician just the right question.

In addition to renewing and expanding the music, the klezmer restoration invested in institutions to ensure its survival. Research and language preservation at the YIVO Institute is bolstered by the rare recordings held at the Mayrent archive. These and other programs offer students the chance to contact elders, to document and encounter oral history, and continue to renew Yiddish language and music.

Among the remarkable products of the klezmer movement are gatherings like KlezKamp, KlezKanada, and Europe's Yiddish Summer Weimar. These camps bring students together with professional and amateur musicians to practice Yiddish culture. For thirty years, KlezKamp was held in New York's Catskill Mountains over winter break (when many Jewish kids had free time). It closed in 2014, but has had its own revival in the annual Yiddish New York gatherings and ongoing projects with the Mayrent Archive at the University of Wisconsin. KlezKanada, meanwhile, continues welcoming students and instructors to Quebec each summer, carrying on the work of communal cultural survival.

Growing awareness of the wider Yiddish theater and ballad culture also continues to expand. Berlin-based Daniel Kahn says the revival groups opened the way for singer-songwriter accordionists like himself by combining traditional forms with new compositions about contemporary issues. "It wasn't until the revival that you would have a band ... that had songs *and* klezmer music ... like what the Klezmatics do, or Brave Old World, bringing together the folk vocal tradition with klezmer dance music."

Twenty-first-century singer-songwriter accordionists like Kahn or Canada's Geoff Berner don't immediately fit the klezmer stereotype. Berner often plays solo accordion and sings what sound like satirical punk songs in English. But personal and political ballad singers were very significant in the Yiddish music that klezmer sprang from. Theater tunes and topical and novelty humor numbers sold more records than the dance pieces that came to be called klezmer. So Berner and Kahn's political ballads are at least as traditional as the klezmer image they don't always fit. This leads to a question: Why did it take forty years for young Jews to pick up accordions? For this, we have to look at the history of rock 'n' roll.

PART FOUR

AMERICAN

WHEEZE:

AN ALTERNATIVE

PRE-HISTORY OF

ROCK

MOST OF THE written story of North American popular music was crafted amidst the extreme anti-accordion stereotypes of the late twentieth century. The stage for this was set by preservationists as early as the late 1800s, who originally planted the idea that vernacular culture was worthy of attention. These early thinkers not only romanticized pre-industrial folk music, but also set it up in opposition to "degenerate" modern culture. Popular accordions were seen as more corrupted than other instruments—regardless of how long they'd been part of local traditions. Never mind whether they'd been purchased from the same mail-order catalogs as banjos or guitars. Misguided by what writer Benjamin Filene called a "cult of authenticity," folk enthusiasts ended up distorting the past while seeking to preserve it.

Later chroniclers inherited this rejection of the accordion. Despite these prejudices, accordions and other "impurities" connected and enriched the journey of white, black, and ethnic music that together fed into the great hybrid, rock 'n' roll. It is easy to find antique accordions that predate every country or blues record we now consider "roots" music. At various times over the last hundred years, the instrument has been played by African Americans, country musicians, and the various "folks" who inspired the folk revival. Let us follow them to their roots.

13

African Americans
Played Accordion before
They Played the Blues

WE THINK OF roots music as being the *deepest* roots. But African American blues, for instance, sprang from more recent origins than is commonly assumed. Blues music developed in various parts of the South around the turn of the last century and spread widely among African Americans in the decades before the Great Depression. But what came before the blues? No answer comes to mind, because the blues and gospel were among the earliest African American music to be widely recorded. Before that there is almost nothing to hear.

Of course free and enslaved African Americans made music for hundreds of years before they were recorded, and by the 1850s some of them had taken up accordions. Before the Civil War, musical training, instruments, and musicians were purchased by slave owners for their households. Some owners allowed enslaved musicians to play for other slaves as a means of pacification. Frederick Douglass wrote that dances, frolics, and holidays "were among the most effective means in the hands of slaveholders of keeping down the spirit of insurrection."

A hint of how slaves' desires conflicted with owners' is revealed by the fact that much of the documentation about black musicians comes from "escaped slave" notices that told of those seeking freedom. Rewards were offered that specifically mention people taking flight who read music and played or even built fiddles. The prices slaveholders were willing to pay for musicians is clear from the case of Solomon Northup, a free black musician, kidnapped from New York and forced into slavery in Louisiana. Northup wrote his famous memoir, *Twelve Years a Slave*, after regaining his freedom in 1853.

Emancipated slaves remembered a great number of blacks playing fiddle, banjo, and percussion, as well as handmade reed pipes called "quills." Robert Winans' remarkable tally from ex-slaves' narratives counted 205 fiddles, 106 banjos, and 30 quills. Only fifteen guitars were mentioned, and there were six accordions.

The African American accordion became more popular later—between 1880 and 1910—well after the antebellum era recalled by former slaves. There had always been African-inspired versions of fiddles, banjos, and other popular instruments. Accordions became the first major African American instrument with no handmade precedent. Expensive imported accordions were initially confined to upper-class parlors. Once they became more affordable, mass-produced, free-reed instruments blossomed.

Accordions were first widely encountered in America in the hands of blackface minstrels (see Chapter 3). These white musicians who pretended to be blacks may have ironically inspired slave owners to give the earliest accordions to enslaved musicians. At the same time, urban blacks were playing accordions in cities like New Orleans (see Chapter 6, "Jazzing the Accordion"), and began developing their own tradition. English-speaking African American accordionists emerged in the 1860s and were popular from emancipation until the advent of the blues in the early twentieth century.

In the years after the Civil War, many rural African American musicians performed for local social dances. Fiddles predominated, along with other instruments including banjos, guitars, and the late-coming accordions. The music these "string bands" played was similar to what we associate with square dances or old-time country or barn dances. Many early country musicians recalled blacks who played the style that was eventually called hillbilly music. Despite how widespread and influential this tradition was, very few black string bands recorded, and even fewer black accordionists.

The earliest African American accordionist to make an audio recording was Walter Rhodes, who released a single disc in 1927. Rhodes was mostly ignored by customers and pretty much everybody else until sixty years later, when researcher Jared Snyder called a famous folklorist and asked if there were other black accordionists besides Rhodes: "The answer I got was a definitive 'No.' Not a 'maybe,' not a 'there is more work to be done.' The finality of that answer just struck me as so wrong."

As Snyder went on to discover, Rhodes was not the only African American accordionist. The trouble was that by the time recording began, the instrument was fading. Most of the black accordionists who recorded were in their seventies or eighties, years after their playing was in demand. The few recordings we have of early African American accordion can all be listened to in a single afternoon. They only hint at a century of parties, dances, and church meetings where the instrument flourished. The last recordings of elderly black accordionists were made in Virginia in 1980. These brought an end to the tradition—as far as we know, the music was never passed on.

Why is this forgotten thread in American music significant? For one thing, blacks played accordions during one of the most dire periods in African American history. After the fleeting hope of Reconstruction, racism continued to corrupt much of the United States between 1890 and 1940, prolonging the torture of slavery until the middle of the twentieth century (and beyond). The African American accordion bloomed between 1880 and 1910, perhaps the harshest years suffered by African Americans after slavery. In the North and South, thousands of blacks were lynched by white mobs—one every three days between 1860 and 1890. The rise of the Ku Klux Klan and other white-supremacist groups compounded the era's Jim Crow segregation laws that denied African Americans basic human rights.

In this time of crisis, few took notice of black string bands and accordionists. Black and white scholars who later brought attention to African Americans' gospel and blues largely passed over these older styles, leaving us haunted by musical phantoms, sounds we can never recover. This is how cultural memory is extinguished.

Accordionists on the Cusp of the Blues

Lead Belly and His Windjammer

Huddie Ledbetter, known as "Lead Belly," was the greatest recorded example of the early African American accordion. He was also among the last. Born in 1889 in Caddo Parish, northwestern Louisiana, he grew up across the state line in northeast Texas. When he was seven years old, his uncle Terrell came back from nearby Mooringsport, and gave the boy his first instrument, a small diatonic accordion. Lead Belly's neighbors called them "windjammers" in the early 1900s and played them at local frolics or "sukey jump" dances.

Lead Belly remembered playing his accordion at dances in the majority-black region where he grew up—when there was "no white man for twenty miles." Old dances were still derived from the cotillions of the years of slavery. His recording "Laura" reflects the poetic dance-calling instructions that blacks developed for these kind of European country dances, "Take your partner, skip on down the line." The few brief accordion records he left behind would likely have been greatly expanded when musicians played dances lasting into the early hours of the morning. Even when Lead Belly (twice) recorded the ballad "John Hardy" on accordion, his relentless bass rhythm would have sustained dancers.

All of Lead Belly's accordion recordings have him performing solo, so we miss any ensemble elements that might have been common in his childhood. His foot keeps rhythm in his dance pieces, but instruments could have included everything from "patting" hand percussion (especially if there were no other instruments) to scraper sticks on the teeth of an animal's jawbone, as recalled in Lead Belly's "Corn Bread Rough": "Jawbone eat and Jawbone talk / Jawbone gonna eat you with a knife and fork." Earlier house dances might have had a pair of fiddles and perhaps a banjo. Accordions were attractive in these situations because they were loud enough to replace one or both fiddles. As Lead Belly grew up, guitars would take over for the banjo, and when blues came to dominate, guitars and pianos replaced almost all the old string-band instruments.

FACING Lead Belly. *Charles L. Todd and Robert Sonkin Migrant Worker Collection (AFC 1985/001), photographer unidentified, American Folklife Center, U.S. Library of Congress.*

It's worth noting that Lead Belly's rural English-language tradition was distinct from French-speaking Black Creole or Cajun accordion players to the south. Unfortunately, Lead Belly's English "frolic" dances faded with the onset of the twentieth century. Creole and Cajun accordion players managed to keep their unique French repertoire despite the changes in "American" music around them.

By the time Lead Belly was a teenager, he had moved to Dallas, where he backed blues legend Blind Lemon Jefferson. He played less and less accordion, and then bought a Mexican twelve-string guitar. For the rest of his career Lead Belly was known as a guitarist.

Years after he'd left his childhood "squashbox" behind, Lead Belly returned to it of his own accord. He may have been nostalgic for the songs of his youth, or perhaps he was inspired by the growing popularity of the accordion in the 1940s. His style had little to do with the Andrews Sisters' "Beer Barrel Polka," but we can't discard the idea that he was thinking about broadening his audience.

Unfortunately, few of his comrades in the early folk revival seem to have showed any curiosity about his accordion. Even Sis Cunningham, who played piano accordion in the Almanac Singers with Pete Seeger and Woody Guthrie, does not mention Lead Belly's windjammer in her biography. No one seems to have asked about this old-fashioned accordionist amongst the crowd of guitar and banjo players trying to popularize folk music.

Out of more than 150 Lead Belly recordings, we have five where he played his accordion. Twelve minutes total from late in his career are the only representation of the first music he ever played. One piece, "Sukey Jump," lasts barely a minute before it cuts off. We can only imagine if he had recorded without the time limitations of 78-rpm records and reproduced something like the hours-long dances of his childhood. As it is, these fragments take us back to the threshold of the last century, a grim time for African Americans, when entertainment was precious and their music was dramatically changing.

Walter Rhodes: Leaving Home Blues

Over the history of more than five thousand "race" records, the only commercial blues recording by an English-speaking African American accordionist was a single disc by Walter Rhodes in 1927, "The Crowing Rooster"/"Leaving Home Blues." Rhodes is significant because he was among the earliest Mississippi Delta blues singers (with any instrument) to record, but also one of the oldest. The recordings contrast his fading accordion technique with fine blues guitar accompaniment by Maylon and Richard Harney. (They were reportedly paired up to balance Rhodes's vocals and "old country racket" with the guitarists who lacked a singer.) Rhodes's accordion struggles through the two slow-blues numbers supported by the Harneys' more agile guitar. Rhodes's bass and melody hands repeated simple phrases that conflict with the harmony of the tune, and he plainly was unable to match the creative support the other instruments offered. Rhodes never recorded again and is said to have been killed years later when struck by lightning.

"Blind" Jesse Harris: Delta Accordion

Ten years after Rhodes recorded, John Lomax spent an afternoon in 1937 with an elderly Mississippi accordionist named "Blind" Jesse Harris. Without commercial studio constraints, Harris was able to play a wider variety of tunes than Rhodes, including blues, ballads, and dance tunes. The recordings are quite rough (with Harris's stomping foot often threatening to overwhelm the proceedings), but together he and Rhodes represent the only audible examples of the Mississippi accordion as it existed at the advent of the blues. Significantly, they each learned to play in the 1890s, near the birthplace of some of the most important later blues performers. The accordionists were, however, the last of their kind, because we know of no young black musicians who took up the instrument in their wake.

Accordions Failed the Blues

At the dawn of the twentieth century, the accordion failed black musicians. Blues innovations challenged the players of many instruments. Pianists, guitarists, and other chromatic instrumentalists mastered novel "blues" scales. Guitars and harmonicas added slurred or bent notes to imitate blues vocals. Early accordions could do none of these things. The positive attributes of African American squash-box accordions—cheapness, portability, and volume—were assets in the roadhouses or street corners where the blues got started, but these positives didn't outweigh early accordions' many negatives when faced with the blues.

The central problem with most early accordions was their limitation to playing certain scales. Accordions with a simple ten-button design suited many European folk musics, but playing most basic blues was a challenge. Players might fake a blues tune by leaving out notes that their accordion lacked, but complete melodies and blues chord progressions were often impossible.

The introduction in the early 1900s of Hawaii's endlessly expressive slide guitar added to the inadequacies that beset black accordionists. Harmonica players could alter notes to achieve blues scales and flavor, but a hundred years later, accordionists still lack this pitch-bending expressiveness.

The bass side of early accordions compounded their inadequacy. Whereas guitarists could play blues melodies while harmonizing bass/chordal accompaniment, accordionists were sometimes limited to as few as two bass buttons and often had to disregard harmony and use them only for atonal rhythm. More capable Stradella bass systems remained unavailable or unaffordable, and blues players discarded the instrument.

The disappearance of the African American accordion coincided with the rise of the piano in black gospel, blues, and jazz. As covered in our discussion of jazz accordion, pianos were available most everywhere: bars, brothels, hotels, clubs, and recording studios, they could even be rolled out onto street corners. The smallest accordion was a burden compared to a piano already installed at a musician's destination—though the on-site piano might well be out of tune.

In the stores and catalogs of the early twentieth century, button accordions cost around the same as guitars and fiddles. But when piano accordions with chromatic scales and full bass accompaniment became available, they were much more expensive than simple instruments like the old button boxes. Facing the cost of quality accordions, blues and jazz players were propelled toward the piano bench.

African American accordions (and black banjo and string bands) vanished in the first decades of the twentieth century. Without young protégés and with few other outlets, accordionists, banjo, and fiddle players became associated with rural backwardness and the stereotypes of minstrelsy. When black accordions didn't travel north in the Great Migration, the style lost any hope of reaching modern ears.

A number of famed jazz and blues musicians are known to have accompanied accordionists or played accordion themselves before switching to other instruments. Delta bluesman Big Joe Williams fondly remembered his grandfather Bert Logan playing fiddle and accordion at house dances. Williams moreover claimed his grandfather was one of the best musicians he'd ever heard.

Charlie Patton, who became tremendously influential in the blues revival, traveled and played with accordionist Homer Lewis in his younger days. Patton made about fifty recordings, half of which were blues. The remainder are an eclectic variety of music that co-existed with the development of the blues. He unfortunately never recorded with Lewis or other accordionists who might have excelled on this earlier material.

Almost nothing is known about a certain Joe Harper, who played accordion in Hazlehurst, Mississippi, in about 1900, supporting guitarist Ike Zinnerman. The only reason we know Harper's name is that Zinnerman became the guitar tutor for a young Robert Johnson. Johnson, of course, went on to make a series of recordings, died young, and was largely forgotten until he helped inspire the white 1960s blues guitar revival. Neither Zinnerman nor his accordionist Harper ("Accordion Joe?") ever recorded, and they slipped away quietly with no revival.

Significant blues players overlapped again with the old accordion tradition with another appearance of the tantalizingly obscure Homer Lewis. Besides playing with Charlie Patton, Lewis played accordion with Patton's apprentice, a young guitarist and harmonica player Chester Burnett who made a name for himself as Howlin' Wolf. After moving to Chicago, Wolf joined others in plugging in and electrifying the blues. Chief of his contemporaries was the guitarist/vocalist Muddy Waters (born McKinley A. Morganfield) who, as a child growing up in Issaquena County, Mississippi, played harmonica and an old broken accordion. By the time Waters was recorded on his front porch in 1941 by John Work and Alan Lomax, he'd long given up the instrument and he earned his fame through his guitar.

The list of blues musicians who had experiences with early accordion players is fragmented because so few were ever asked. Besides Muddy Waters and Lead Belly, famous bluesmen who played accordion in their childhoods included Big Joe Williams (who learned from his grandfather), and twelve-string guitarist Blind Willie McTell.

The connection of these pioneers of blues and folk music to accordions has been treated as a footnote at best. The *Encyclopedia of the*

Blues says, "Muddy Waters started on a beat up button accordion." That is almost all that's known of the Chicago bluesman's history with the instrument. Once artists picked up guitars, the accordion was dispensed with. Lead Belly was the only player who returned to the instrument with affection late in his life. After the coming of the blues, no young players we know of took up accordion, and the African American windjammer faded and died. When the blues scale became a mandatory part of African American music, the fateful lack of a few critical buttons cost the accordion its place in nearly a half-century of American music.

Sacred Black Accordion

African American accordions probably lasted longest in church. "It is thought unbecoming for a *chu'ch member* to play the violin, if not actually an audacious communication with Satan himself. But it involves neither deadly sin nor any spiritual risk whatever to play the accordeon or 'lap organ' as they call it," read an item in the *Boston Evening Transcript* in 1892.

African Americans had played accordions at secular dances since the late 1800s. At the same time, these "lap organs" were used for sacred music. Unlike the unsavory fiddles, stigma-free accordions were easily adopted for playing in church or respectable homes. Guitarist John Cannon, who married the sister of blues icon Charlie Patton in 1904, stopped playing all but accordion in support of his religion. John Jackson of Rappahannock, Virginia, "attested that his mother played only spirituals on the accordion, such pieces as 'Swing Low, Sweet Chariot' and 'I Shall Not Be Moved.'" Flora Moulton, from Louisa County, Virginia (who played accordion before switching to guitar) remembered her father, "a Baptist minister who felt comfortable playing spirituals on the accordion ... and apparently disapproved of his fellow accordionists in the area who mixed the spiritual with the secular."

Not everyone made such distinctions: Bert Logan, grandfather of blues singer Big Joe Williams, played fiddle tunes on accordion but also "[as] a church deacon, seems to have been among those performers who could reconcile singing spirituals and performing secular music." Similarly, Emily Jackson, the mother of South Carolina medicine-show harmonica player Peg Leg Sam, was remembered as a fine player of both sacred and secular music on organ and accordion.

Gospel music and the blues developed as close musical cousins. Gospel piano brought the same technical obstacles that button accordions faced with blues guitars. By the mid-1920s, accordions had been almost completely silenced in black churches. A very few survivors remained—unrecorded and largely unnoticed. In 1972, Sister Sadie B. Saddlers, who played in her church in Shaw, Mississippi, was photographed with her button accordion. She may have been the last survivor of the black accordion tradition in the state.

The instrument did live on as a sacred instrument in scattered areas. Years after the coming of gospel, a few audio recordings were made of sacred African American accordionists, some that harkened back to the nineteenth-century button box. The last known recordings of English-language, black, diatonic button accordionists were made by folklorist Kip Lornell in 1981. The Toms Family Singers in Piney River, Virginia, were a unison choir with a dozen members of different ages supported by patriarch Walter Toms Jr. playing an old two-row button accordion. His bass-driven rhythm and rough melody seems unassuming, until you realize it was the fading echo of button accordions that played for African American churches and dance floors since the 1880s.

The black button accordion fell into obscurity, but piano accordionists still occasionally turned up playing African American sacred music. The instrument was especially suited for open-air street preaching, and that's where folklorists encountered several great performers. Blind Connie Williams (born 1915) was a lively street singer who played guitar and piano accordion and was recorded in Philadelphia in 1961. Originally from Florida, in the 1930s he played with famed blues and gospel guitarist Reverend Gary Davis in New York. Thirty years later, Williams's repertoire included blues and sacred songs on guitar, but only spiritual numbers on accordion. He claimed the police harassed him less if he sang religious songs, and he preferred the accordion because it was less work to play loud. As a child he learned music at the Florida School for the Deaf and Blind (Ray Charles's alma mater), but no one seems to have asked Williams if he played the older button box as well as the newer piano accordion. Besides his one soulful recording session, little is known about him—even when or where he died.

Representing a slightly younger generation, Clarence Clay and William Scott sang on the streets of Philadelphia in the 1950s and '60s. Clay played piano accordion and harmonized gospel songs with Scott. Born in the 1920s, the duo had been playing on the streets of Philadelphia for a decade when they recorded their 1963 album *The Blues of Clarence Clay & William Scott: The New Gospel Keys* for folk researcher Pete Welding's Testament record label. Clay's weaving, almost droning accordion combines with the duo's raw counterpoint to create a stirring resonance one can only hope was appreciated on Philadelphia street corners. Along with Blind Connie Williams, Clay and Scott's gritty glory fulfilled the promise of the accordion as an instrument that took music to the people while lifting the spirits.

Father Augustine John Tolton: On a Sacred Path

Stepping back from the gospel tradition, accordionist John Tolton (1854–97) was the first recognized black Catholic priest in America. He was born in Missouri into an enslaved family. When Tolton was eight, he and his family escaped their Catholic slaveholders and fled to Illinois. His father died fighting for the Union army.

After he applied to and was rejected by U.S. seminaries, Tolton studied for the priesthood in Rome and was ordained in 1886. He wanted to serve in Africa but was ordered to return to the U.S. He became known for his sermons, his singing, and for the accordion that a fellow seminarian had taught him to play. As a lone black priest, he faced prejudice and isolation and would often read or play hymns on his accordion long into the night. Working tirelessly to increase his flock, he died in a Chicago heat wave at age forty-three. Tolton has been proposed for canonization for his role challenging discrimination. Assuming success, he will also be the first sainted accordionist from the United States.

Integrated Accordion in the South

Thanks to the work of Jared Snyder and a few others, we have an outline of the African American accordion, but information about rural white players in the South remains scarce. What is known is that accordions were part of the old-time fiddle dances where musicians of different races played together on occasion. The very few recordings we have of European American button box players seem closely related to the African American style.

Was there an unexplored Southern white old-time accordion tradition? Were button box players like Malissa Vandiver Monroe, mother of bluegrass founder Bill Monroe, part of a wider Southern accordion style? There were (to my knowledge) no commercial recordings of Southern white button accordion players. The instrument may have been rare or it may not have fit the stereotypes of "hillbilly" music that record scouts wanted. Several elderly white accordionists were, however, recorded by folklorists over a span of decades, indicating the tradition may have persisted in out of the way places.

Emit Valentine was a white accordionist from Centerville, North Carolina (born 1891). He had given up playing for years, but his daughter gave him an accordion in 1971 and he recorded an hour's worth of old-time and religious tunes that seem closely related to African American accordionists' from the region. Similarly, Reed Eddie and John Davis were a mixed-race accordion duo who recorded religious music in Buckingham County, Virginia, as late as 1986. These old men brought together remarkable strands of musical history that remain almost entirely overlooked.

The Silencing of the Black Accordion

Record companies began profiting from the work of black artists in the 1920s, but accordions were not part of the sales strategy. Producers focused on African American gospel, jazz, and blues players, turning away old-time string bands, black fiddlers, banjo players, and the occasional accordionist. As Elijah Wald has said, "In a less race-conscious world, black fiddlers and white blues singers might have been regarded as forming a single Southern continuum."

To make things worse, non-commercial field recordings also neglected black accordionists. Folkloric "song-catchers" too often assumed accordions were recent interlopers and, ironically, they sought out more modern blues stylings instead. Thinking they were plumbing the roots of African American culture, they bypassed an instrument that had been played by Southern blacks since the time of slavery.

Race Records' Erasure

The recording industry sold millions of blues, jazz, and gospel records to what they called the "race" market during the pre-Depression 1920s. "Race records" were named to appeal to the pride of black people striving for a better future. Being a "race" man or woman in the early twentieth century implied that you were part of the struggle against the insults of racism. The new commercial record companies didn't necessarily care about that. They were interested in black dollars.

In those same early recording years, ethnic record labels were capturing the attention of niche markets in Irish, Polish, Yiddish, Italian, and other communities. Some produced artists who ascended to become stars. But during the rise of the accordion in mainstream music, almost no black examples were recorded, and there were certainly no well-known black accordion stars.

The coming of the recording industry drastically changed music in the southern United States. Prior to the 1920s especially, black bands might play for white audiences, and white songs were popular with black musicians. Integration of players or even audiences was not unknown. Musical influences flowed back and forth across (still very significant) racial barriers. Basically, black and white players would both play whatever music was fashionable: Tin Pan Alley, minstrel tunes, folk songs, and dance numbers. Smart musicians prepared for any request, whether for ballads that were one hundred years old or new songs based on recent disasters and events.

Beginning in the 1920s, record companies' sales branches decided they wanted boundaries. In effect, record stores invented genres in order to funnel customers toward the music they were most likely to buy. Companies divided Southern music based on race. Blacks would purchase "race" records, while white customers were directed to "hillbilly music." Despite the fact that "hillbilly" music was made by both races, African American fiddlers, banjo players, and accordionists were marketed out of history. In the words of recent commentator Eric Brightwell, "black hillbilly musicians ... quickly learned some other tunes if they hoped to cut music for anyone besides field recorders and ethnomusicologists." This market-driven purge of non-blues instruments from black music drove the African American accordion into obscurity.

Folklorists and the Black Accordion

Folk historians might have acknowledged black accordionists who had been locked out by record companies. It never happened. Initially, in fact, many nationalist folklorists didn't appreciate African American music at all. This slowly changed as progressive values spread. By the 1960s, researchers were tracking down older musicians based on commercial records from the 1920s and '30s, but they often missed traditions that weren't captured on 78s.

Mentions of accordions and accordionists were repeatedly over-looked by writers and researchers. Bill Greensmith, in his excellent biography of blues guitarist Henry Townsend, mentioned that Townsend's father had played accordion in Missouri in the early 1900s: "He could do a lick or two on guitar, but he played an accordion. He played blues something like Clifton Chenier... But back then that word wasn't used, blues. I never heard that word used. They called them reels back then." This was a glimpse into the music that predated the blues, but follow-up questions didn't follow. Did Townsend's father play button accordion? Were there other accordionists around? What was the difference between "reels" and the blues? After Townsend died in 2006, there was no one left to ask.

Blues artists were seldom asked about the music they heard when they were young. Muddy Waters might have told what kind of accordion he had as a child or who he remembered playing them. Howlin' Wolf might have recalled Homer Lewis and how the accordion sounded behind Charlie Patton's guitar. In separate interviews, blues men Big Joe Williams, K.C. Douglas, Jim Brewer, and Eli Owen (all born between 1900 and 1921) mentioned older relatives who played accordions and in many cases taught them their first music.

These black accordionists faded in the early twentieth century but the death of the tradition was not inevitable. Between the initial decline and the very last known players, sixty years of possible interviews and recordings were missed. Surviving black accordionists could have played at 1960s folk festivals, but they remained undiscovered.

Windjammer Century

Black accordionists and the string bands they were part of exist largely as inaudible ghosts today: dances played by slaves for their owners' entertainment; marches of black soldiers through the Civil War; square dance calls by freed blacks during the shifting racial ground of Reconstruction; and struggling generations of black musicians trying to accommodate the challenge of the blues amidst the terror of Jim Crow.

In 1981, in the small community of Massies Mill, in Nelson County, Virginia, folklorist Kip Lornell visited with three accordionists. Frank and John Tolliver and Hiawatha Giles were probably the last English-speaking, African American accordionists ever recorded. For younger family members, their music must have seemed a world apart—three old men with their funny songs and accordions—but the elders carried the echoes of a century. The black accordion had begun its slow fade back when the blues arose, but it survived in rural pockets through the coming of jazz, R&B, rock, and soul. But after the men played and joked that afternoon in Virginia, when no young person picked up the old instruments, the African American accordion tradition was silenced.

14

Country and Western: Cowboys and Squeezeboxes

C OUNTRY MUSIC SPRANG from a mix of multi-ethnic folk songs and fiddling, black blues and banjo, Hawaiian guitar, vaudeville and minstrel yodeling, and a dash of ethnic polkas and waltzes. Together they turned out perhaps the richest musical miscegenation in American cultural history. Claims that innovation goes against country tradition defy the music's origins.

The golden age of country music began a few decades into the twentieth century and overlapped with the apex of the accordion. Between the 1930s and 1950s, squeezeboxes were common on country radio, especially in the "western" half of country and western. At least one rhinestone accordion resides in the Country Music Hall of Fame. Even hardcore honky-tonkers and conservative bluegrass players have a few squeezeboxes in their closets. The accordion can't claim to be a central instrument in country, but for years it filled the musical roles of a portable keyboard and a chordal instrument while taking the occasional hot solo.

The Accordion's Place in Country

Almost everything I know about country music I learned while researching accordions. It turned out to be a reasonable introduction to the genre. Far from being out of the ordinary, the squeezebox was a regular part of country and western throughout its expanding years in the 1920s–50s.

It remains unclear how common accordions were among Southerners before recordings began. Fiddles reigned supreme but "windjammers" were fairly widespread among Southern blacks by the 1880s. Other instruments like the guitar, mandolin, and store-bought banjos joined the folk music of the region—why not accordions?

Pressure may have come from outside. Academics searching for "pure" Anglo-Saxon ballads in the South regularly lamented the presence of Tin Pan Alley and vaudeville songs among rural musicians. Some complained about non-traditional instruments like banjos and guitars. It's easy to imagine even a family heirloom squeezebox being regarded as out of place. The few mentions of early white Southern button accordionists offer little background about who the musicians were, where the instruments came from, or how they were played.

Once country recording started in the 1920s, a growing number of piano accordionists appeared. We have evidence of more than 150 accordionists playing various country styles. By the 1960s, though, the country music industry was consolidating in Nashville. There, modern producers like Owen Bradley and Paul Cohen excised accordions from the "sound" they were crafting, and country accordion found itself without a home.

The accordion was not banished alone. Entire "country" regions were forgotten. Chicago and the industrializing Piedmont South had been major contributors to early country. Westerners from Texas to California produced tremendously influential music. The rest of rural America, Canada, and even Mexico all had early input into the genre that was celebrated by Nashville. Listening with an ear for the accordion draws listeners to these other centers that didn't always fit the simple Southeastern "hillbilly" story.

Old-Time Accordion

Despite stereotypes about its supposed remote rural roots, country music as we know it would not have come about if musicians in the American South had been isolated from the rest of the world. The region's early music grew from a rich patchwork of English, Scottish, European, and African American traditions. After the Civil War, railroads further breached the isolation of the rapidly industrializing South by bringing touring musicians and store-bought sheet music and instruments within reach of most Southerners.

The earliest accordions arrived with minstrel performers and expensive imports. Once mail-order catalogs and general stores stocked them, accordions became available to any adventurous musician. They were not however the only new sounds. Based on African instruments, modernized versions of the banjo became the most famous symbol of the minstrel shows. If they hadn't been there earlier, they were soon heard throughout the South. Country players who performed in blackface as young men included Bob Wills, Jimmie Rodgers, and Roy Acuff—they all would have seen minstrel banjos and may have had contact with accordionists there.

Guitars were a more recent import for many Southern communities. They were primarily spread by the new mail-order catalogs and then joined country's core instrumentation of fiddle, banjo, and guitar in the early twentieth century. The Southern squeezebox had a fraction of the impact of these other instruments, but references to accordions hint at their early use.

In Clay County, Tennessee, longtime resident Marvena Lynch remembered two accordionists, Helen Wells and A.T. Arms, playing in the late 1800s and early 1900s. They may have been part of a Southern accordion style that was never explored or documented. Individual players would likely have taken up the instrument after the 1860s and learned to play from printed tutors or by adapting it to existing music. Others may have had direct connection with immigrant communities developing their own traditions.

Several country stars remembered family members who played accordions. Grandpa Jones of the *Grand Ole Opry* (and TV's *Hee Haw*) was born in 1915 and recalled his mother playing concertina. Western swing bandleader Adolph Hofner's mother also played concertina, and bluegrass pioneer Bill Monroe's mom played accordion.

Besides these ancestors of famous figures, very few early Southern white accordionists are known. In rural Virginia, local banjo player Sam Connor (born 1910) learned his repertoire from his father, an accordionist who played in the early 1900s. On the Outer Banks of North

Carolina, seventy-year-old accordionist Charles K. "Tink" Tillet was recorded in 1940 playing old-time ballads and tunes like "Somebody's Waiting for Me." Decades later in 1971, Emit Valentine (born 1891) was recorded playing country and gospel songs in Centerville, North Carolina, by folklorist Tom Carter.

To my knowledge, no examples of Southern whites playing early button accordions were professionally recorded. Curiously, though, Columbia Records' first catalog aimed at rural whites in 1924 was entitled *Familiar Tunes on Fiddle, Guitar, Banjo, Harmonica, and Accordion.* An advertisement that appeared in *Talking Machine World* magazine promoted it to audiences looking for "rustic talent . . . known where the square dance has not been supplanted by the foxtrot."

Community dance music would likely have been the home for any unrecorded "rustic" Southern accordions, and a few early country artists remembered playing squeezeboxes before they took up other instruments. Jimmie Tarlton was a blues singer and influential early slide guitarist from South Carolina. (He learned slide directly from touring Hawaiian artist Frank Ferera.) As a youngster, Tarlton also played harmonica and accordion. His story includes the rare detail that he played a "small" accordion, presumably an early diatonic button box. In a pattern similar to African American blues artists, when Tarlton blazed a trail for country slide guitar with his 1927 hits "Birmingham Jail/Columbus Stockade Blues," he had long since laid down the squeezebox.

Earliest Country Accordion Records

The country music industry was born from a competition between radio and recording. Initially, radio stations and record companies both targeted concentrated urban audiences. This began to change in the 1920s, as record companies reached out to more isolated ethnic, country, and blues audiences. They targeted the rural South because there was far less access to electricity to power radios there. The prevalence of hand-cranked Victrolas turned early country and blues into Southern music.

The first country accordionists now qualify as "shrouded in mystery," though they were probably pretty ordinary at the time. A mysterious Raney Van Vink played accordion on what might be the earliest country accordion records in 1927. A cabinetmaker named Homer Christopher played guitar on these recordings. It may have been Van Vink's influence that led the guitarist to pick up the accordion himself. In the 1940s, Christopher moved to North Carolina to play accordion with the Crazy Buckle Busters and to join Unit 2 of the Briarhoppers, a group in so much demand that they cloned themselves to cover all their engagements. Most of what we know about Christopher is from a single letter he wrote summarizing his musical career before he died in 1977.

Among the other early country accordionists was the German-born Fran Trappe, who played expressively behind the great Bowman Sisters. There was also a certain Fred Shriver, who backed up the fiddler Blind Joe Mangrum on the *Grand Ole Opry* and on two fine square dance numbers for Victor Records in 1928. We don't know much about Shriver, but he was certainly a more skillful player of traditional tunes than some of the era's "hillbilly" musicians. His enthusiastic chording sounds as if he'd played accordion for dancers, rather than just being a pianist who picked up the squeezebox on the side.

☞ How "Country" Was the Accordion?

THE ACCORDION BECAME COMMON, but was not central to country music. On the other hand, country music wasn't entirely central to a lot of country accordionists. Their work with western bands or hillbilly acts was usually just one stop in careers that might have included other types of musical employment. Pee Wee King was a country and western bandleader who played accordion, not a distinctly country and western accordion player.

Many country accordionists were immigrants or the children of immigrants and took to country music as a national phenomenon and a potential paycheck. Thanks to the piano accordion's network of teachers and classes, these well-trained musicians with roots in ethnic communities suddenly found themselves uniquely positioned to take their accordion to the country.

Surprisingly hot sales of Southern hillbilly recordings quickly inspired Northern copycat artists. These included a young Charles Magnante, who before introducing classical accordion to Carnegie Hall, appeared as "Charlie Briggs" in Fred Hall's Mountaineers, a "city-billy" band in New York. They were a studio crew in the 1930s that operated under various names and styles for radio and records. When asked once what kind of mountaineers they were, their response was, "Phony!" and added, "When they put escalators on mountains, we may decide to spend the summer up there."

Country Radio

Country music listeners really discovered accordions over the airwaves. From the mid-1930s until the early 1950s, accordions became a predictable part of country and especially western cowboy-style acts. Both of country's biggest radio programs, Chicago's WLS *National Barn Dance* and Nashville's *Grand Ole Opry*, had house bands with accordionists. At the same time, Hollywood's singing cowboys introduced accordions into their modern revisions of the Old West. In a nod toward range-roving practicality, movie props sometimes included more portable concertinas, but the soundtrack invariably featured full-size accordions.

Beginning in the 1920s, scores of accordionists played country music professionally. None of these artists are well known today, but judging by photographs taken before 1960, ten to twenty percent of country bands seem to have included squeezeboxes. Narrowed to "western" bands between 1935 and 1955, the numbers were significantly higher.

Instrumentally, fiddles and strings were the basis of the country sound, but though not every group had one, accordions became nearly as common as the mandolin or even the banjo, both of which fell from fashion before bluegrass lifted them up in the 1940s. Accordions were certainly less exotic than Bob Wills's use of horns and saxophones in his western swing band, or Spade Cooley's truly eccentric concert harp.

Accordionists provided chordal sweetening or cheaply filled in for a sax or string section. Like modern electronic keyboards, they rounded out the sound between singers, rhythm, and melody players. Some accordionists stuck with their backing role without pushing the instrument beyond the basics. Others were top-flight soloists who traded off with the best musicians on the air.

The WLS *National Barn Dance*: Country Music in Chicago

The first major country radio show was broadcast from Chicago, an unlikely center for what we think of as Southern culture. In fact, Northern farm families had more radios in the 1930s. The Windy City's radio stations reached rural communities across the Midwest and beyond.

It's well known that Southern blacks fled north in the Great Migration. The urban and rural areas of the northern Midwest were also the destination for many whites who combined their songs, instruments, and styles with Northern regional and immigrant music to create what amounted to a "hillbilly" parallel to Chicago jazz and blues.

Chicago's WLS radio, owned by Sears-Roebuck, the "World's Largest Store," broadcast at fifty thousand watts AM, and on a clear night could be heard from the Atlantic Ocean to the Rocky Mountains. At first Sears sponsored the entire station to promote sales over the wide swath of listeners. Their mail-order catalogs reached almost everywhere in rural America, selling both needs and niceties—including a selection of accordions, guitars, and banjos. One of the station's most engaging announcers, "Judge" George Hay, created the WLS *National Barn Dance,* a rural-oriented show that set the mold for much of country music to come. When Hay jumped ship in 1925, he moved to Nashville and premiered his longest-running endeavor, the *Grand Ole Opry*.

The original *Barn Dance* was a variety show with comedy, music, and songs that acknowledged migrants' longing for home and family. It included Southern string bands and frequently incorporated accordion accompaniment along with other band instruments not usually associated with country music. The *Barn Dance* offered a more eclectic sound than Southern relatives like the *Opry* would. Patsy Montana and her Prairie Ramblers might be featured alongside "Soprano Helen Morris doing songs from *Faust*," followed by the Hoosier Hot Shots, a slide-whistling Midwestern precursor to Spike Jones's comedic City Slickers.

Decades after it went off the air, the WLS *Barn Dance* has now faded from "legendary" to "historically important," but during its run from 1924-60 it was a major contributor to country music's spread from the South to national popularity. Musically it represented an irreplaceable strand in country's early story: along with Southern hillbilly musicians, the hybrid Northern groups on the *Barn Dance* combined western cowboys and swing bands and laid the foundation for American country and western tradition.

Grand Ole (Accordion) Opry

When the *National Barn Dance* closed down in 1960, it was the longest-running country show on radio and one of the longest-running radio shows in the world. Its main competition was Nashville's *Grand Ole Opry*. The *Barn Dance*'s announcer, "Judge" George Hay, had taken the old-time country formula from WLS to the new powerhouse station WSM in Nashville. There he began a national institution with an ongoing mythology flexible enough to adapt to the changes from hillbilly to western swing to modern country. A significant portion of the *Opry*'s audience had migrated out of the South, but the show remained rooted in the region. Even as the *Opry* incorporated influences from popular and immigrant music, it presented the combination as part of an old-time Southern tradition.

In the late 1920s, the early *Opry* featured the skillful accordionist Fred Shriver with fiddler Blind Joe Mangrum, but it wasn't until the '30s that the accordion became a mainstay. As the *Opry* rose to prominence it featured two major accordion acts, Jack Shook's Missouri Mountaineers and Pee Wee King's Golden West Cowboys. The Mountaineers are almost totally forgotten, but Pee Wee still echoes in modern music. Together they kept the accordion on nearly every episode of the *Opry* during the latter half of the 1930s, and Pee Wee's band continued there until the mid-1940s.

The widespread uptake of the accordion included acts we seldom associate with the instrument. Roy Acuff, Bill Monroe, and Hank Williams were all backed by accordionists at one time or another: Jimmy Riddle and Sonny Day played with Acuff's Smoky Mountain Boys; Sally Ann Forrester was one of Bill Monroe's original Blue Grass Boys; and Cois "Pee Wee" Moultrie and Vic Willis both played and recorded with Hank Williams Sr.

As accordions entered American music they became commonplace backup instruments on the *Opry*, but few flashy or innovative instrumentalists appeared to make the instrument "stick" in country. The sound of country accordion remains mostly a nostalgic flavor rather than an unforgettable favorite. Nevertheless, backing the era's greatest artists, accordionists held their own on country radio.

Accordionists on the *National Barn Dance*

Louise Massey and the Westerners, ca. 1934. L to R: Milt Mabie, Larry Wellington, Louise Massey Mabie, Curt Massey, and Allen Massey. (Milt Mabie presumably changed his chaps a few years later when the traditional Southwestern Native swastika was tarnished by Nazism forever.) *Historical Society of Southeastern New Mexico.*

Larry Wellington with Louise Massey and the Westerners

The family band known as Louise Massey and the Westerners were stars on the *National Barn Dance* when it dominated country radio in the 1930s and '40s. They were also one of the first country bands who had real experience with western ranching, having grown up with horses, cowboy hats, and such in New Mexico. Despite their origins, musically they leaned more toward sophisticated and cosmopolitan variety than down-home hillbilly. After stints in Chicago they took their act to New York City, where they were in effect the first pop-country band, easing the way for future artists to play both big towns.

With acts like the Westerners, the *National Barn Dance* was the first big country venue that encouraged a stylized cowpoke image. The Masseys took their trend-setting western-wear to an ostentatious extreme. Louise was known as the "original rhinestone cowgirl" and claimed all her boots were satin. The Masseys performed in spotless white suits— even while sitting on hay bales—or in fanciful western outfits created by a French designer.

Accordionist Larry Wellington, who was the band's only non-family member, joined after the founder of the act, "Dad" Massey, retired. Wellington had been a music teacher and led a harmonica band before he joined the Masseys; his accordion helped sustain their success on radio and records over the Great Depression (while most acts were struggling). They were lucky enough to premiere on the *Barn Dance* the week it went national on the NBC network, and eventually garnered 200,000 fan letters a month. Wellington's technical ability matched the band's "uptown-hillbilly" music, which included horns and clarinet with ears open to jazz. At the same time, the group demonstrated their genuine Southwestern origins by singing in both Spanish and English for songs like their hit "My Adobe Hacienda," which went beyond typical Hollywood screenwriters' whitewash.

The Masseys' music ranged from light-hearted Southwestern tunes like "Out on the Loco Range" (1934) to jazz-flavored pastiches like "Sweet Mama Tree Top Tall," with vocals suggesting a hep minstrel show. Wellington traded breakneck solos on tunes like "Buckaroo Stomp" and added jazzy backing to the playful "Bunkhouse Jamboree." His "Squeeze Box Polka" was a light-hearted and precise pop fancy that matched the band's western-swinging nursery rhyme "Pop Goes the Weasel." Their eclectic catalog brought country music to a wider audience than ever before. In the late 1940s while they were still riding high, Louise chose to retire to her New Mexico hacienda.

Wellington hung around in Chicago, where in 1947 he played accordion with the remarkably named Funk Serenaders, who promoted seed corn for Iowa's Funk Brothers Seed Company. The Serenaders backed a historical show called *The Great Corn Story*, which dramatized industry-friendly and occasionally racist stories about crops and the conquest of the west. Wellington continued performing and composing for radio and film and ended up doing music and acting in a string of 1960s B-movies, including 1964's exploitation landmark *Two Thousand Maniacs!* He died in 1973 leaving behind a remarkable journey through twentieth-century pop culture.

Art Wenzel, from *Barn Dance* to Sunshine State

With exceptions like bandleader Pee Wee King, most professional country and western accordionists worked mostly as backing musicians. One such story is that of Art Wenzel. Born in 1907, he did radio in Milwaukee and Chicago before moving to California, where he recorded and broadcast with his own group and others. He's known to have played on dozens of records by country artists.

A rare 1936 front-page story in Chicago's WLS radio's *Stand By* program guide gave *Barn Dance* fans an uncommon look at the young accordionist: Wenzel's mother started him on piano lessons, and after picking up banjo and saxophone he landed his first professional dance-band job at fourteen. He later worked in insurance and then ran a music store teaching piano and did radio in Milwaukee. He picked up a friend's accordion at a Halloween party and had his first gig on the instrument only two months later. It started as a laugh, but more bands wanted accordionists than piano or sax players, so he stuck with it. On a sad note, his wife of six years died, leaving him with a two-year-old son who Wenzel's mother and sister helped raise.

His luck turned toward the *Barn Dance* when he drove a female singer (with a chaperone) to Chicago for her WLS audition. He planned to pick up accordions for his music store, but the agents asked if he played. They liked him and within a week he had moved to Chicago and was on the air at the *Barn Dance* with Otto and the Novelodeons. They were a novelty band that wore suits rather than hillbilly outfits, and played the kind of slapstick music that requires great skill and gets little appreciation. They were successful enough that he was able to buy a $1,000 accordion—which seems unimaginable, as it might cost more than $10,000 today.

He continued on WLS until the lure of musical cowboys drew him to Hollywood, where he appeared in more than a dozen western movies. In 1942 he played with Johnny Bond and His Red River Valley Boys (with Spade Cooley on fiddle) on a cover of the anti-Nazi propaganda hit

"Der Fuehrer's Face." By 1944 he was on the radio in Pasadena with his own band, Art Wenzel and His Ragtime Cowboys. He played with a stack of different stations, bands, and artists including the Texas Rangers, the Saddle Pals, the Colorado Hillbillies, the Rhythm Rangers, and the Pals of the Golden West. He recorded with Tin Ear Tanner, Merle Travis, Tex Ritter, and the "Yodeling Blond Bombshell" Carolina Cotton (who sang with all the great western accordionists). His nimble arpeggios spiced up a style of swinging country pop that audiences loved.

With his own band, there were a couple of recordings. A single 78-rpm disc, mislabeled "Art Wengel's Ragtime Cowboys," paired a cheerful "Yodeling Polka" and a light orchestral "Just Lonesome for You," with smooth vocals by Colleen Summers (a.k.a. Mary Ford, prior to her work with guitarist Les Paul). Despite their name, neither track was terribly ragtime or cowboy.

Wenzel's career traced the rise of country radio and the singing-cowboy movies that drew musicians of all types to create some of the most popular music of the day. Most of the players came and went with even less of a trace then Wenzel, but few people leave a career's worth of recordings and film bits to reflect on, so the ragtime cowboy did all right.

The Kentuckians at a road show, 1936. *Courtesy of James Buchanan (thanks, Steve Perry).*

The Klein Brothers, Sunshine Sue, and More

An extraordinary number of female artists were involved with the *National Barn Dance*. Patsy Montana and the comedian Lulu Belle are perhaps best remembered, but scores of women performed on the show over the years. When the Depression's mass unemployment devastated home life, female radio artists were welcomed like sisters, mothers, aunts, and caring spouses. This may have helped reassure listeners, but didn't cover up the fact that more women were supporting families on their own. Behind the scenes at the *Barn Dance*, dozens of young performers carried on as might be expected, and marriages and births amongst the cast and musicians were regularly noted in promotions for the show.

Amongst the more remarkable performers at the *National Barn Dance* were the "trick yodeling" DeZurik sisters Carolyn and Mary Jane (with sisters Eva and Lorraine as needed). Their act involved duet harmonizing of sung bird-calls, chicken-cackles, and nonsense sounds. Some of their performances featured talented accordionist brothers Augie and Ray Klein, who eventually married sisters Mary Jane and Eva. Ray Klein started on fiddle as a kid, but stole chances at his brother Augie's accordion and eventually played the hand-me-down onto the airwaves as a staff accordionist in the *Barn Dance*'s Sage Riders. He sometimes doubled with his brother for sophisticated but crowd-pleasing updates on old-time numbers like "Camptown Races."

Augie Klein played with the WLS Rangers and recorded with Rex Griffin, Red Foley, and others all around Chicago. After serving in World War II, he traded tasteful riffs with Chet Atkins on a series of records. Klein also played with the Dinning Sisters, country music's answer to the harmonious Andrews siblings. The Dinnings were stars on WLS, but their biggest squeezebox moment was probably their 1948 hit "Buttons and Bows," which sold millions and featured duded-up jazz accordionist Art Van Damme.

Mary Arlene Workman, who became known as "Sunshine Sue," played accordion (and ukulele, guitar, and piano) on WLS and then became the only female host and general producer of a major country show at the *Old Dominion Barn Dance* on Richmond's WRVA. The governor of Virginia dubbed her "Queen of the Hillbillies" and had a reserved seat for the show each night. Sue and the *Old Dominion* crew made it all the way to Broadway for a short 24-night run of *Hayride: A Hillbilly, Folk*

Musical in 1954. The playbill mixed the mythology of folklore with exoticism: "The true hillbilly musician is an untrained entertainer, usually both an instrumentalist and a vocalist ... It is rare indeed if he has any formal knowledge of music ... he is, in every sense a 'primitive.'" No word on what cast members Lester Flatt and Earl Scruggs (and Sonny Day, who played accordion with Roy Acuff) thought about being called primitive entertainers with no knowledge of music.

At least two other female accordionists toured with the *National Barn Dance* roadshow in the mid-1930s. Lillie Buchanan and Rena (possibly Rena Staas) played accordion duets for the multi-ethnic rural communities of Wisconsin and northern Illinois. Known as the Kentuckians, most of the performers were from Illinois, and the repertoire came from the rural Midwest country/pop/ethnic mix that made the *Barn Dance* so popular. The road show was separate from the starring radio roster, and when not performing, the less-than-celebrated players went door-to-door selling *Prairie Farmer* and WLS *Barn Dance* magazine subscriptions.

Lee Morgan and the Midwesterners Close the *Barn Dance*

For the final two years of the WLS *Barn Dance*, and the very last broadcast in 1960, bassist Lee Morgan's group the Midwesterners featured "Dusty Sands" on accordion. "Dusty" turned out to be jazz virtuoso Leon Sash, moonlighting with his wife's western outfit. Without mentioning the connection, an edition of *Billboard* magazine featured both the Midwesterners' country-polka album and Sash's bebop jazz *Hi Fi Holiday for Accordion*. When the *Barn Dance* closed its doors after thirty-six years on the air, Morgan sang Patsy Montana's "I Want to Be a Cowboy's Sweetheart" and the show went silent. "Dusty Sands" retired, and from then on it was straight jazz for Leon Sash.

Chad Berry's book and film *The Hayloft Gang* chronicles the history and artists of the *Barn Dance* and the fact that their influence and even existence are largely overlooked today. Chicago shifted from a hub of Midwestern farm culture to an urban region of its own, and more and more the western migration of Southerners led them to California, beyond the range of the WLS signal. After the 1940s, Nashville consolidated its position as the music industry's country headquarters, and today the *Grand Ole Opry* is the last survivor from early country radio.

Grand Ole Opry Accordionists

The Missouri Mountaineers' Bobby Castleman, Elbert McEwen

One of the widely heard but little remembered country bands of the *Grand Ole Opry*'s classic early era was the Missouri Mountaineers. At a time when country music was developing its foundation, guitar player Jack Shook led his boys with first Elbert McEwen and then Bobby Castleman on accordion. According to *Opry* historian Byron Fay, they were among the most popular bands on the show for years.

Shook's Mountaineers formed just as country music was recovering from the failure of the recording industry in the Depression. Radio shows like the *Opry* promoted acts that made most of their money on tour, while the new jukeboxes—which even the poor could afford—built profit back into the record industry. Unfortunately, Shook's Mountaineers never toured or recorded professionally. In between big Saturday *Opry* shows, the band held day jobs at the *Opry*'s WSM radio station, so the Mountaineers didn't need extra income from promotional recordings. They also avoided the grueling midweek tours other *Opry* stars did to supplement their $5 Saturday-night *Opry* stipends. The Mountaineers simply played the weekly show, were great favorites with *Opry* audiences, and faded away when their appearances ended in 1939.

The Mountaineers created some hot tunes in their day, but can only be heard on about fifteen minutes of low-quality test records made by a radio technician in the 1930s. Through the scratchy, distorted sound we can hear expert fiddler Mac McGar standing out in a set of frenetic dance numbers: "Fire on the Mountain," "Up Jumped Trouble," and "Pritchett's Hornpipe," any of which would have spiced up the *Opry* between vocal numbers or sponsors' plugs. The recordings include one religious tune, "Open Up Them Pearly Gates," with western-style harmonizing in the manner of the Sons of the Pioneers. (The ten raucous dance tunes that surround the spiritual might lead one to question the band's commitment to the moral life.) Throughout, the accordionists follow the rhythm, nothing fancy to distract from the fiery fiddle that's the obvious centerpiece. It would take a bandleader named Pee Wee to take the accordion to the front of the stage.

Pee Wee King and His Golden West Cowboys

"King of Western Swing" Bob Wills once asked, "Pee Wee, how in the hell can a Polish boy from Wisconsin play the accordion, write 'The Tennessee Waltz,' be a star on the *Grand Ole Opry*, and lead the country's most popular western swing band? It just doesn't add up."

If you're a country or rock music fan and appreciate a bit of electric guitar or drums, you can thank artists like Polish American accordion player Pee Wee King. Born Julius Frank Anthony Kuczynski, Pee Wee got his moniker in the early 1930s while fronting a Milwaukee band called the King's Jesters with three other guys named Frank—and he was the shortest. "Pee Wee" became the most well-known country accordionist as modern country music rose around him.

As a youngster, Pee Wee was surrounded by Wisconsin polka bands that mixed ethnic traditional flavors with pop music. He got a break when Gene Autry hired him for his touring group in 1934. King adapted to the country and western trend and when Autry left for Hollywood, Pee Wee renamed the band the Golden West Cowboys—even though none of the players had been west of the Mississippi.

They straddled the lines between hillbilly, western, and jazz with ties to the polka belt thrown in. It was not uncommon then for American groups from New York through the Midwest and down into Texas to mix accordions, polkas, and cowboy hats. Pee Wee's group acted as a bridge from what was still dismissed as "hillbilly" to more fashionable pop music. Similar to the Massey family a decade earlier, he opened doors for later country artists who might otherwise never have broken into the pop charts.

Pee Wee wasn't a stylistic radical, but he was willing to try new things to see what worked. The results of this kind of practical experiments survive in the music we hear every day. The Golden West Cowboys were not the first band to have an electric guitar or drums or fancy western outfits on the *Grand Ole Opry* (Bob Wills literally snuck a drummer on stage one night in 1944). But Pee Wee's band stuck around and helped make these things acceptable in country music over the ten years they spent on the show.

The band played a steady mix of country tunes, swing, polkas, and comedy. In the 1940s they added cowboy-boogie numbers that edged toward rockabilly. Their 1947 "Ten Gallon Boogie" may be the earliest rock 'n' roll accordion. Pee Wee himself never claimed to be a virtuosic player, but he happily allowed his skilled musicians to overshadow him. A series of electric guitar players like Roy Jewell Ayres and Robert Koefer were among those who drove the group toward the future of music.

Pee Wee's band could swing when they wanted to, but playing for seated (non-dancing) audiences in theaters, live radio, and later TV, their style was often more eclectic than "hot." His populist formula led Pee Wee to write one of the bestselling country songs of all time, "The Tennessee Waltz." It was to a tune the band had been calling the "No Name Waltz," and legend has it the lyrics were written on the back of a matchbook on the way to a show. The group's "Tennessee Polka" was a hit as well, but only the waltz became a state song.

Pee Wee became the twenty-third member of the Country Music Hall of Fame, representing the era when waltzes, polkas, cowboy songs, electric guitars, drums, accordions, and rhinestone cowboy suits became part of the music. When Bob Wills asked how "a Polish boy from Wisconsin" got there, the savvy Pee Wee's response was, "Bob, all you got to do is please the people and sell records."

Helen Carter of the Carter Family

The original Carter Family—Sara, Maybelle, and A.P. Carter—produced some of the most influential recordings in American history. Maybelle's young daughters began their own careers as part of the family, via super-powered Mexican border radio in 1939 when Helen (the oldest sister) was only twelve. Stations like XERA and XERF flouted U.S. regulation by broadcasting at up to a million watts of power, at a time when local stateside stations were limited to a few thousand watts. Border radio reached almost all of North America; when conditions were right, the young Carter Sisters' first regular gig was heard quite literally around the world.

When the original Carter Family split after Sara divorced A.P. (remarkable at the time), country guitar pioneer Maybelle renewed the act around her daughters. Middle child June Carter provided comic relief and grew into the darling Johnny Cash begged to marry. Anita Carter, the youngest, was the best singer and later had top-ten hits with Canadian country star Hank Snow. Of the three sisters, Helen was the best overall musician. She created arrangements, sang the trickiest harmonies (but seldom lead), and played at least five instruments—including accordion.

The girls' father, Eck Carter, had pushed his daughters' musical training, exposing them to classical music at home in Poor Valley, Virginia.

Maybelle and the Carter Sisters (June, Helen, and Anita); with the Virginia Boys, Doc Addington and Carl McConnell. *Courtesy of Ronald Carl McConnell.*

He also chose instruments for them, assigning Anita a bass she had to stand on a chair to play, and saddling Helen with the unfamiliar accordion. She complained, "This thing is just totally backwards to the piano," until the Carters shared a date in Louisville with Pee Wee King, who offered, "Hey, did you know you got that on upside down?"

A young guitarist named Chet Atkins joined the act and added virtuosic jazz elements. Even hymns like "I Am a Pilgrim" gained a modern shine with McGuire Sisters–style harmonies over Atkins's loping but intricate guitar. The act was a hit, and when Helen was twenty-three, in 1950, the Carter Sisters and Atkins finally landed on the *Grand Ole Opry*. Atkins later became central in creating the pop-oriented "Nashville sound," but he always credited the Carters for his start.

During the 1950s, the sisters opened shows for a young Elvis Presley as he began to get wider attention. He asked Anita to marry him; already married, she said no. As the sisters started families of their own, Becky Bowman was called in to play accordion when Helen had a baby. Bowman then stayed with the group for four years, spelling whichever sister needed a break.

Maybelle and Sara of the original Carter family died in the late 1970s. Helen lived until 1998, carrying on her mother's vision of the musical heritage her family came to stand for. When Helen died, the only negative story anybody shared was from Chet Atkins, who recalled that touring with the Carter Sisters he'd often be relegated to roadie: "Helen, don't you carry that ... Chester, get that accordion!"

Bluegrass: Roots as Artifice

Bluegrass is often thought of as one of the most custom-bound branches of country music. Over the years, some fans have gone so far as to emphatically bar instruments like accordions from performing at their events. This antipathy to innovation is curious, because bluegrass itself was a purposeful break with tradition. The irony is compounded because Bill Monroe's original bluegrass band had an accordionist, Sally Ann Forrester, who played on their first and most popular recordings.

Bluegrass was a modernist 1940s revision of country music. Its contemporaries included bebop jazz, electric jump-blues, and even early rockabilly. It is interesting that bluegrass is often assumed to come from an earlier century than the others. The music Monroe and his followers made has been invested with an aura of ill-defined authenticity. If we examine the formative stages of the style in the 1940s, it's hard not to see different ways it might have been, and how it might develop in the future. The next time someone says a good accordionist can't play in a bluegrass band, it's tempting to ask when exactly the rules of bluegrass were set in stone.

Unusual Bluegrass Instruments: Mandolin, Banjo, Accordion

Bluegrass founder Bill Monroe's famous mandolin may have been more modern than the accordion in his native Kentucky. Southern European immigrants had introduced mandolin orchestras at the turn of the century. Critic Mark Humphrey noted, "[The mandolin's] connection to Monroe's Scots and Dutch roots is nonexistent. And by the time he was playing mandolin, circa 1922, its antiquity in his culture was approximately that of the synthesizer in rural Kentucky today." The solo mandolin had taken hold in Southern string bands by the 1930s, but it was partially thanks to Monroe himself that the instrument didn't fade from the tradition.

Monroe tried several instrumental combinations while crafting what became known as bluegrass. Besides his mandolin, banjos were at the time somewhat unusual. Over the 1920s and '30s, banjos had lost ground in country music and Monroe himself did not add one to his band until 1942. The "bluegrass" banjo was thus only a year or two old when multi-instrumentalist Sally Ann Forrester started playing accordion with Monroe in about 1944. At the time, her instrument was a reasonable experiment. Some of the most popular country acts were using it. Even conservative artists like Roy Acuff tapped harmonica player Jimmy Riddle and then Francis "Sonny" Day to play accordion in the early 1940s.

Monroe's bluegrass formula emerged while he was trying to see what would sell. It turned out that the most popular record of his career was "Kentucky Waltz" (1945), recorded with Forrester's accordion before his "classic" bluegrass sound solidified.

There's no indication that country players like Forrester based their style on earlier Southern accordionists. The reissue of the first Blue Grass Boys recordings does mention that "purists who have asked Monroe about the unholy presence of a reed instrument ... have been solemnly told that Forrester's accordion reminded him of that played by his mother," Malissa Vandiver Monroe, who was a fine fiddler, and played harmonica and button accordion.

After the 1950s, bluegrass developed into more of a subcultural social movement than a commercial project. Festivals, newsletters, and independent record labels replaced the hope for jukebox hits. Emphasizing the recreation of a set style and a manufactured aura of history, the bluegrass community succeeded admirably in sustaining a modern form using folk preservation methods. Even so, Monroe's own career included recordings with electric organ and other "unorthodox" instruments. These make experiments less of an aberration, and hardline objections less defensible.

(The) Bluegrass Accordionist

Sally Ann Forrester: Bluegrass Accordion Ground Zero

Sally Ann Forrester was the first woman in bluegrass and the first accordionist in bluegrass. More than that, she was one of the first musicians in bluegrass. She has only recently begun to be acknowledged for these pioneering roles. Forrester played professionally for more than ten years, better than average among country players at the time, and yet critics often haven't known what to do with her or her instrument. It wasn't until the 1970s that women equaled her prominence in bluegrass bands, and another decade passed before musician/researchers like Murphy Henry began championing Forrester as a pioneer. Henry's book *Pretty Good for a Girl: Women in Bluegrass* (2013) details the lives and carriers of dozens of bluegrass women from the 1940s to the twenty-first century. They all trace their roots back to Forrester and her accordion.

Born Goldie Sue Wilene Russell on December 20, 1922, she was named after her grandfather William, who had wanted a boy. (Wilene was always called Billie until she got her stage name, "Sally Ann," from Bill Monroe, possibly because he didn't want two "Bills" in the band.) Her grandparents raised Wilene in Oklahoma after tuberculosis killed her mother, her aunt, and, before that, five of her grandmother's brothers and sisters. Wilene's grandfather played fiddle and would take her to see Bob Wills thirty miles away in Tulsa. The youngster had to promise not to let on that her grandfather danced with other women. "I kept my mouth shut because I wanted to go to those dances!" she recalled.

Growing up, Wilene played fiddle, guitar, piano, and sang, and eventually used all these professionally. Her music career started on local radio, where she met her future husband, fiddle player Howdy Forrester. They joined the *Grand Ole Opry*'s traveling "tent show," which toured the South during the summer seasons, and there met Bill Monroe. Starting in 1943 she performed with Monroe for more than three years.

Life on the road was rough. They sometimes traveled three thousand miles a week while returning to Nashville every Saturday night to play the *Opry*. Besides performing, Sally Ann (now using her stage name) handled ticket money and the door without being paid for the extra work. Her son Bob Forrester related that since Monroe didn't read music, she also transcribed his lead sheets in order to copyright his songs. In the show she sang the high-tenor parts. Years later, some male singers had difficulty accepting that women could sing the "men's" parts Forrester had premiered.

When the first Blue Grass Boys records were cut, Forrester had only been playing accordion for a year. It may have been Monroe who asked her to pick up the instrument, or she might have suggested it as a way to expand her role in the band beyond just singing. Murphy Henry's research shows, "It is almost certain that the accordion was added to the show because Monroe thought it would sell." Roy Acuff and other popular country artists had added accordion, and in Hank Williams's words, "For drawing power in the South, it was Roy Acuff and then God!" If Monroe wanted to succeed, Acuff was a good model.

On Monroe's original 1945 Columbia recordings, Forrester doesn't sound like an expert on the squeezebox. She mostly fills out the sound with backing chords and takes a few solos, including one on a version of Monroe's biggest hit, "Kentucky Waltz." The accordion she played seems to have had a fairly "wet" tremolo tuning that was typical for the time, but may have been unsuitable for the intricate interplay of blue-grass music. It would have been interesting to hear her on a cleanly tuned instrument.

Forrester's husband, Howdy, missed playing fiddle on the first Blue Grass Boys recordings because he'd enlisted in World War II, but he rejoined the group when he got out. By the time Columbia released the records a year later, Sally Ann and Howdy had quit. Tired from years of touring, she, her husband, and his brother Joe (who'd joined on bass), all left the Boys in the spring of 1946. She was twenty-three and pregnant.

They kept performing, mostly in less road-intensive jobs in Tulsa and then Dallas, where her grandmother helped raise their baby. In about 1948 she filmed a series of short musical clips that showed at theaters between movies. Soloing on her accordion, by then she stood out as probably the most interesting musician in the standard country show band. Later, these films were made available as some of the earliest TV programs.

For a while her husband was a letter carrier for the post office before going back to fiddle for Roy Acuff for what turned out to be several decades. Sally Ann—once again called "Billie"—retired from show biz in the 1950s and held a job with Social Security for the next thirty years. She took on the role of "unofficial *Opry* retirement analyst" for Nash-ville's musicians. The family kept doing music at home, and she played accordion with Acuff a few times, including a USO tour to Alaska in 1954. By the time she began to receive recognition for her work, Billie had Alzheimer's and lived in a nursing home near her son. She passed away in 1999.

As for Bill Monroe, he likely never made an aesthetic decision to "get rid of the accordion"—he simply didn't seek out a replacement when

Sally Ann and her husband left. Forrester's role in the formation of bluegrass reveals how experimentation and creativity (and at least one accordion) were at the heart of this very modern music.

Western Squeeze: Accordions Head West

When Judge Hay disapproved of accordions at the *Grand Ole Opry*, Pee Wee King responded, "Well, it's a western instrument, and we play country and western music." There was a real division between "country" and "western" then. Country was a politically correct (i.e., less insulting and more likely to attract customers) way to refer to what had been known as "hillbilly" music, rooted in the rural Southeast. Western, meanwhile, included western swing dance music and cowboy songs associated with radio and Hollywood. Dozens of these western musicians and devotees far from the west somehow fit squeezeboxes in their saddlebags.

Old Western Accordions?

America's cowboy myth of independence and adventure (with a side of violence and casual racism) was spread by cheap magazines beginning in the mid-1800s. Cowboys in the Old West certainly would pass time with music on occasion, but the twentieth-century country and western sound, with electric steel guitars and such, is modern.

The west rolled into musical culture spread by hit songs and sheet music. Cowpoke acts like the Massey Family reinforced the image on records and radio. Finally, yodeling stars like Gene Autry and Roy Rogers became national icons in the 1930s and '40s. They and others appeared in thousands of cowboy movies and sold hundreds of millions of dollars of merchandise. (Autry made more selling capguns than movie tickets.)

Historically, compact harmonicas—and possibly their relatives the accordion and concertina—would have entered the west when railroads expanded during the latter half of the 1800s, but there's little documentation of cowboy accordionists on the actual range.

Modern Media and the Singing Cowboy

Singing cowgirls (and boys) came into their own as radio audiences har-kened to a past that seemed to predate newfangled things like radios. Western stars were featured heavily on Chicago's *National Barn Dance*, where Patsy Montana, the Massey Family, and Gene Autry held forth. Meanwhile on the *Grand Ole Opry*, western regalia remained a curios-ity until acts like Pee Wee King and His Golden West Cowboys helped replace "hillbilly" music with "country and western" in the 1940s.

Meanwhile back in the Southwest, territory bands grew larger and louder to fill halls with thousands of dancers. "Western swing" com-bined swing arrangements with string band fiddle tunes to create cowboy jazz unlike anything ever played around a chuckwagon campfire. Some eastern hillbilly acts headed west to be in pictures, but western musicians had geography in their favor; and many of the cowboy movies relied on a roster of local California players.

Singing-cowboy movies were made on the cheap, and a lot of the music was disposable. Far fewer sagebrush, cowboy, and cattle-drive tunes became hits than country's more memorable standards about heartbreak and such. This may have been because songwriters and audi-ences had more first-hand experience with romance than ranching, or because western-themed songs were seen as "filler" in cowboy films, but had to earn their keep to stay on the radio.

Throughout the western music boom, accordions showed up nearly everywhere. The tough-guy morality tale *High Noon* won four Oscars in 1953, including Best Soundtrack, after composer Dimitri Tiom-kin called in classical innovator Anthony Galla-Rini for the accordion bits. Serious films like this were pretty far from the standard yodeling cowboy, but as long as the western music fad lasted, accordions were part of it.

The longest-lasting cowboy accordionist of the era was probably Jimmy Dean, who carried western style into the 1960s. Rising from a childhood in poverty, he played accordion with his Texas Wildcats on radio and TV in the 1950s. His international hit "Big Bad John," and subsequent televised *Jimmy Dean Show*, helped bring country music per-formers into the mainstream in the 1960s. By then Dean was wearing suits rather than cowboy hats, and laughed himself silly doing come-die duets with Rowlf the Dog in some of the earliest TV exposure for

Jim Henson's Muppets. In a final career shift, Dean partnered with his brother in a meat-packing company. Shockingly, he's more famous today for his sausage than his squeezebox.

Cow-Pop Goes Accordion

Back in the 1940s it had been the wild west in Hollywood's recording studios. Western-themed radio and films needed pop music for their heroes, so accordionists in western duds headed out onto the range. Foy Willing's Riders of the Purple Sage were a typical cowboy band that combined close harmony singing in the style of the Sons of the Pioneers, with accordion, clarinet, upright bass, and rhythm guitar.

Buck Page, who founded an entirely different Sons of the Purple Sage group, said, "Most of the cowboy bands until we came along were fiddles, guitars and banjos. But it sounded kind of empty behind the vocals, so there was a good accordion player in town and I got him into the group. It really filled up the sound."

California musicians didn't have to know how to ride to become cowboys. Eddie Carver was an exceptional accordionist who played with the Red Rowe's Ridge Riders. He also played in the San Fernando Playboys with session-guitar icon Bob Bain. In 1949, the Playboys cut remarkable jazz versions of old-time tunes like "Aunt Dinah's Quilting Party" at guitarist Les Paul's home studio. Carver was slick and swinging as they turned "Happy Roving Cowboy" into a polished technical workout. When the western fad faded in the 1950s, Carver went on to play piano and studio accordion with Dean Martin. He is said to have died in 1959 at age thirty-five.

Amidst many male cowboy musicians, female accordionists also appeared. Eleanor Clements held her own in Doc Schneider's Texans, broadcasting from WFBC in Greenville, South Carolina. Cleo Hoyt played accordion in the 1940s with Texas groups Bill Boyd and his Cowboy Ramblers and with Richard Bills and his Radio Texans. "Calico" Ted Graves played her piano and accordion with Red Woodward's Red Hawks in Fort Worth, Texas, joined by another woman on pedal steel in at least one photo. LaVida Dallugge Brickner was known as "Sally Montana" when she played with the Montana Cowgirls. They also went by the Rangerettes, Cactus Cuties, and the Lariettes.

L to R: Charles "Ezra Ford" Hetherington, Zeke Manners, Ted "Pappy" Below, and Elton Britt moseyed all the way over to London, England, in 1934. *Courtesy of Kevin Coffey.*

Lacking the cachet of blues or Appalachian folk players, most cowboy musicians didn't enjoy a revival in later years. The work of these talented instrumentalists remains tucked away on radio-show and movie soundtracks or never-reissued recordings. Of all the accordion genres in America, western musicians may have suffered the most from lack of research and attention.

Western Country Accordionists

Zeke Manners and the Original Beverley Hillbillies

Among the earliest country accordion acts were the original Beverly Hillbillies. They were a gimmick band started in 1930 as a radio publicity stunt with accordionist "Zeke Manners" (Leo Ezekiel Mannes). The Hillbillies claimed to be an Appalachian family living in an isolated "holler" near Malibu Beach. Audiences were so convinced that when one of the Hillbillies lamented that their (fictional) log cabin had burned down, the radio station's parking lot filled up with lumber and supplies to rebuild. The group carried on the act through radio, recordings, and personal appearances before breaking up a few years later. By that time Manners's "hillbilly" squeezebox had set a precedent that influenced the accordion's prominence in western music for years to come.

During the 1940s, Manners headed out east and built a career playing rural characters for newly urbanized radio audiences. Calling himself "the Jewish cowboy," he played daily on at least three New York stations. The Andrews Sisters made his song "The Pennsylvania Polka" a hit in 1942. (Frankie Yankovic's version appears repeatedly in the 1993 film *Groundhog Day*.) In the 1960s, Manners sued a certain TV show over the group's name, a reminder that the days of old-time country accordion should not be forgotten.

Al Dexter: Country-Accordion's Hitmaker

A series of chart-toppers by Texan Al Dexter helped further stake the accordion's claim in country. His sensational "Pistol Packin' Mama" took airwaves and jukeboxes by storm in 1943. As writer Tony Russell put it, "Wartime America heard one shot of 'Pistol' and surrendered to it." The song's title was a turn on Jimmie Rodgers's 1930 gangster yodel, "Pistol Packin' Papa," and became the first number one on Billboard's folk music chart. (It was only after postwar McCarthyism dictated that "folk" was communistic that "country" was drafted to replace the disparaging "hillbilly music.")

Contrary to modern expectations, Dexter's song was driven to its great success by the jaunty instrumentation of Paul Sells's accordion and Holly Hollinger's trumpet. "Pistol Packin'" was also aided by the Musicians' Union recording ban. The strike prevented major labels from releasing quick covers of regional and niche records like Dexter's. For the first time, some original artists were able to profit off their creations. This boosted independent labels and smaller genres like country and R&B. Dexter's tune was eventually covered by stars like Bing Crosby, and it became the signature song of R&B accordionist Julie Gardner on her wartime USO tours.

Dexter's other hits during the war years included "Guitar Polka" and "I'm Losing My Mind over You." Paul Sells played accordion on many of these and then joined Foy Willing's Riders of the Purple Sage. "Pistol," though, remains the phenomena that, for a spell, made the accordion one of the most audible instruments in country.

"Smiley" Burnette: Sidekick Star

The highest-profile cowboy accordionist was a movie sidekick who outshone the stars. Lester Alvin "Smiley" Burnette was billed as "Frog Millhouse" for his singing voice, and starred in western TV, radio, and more than a hundred movies. His career began back when "hillbilly" music still centered on the *National Barn Dance* in Chicago. Gene Autry became the show's biggest cowboy star, and was looking for an accordion player. He hired "Smiley" to premiere on Christmas Eve 1933, reportedly after an interview that went like this:

A: "This is Gene Autry."
B: "Sure, and I'm General Grant!"...
A: "I can pay you $35 and all your expenses. You think it over and let me know."
B [without a pause]: "I've thunk it over. You've done hired yourself an accordion player."

"Smiley" had never been west of Illinois before he and Autry took their cowpoke act to Hollywood a year later. There he co-starred in more than fifty of Gene Autry's westerns. The accordion was just one of dozens instruments Burnette played on the trail, sometimes several at a time. These included ones he invented himself, such as the "jassass-a-phone," a contraption that looked like a chest of drawers with trumpet horns that rode on the back of a mule. Despite his versatility, Burnette wasn't the greatest accordionist. As "Ranger Doug" (Douglas B. Green) of Riders in the Sky noted, "It's amazing how much better Autry's records got after he got a pro accordion player."

"Smiley" wrote hundreds of songs which he would sell to the film studios by singing them over the phone. His most famous was probably "Mama Don't Allow No Music Playin' 'Round Here," adapted from an earlier song with racier lyrics. He and Autry premiered it in their first picture, *In Old Santa Fe* (1934), and it quickly entered the folk tradition.

When TV arrived in the 1950s, cheap cowboy films dried up. Burnette continued on radio and in thousands of personal appearances where he sold novelty publications like his DIY instruction guide, *My Friend the Coat Hanger.* His last role was as a railroad engineer Charlie Pratt on TV's *Petticoat Junction* and *Green Acres.* He died at age fifty-five in 1967 from leukemia.

Burnette was billed as a supporting actor, but often brought in more fans than the lead. He took a job as an accordionist and rode it pretty far without needing to be the greatest: "I never wanted to be an actor and to this day I don't consider myself one. I just played this one role, I never knew how to play anything else."

"Bud" Sievert: Western Pop and "Hillbilly Bebop"

The New Riders of the Purple Sage were a hip 1970s Bay Area country rock band. They sought out the roots of old-time and country sounds—which for them included electric and steel guitars from the 1930s and '40s. (The Grateful Dead's Jerry Garcia taught himself pedal steel playing with them.) Country rockers like Gram Parsons, the New Riders, and the Dead didn't however revive western accordion. This was not for lack of inspired examples. Some of the best accordionists in popular music had played for jazz-influenced western bands in the 1940s and '50s.

The "old" Riders of the Purple Sage, for instance, had a damn good accordion player. Burton "Bud" Sievert was the cool western accordionist who played in Foy Willing's 1948 version of the Riders. On sweet tunes or hot numbers, his polished sound jumped out of old-time radios. Going off on a tear, he was light and smooth but up front and audible.

Western musicians like Sievert could be ridiculously busy. The Riders of the Purple Sage played on hundreds of radio shows and records and appeared with Roy Rogers and others in dozens of movies. The *All Star Western Theater* radio show featured Sievert and the Riders acting out radio dramas and filling in with musical interludes. "Smiley" Burnette joined an episode in 1947, where he foiled a bank robbery as a "Cowboy Dentist" with a song imitating the grinding sound of a drill.

In 1948, Willing snuck Sievert and the Riders over the border into Tijuana, Mexico, to get around the Musicians' Union's recording ban. They cut sixty songs in two days for use in radio broadcasts. On the way back, Customs asked if they had anything of value to declare, so Willing estimated the tapes were worth about $7, by weight. He and the band then added dialogue and assembled the smuggled songs into complete shows for radio stations to broadcast as if they were being performed live.

Musically, the Riders did everything from hot intros to slow ballads. They also added rich instrumental backing behind commercials: "Webers's Bread Is Good Bread" was one plain-spoken sponsor's slogan. The Riders' close harmony vocals lifted up whatever they touched, whether it was old-time numbers or recent western knock-offs. They'd also let loose with small-group jazz, moving from atmospheric Hawaiian guitar to hip swing fiddle added by Johnny Paul (John Paul Gerardi). A remarkable breadth of music grew around their cowboy shtick.

After leaving the Riders, Sievert played with Hank Penny's intensely eclectic band. Penny played everything from western swing to rockabilly in what's been called "big band swing on a hillbilly budget." Frank Buckley, Billy Liebert, Kelland Clark, and the masterful Stan Ellison traded the squeezebox chair behind Penny's sometimes humorous, often musically adventurous songs. His "Hillbilly Bebop" with Billy Liebert is a western swing classic. Other titles of note include the swinging "Penny Blows His Top," with Bob Caudana on squeezebox, and the early 1950s instrumental, "Progressive Country Music for a Hollywood Flapper."

After 1950 or so, the bottom dropped out of the cowboy market and most of these artists went on to other things. Some continued in the industry, but for many the fantasy of Hollywood's west ran dry. Back in the 1940s though, before the trail ran out, cowboy vocal groups had their parallel in the dance hall music of western swing.

Western Swing: Nostalgia for the Future (in a Ten Gallon Hat)

Cowboy pop overlapped with the age of dance bands in the 1920s–40s. It was natural that the two styles bore musical fruit. As the Depression lurched toward World War II, country and western dance bands sprang up along the route of economic refugees from Texas and Oklahoma into California. They featured singers with cowboy hats fronting what amounted to jazz bands that played hot fiddle music. The sound was designed for enormous dance halls that sometimes fit thousands of people, and they kept an ear open for record sales in the booming new jukebox market.

Many western swing groups touched on cowboy nostalgia, but others dressed in modern suits like any other combo of the day. They relied on strings with a country feel, but were also the first musicians to use electric guitars. The bands were a contradictory mix that produced wildly innovative music that later fed directly into rock 'n' roll. Emerging just before the high-water mark of the accordion age in America, it's no surprise that many western bands had a squeezebox chair.

Bob Wills is the most famous exemplar of western swing. I found only one photo of Wills's 1930s band that included an accordion (and horns) along with his standard fiddles and guitars. Beyond Wills, though, accordions were musically central to many of the most important western bands.

Out in California, Wills's closest competition may have been the bands led by Spade Cooley and Tex Williams, both had top accordionists. Musicians frequently jumped from group to group but certain bands and players stand out clearly as key examples of the accordion in the swingingest branch of country music.

Western Swinging Accordion?

In photo after photo and documented in discographies, recordings, and record company session rosters, dozens of western bands included accordionists. Fiddlers and the newly invented electric guitars commanded the most respect, but the squeezebox was far from unusual and eclipsed things like traditional country banjos entirely. When Spade Cooley used a full-size concert harp, *that* was unusual.

Western music was enriched by contact with the immigrant musicians who fed the accordion's golden age. The so-called polka belt (see Chapter 5) reached from Midwestern cities like Cleveland and Chicago across the Prairies down into Oklahoma and Texas. Players like Swedish-born accordionist Joe Strand climbed aboard the singing cowboy bandwagon, where they ended up backing Hollywood groups with names like the Texas Rangers. As Elijah Wald put it, "[Accordions] can be heard on two-thirds of the hillbilly records that reached the top of the *Billboard* folk chart in the mid-1940s... the accordion provided a bridge to a broader audience: not the pop mainstream but listeners who had grown up around ethnic waltz and polka bands."

The instrument wasn't the centerpiece of most western bands, but accordionists took their share of solos and added depth and color similar to a horn section. Sometimes pianists switched to the unfamiliar squeezebox, which may explain a few less than stellar performances, but there were more than enough hot players worth remembering.

☞ Where Have All the Big Bands Gone?

WESTERN SWING GROUPS witnessed the fade of the last large dance orchestras. This happened mostly because of economics: bigger bands cost money. During the Depression, orchestras were able to survive thanks to musicians' willingness to travel rough for cheap wages. World War II brought gasoline rationing, which put at least a temporary halt to most groups.

The draft and high wartime employment also meant steeper payroll (and an unprecedented number of professional female musicians). A short postwar recession drove wages back down and re-energized bands who were entertaining returning troops. But when the economy improved after 1946, orchestras struggled. The rise of amplification finally made most big bands superfluous. Small combos could fill everything from bars to stadiums.

Then audiences began staying home to raise the baby boomers. Venues closed, bands folded, and the craze for couples dancing that had lasted since the advent of the waltz in the 1800s faded away.

Ghost Riders in Western Swing

Folk-based country and black R&B from the South are often seen as the twin rivers flowing into rock 'n' roll. It's a mistake, though, to see them as the only streams. Complex mixtures of Anglo and African American, but also Hawaiian, Mexican, and ethnic music predated the mess that became rock 'n' roll. Generations of musicians in different traditions created the foundations for rock. Western swing and other sources seldom get acknowledged as invisible threads in this fabric of modern music.

Western swing is easy to overlook now because it combined genres we've grown accustomed to think of as separate. Cowboy jazz musicians premiered the electric guitar? Hawaiian music brought the slide to country and blues? Trend-setting players (guitarists, fiddlers, and accordionists) lie submerged beneath layers of pop music they inspired.

The Door Swings Closed on Western Swing

By the 1950s, the huge audiences of the war years were gone. Big dance halls closed and western swing's "Southwest jazz" faded from the cultural memory of most Americans. The country accordion went the way of the big bands. Accordionists had been the heart or at least the brains of several bands, doing arrangements and contributing musical education. But they never developed a distinctive "country" style that audiences grew attached to. As times changed, when nostalgia led people back to western music, the accordion was usually overlooked.

Western swing had laid the groundwork for its replacement as players embraced new sounds and new instruments. Western groups welcomed accordions, drums, and electric guitars into country and created some of the most forward-looking music in the world. Pared-down amplified groups then took country and western's nostalgic futurism to honky tonks and rockabilly. Before we forget, let's take a look at some of the players.

The Westernest-Swingingest Musicians

Take away the cowboy hats and it's hard to know if western swing was more jazz than country. Some western players in fact considered themselves above their "nitty-gritty" country counterparts. The best of them were well equipped to play "sophisticated" show tunes, jazz, or orchestrated film music when called upon. They were modern musicians who happened to play country, mostly because it paid better in the late 1940s than the fading swing bands.

Keep in mind that the lines between sweaty western swing, singing cowboy, and other kinds of western music were pretty vague, with no uncrossable border when a musician was looking for a paycheck. Pros worked with many different groups in different styles. Some settled in Hollywood to do session work, others traveled to play for dance hall fans across the country. Wherever they were, western musicians tended to bring jazzy stylings and musicianship to the country scene.

Some western accordionists played rhythm-section roles without challenging the fireworks of hot fiddlers and up-and-coming electric and steel guitarists. In quieter moments the instrument might replace a

Tex Williams's Western Caravan: (L to R) Paul "Spike" Featherstone (on harp!), Tex Williams, Larry "Pedro" DePaul (accordion), Rex Call, Muddy Berry, Cactus Soldi, Smokey Rogers, Gibby Gibson, Ossie Godson, Johnny Weis, and Deuce Spriggins, ca. 1946–47. *Courtesy of Kevin Coffey.*

harmonica for a "lonesome cowboy, home on the range" sound. They'd support soloists and take turns of their own, but weren't show stoppers. Like most rhythm instruments, their role was significant but often understated as they blended into the western veneer that masked this modern industrial music.

George Bamby, Frank Buckley, Larry "Pedro" DePaul, and others, on the other hand, were at the forefront of California's "cowboy culture" soundtrack. Theirs were the phones that rang when people wanted a squeezebox that could stand up to the electric guitars out on the range.

The Light Crust Doughboys

The roots of western swing sprang from a band with an unlikely name: the Light Crust Doughboys. Sponsored by a flour mill in 1931, the Doughboys included the pre-coronation "King of Western Swing" Bob Wills, as well as the great Milton Brown. Brown left the Doughboys and then died in a car wreck, but not before his later group the Musical Brownies influenced a generation of hot western players. After seeding these leaders, the Doughboys played on in one form or another for more than sixty years. Photos of the band reveal a string of accordionists sitting in on their rhythm section.

The Doughboys had at least three accordionists during the 1930s and '40s, mostly after their most influential alumni Brown and Wills left to make their marks. The first was Kenneth "Abner" Pitts (who usually played fiddle). The guys all got nicknames: "Bashful," "Doc," "Sleepy," "Snub." Their next accordionist was John "Knocky" Parker. He was an excellent blues piano player who taught the band tunes from his favorite R&B records. Their banjo-player/leader Marvin Montgomery then did arrangements for guitars and fiddles in imitation of jazz horns. On the road, since Knocky "couldn't put a piano on that bus very well," he took an accordion as a substitute. Parker later earned a doctorate and became an English professor, but would still pound out blues piano at any opportunity.

Charles Godwin took up the squeezebox in a postwar Doughboys and was also dubbed "Knocky" (to confuse future researchers and perhaps fool fans). Among the Doughboy recordings with "Knocky II" there's a version of Charles Magnante's showpiece "Accordiana." Godwin left the band and died some years later in an airplane crash. After him, they retired the name along with the accordion slot. Ever since, the Doughboys' 1930s-40s recordings with the two "Knockys" have been among the classics of western music.

Versions of the Doughboys performed with many personnel changes over decades of music-making—including the time in the 1950s when they met and enticed onto the bandstand the unlikely duo of Sergey Vaschenko on balalaika with Vladimir Kaliazine on Russian classical bayan accordion. This "eastern swing" was certainly one of the more unusual experiments in country music from that era, and one I would love to have witnessed.

Adolph Hofner and Polka Country

The swing era was complicated. Many audiences listened to more than one type of music, and traveling bands learned to play more than one style. Adolph Hofner grew up in a Czech and German immigrant communities near San Antonio, Texas, and spoke Czech before he learned English. His mother played concertina and his father played harmonica, but Adolph and his younger brother started their career playing Hawaiian music. Out of this eclectic background he grew up to be a country guitarist who sang like Bing Crosby.

Milton Brown's western swing inspired Hofner to form a band. They replaced Czech-style hammered dulcimer with western fiddles, guitars, and occasional accordion and sang mostly in English. Despite its close ties with immigrant "polka" communities, Hofner's band was ironically less associated with accordions than many of its peers. Their regular piano player, Charlie Poss, only played it on occasional live dates. A few Hofner records feature Walter Kleypas, who was an influential country accordionist in Texas. Their later recordings featured accordions, but it doesn't seem to have been a mainstay of the Hofner sound. Their western-style version of the 1920s nugget "Sam, The Old Accordion Man" features solos by honky-tonk piano, electric and steel guitar, but no accordion at all. Hofner nevertheless acts as a bridge between country, European ethnic, and even the region's Mexican American accordion.

Caught with an unfortunate name after the start of World War II, Hofner rechristened his band Dolph Hofner and His San Antonians. After a wartime stint entertaining troops in Los Angeles, he returned to Texas and began to play more polkas and sing more tunes in Czech. "Alamo Schottische" (1947) typified this regional crossover between Texas and Bohemia. For the next forty years, Hofner and various versions of his band became a fixture around San Antonio as he played on into the early 1990s. Not bad for an immigrants' kid named Adolph.

Swift Jewel Cowboys

The Swift Jewel Cowboys, named after a sponsor's salad oil, played western swing based out of Memphis, Tennessee—which hadn't been called "the west" since the late 1700s. Barreling through hillbilly country with jazz-influenced western style, they dressed like cowboys and weren't kidding. Billed as the "Only Mounted Cowboy Band in America," they bought and broke seven horses to ride while performing at rodeos. Reeds player Lefty Ingram explained, "We played a short musical program, did a few horse stunts and each of us rode a steer out of the bucking chute." One of the most sophisticated western bands in the country had the chops on horseback too. Pioneering the country-rodeo circuit, they may also have set a record for sending the most members to the hospital with broken bones.

Part of their act had the band playing music from horseback. A photo shows precarious accordionist Clifford "Kokomo" Crocker and even double bass player "Cactus Pete" posing atop their horses with their instruments. Non-musical stunts had Crocker and guitarist Slim Hall clowning while riding the same horse together. Kokomo's horse also did mathematical calculations for the crowd. Assuming no injuries, the band would then play for dances.

Musically, these Cowboys were formidable. They could stomp off a blues number that sounded more like a 1930s jazz band than any kind of country act. Dispensing with steel guitar, lines were drawn with horns, fiddle, Crocker's accordion, and Lefty Ingram's brilliant clarinet. Jimmy Riddle, who later played accordion and harmonica with Roy Acuff, filled in while band members took time off. "Kokomo" provided clever accordion fills and understated support for the clarinet and horn solos. If Duke Ellington's band had worked day jobs herding cattle, they might have sounded like this.

Like most early accordion artists, Crocker's tone was a bit harsh, but he carried it off with style. All that remains, though, is about two dozen sides the band recorded over a few days in 1939. On instrumentals like "Bug Shuffle," Crocker's accordion solo ends with haunting chords well outside the typical western theme. On other tunes he sings or trades playful reed riffs with Ingram's virtuosic clarinet, creating music, whether western or not, that drew thousands of dancers and radio listeners.

In 1939, the Cowboys played 765 gigs, not including radio appearances. Audiences collected boxtops from the sponsor's salad oil, which served as tickets to shows at schools, country fairs, vaudeville theaters, dance halls, hospital benefits, and supermarket openings. It's no wonder they couldn't keep up the pace. When World War II began, rubber-tire rationing restricted their travel and conscription took several members. The group sold their horses and split up. Seventy-five years later, their uncommon blend of country, jazz, and blues still sounds like it's ready to leap off a horse and start dancing.

Western Accordion King: Larry "Pedro" DePaul

In Texas, Bob Wills was the uncontested "King of Western Swing," but in California, Spade Cooley claimed the title. Wills's players tended toward group and solo improvisation, famously triggered by a wave of Wills's violin bow. Cooley's outfit instead played turn-on-a-dime arrangements—often written by accordionists Larry "Pedro" DePaul or Frank Buckley. These charts minimized improvisation outside of solos. The band made up for it with players like steel guitar genius Earl "Joaquin" Murphey, guitarist Johnny Weis, and an array of fiddlers.

Commercial recordings from Cooley's most creative period are patchy, due to wartime shellac rationing, conscription, and the musicians' recording bans of 1942–44 and 1948. On radio-transcription discs, though, accordion players "Pedro" DePaul, George Bamby, and Frank Buckley were some of the standouts of western swing.

Accordionist and arranger Larry "Pedro" DePaul rode in from the western outpost of Cleveland, Ohio. During the Depression, DePaul had taken violin lessons as long as his family could afford it, then started playing his uncle's accordion. By age seventeen he was getting paid to play local radio before and after school.

The youngster joined Texas Jim Lewis's touring band and found his way out to Hollywood. There he helped craft Spade Cooley's iconoclastic sound. DePaul suggested that he could write arrangements for use at the vast oceanside Venice Pier Ballroom. The promoter didn't want horns like Bob Wills was using, so DePaul's arrangements called for up to four fiddles in close harmony, electric lead and steel guitars, a swing rhythm section with drums, and as many as four vocalists. The whole thing was topped off with Paul "Spike" Featherstone's elegant full-size harp. After the war, they added vibes.

Juggling all this, DePaul's rhythmic accordion led the band through mid-song key and tempo changes that were impossible for lesser groups. They were the tightest ensemble in country music, and filled ballrooms five nights a week. Radio recordings reveal the full power of the musicians playing DePaul's charts, with lightning-fast versions of waltzes, schottisches, and polkas—"Cowpoke Polka," "Yodeling Polka"—even a "Hornpipe Swing."

As World War II ground on, Cooley's band members worked day jobs making airplane parts while playing for crowds of eight thousand dancers each night. DePaul was near exhaustion from this schedule when he was drafted in 1945. Hotshot accordionists Frank Buckley and George Bamby filled in for the duration of the war.

Cooley was legendarily difficult to work with, and his band went through frequent tumultuous changes.* When DePaul returned from the war, he joined a mass exodus of band members who followed singer Tex Williams when he quit (or was fired, depending on accounts) to form the Western Caravan. The Caravan was a "co-op" band with DePaul as

---

* In 1961, after years of drunken violence, Spade Cooley murdered his wife Ella Mae Evans and spent the rest of his life in prison. If someone you know is at risk, www.hotpeachpages .net has information on family violence prevention in every country in the world.

one of four owners. They carried on many of Cooley's musical innovations, with DePaul's arrangements and many of the same musicians. Out from under Cooley's control, DePaul created even more elaborate experiments, including a reworking of jazz maestro Stan Kenton's "Artistry in Rhythm" as "Artistry in Western Swing" in 1948.

Williams and the Caravan had several pop hits, including the inescapable "Smoke! Smoke! Smoke! (That Cigarette)," but in 1951, rising expenses and shrinking crowds finally split what had been one of America's most exciting groups.

In the 1950s, DePaul and some of his bandmates opened a music store together where he gave lessons to 150 accordion, violin, and trombone students. (He taught himself flute in order to teach that, too.) In the 1990s, DePaul moved to Spokane, Washington, and thanks to the dedicated western swing revival scene he became one of the few 1940s accordionists to be interviewed about their lives and the music they made.

Billy Liebert: "You Play Too Goddamn Good"

Cliffie Stone, bandleader for the *Dinner Bell Roundup* radio show, introduced a song in 1947, "We're gonna have Billy show off a little bit here on his accordion." From the hands of accordionist Billy Liebert, the standard "St. Louis Blues" meandered like the Mississippi River, overflowing the melody, incorporating segments of "Rhapsody in Blue," and rushed on to an almost ragtime, nearly bebop finish.

Liebert was a Los Angeles session player who was the perfect embodiment of the masterful musician who escaped most public attention. Growing up in Detroit, Liebert had played in bands since he was fourteen. Like Pedro DePaul, he hitched up with Texas Jim Lewis on a Midwest tour and followed him to California. After time in the Navy, he began his recording career in 1946 and eventually worked with almost everyone in West Coast country.

He found a musical base in radio announcer Cliffie Stone's *Hometown Jamboree* band. They played swing jazz with a western twang and doubled as Capitol Records' country music outfit. When Liebert enlisted steel guitar hotshot Speedy West into the group, he conveyed a lesson he'd learned from Stone: "You know your trouble? You play too goddamn good." Playing what the producer wanted (even if you didn't like it) got you more work.

Following the whims of the studios, Liebert largely played piano in the 1950s and kept the accordion for after-hours jamming. One amusing foray back to the squeezebox was Stan Freberg's 1957 novelty record "Wun'erful, Wun'erful!" which mocked *The Lawrence Welk Show*. Liebert provided a hesitant and clumsy accordion part that adds musical satire to a sketch about a wayward bubble-machine floating the Avalon Ballroom out to sea. Welk was reportedly not amused.

Liebert was musical director for CBS from 1964–69, and was voted Best Country Piano Player by the Academy of Country Music in 1966 and 1967. He played with Merle Haggard, Roy Rogers, Kay Starr, Mel Tormé, Merle Travis, proto-rocker Ella Mae Morse, the Everly Brothers, Johnny Cash, Flatt & Scruggs, and dozens of other country artists over three decades. In the 1970s he wrapped things up behind the scenes working on John Wayne's only album, *America, Why I Love Her*.

Amidst a career of high points, Liebert played accordion on some of his friend Speedy West's fantastic early 1960s "space-guitar" records. These were so musically intense that Cliffie Stone's fingers bled when he sat in on bass. Afterwards, Liebert got the daunting task of notating Speedy's and Jimmy Bryant's lead sheets so they could be copyrighted. Every improvised riff had to be sorted and written down. "All those damn notes, I wrote those things down," he said. "I played some of those licks and they were correct as hell, but they weren't easy to do. There aren't too many guitar players who could play that."

Bill Haley's Aces of Western Accordion: Al Constantine and Johnny Grande

The late 1940s saw the earliest signs of rock 'n' roll, when American music mixed country and western, R&B, and a mashup of Latin and other ingredients. As musicians buckled down into smaller groups, amplified western combos brought "hillbilly boogie" to the doorsteps of the *Grand Ole Opry*. They traded repertoire with the jump-blues combos playing the R&B circuit and together foreshadowed the future.

One artist made the leap from small-time western music to global fame. Bill Haley and the Four Aces of Western Swing were a combo from northeastern Pennsylvania. Haley got his start as a kid imitating Gene Autry as part of the great cowboy music phenomenon. (A childhood group, the Texas Range Riders, included his friend Dorothy Heavlow on accordion.) Billed as Yodeling Bill Haley, he played Chicago's *National*

Barn Dance, then traveled through St. Louis, New Orleans, and Texas, taking in R&B, jazz and western swing.

In the late 1940s, he became music director of a radio station in Chester, Pennsylvania, with a mixed audience of black, country, and ethnic listeners. Playing live, his Four Aces band filled the "country" slot. Al Constantine joined on accordion, an instrument practically required in western groups in the Northeast. The Aces showed bare hints of the revolution that was to come, but players like Constantine laid the groundwork for the earliest attempts at rock accordion. The group may have been privileged to flip the switch on the future of music a few years later, but listening to their records it's tempting to say that Haley was more convincing as a yodeler than he was as a rocker.

With little fortune in sight, a frustrated Haley broke his hand picking a fight with a wall—his arm in a sling, he broke up the Aces. Around that same time, though, a guitarist named John Williamson and his accordionist friend Johnny Grande heard Haley had been trying to mix western swing with R&B, and they enticed him back to the stage.

The new group was Bill Haley and the Saddlemen and they called their experimental music "cowboy jive." During the Korean War they played for workers in Philadelphia, and started performing at high schools to see how their material went over with youngsters. Their direction turned toward translating R&B for white kids. In 1952, with the future in mind, they became Bill Haley and the Comets. Their "Rock around the Clock" was still two years away but their days of western swing were officially over.

15

The Folk Revival:
The Accordion
Betrayed

I N THE LATE 1800s, accordions were adopted by an extraordinary
number of folk musicians around the world. In many places they
went on to become symbols linked with the survival of regional cultures. But they weren't always seen as saviors. Early European critics called the squeezebox "the archenemy of folk music." People were
urged to "rise in protest and take up the fight against the savage accordion." Outraged opponents exhorted, "Do not dance to the screeching,
insidious accordions. Burn them." In response, as modern writer James
P. Leary wryly commented, "Folk musicians everywhere ignored their
admonitions."

Years later, however, the North American folk revival in the 1950s
and '60s almost totally neglected the instrument. This was not because
they were uncommon. As we've seen, accordion players brought tremendous vigor to polka, Irish, klezmer, conjunto/norteño, and Louisiana
French styles. But when representatives from these traditions were
invited to 1960s folk festivals, they came as outsiders and their music
was seldom taken up by revivalists.

The irony of accordions being rejected by North American folk aficionados was that "folks" were playing them everywhere. Hundreds of
thousands of young people were taking accordion lessons at the time.

Revivalists could have incorporated the instrument in an instant. For middle-class whites though, accordions had become so established that they hardly registered as folk instruments. There was no romance or rebellion in televised accordionists. Even cool musicians who played it were suddenly "square."

Folk revivalists thought of themselves as preserving music rooted in the past. Simultaneously, they rejected significant swaths of historical and ethnic diversity, including most accordion-centered traditions. In their place, with remarkable diligence, folk fans sought out Southern and black artists and promoted them as America's universal folk heritage.

This is not to say that folklorists and revivalists didn't contribute uniquely valuable work. There is no denying the vibrance of the African American and Southern music that they focused on. Nevertheless, when urban (mostly middle-class and white) revivalists spurned accordion-related genres it had far-reaching effects. Their countercultural folk heroes became rock stars, and the rejection of the accordion was amplified worldwide.

Ironically, much of today's renewal of interest in the accordion is inspired by genres like zydeco and klezmer, which the mid-century urban revival initially ignored. It's interesting to imagine what might have followed if the revival hadn't limited itself to only some regions, some languages, and some instruments.

The Lost Accordion Revival

When revivalists' versions of old recordings rose to international popularity in the 1950s, the accordion was nowhere to be heard. David Guard of the Kingston Trio recalls that after the Weavers came out in 1950, "Everybody bought guitars." (Guard himself purchased a banjo.) If the Weavers or the Trio had included folk accordionists, many more might have followed (and somebody probably would have written this book years ago).

As it is, most participants in the youthful folk movement were less interested in ethnomusicology than in entertainment and mild non-conformity. As author Sheldon Posen described, Northern revivalists who looked south created, bought, and sold an idealized history. "People became tourists ... in someone else's culture."

While folk revivalists were neglecting the accordion, some accordionists were rejecting folk music. Mid-century accordion boosters made the telling choice to distance their instrument from its folk origins, aiming to assimilate into the world of "serious music." This turned out to be a grave error. While several European countries found ways to combine concert music with the study of folk traditions, in North America, folk and "serious" musicians seldom converged and the accordion was excluded from both.

From the beginning, folk fans' emphasis on authenticity masked an artificial tradition. They left things out, they romanticized, they pretended and imitated. Eventually, to some fans' chagrin, pop music swallowed the bankable parts of the revival. Following the revivalists' example, rejection of the accordion was fixed for decades to come.

Early Folk Revival (pre-1930)

Back in the Industrial Revolution, opposition to the accordion had been common in regions where the new instrument encroached upon long-standing folk traditions. Early twentieth-century Swedish composer Hugo Alfvén memorably recommended: "Chop up all the accordions that come in your way, stamp them to a jelly, cut them into pieces and throw them into the pigsty, because that is where they belong!"

This opposition to outside influences was blazing as nationalist mythologies claimed ownership of folk music. Early accordions were condemned in Finland as part of the cultural and political threat from imperialist Russia. French bagpipers and Italian immigrant accordionists fought legendary battles that echoed their communities' economic competition. Supporters of Irish pipes damned the accordion, while emigration and industrialism drastically altered their music.

In North America, ethnic folk cultures that employed accordions were more often ignored by folklorists than railed against. Nativist researchers may have feared the influence of Irish and Italian immigrants and non-English speakers, but said much more against the pervasive impact of popular music, especially music influenced by African Americans. Rather than accordions, nationalists targeted minstrel shows, Tin Pan Alley, ragtime, and jazz.

Nineteenth-century folkloric "ballad hunters" like Cecil Sharp sought to discover, purify, and raise the status of supposedly ancient English folk culture in order to "civilize the masses." Sharp expanded on the work of researchers like Francis Child, who preserved only the written words of what they estimated were the oldest songs. When musical content was included, curators decided which instruments were deemed appropriate. This search for authenticity often resulted in inaccurate views of the eclectic musical world.

A few supporters of folk preservation did set out to include ethnic or other music. The first issue of the *Journal of American Folklore* in 1888 advocated the collection of material from "English folklore," "Negroes in the Southern States," the "Indian Tribes of North America," and "French Canada, Mexico, etc." That "etc." could easily have included accordions, frequently played by more recent ethnic immigrants.

Similarly, settlement schools that did social work in impoverished communities sought to "improve" urban immigrants by encouraging varied folk customs. The accordion, though, had lost some of its connection with folklore as immigrant musicians found a place within popular music. Commercial success deflected folklorists' attention.

Rather than folklorists, it turned out to be commercial recording companies that preserved the majority of early folk and ethnic accordion music. In a reversal of Frances Child's collections of only the lyrics of old songs, recording made it easier to preserve tunes than texts. In the 1920s, companies happily recorded any ethnic content that seemed likely to sell. Even the customers didn't have to understand the words for songs to succeed. Ethnic styles passed from one audience to another, befuddling folkloric purists as never before.

Pre-war, Pre-revival Folk, 1930s–40s

Leading up to World War II, commercial and folkloric recordings captured tens of thousands of performances from a profusion of styles, languages, and regions. For the first time, regional music could be heard far from its original cultural context. Before they reached audiences though, even the most authentic folk recordings were compromised.

Record producers and folklorists filtered what was preserved and distributed. The limited quality and length of recordings also influenced playing styles. In even the best cases, only fragments of larger traditions became available to outside audiences. Despite these shortcomings, when the 1950s–60s folk revival came along, a canon of artists, genres, songs, and instruments were being argued over, annotated, lauded, and discarded, often with little or no consultation with their original sources. Accordions were generally excluded from this canon.

Another America:
Folk Music's Missing Midwest

In 1976, a huge map detailing the nation's folk music hung over the stage at the Bicentennial Festival of American Folklife in Washington, D.C. Folklorist James P. Leary noticed something missing, "The Upper Midwest was terra incognito. Complete voids yawned in Iowa and the Dakotas, while the only place dotting Wisconsin was, erroneously, Northfield [which is actually in Minnesota]."

Based on Alan Lomax's work, this map of North American folk music ignored half the continent. The states of Michigan, Minnesota, and Wisconsin, and immigrant musicians from the Ohio-to-Texas "polka belt" were cartographically silenced. Tellingly, these gaps in the map of American folk music almost exactly match the regions where accordions and polkas were most popular (see Chapter 5).

It didn't have to be this way. In 1938, Alan Lomax mounted an expedition to the Upper Midwest for the Library of Congress. It was part of a concerted attempt to broaden folk music's focus beyond the Southeast into other regions of the country. Intended as a "rapid reconnaissance survey" of the three Great Lakes states, after a month Lomax had hardly made it out of Michigan.

Effusively he reported to his superiors in Washington that "the Upper Peninsula of Michigan proved to be the most fertile source ... There was enough material in the region for years of work." He was able to preserve about a thousand songs, saying there was "more material than [he] had time to record." Lomax wrote that he believed the Upper Midwest might be "the most interesting country I have ever traveled in," and "the most richly varied area for folk music that I had ever visited." And yet in all the years after, he never returned to the region, and his research and recordings from his trip remained unavailable during his lifetime.

It says something about the depth of Lomax's achievements that a thousand recordings were forgotten amidst the clutter for seventy five years. But it wasn't only his research that was neglected. Two women, Sidney Robertson Cowell in the 1930s and Helene Stratman-Thomas

in the 1940s, collected a total of nearly a thousand more folk performances from Minnesota and Wisconsin. Like Lomax, they endured the
rigorous conditions of rural Depression and wartime America, cover-
ing thousands of miles on unpaved roads. Their adventures included
occasional harassment from what Robertson (who'd spent time in the
slums of New York) called "the toughest-looking characters—I swear
my Lower East Side gang couldn't touch 'em." Despite their remarkable efforts, almost no one was aware of their work until the beginning
of the next century.

Throughout the 1930s–60s, amateur and professional musicologists like these three combed the nation for traditional musicians. They
helped make blues and old-time country into "American" folk music
archetypes. Why, then, did their influence pass over some regions of
the country? The music of the Upper Midwest presented three obstacles
for folk revivalists: First, the baffling mixture of cultural sources in the
region was—baffling. In addition, language barriers were a huge obstacle. Finally, the blurry crossover between "folk" and commercial music
made it easy to see some traditions as suspect. Each of these challenges
deserves attention.

Lomax scholar James Leary explains, "The Upper Midwest was not
the America of New England villages, New York tenements, Pennsylvania Dutch farms, Appalachian hollows, Southern cotton plantations,
or Western plains celebrated by folklorists and familiar to the nation."
Local listeners, dancers, and players called what they played and heard
"old-time music" but it wasn't Appalachian, it was Northern fiddles and
ballads and square dances in dozens of languages, with ethnic instruments, homemade lumberjack guitars, accordions, and a healthy dose
of polkas and other European dances.

The hundreds of artists on these three researchers' (Stratman-
Thomas, Robertson, and Lomax's) two thousand recordings spoke
and sang in more than twenty-five languages. As one example from
this inter-ethnic jumble, Henry Mahoski, the son of Polish immigrants,
played a tune on a German Chemnitzer concertina. He had learned the
song "Kauhavan Polka" from a record by Finnish American Viola Turpeinen, who grew up nearby and played piano accordion because she'd
learned it from her Italian neighbor.

In many ways, this overflowing diversity was the unifying charac-
teristic of the region's music. The ethnic mix of the Upper Midwest led

musicians to play for a tangle of audiences and create a style based on a confluence of influences as rich as any in America. The Upper Midwest's "old-time ethnic" bands did tunes from many countries, often played by musicians of one ethnic/language group for audiences of another. The lack of conformity presented a problem for those interested in documenting distinct types of folkloric music, and the region's remarkably American tangle slipped past the architects of the folk revival almost entirely.

An even greater practical barrier for wider uptake of the region's style was language. Germans playing "The Irish Washerwoman" on accordion while calling square dances in English were confusing, but at least it was in English. Robertson, Lomax, and Stratman-Thomas published a few English lumberjack songs they collected in the Upper Midwest, but none of the non-English material. The twenty-five languages these folklorists encountered in the Upper Midwest didn't just challenge nativists' English-only prejudice. Faced with the work necessary to present the two thousand recordings to the public, the task defeated the collectors. Robertson shifted her focus to California, Lomax headed to Europe, and even though Stratman-Thomas worked for years to promote the region's multilingual music, her posthumous *Folksongs Out of Wisconsin* (1977) contained only English lyrics. Seventy-five years passed before teams of grad students were marshaled to accomplish the monumental undertaking of translating, annotating, and publishing the songs that Robertson, Lomax, and Stratman-Thomas recorded.

The music of the northern Midwest faced a final obstacle because of its relation to the polka boom in the 1940s. Folklorists had spread the idea that folk music was an alternative to bland pop music. The core irony of the later 1960s folk revival was, of course, that it attracted millions of listeners in part because the music was marketed as unfashionable.

Musicologist Charles Seeger (Pete's father) had urged Sidney Robertson, "Record EVERYthing! We know so little! Record everything!" But even the most open-eared folklorist had preferences as they selected what to record, which questions to ask, and what to promote and distribute. Lomax's own Midwest field notes relate his dissatisfaction with "hillbilly" country music at a folk festival sponsored by a local radio station. He also mentions his encounter with "the worst jazz I ever heard" at a Polish picnic.

Since Lomax chose not to record this terrible picnic jazz, we have no way to know what his "worst" band sounded like. Would they have played polkas associated with "corny" contemporary superstars like Lawrence Welk or Frankie Yankovic? If Lomax was uncomfortable with such trendy polkas (which seems likely), that might help explain why Welk's home state of North Dakota was left entirely blank on the *Folk Songs of North America* map. Like many collectors, Lomax was a connoisseur. This sometimes led to uncomfortable attempts to champion people's music while impulsively ignoring what was actually popular.

During his five weeks in Michigan in 1938, Alan Lomax recorded 147 discs. One writer called it "twenty-four hours of music, five minutes at a time." Lomax described the experience as "musical vertigo." He encountered young people's jazz, older folks' polkas, and local folk musicians whose defining quality was a lack of conformity. This hybrid syncretism had accordions, polkas, and layered songs from different languages unified by their wild divergence from the idea that folk styles had to be static and unadulterated. This unique collage of music from the Upper Midwest could have been the basis for a more lively, inclusive, and authentic revival, if only it had been heard.

Alan Lomax and "This Pestiferous Instrument"

In 1960, folklorist Alan Lomax wrote, "When the whole world is bored with automated, mass-distributed video-music, our descendants will despise us for throwing away the best of our culture." Given his stirring words, it's ironic that Lomax was partially responsible for the accordion's erasure from the American folk revival.

By the end of his life, Alan Lomax left a legacy of recordings that will far outlast any faults he may have had. That said, as America's most well-known folklorist he did the accordion few favors. Lomax started his career in the 1930s, following his father, John Lomax, on legendary expeditions that documented musicians like Lead Belly for the first time. The young Lomax eventually grew to be one of the most influential movers behind the mid-century North American revival. He did field recordings all over the world, worked with the U.S. Library of Congress's Archive of American Folk Song, and published extensively on the origins and development of people's music. He never had much good to say about the squeezebox, though.

Lomax may have developed this antipathy to the instrument while traveling in Europe after the Second World War. He went there after fleeing the U.S. to escape the Red Scare many of his friends in the folk music community endured during the McCarthy era. It's a little bit tempting to ponder how his condemnation of accordions sounds reminiscent of the all-too-real political persecution he himself was avoiding:

> During the nineteenth century the accordion, which has done such severe damage to the old folk music of Central Europe, penetrated every region of Italy. The Southern Italian folk musicians, however, have worked out ways of playing this pestiferous instrument so that it supports, rather than injures their old tunes.

Lomax quit North America at a time when anti-accordion opinion was strong among European folklorists. In their eyes, the instrument was displacing ancient and valuable bagpipes, fiddles, and other traditions. If he didn't have this prejudice before, Lomax seems to have adopted and applied it after returning to his own country. He ended up shortchanging American accordion styles that were older or more threatened than some of the music he championed.

For example, Lead Belly's non-traditional Mexican twelve-string was given precedence over his childhood windjammer. The fact that accordions had supplanted bagpipes in Italy did not reflect the way nineteenth-century African American accordion players were replaced by blues guitarists. By misapplying these preconceptions, Lomax and others effectively erased the English-speaking African American accordion. Thankfully, such prejudice didn't succeed in all traditions. Chris Strachwitz recalled Lomax lamenting the presence of accordions in Mexican American music. The border accordion proudly outlived Lomax's opinion.

Besides his judgment of the accordion, Lomax's later work closed its ears to much of America's Midwestern and non-English ethnic music, including the wide varieties of polka. A casual follower of Lomax's work might never have given folk music outside the South a thought. Lomax scholar James P. Leary commented, "I have long wondered what might have happened had Alan Lomax been raised in Ishpeming[, Michigan], Eau Claire[, Wisconsin], or Eveleth[, Minnesota]."

Lomax's regional orientation and his negative feelings about the accordion's invasive influence shaped the future of American folk music.

Northern kids who had never before picked up guitars began playing Appalachian songs from Lomax's songbooks. Many of these same youths' parents and grandparents might have sung and danced to their own multi-ethnic folk music with fiddles or accordions. Lomax's famous interviews with artists like Lead Belly and Muddy Waters skipped over the fact that both played accordion as children before taking up guitar. This excision of the instrument became so ingrained that folk fans and researchers presumed accordions had no role in American music.

Over more than sixty years of field work, Alan Lomax helped pioneer the appreciation, documentation, and preservation of the sounds of humanity. He was jailed in Mississippi, detained by fascists in Spain, and repeatedly robbed of notebooks, recordings, clothes, and cars. It's important to acknowledge, though, that people who persist in such uniquely valuable work can do so imperfectly.

Cajun musician and scholar Barry Jean Ancelet discussed Lomax's interpretations of the irreplaceable recordings of early Creole and Cajun music he collected in the 1930s: "Even in the cases when he was obviously wrong, he inspired those around him who were frustrated by his opinionated wild guesses to find out the real story."

Activist Accordions and Squeezebox Politics

Folk music was changed forever by the growing tide of commercial and academic recording in the 1920s. Alongside the new technology, politics also reshaped the music. Throughout the 1930s and '40s, the ideological left in the United States took up folk music as a means of spreading their message of social change. Occasionally this involved the squeezebox.

In fact there was a folk history of radical accordionists dating back to the early 1900s. Long before the folk revival, musical street battles raged between Salvation Army bands (known for horns and concertinas) and union activists of the Industrial Workers of the World (IWW, or Wobblies). The Wobblies' most famous songwriter was Swedish immigrant and eventual martyr, Joe Hill. Hill learned accordion and fiddle as a kid— he once said that he'd rather play fiddle than eat. He became famous for radicalizing the words of well-known hymns. When Salvationist bands drowned out union meetings with "The Sweet By and By," IWWs joined in by singing Hill's "That's a Lie!" lyrics.

In Depression-era New York City, socially conscious folk singers like Woody Guthrie and Aunt Molly Jackson were lauded for creating new songs in the style of the old. They laid the groundwork for topical political music, but also for singer-songwriters like Bob Dylan, who would use traditional styles to tell personal stories. As the revival progressed, folk singing wasn't limited to old ballads: it could talk about labor struggles, current events, or personal heartbreak.

Before the anti-communist witch hunts of the 1950s, "folk music" of various sorts had become so mainstream that it briefly replaced the less-than-respectful "hillbilly" as the generic name for country music. This changed when million-selling groups like the Weavers were targeted by grandstanders secretly fed reports by J. Edgar Hoover's FBI. If folk singers wanted to stay in business, they had to remove politics from their act. At about this time they were also removing accordions.

The Folk Revivals of the 1950s–60s

After World War II, academic ballad hunters and Depression-era political folk singers faced a growing conformity in American media. Unexpectedly though, folk music was on the rise. This mid-century movement earnestly prized "authenticity," but it also ignored music that didn't fit its guitar-and-string band formulae. Despite a few proponents like Zilphia Horton and Sis Cunningham, young folk fans almost completely abandoned the accordion.

Looking though photos of famous 1960s folk musicians, banjos were token, fiddles rare, mountain dulcimers exotic, and accordions anathema. The folk revival started as a reaction against conformity but fell in line behind a single instrument. The twang of a $20 Roy Rogers six-string was the romanticized bridge to a commodified folk culture.

There was infighting within the movement as it developed. Extraordinarily successful revival singers like the Kingston Trio faced derision from less pop-minded aficionados. Name-calling hid the fact that few, if any, players in the folk revival were really traditional, and all the factions overlapped and inspired each other. One thing that unified the parties was the absence of squeezeboxes.

Folk vs. Popular—but No Accordion

Historian Grace Hale's study of middle-class rebellion stated, "In the late nineteenth century, educated and wealthy whites cultivated an interest in folk ballads to separate themselves from the many Americans who preferred Tin Pan Alley hits and coon songs." Minstrel songs were rejected by prejudiced folklorists because they were associated with African Americans; later revivalists would revile those same songs as inauthentic and racist.

Researchers, record collectors, critics, and fans combined efforts in an attempt to get American folk music organized. Almost all of them started by rejecting the trends of their time. "Folk music" was invented when it was removed from its creators and purified of commercial influences— or so the purists thought.

Revivalists—whether of folk, jazz, or blues—usually had markedly different intentions than the creators of the music they sought to preserve. Elijah Wald notes that 1960s blues revivalists "were looking for an alternative to the light entertainment of the pop scene and for insight into vanished or foreign worlds." By contrast, the original blues musicians were intentionally *creating* light entertainment for their 1920s fans, many of whom were working to escape the all-too-real world of the segregated South. Hale notes, "Revivalists were interested in country blues and early hillbilly music, in forms forgotten enough to give free rein to their fantasies. They needed an alternative to the present." Preservationists argued about artistic and historical merit, whereas most creators simply wanted to have a good time and get paid.

Throughout these debates, archaic folk and ethnic accordion traditions were ignored by students who were thrilled to learn more modern guitar and banjo picking styles. Ethnic records like polkas and klezmer with "unintelligible" titles defeated language-deficient collectors and were, in some cases, used as disposable "packing" to protect blues and country discs.

Harry Smith (Mostly) Left Accordions Out of American Folk Music

Harry Smith's remarkably influential collection of recordings, the *Anthology of American Folk Music* (1952), helped shape the 1950s-60s revival. Smith, a white kid from way out in Washington State, crafted a personal national geography that pretty much ignored America outside the South. One tune from Minnesota, Frank Cloutier and the Victoria Café Orchestra's "Moonshiner's Dance Part 1," sits isolated from the other eighty-some Southern songs. Smith's choices set the accepted boundaries of "folk music" for the most influential decade of the revival.

Beyond its regional limitations, the central irony of Smith's countercultural collection is that it was entirely composed of commercial recordings. Smith's sources—Southern white hillbilly, black blues, and rural religious music—were the harvest of the entertainment industry in the 1920s and '30s.

The only accordion tracks in Smith's vision of America were four lonely Cajun French numbers. He didn't demonstrate much knowledge of the squeezebox, either. His quirky comment for "Arcadian One Step" asserts, "The accordion, one of the most basic Arcadian instruments, is seldom heard in the states north of Louisiana." While Smith was compiling his collection in the 1950s, 200,000 accordions were sold every year in the United States. Music north of Louisiana was rife with them. This high profile, though, may have been the problem.

Smith was a Beat-era bohemian iconoclast, to say the least. His desire was to promote an alternative to contemporary music, identifying with what Greil Marcus mythologized as an "old, weird, America." Smith is said to have avidly collected polkas, reels, and klezmer records, but these didn't make the cut. He passed over Yiddish and ethnic material that was at least as "weird" as the hillbilly and blues songs he included. Immigrant polkas that appealed to American pop audiences didn't need his revival.

The Southern boundaries of the anthology excluded plenty of familiar and accessible folk music from other regions. Old-time bands from Upstate New York habitually included accordions with their fiddles and guitars. But folk fans like Smith, who lived in New York City by then, fell in love with Southern string band records. As a result, all over the country kids picked up guitars and cast aside local accordion traditions.

Smith famously said he had set out to change American music and succeeded. "Hillbilly"-based folk and African American blues were lifted up and inspired millions. Meanwhile, music Smith had bypassed survived without mainstream support, or faded away. An ironic result is that a lot of the music Smith rejected sounds "older and weirder" today than the songs on his anthology. Given his taste for non-conformity, if he was working today Smith might be putting out hipster compilations of celebrated 1950s accordionists.

Class and Contradiction

Canadian Ian McKay noted of early folklorists, "One could easily combine a career collecting the traditional ballads sung by ordinary working people with the utmost contempt for those who had come into possession of such aristocratic heirlooms." "Folk reviving" as far back as the 1800s began with academics extracting musical artifacts from rural singers. The revival grew to prominence based on collectors like Smith's reaction against modern conformity. Of course, by then regular folks weren't listening to "folk music."

Smith, like Lomax, passed over rural and working-class accordions that conflicted with what writer James Leary called an imagined "golden age of unsullied folk authenticity that had been polluted by machines and mass production." Critics perennially anointed and advocated "good" music and fretted when the masses didn't fall in line. Of course when any authentic style became popular, advocates might well abandon it in favor of some new obscurity.

Prophetic Folk Accordionists

The conflict between populism and elitism became more complicated when leftist political activists adopted folk forms for their topical songs. Early in the Great Depression, Charles Seeger and other communist supporters formed the classical Composers Collective. When their modernist orchestral propaganda failed to sway the masses, they turned to folk music. As the years passed, political folk songs would be celebrated, suppressed, and—after the passing of the 1960s revival—dismissed as passé.

At least three accordionists played significant roles in the mid-century revival. All three have been widely overlooked. Zilphia Horton was music director at the Highlander Center; Sis Cunningham sang with the Almanac Singers and founded *Broadside* magazine; and Jenny Vincent was an activist for years in New Mexico. All were pianists who switched to the squeezebox to play in political contexts. Each joined artists in the popular front of socialists, leftists, and communists during the Depression and World War II. All three offered music to their movements using their accordions.

These women weren't well-known solo performers. They weren't folk stars who dropped in for fundraisers then set off to make trend-setting albums. Instead, they were political organizers. They didn't change the world through their unique brilliance. Rather, they worked with others and played parts in greater things.

Zilphia Horton: On the Line for Justice

From a tiny school in rural Tennessee, an accordionist inspired people around the world, and almost none of them know her name. Zilphia Mae Johnson Horton (1910–56) was the music coordinator at the Highlander School, a small activist training center founded in the Appalachian mountain region in 1932. Highlander faced down violence and hatred while organizing for the labor and Civil Rights Movements throughout the South.

Folk music at Highlander wasn't just enjoyed by locals or studied by outsiders. It was a source of power for people with little else. Horton lifted music up as a demonstration of the value of people long denied. Following her guidance, Highlander continues today where other labor colleges of the time quickly failed. After her death in 1956, music that she championed became central to the Civil Rights Movement.

During the folk revival's long development, Zilphia left a mark for using folk music in political action and education. This was not without personal cost. Her father was a mine-owner in Arkansas, and she was privileged enough to study music and go to college. One legend has it that her father disowned her after she declared support for the Progressive Miners of America. He may have been more concerned that she was smoking in front of her sisters. They later reconciled, but she left home in 1934.

Zilphia found her way to Highlander in Tennessee. The two-year-old school wanted a musician but hadn't found one interested in local folk music. She brought her voice, accordion, piano, and guitar skills to a workshop in 1935 and stayed for twenty years. Two months after she arrived, she married Highlander founder Myles Horton. "It was not love at first sight as many thought," Myles later said. "Zilphia had been at Highlander almost a week before we fell in love."

She joined the school to teach and perform, and she encouraged the gathering of folk music. Unlike academic collectors, she promoted the use of songs as anthems of social change. Organizers around the country

sent hundreds of lyrics and tunes that she published in songbooks for progressive unions. Photos show her demonstrating the portability of the accordion, playing at union meetings, picket lines, and singalongs.

In the 1930s, the "hillbillies" of Appalachia had often been ridiculed as isolated, pre-industrial, and impoverished. Ballad-hunters idealized the region's music as a holdover from ancient European times. As scholar Alicia Massie-Legg recently framed it, Appalachia "became, for urban middle-class people, a mythological culture untouched by modern commercialism." For outsiders, the mountains were, like the mythical Old West, an imaginary alternative to the alienation of modern life.

Activists like Horton grounded local traditions in two ways. First, familiar music helped the people who created it recognize the value of their communities. Next, the idealized community values often portrayed in the music opened a door to critique worldly problems. Massie-Legg says folk music helped people "develop an awareness of themselves as a cultural group separate and apart from those who wielded political and economic power." Mountain culture, which had been ridiculed, was reclaimed—its deep roots made activists' hoped-for revolutionary future seem more realistic and attractive.

Along with teaching the value and power of singing together, Horton's most lasting contribution was collecting, modernizing, and spreading songs. She published them in mimeographed "songsters" beginning in 1935. They were sold for a nickel, so even striking workers could afford them. In 1939, she published a larger hardbound book, *Labor Songs*, with help from the Textile Workers Union of America, and it was passed around on picket lines throughout the 1940s.

The songsters' intent was that singing would strengthen picket lines and union meetings to encourage a culture of hopeful change. Horton started with folk, popular, or religious songs that people already knew. New words were applied to these to make them relevant to social causes. Massie-Legg described this *contrafacta* as "lyrical surgery," that reflected a kind of "deliberate folk process" that changed the songs for a purpose, rather than over long years as idealized by folk music theorists.

People who remember Horton say her true genius was for rousing groups to sing. She led workshops with her accordion at Highlander, but also during picket-line study groups. She called them "field trips," when

FACING Zilphia Horton singing on a picket line in the 1940s. *Highlander Research and Education Center Archives.*

students would join union protests as early as four or five in the morning to offer classes on labor history, law, and current events. At one such picket, mill owners opened fire with machine guns that injured women standing on either side of Horton. When the firing stopped, she and a few others faced the mill gates and sang "We Shall Not Be Moved." Horton remembered how people "began to come out again from behind barns and garages . . . and they stood there and were not moved and sang. And that's what won their organization."

In 1948, the national Congress of Industrial Organizations (CIO), under pressure from a renewed Red Scare, abruptly canceled what had been Horton's two-year project to publish an expanded labor songbook. In the anti-communist climate of the 1950s, she never worked with mainstream unions again. Horton had traveled the country for most of her adult life working for labor rights; her husband said suddenly she was "a singer without a movement."

A new crusade arose. Horton learned "We Will Overcome" in 1945 from Lucille Simmons and other women on strike against the American Tobacco Company in Charleston, South Carolina. It became Horton's favorite song and she closed meetings with it each evening at Highlander. Visitors like Pete Seeger learned it and republished it in *People's Songs* magazine in New York in 1948. Martin Luther King first heard it at Highlander in 1957 at a training for civil rights activists.

Just as this new movement was growing, Zilphia died in 1956, after drinking typewriter-cleaner that looked like a glass of water. She was forty-six years old. As she lay in hospital, she worried about her children and hoped some of what she'd done would continue to be useful.

After her death, Myles Horton lamented that they had no one to lead them in singing. Guy Carawan took over as Highlander's musical director and helped carry the music Horton had gathered into the Civil Rights Movement: "We Shall Not Be Moved," "Keep Your Eyes On the Prize," "We Shall Overcome." Songs she had taught to small groups with her accordion were sung by millions. Dozens more new movement songs were created using the methods Horton had developed.

If Horton had chosen, she might have been as famous as her friends Woody Guthrie, Pete Seeger, or Alan Lomax. Her gift was sharing the power of songs without seeking fame or attention. She encouraged communities to gather and sing and feel their strength. Her accordion played only a support role in Horton's story. After she died, it didn't spread in

Sis Cunningham of the Almanac Singers, ca. mid-1940s. Appeared in the Communist Party's *Daily Worker*. *From the photo collection held at the Tamiment Library,
New York University, by permission of the Communist Party USA.*

the Civil Rights Movement. Perhaps if she had lived, or if successor Guy
Carawan had played squeezebox instead of guitar, the folk revival would
have had more singing accordionists. Inspired by Horton (and without
needing microphones) they might have led political songs on through
the following turbulent decades.

Sis Cunningham: Bridge from Old to New

Agnes "Sis" Cunningham (1909–2004) set out to change the world with
her accordion, and in some ways she did. Her work onstage and off influenced the music and lyrics of activist artists around the world. She and
her husband, writer Gordon Friesen, founded and published *Broadside,* a
tiny but remarkably influential American political folk-song publication
that debuted unknown songwriters like Bob Dylan. Political songs that
premiered in her living room are sung decades later. Her accordion is

little remembered outside a few photos in folk music history books, but any time we hear a song from that era with political teeth, she helped spread it.

Growing up in poverty, she was driven to tell stories about common people and injustices. In the 1930s, Cunningham played accordion and composed activist songs for the Red Dust Players, an agitation-propaganda theater troupe that performed for desperately poor agricultural workers in the Midwest. They played on creaking porches in the light of the actors' car headlights for audiences who'd never seen a movie. Their shows featured songs and broad melodramas that were pitched to literally dirt-poor tenant farm-workers. One starred a farmer, his wife, and their beautiful daughter "Tillie" being chased around the stage by a black-cloaked and mustached Mr. Mortgage.

Cunningham recalled, "I took up my little accordion and started fooling around with tunes. In almost no time I had a whole song put together, and in a couple of hours I had four more ready. I had to do my memorizing while washing and ironing the week's working duds ... I had to look fairly presentable." Unfortunately, the response from nearby landowners was violent. Her song "Sundown" reflects the terrorism unleashed on anyone brave enough to speak for change:

> Well the very first meetin' we did call,
> Them bullets came through the church house wall,
> Planter don't 'llow no Union here,
> Machine gun's speakin' it mighty clear.

Activists faced brutality, disappearance, or murder by the racist, anti-union KKK and by vigilantes hired by landowners. In 1941, on the eve of America's entry into World War II, four people in Oklahoma were sentenced to ten years in prison for the possession of leftist literature—including the U.S. Constitution. Cunningham's story was not an American fairy tale of underdogs triumphing over grim adversity. The Red Dust Players were popular with their isolated audiences, but the campaign of threats put an end to their touring. Faced with arrest and violence, they disbanded and fled the region.

Retreating from the Midwest, Cunningham came to New York and joined the Almanac Singers, an early folk group that included Pete Seeger, Woody Guthrie, Millard Lampell, Bess Lomax (Alan's sister), and Lee Hays (who'd gone to church as a kid with Zilphia Horton and later formed the Weavers with Seeger). The Almanacs were hobbled by their association with Communist party politics. Over the span of 1941 (before Cunningham's arrival), the group's first album *Songs for John Doe* briefly preached non-intervention when the Soviets were in accord with the Nazis. After Hitler invaded Russia, the group quickly switched to pro-war songs. By the time Cunningham and her accordion joined in 1942, they were recording "Round and Round Hitler's Grave," and performing on radio for the overseas broadcasts of the Office of War Information. Uncompromising even when they were most popular, they lost at least one domestic gig because they refused to dress up as hillbillies. The band folded by 1943 as members took jobs in the war effort.

In the years after the breakup of the Almanacs, Cunningham's family was forced into unemployment and poverty by the anti-communist blacklist. Through the 1940s and '50s they suffered real hardships for their unpopular ideas, and the couple lived in economic precarity for the rest of their lives. With two children to care for in a city where they were banned from their professions, life was bitterly hard. A never-published song Cunningham wrote at the time went:

Have you ever dug around in your old coat pockets
In your old coat pockets for a dime!
You're plain flat broke and it ain't no joke
And you dig around one last time.

You've done it before but you do it once more
Keep pokin' your fingers through the holes,
And from a fuzzy corner if you dig out a quarter
It shines in your hand like gold.

She later recalled, "The singing phase of my life came to a slow, painful end during this period ... My accordion got heavier and heavier." It took years for blacklisted former folk stars like Pete Seeger to regain any kind of viable career. Some, like Cunningham, never returned to the stage. "To say that it was painful is an understatement. I suffered deeply; I couldn't stop blaming myself. I felt I had failed. I went on for years under the cloud of failure, unable to sing, unable to write. My silence was total."

Eventually she saw the labor songs of the 1930s give birth to singing movements for civil rights and ongoing social change. In 1962,

Cunningham and her husband founded *Broadside* magazine in their public housing apartment. The first issue had Bob Dylan's "Talkin' John Birch Society Blues," and Malvina Reynolds's "Come Clean Blues" (about a strike at the Colgate toothpaste plant in Berkeley). They printed three hundred copies on a mimeograph machine and sold them for thirty-five cents.

Broadside was what we would today call a zine, a tiny magazine with a few thousand subscribers, hand produced around Cunningham and Friesen's dining-room table. Each issue included articles about "topical" political/protest songs and songwriters, along with the texts and music of timely tunes. Little-known songwriters who appeared in its early pages included Phil Ochs, Bernice Johnson Reagon, Buffy Sainte-Marie, Pete Seeger, and Nina Simone. Artists came by the *Broadside* apartment/office and sang songs into the Revere tape recorder Seeger donated, then Cunningham transcribed the songs for the magazine. Issue six featured the unreleased "Blowin' in the Wind."

The magazine was sustained throughout its years by volunteers and donations from benefactors like Toshi Seeger and her husband, Pete. Cunningham and Friesen lived on a shoestring "that stretched over the entire expanse of *Broadside*'s existence." Even within the folk music community, support was intermittent. The rival *Little Sandy Review* dismissed *Broadside* as too political with not enough real folk, disliking Dylan's topical songs specifically. Cunningham defended the new crop of songwriters even when they wrote about things they'd never experienced. She once dryly cited nuclear war as a topic begging for authorial distance.

Lost amidst the larger task of promoting peoples' songs was Cunningham's accordion. She had packed it away decades earlier in the cramped world of the blacklist. She knew and corresponded with other picket-line accordionists like Zilphia Horton of the Highlander Center, and union singer Jenny Vincent. *Broadside* continued the tradition Horton's sing-along songsters and the IWW *Little Red Songbook*, but gatherings of protest singers were turning toward solo performers with guitars, with no accordions in sight.

Broadside continued publishing until 1988, when Sis and her husband were in their late seventies. Songs by Leon Rosselson, Lucinda Williams, Vanessa Redgrave, and Johnny Cash all appeared in the magazine. Cunningham reflected, "Time only will tell whether our efforts through the years served to bring about a modicum of change." About her earlier years, she reflected, "I will not say I have no bitterness about what happened to us; I would be lying if I said that. The blacklist was a death that we lived through."

> I wish I had been this clear-headed about my inability to continue singing. My talent in music had already started to die of neglect some years before Gordon was blacklisted, and I saw the trouble as stemming from something within me instead of two primary outside forces: working-class oppression and women's oppression, both killers. The circumstances of the blacklist was for me only the final pull into silence.

The adversity Cunningham relates in her biography never really let up. Like too many of the people she advocated for, her life was one of struggling to get by, including eventually the trials of aging in the New York neighborhood she and her husband had contributed to for years.

In the midst of *Broadside*'s run, Cunningham was finally convinced to record an album of her own for Folkways records, *Sundown* (1976). She sang songs from the Red Dust days and told stories of hard times and struggles. It's mostly her alone with a bit of guitar. She didn't play her accordion.

Years later, accordionists were part of Occupy Wall Street, Black Lives Matter, anti-government protests in Egypt, and refugee resistance in Europe. The instrument remains well equipped and ready to lead songs indoors or in the street. Sis Cunningham's work for a hopeful future continues. As she put it: "They would have folks like us die without a fuss; just break down and dissolve. We didn't oblige."

Jenny Vincent: The Long View

Lifelong political activist Jenny Vincent (1913–2016) was another musician unafraid to incorporate ethnic music and an accordion into her repertoire. In sync with Sis Cunningham and Zilphia Horton, she took up folk music in the 1930s, and, like them, she never gained fame or fortune.

Vincent took her accordion where you couldn't take a piano and played folk songs that reached people when formal music wouldn't. She played hootenannies, fundraisers, and picket lines with Pete Seeger, Woody Guthrie, and Paul Robeson. Throughout her career, her instrument was a little Hohner Imperial IIA, a 32-bass accordion she found at

a New York pawnshop in 1948. It was ideal for playing simple music in the open air. The logo on hers read, "PERIAL," and I wish someone had asked if she modified it to avoid playing an "imperialist" instrument.

During and after World War II, Vincent played veterans' hospitals where one GI told a Red Cross volunteer, "That girl did more for the morale of the men than any movie actress could." Rather than focusing on music from her classical background, she played folk tunes that soldiers knew. At war's end she returned to her adopted home in New Mexico to continue campaigning and researching traditional music.

Playing for the Rocky Mountain Farmers Union, she met Taos Public School teacher Rufina Baca. With Baca's help, she introduced Spanish American songs to local public schools. At that time in the 1940s, speaking Spanish was forbidden for students or teachers. As a volunteer, though, Vincent sang Spanish and other songs and continued to do so for forty years. Decades later, adults recognized her in the street and remembered her singing in their grade school classrooms.

Vincent's own son once came home from school and said the other kids were swearing at him in Spanish and he felt like he was being discriminated against. Vincent asked what language they had to speak in the school. When he said "English," she replied, "So who is being discriminated against?" She suggested he pick up some Spanish: "We told him to go ahead and learn the dirty words first." He became fluent, made lifelong friends, and eventually was a Fulbright scholar in Venezuela.

In 1950, the "Salt of the Earth" strike began when Latino zinc miners protested the fact that they got lower wages, from separate payroll windows, for more dangerous work than white workers. When strikers were ordered to stop picketing, their wives and family members took over the strike lines. For fifteen months they faced violence, imprisonment, tear gas, and death threats—and then they won a contract.

Vincent had played at the mine workers' union convention before the strike began. She took her accordion to the women's picket line to sing "Solidarity Forever" and "Union Maid." When unionists were imprisoned, Vincent, her husband, and their neighbors risked their property to post a $27,000 bond to free them.

The strike was immortalized when blacklisted filmmakers created the movie *Salt of the Earth* (1954). The film stared members of the union and their families, and the production faced violent opposition as two

FACING Jenny Vincent in New York City, 1947. *Courtesy of the Vincent family.*

union halls and a union leader's home were burned by arsonists during the filming. Banned by distributors for years in the United States, only a few copies passed from one union-hall showing to another. Now it is seen as a landmark of independent filmmaking and the portrayal of working-class and Latino issues.

Vincent herself faced the blacklist for joining the Communist Party in 1943, when the U.S. was allied with Russia against the Nazis. In that brief time, supporting the Soviet Union seemed almost patriotic, but such excuses weren't admissible during the J. Edgar Hoover–led witch hunt that followed.

The anti-communism of the 1950s meant choosing between threats of prison or informing on friends. There were so many undercover investigators sent to Vincent's home that they unknowingly reported on each other. In Vincent's case, infiltrators were paid for stories they simply made up. At least one, Harvey Matusow, served time in prison for false testimony.

Just as folk music was reaching the pop charts in 1960, Vincent was subpoenaed backstage at the National Folk Festival to appear before the Senate Internal Security Subcommittee. Facing a negative right-wing press campaign, she quoted President Eisenhower's words about the folk festival: "It is a dramatic reminder that our individual freedoms and national strength come from the interplay of diverse social forces directed toward a common goal." Vincent added, "I believe our country needs to breathe the full fresh air of freedom, and we will be able to breathe better when this committee, and its counterpart the House Un-American Activities Committee, are abolished." The Senate's investigation produced nothing and she happily returned to the festival a few years later.

In 1956, she formed the Trio de Taos with Hattie Trujillo and Nat Flores. For thirty years they played dance music together on mandolin, guitar, and Vincent's accordion. When she turned one hundred years old in 2013, her recordings, publications, and support of New Mexican folkloric music garnered her recognition from the governor for doing what had been illegal when she started seventy years earlier.

Vincent lived through more than one lifetime of the country's politics. In 1969, while visiting the Highlander Center in Tennessee, she and Puerto Rican poet Miguel Torres translated a verse to the song "De Colores," anthem of the Hispanic Civil Rights Movements in the U.S. "*Los grandes amores de muchos colores me gustan a mi* / Love that embraces all colors, all races is greatest for me."

Jenny's correspondence with one-time accordionist Sis Cunningham praised her perseverance in the cause of activist folk music. Like these others, Vincent faced suffering, hatred, and repression in her activist work and her life. She responded with music and joy and carried on.

The 1960s Folk Revival: This Machine Kills Accordions

I wished I had used it more on some of my past records...
Actually accordion players were the first
musicians that I had seen a lot of growing up.
BOB DYLAN

The 1960s folk boom sprang out of young people's alienation from commodified culture. Then it became part of that culture. Folk fans felt called toward older rural styles as an alternative to mass-produced entertainment. They didn't mind that what they called "folk music" was a fairly modern creation purchased by millions of people on records made in industrial factories.

Folk-style songwriters had more in common with professional country artists like Hank Williams and Jimmie Rodgers than with isolated "primitive" musicians. Originally it was urbane rustics like Vernon Dalhart (1925's "Wreck of the Old 97") who pioneered the techniques that folk revivalists emulated. Country scholar Patrick Huber wrote that, "New York citybilly singers [in the 1920s] redefined recorded hillbilly music from a primarily instrumental genre to a vocal-oriented one, a listening—as opposed to a dance—music... [They] paved the way for the subsequent rise of such Southern singing stars as Jimmie Rodgers."

The instant 1960s folk musicians began writing and copyrighting their own songs, they learned the lessons that rural-style artists like the Carter Family had: to make money you had to own your material. This was a profound breach from the folk ideal, where music was an age-old community property. The music industry practically mandated this change, as technology allowed artists to reach huge paying audiences.

The folk revival went electric as soon as performers played for more than a handful of people. Pete Seeger himself said, "Anyone who uses a microphone is electrified." Before the 1920s, vocalists had to shout. Electrical recording and live amplification made way for laid-back "crooning" singers who didn't need operatic training to be heard. The nuanced performances and personal connection that crooners, cowboys, and country blues singers gave to record and radio listeners were impossible without this modern technology. Years later, when Joan Baez sang into microphones at folk festivals, she drew as much from Bing Crosby as she did from primordial folk singers.

The music of the folk revival was an inviting combination: exotic, but not overwhelmingly demanding. The tunes followed accessible patterns of style and structure. There were few thorny ethnic rhythms. The language was English (even if shaded with Southern dialects).

The folk revival was perhaps the accordion's best opportunity to join the flood that became rock music. In theory, some white kid could have cleaned up playing unruly accordion. Popularized versions of zydeco, Irish button box or rowdy polkas could have made somebody a star, but there was no Dylan of the squeezebox.

A Traditional Conundrum

The accordion was so entrenched in the glamour of mid-century pop music that spectators could easily overlook the instrument's traditional past. For white middle-class youngsters, the accordion wasn't an old-fashioned instrument to be discovered, it represented the status quo. Parents paid for accordion lessons. It was on television every night. There were classes in schools: you could get a college degree in classical accordion. Those wanting an anti-establishment alternative looked elsewhere.

The brand name of one chrome-trimmed 1950s-era accordion was "Futuramic." This ran directly counter to nostalgic folk ideals. For middle-class kids struggling against pervasive consumerism, accordions' space-age designs hurt their marketability. Buying a new guitar or a banjo may have been just as commercial as shopping for an accordion, but it felt like you were exploring a bygone era, not an appliance store.

Urbane Folk

When Wisconsin old-time fiddler Bernard Johnson was asked what he thought about folk music, he replied, "I never tried to play that." By the late 1950s, polished groups like the Kingston Trio and the racially integrated Tarriers had adapted the Weavers' lively style for new audiences. Their trimly harmonized records bore little resemblance to traditional styles, but they sold remarkably well.

As performers gained fame, concerts became profit-oriented rather than community events. Public gathering places like New York City's Washington Square Park were gradually replaced by folk festivals in Newport or Berkeley, where much of the audience came to see the stars.

A division grew by the early 1960s between popular folk singers and traditional instrumentalists. Some said that songwriters like Bob Dylan strayed when they started creating original material. Throughout this clash, the accordion was otherwise occupied. Rather than arguing about folk music, hundreds of thousands of Dick Contino imitators were competing to see who could play the fastest version of "Flight of the Bumblebee." The social-climbing accordion scene stood in stark contrast to the folk revival's earnest struggles over authenticity.

Rudimentary folk squeezeboxers would have been laughed off accordion stages in the 1950s. We'll never know if singer-songwriter accordionists would have been rebuffed by baffled folk musicians as well. It would be almost fifty years and a new century before Edmonton's Maria Dunn, Seattle's Jason Webley, and others would finally demonstrate the accordion's potential as a solo singer-songwriter instrument.

New Lost Squeezebox String Bands

Much of the long-lost music that folk revivalists went to such great lengths to recover in the 1950s and '60s had been popular only twenty-five years earlier. The global economic failure of the Great Depression, followed by the trauma of World War II and the resultant leap of electronic and manufacturing technology had created a cultural chasm that is difficult to fathom. Children raised in this new world found the old one distant, and, for some, entrancing.

Old-fashioned acoustic guitars were the overwhelming choice for young folk songwriters and singers. The revival also involved string bands modeled on Southern "old-time" recordings. They featured guitars, banjos, fiddles, and mandolins, with an occasional autoharp or dulcimer. Limiting their repertoire to Southern music, revival string musicians bypassed accordion-friendly regions where many of them actually lived.

John Cohen of the premier revival string band the New Lost City Ramblers had seen New York State string bands with accordions in the 1950s. That rural New York tradition went back at least to African American fiddle player Alva Belcher, who used accordion in his band in the 1880s and '90s. Northern old-time music also included Pennsylvania mountain players described as having fiddles, harmonicas, and accordions in 1900. A survey of rural Midwestern country fiddlers who played between 1900 and 1940 showed many who doubled on accordion. But their accordions didn't make it onto records, and the revivalists wouldn't hear it.

Uprooting the Folk Accordion: Prehistoric Shellac

The biggest historical difference between string bands from different regions was that old-time musicians in the South recorded more. Researcher Simon Bronner remarked, "It is curious that almost no recorded legacy exists for the pre–World War II era of country music in New York [State] considering the ... large amount of country music activity." This lack of regional diversity led to the mistaken assumption that Southern recordings represented old-time rural styles everywhere.

Revivalists took inspiration from historic rural music based on the authority of aged shellac—whoever spent an afternoon in a recording studio in the 1920s. Southern old-time songs and hot square dance fiddles earned places in the revival canon. Similar music and even the same tunes in the style of the Upper Midwest, New York, Pennsylvania, and Connecticut—home to many folk revivalists—were often passed over. Even after Tracy Schwarz joined the New Lost City Ramblers in 1963 and began promoting Cajun accordion, old-time Northern and Midwestern squeezebox traditions lost their place in the new "folk" treasury.

☞ Harmonica: Cousin to the Blues

IT IS WORTH commenting on why harmonicas did not suffer the fate of their cousins, the accordions. The mouth-harp's success parallels the challenges that brought down the accordion. They both appeared in the industrial 1800s and spread rapidly as the nineteenth century progressed. Firmly associated with folk music, harmonicas were very seldom burdened with the efforts of some accordionists to raise their instrument's stature. When the folk revival arrived, harmonicas were already in millions of pockets.

Today, harmonicas are primarily associated with the blues. This dates back to the ability to bend notes and play blues scales, which let harmonicas survive where the African American button box failed in the early 1900s. With harmonica on board, the blues of course was ready to become a key building block of twentieth-century music.

Blown into a microphone, the humble mouth-harp roared. Chicago blues harmonicas sparred with the new electric guitar and created the blueprint for the future. The unprecedented volume of electric blues cross-bred with country music's pre-industrial nostalgia and pushed the folk revival toward rock 'n' roll. Pocket-sized harmonicas successfully adapted and survived—accordions, not so much.

Anti-immigrant Prejudice and the English-Only Revival

There were other reasons Southern old-time or country styles came to represent white folk music. There wasn't really much purity involved, though. African American musicians taught some of the most well-known early country fiddlers and guitarists. This kind of musical integration made Southern music unique and exciting. But in the North and Midwest, a different breed of multi-ethnic cross-fertilization prevented the region's adoption by the folk revival.

Starting back in the 1800s, North American folklorists sought to defend Anglo-Saxon culture against what one scholar has termed "potential cultural dangers which, if left unchecked, might mongrelize and debase the American populace." In 1899, the multi-ethnic mix in the Upper Midwest had journalist Wardon Allan Curtis calling for an end to its "strongholds of foreignism." His hope was that "in another generation it will all be American."

Nationalist and racist pressure vastly reduced immigration in the 1920s. Assimilation was encouraged and Anglo-American folk culture was promoted at the expense of others. Folklorist Archie Green wrote years later, "Some ballad scholars held an imbedded belief that Anglo-Saxon lore . . . was not only quintessentially American, but also an antidote to Catholic, Celtic, alien, radical or assorted dark-skinned terrors."

Northern folk revivalists in the 1950s unwittingly furthered this assimilationist initiative. Many of them were second or third-generation children of immigrants who no longer had Irish, Yiddish, Finnish, or Slovenian as their first or even second language. When children of immigrants were familiar with their parents' songs, few had gateways to other traditions. Uprooted from their multi-ethnic heritage, Northern and Midwestern revival audiences embraced a romanticized version of monolingual Southern music.

Nativism, assimilation, and the obstacles of language accelerated the downfall of the accordion. Two generations had danced to Frankie Yankovic's "Americanized" polkas and watched Italian Americans like Dick Contino pump out accordion records. When children of immigrants were cut off from their heritage, the accordion was stripped of its circumstance. In the worst cases, young people internalized nineteenth-century aversions to their ancestry. Without a strong community context and vital folk repertoire, young players were unprepared to make traditional accordions contemporary.

European immigrants weren't alone in their exclusion from the folk revival. Most Spanish-language music was ignored, as was the century-plus history of Chinese and other Asian American musicians in North America. With notable exceptions like Buffy Sainte-Marie, Indigenous cultures were known to only a few outside Native communities. Many of these traditions suffered, while a few survived or even prospered outside the white, middle-class realm of the folk boom.

Among the rare exceptions to this ethnic erasure were Irish ballad groups like the Irish Rovers (who sang in English). The Newport Folk Foundation also laudably used some of its profits to support Louisiana

French culture. Folk stages did welcome some ethnic players in the 1960s, and progressive folklorists gathered irreplaceable recordings. But it wasn't until the 1970s that Jewish, Mexican American, Creole, and Cajun accordions really began to get attention beyond their regions.

When voices did rise in support of ethnic music during the revival, their efforts benefited the accordion. Most important were several prescient collectors and preservationists. Chris Strachwitz, the Austrian-born founder of Arhoolie Records, consistently released zydeco, Cajun, and conjunto accordion music beginning in the 1960s. The careers of Flaco Jiménez, Clifton Chenier, and others received some of their first exposure outside of their own communities through Arhoolie and other revival labels like Moses Asch's Folkways Records.

Richard Spottswood was another eclectic record collector who, in the 1970s, recognized the lack of attention ethnic music was receiving. He compiled the Library of Congress's fifteen-LP *Folksongs of America* anthology for the U.S. bicentennial in the 1970s—specifically including immigrant and ethnic dance music. Spottswood was also one of the main contributors to the Library of Congress's book *Ethnic Recordings in America: A Neglected Heritage* (1982). This culminated in his epic work, published in 1990, *Ethnic Music on Records: A Discography of Ethnic Recordings Produced in the United States, 1893–1942.*

Kip Lornell, Anne Rasmussen, and others also worked over the years to cover the full range of North American ethnomusicology. Even as far back as 1961, folk researcher Bruno Nettl's *An Introduction to Folk Music in the United States* included significant ethnic music content. Revivalists, however, failed to integrate these multi-regional riches. Years later, James Leary commented, "Perhaps matters might have been different had Nettl not adorned his cover with an accordionist during a guitar- and banjo-dominated era."

And No Dancing...

Peter, Paul, and Mary's debut album came with a warning that "it deserves your exclusive attention. No dancing, please." As singers and guitarists stole spotlights and recording contracts, lively accordions maintained a toehold at the edge of the folk revival in some traditional dance gatherings.

Cursory histories of modern country and folk music often start with the songs of the Carter Family and Jimmie Rodgers, but the earliest rural music on record was dance music. Hillbilly recording began in the 1920s with instrumental fiddle soloists. Only in 1923 did radio artist Fiddlin' John Carson have the first country hit by adding words over his fiddle playing. By 1924, professional New York singers like Vernon Dalhart were shifting the genre from predominantly dance instrumentals toward sit-down music for listening.

Whereas dance bands and upbeat jukebox hits still had a huge impact on country music, the emphasis on lyrics lasted. Folk revivalists intensified this pattern of listening rather than dancing. Young people sang ballads with an earnest sincerity, but largely dropped folk's dancing fiddles, banjos, and the regional squeezeboxes. In doing so they abandoned more than half of the folk repertoire—skipping over tricky dance steps in favor of coffee-house choruses.

This refashioning also affected revivalist string bands. Prior to the recording era, dance tunes were often played by only one instrumentalist. Back in the early days of Chicago's *National Barn Dance*, solo fiddlers proved too monotonous for early radio. More complicated and interesting arrangements made old tunes entertaining for modern audiences who weren't dancing.

Modern changes affected other instruments besides the accordion. Percussive banjo was slowly ostracized from commercial folk. Almost no fiddle players appeared outside the few old-time bands like the New Lost City Ramblers. The folk music that dominated the market sold records and advertising, not dance manuals and classes. Community-oriented music gave way to an individualist emphasis on singers who made records you could listen to at home. This didn't require dancing or accordions.

Folk dancing has its own tumultuous history paralleling the development of the music. It included black string musicians who developed traditional dance-calls; a racist Henry Ford promoting square dancing as a bulwark against the corruption of Jewish and African American jazz; modern promoters advocating for dancing in school physical fitness programs; and various battles over style and authenticity. Suffice it to say, folk dancing has its own racial and social history that continues to this day.

There are photos of square dancing at Washington Square Park, the epicenter of the folk revival in New York. There were also dances at the

Highlander Center and at other folk cultural gatherings for years. Pete Seeger and his future wife, Toshi, met at a dance put on by the influential square dance evangelist Margot Mayo in the 1930s. But dance is ephemeral, and it is challenging to mass-produce and commodify. Square dance callers seldom made fortunes on hit records.

Folk and square dancing did survive, though, and included more accordions than any other aspect of the revival. Square dances in New York State frequently kept accordions within the reach of revivalists. Beginning in the 1930s, accordionist Floyd Woodhull's old-time band played six nights a week for years around Elmira in New York State.

In cold New England winters, dances were hosted by families for generations. They'd welcome dancers into their home or a local hall, teach steps and provide the music. Fiddler, accordionist, and dance-caller Dudley Laufman recalls dances in New Hampshire in the 1940s that sparked a lifelong passion. Through his and others' efforts, folk dances worked their way into the late-1960s "back-to-the-land" aesthetic and held a place for the accordion on the periphery of the wider folk music boom.

Millions of people were, of course, dancing during the folk revival, just not to folk music. Dancing was pretty much the basis for the usurper rock 'n' roll, and novelties like "The Twist" even came with instructions that echoed square dance calls. Folkies like Phil Ochs got laughs in coffee houses by mocking the early Beatles, but he acknowledged that pop music gave people something his topical political songs didn't. There never was a chart-topping folk-rock dance craze, but when Dylan finally hit the pop charts, he did it by channeling Chuck Berry rather than the Carter Family. His "Subterranean Homesick Blues" carried a debt to rapid-fire dance callers, but the barn (and the accordion) had been abandoned with the squares.

The Ballad of the Lost Polka

In 1965, when folk rockers the Byrds recorded their massive hit "Mr. Tambourine Man," they shifted Bob Dylan's original slow 2/4 demo to a swaying 4/4 rock beat. What would the Byrds have sounded like if they'd kept the 2/4 and become a psychedelic polka band?

The folk revival's indifference to dancing fed a disdain for polka in mainstream North America. The intense distaste for accordions that many pop music fans developed after the 1960s was only rivaled by the casual ridicule heaped on this jaunty folk dance.

The polka had been an international dance craze twice: first in the 1840s and again in the 1940s. Between these waves it fit most definitions of folk music, but its climb to the pop charts in the 1940s came right as the folk canon was coalescing. As far as folk preservationists were concerned, popularity cost the dance its credibility.

Polka's misfortune was compounded because its 1940s–50s window of mainstream success happened just prior to the artistic revolution of rock 'n' roll. In 1950, waltzes were calmly overtaking polkas on the hit parade. Such orderly transitions were shattered as technological and stylistic changes altered music irreversibly.

The polka found itself forsaken, shut out by popular music and cut off from the folk revival. Mainstream enthusiasm deteriorated into widespread derision. "The Twist" revolutionized social dance and many music fans gave up coordinated couples dances entirely. The loss of the frivolous polka was part of the gelding of folk music of Anglo North America, and presaged rock's own sit-down orientation that began with the Beatles' *Sgt. Pepper* and lasted until the rise of disco in the 1970s.

It is jarring today for Anglo listeners to discover polkas as the basis for "non-Welk" styles such as Mexico's *narcocorrido* "gangster polkas" with their lyrics about drug-war violence. Such outrageous content challenges the prejudice that has restricted polkas to punchline clichés. Barring a few experiments from groups like Brave Combo or avant-garde artist Guy Klucevsek, few musicians breached the barriers isolating the polka world. Even "Weird Al" Yankovic's parody humor engages with polka's joyful spirit without leading audiences beyond stereotype.

Rejected by early preservationists for being *in* fashion, polka was dismissed by the public as *old-fashioned*. Revival audiences missed the chance to create new kinds of polkas, and polka missed a chance for renewal. By the time rock 'n' roll arrived, both the polka and the accordion had left the building.

PART FIVE

THE

ACCORDION

EXILE IN THE

AGE OF ROCK

ROCK 'N' ROLL is simplistically formulated as a blend of white country music and black R&B. As we've seen, country was deeply influenced by black string bands and African American blues, as well as the tangle of minstrelsy, vaudeville, religious, and older folk traditions. Meanwhile, R&B artists contended with the nation's system of segregation but attracted their share of cultural collaborators as well, including influences from Cuban, Mexican, and Hawaiian music and hundreds of years of contact with Europeans.

Before rock 'n' roll, accordions found their way into pop music, western bands, and broad swaths of ethnic folk music. On the other hand, the instrument was mostly rejected by blues players and much of African American jazz. After slick electric guitars drove accordions out of Nashville, the squeeze-box was in for a rocky road.

Early rock reunited the artificially split "race" and "hillbilly" strains of Southern music. Marginalized artists from both genres had found it difficult to penetrate the big-money pop charts. When R&B and country songs started crossing over in the 1950s, it opened the floodgates. Suddenly lowdown country and formerly segregated R&B artists were heard indiscriminately on radio from the Canadian border to the Caribbean, and on record in every port where U.S. ships docked. A young accordion player named John Lennon heard blues records brought to Liverpool by American sailors. No accordions appeared on those discs, and he begged his mother for a guitar. As rock 'n' roll swept the airwaves, the accordion started a decades-long decline.

16

Rockin' the Accordion

ROM THE 1960S to the '80s, a generation of journalists and scholars were unyieldingly oblivious to the accordion's place in American music. This included its presence in the earliest rock 'n' roll. Debates rage over which version of "Rocket 88" was the original rock 'n' roll song. An entire book by Jim Dawson and Steve Propes lines up fifty candidates to ask *What Was the First Rock 'n' Roll Record?* Online partisans trace influential recordings as far back Jim Jackson's "Kansas City Blues" in 1927.

Eight years before Bill Haley's contender "Rock around the Clock," though, Pee Wee King and His Golden West Cowboys' released "Ten Gallon Boogie" (1947), perhaps the primordial rock 'n' roll accordion recording. The vocals aren't very aggressive, but the rhythm of Harold Bradley's electric guitar only needed a snare backbeat to take off. Meanwhile, Pee Wee's sloppy squeezebox boogie solo has the spark of acoustic punk thirty years early—there's hot fiddle and pedal steel too.

On the R&B side, Chifton Chenier's "My Soul," released on Chess Records in 1957, had Chenier playing Chicago blues accordion at the base of the rock family tree. Pity that British and American artists who worshiped Chess blues players like Muddy Waters didn't notice this electrified accordionist amidst their idols.

R&B and country had both largely shed their accordion connections by the mid-1950s. Clifton Chenier and other Creole players kept accordions percolating in nascent zydeco, but their French Creole touring circuit never brought them R&B stardom. Meanwhile, non-Creole blacks had basically given up on accordions long before they could influence rock.

From the country side, when Bill Haley and the Comets played "Rock around the Clock" live, Johnny Grande played accordion. But on the Comets' recordings, the squeezebox was replaced by piano. Outside of a very few exceptions, accordions were uniformly dropped by later white rock bands.

Electric guitars were the instrument of the day. Even R&B's mighty saxophone could not compete as amplification cut the number of musicians needed to fill dance halls. After Little Richard joined the ministry and Jerry Lee Lewis married his cousin, pianos dropped out and guitars took the lead. When the Beatles hit as a self-contained group of four, they established the simplified, accordion-less combo as the standard.

Like most cultural changes, nobody planned the rise of rock or the fall of the accordion. Without malign intent, musicians and entrepreneurs simply struggled by trial and error to create what would sell. The resurrection of interest in accordions today invites a long-neglected accounting for its rather spectacular demise. Of all the ensemble instruments that lost ground to rock 'n' roll—saxophones, piano, fiddles—why did accordions become such a pariah for almost half a century?

The Dawn of Accordion Rock

The writers who created the story of pop music ignored the accordion partially because its ubiquity made it uninteresting. No one could predict how quickly the instrument would fall from grace. Today we sift through historians' discard bin to find the seeds of rock 'n' roll accordion that were planted while the instrument reached pervasive popularity in the 1950s. Sadly, they did not bear fruit.

Pee Wee King: Returning to Rock

Country star Pee Wee King (who we met in Chapter 14) kept up with the times. In the 1930s he joined those in Nashville who welcomed drums, electric guitars, and of course his own accordion. He hitched onto more trends in the 1940s, adding the early electronic Hammond Solovox organ.

Bands cashing in on new trends can be cringe-worthy, but Pee Wee and the Golden West Cowboys regularly hit the sweet spot mixing country with jive-jazz to become hillbilly boogie. They displayed their take on the burgeoning genre in great late-1940s tracks "Ten Gallon Boogie" and "Bull Fiddle Boogie." In the mid-1950s, a hopped-up version of the *Dragnet* TV show theme and a cover of "Blue Suede Shoes" confirmed their credentials as squeezebox explorers in the early rock 'n' roll wilderness. More was to come.

Johnny Grande: Accordion in the "First Rock and Roll Band"

It was a Bill Haley and the Comets record that white Cleveland DJ Alan Freed first called "rock and roll." There was a long, mostly sexual etymology for the term, but Haley's bassist Marshall Lytle remembers Freed playing their version of "Rock This Joint" in 1952 while repeatedly yelling over the air, "Rock and roll, everybody!" until the phones lit up with requests.

Bill Haley's earlier group, the Four Aces of Western Swing (featured in Chapter 14) had split in 1949. His follow-up venture, the Saddlemen, streamlined into the space-age Comets in 1952. Billing themselves as "cowboy jive," they were what blogger Marcello Carlin calls western swing's "rumbustious" answer to R&B's jump-blues combos, which took off as the big bands tightened their belts in the 1950s. The best-looking guy in the band was the accordionist.

Johnny Grande was born in South Philadelphia to an Italian family. He joined the Four Aces in 1949 and stuck with Haley all the way until 1962 (because he was a full partner paid a percentage, rather than the lower salary for backing musicians). Grande was important to the group because he read music and kept the arrangements. He played accordion and piano—mostly using the squeezebox while touring and on TV and movies, since it was portable so he could do dance routines with the rest of the band.

The Saddlemen had been one of the first white bands that attempted to play black R&B numbers. In Philadelphia, during the Korean War, they played country music for servicemen until 10 p.m. then switched to their hillbilly-R&B mix. Audiences packed clubs to see them.

Their early R&B cover recordings were curtailed by distribution problems and struggled to match the success the original black artists had on the segregated R&B charts. The Comets' covers though, with their hillbilly guitar, rattling bass, and palatable but not-too-threatening energy,

were the ones that eventually sold millions. White bands like the Comets carried the music across racist barriers, but it's clear the color line kept R&B artists like Jackie Brenston ("Rocket 88") and Jimmy Preston ("Rock This Joint") from the potential of their original records.

The Comets recorded only a few accordion (rather than piano) tunes, including 1954's sloppy-hot and rather absurd "Straight Jacket." Their 1956 album *Rock 'n' Roll Stage Show* featured the instrumental "Rockin' Little Tune," which jumps nicely, with false endings and smart guitar, sax, and accordion solos. It was a showpiece written by Grande, and if his name is on the birth certificate for rock 'n' roll accordion, it's right there.

After relentless international touring for fading audiences, a worn-out Grande retired. Closer to the sexy image of a rock star than Haley ever was, Grande's accordion went along for the ride as they helped white kids start rolling.

In 1987, Haley was inducted into the Rock and Roll Hall of Fame without the Comets. Grande took this as inspiration to reform the group as "the World's Oldest Rock and Roll Band" and toured internationally. He was playing into his seventies, before his death in 2006.

Clifton Chenier: Louisiana Rock

Clifton Chenier is known as the King of the Zydeco (see Chapter 9), but he was also the most important early R&B player to play rock 'n' roll accordion. Beginning in Louisiana and East Texas, Chenier brought the blues to the instrument, but he wasn't the first R&B act to embrace the squeezebox. The Creole Musical Three, Julie Gardner, and Christine Chatman (see Chapter 6) left tempting testimonials to blues accordion, but no known recordings to preserve what they sounded like. Chenier recorded prolifically and his influence is heard in every zydeco band in the world.

For years, Chenier played with just his brother Cleveland on rubboard: no bass, or drums. Mastering the accordion's left hand, he proved you could play boogie-woogie on the Stradella system that had been designed for waltzes and polkas. By the time rock 'n' roll broke, Chenier had electrified his accordion to compete with electric bass and guitars. Chris Strachwitz remembered later, "The guys who would repair

FACING Johnny Grande promotional photograph for Hohner accordions, 1957. *Courtesy of Hohner Accordions/D.M. Gregoire.*

accordions, they would put the pickups into the instruments, just like they did later with the Cajun ones."

Chenier said he wanted to sound like Ray Charles, aiming for both the R&B and pop charts with music that crossed boundaries. Even one hit in the 1950s could have made Chenier and his accordion as influential as Little Richard or Fats Domino. The closest he came was the crushing "My Soul," released by Chicago's Checker/Chess Records in 1957. It churned out intense Chicago blues with a young Etta James on backup vocals and Chenier's raw accordion as what might have seemed a bonus novelty. Released alongside labelmates Chuck Berry and Bo Diddley, it sold well, but never crossed over to the wider white market.

Imagine a million youngsters coming home from their accordion lessons and seeing this tall black man with gold teeth playing electric accordion on TV. Years later zydeco helped revive the instrument, but if Chenier had hit in the 1950s, the accordion might never have gone away.

As the first wave of rock 'n' roll faded, Chenier returned to his Southern (Louisiana–Texas–California) circuit. His star shone in the Creole community, but for years the music that was beginning to be called zydeco was little-known to outsiders. Chenier was the explosive squeezebox icon America never knew. Without him in the spotlight, rock 'n' roll accordion missed its greatest champion.

The 1960s: Garage Bands and the Accordion's Last Stand

Before William Schimmel became a classical composer (and played on several classic Tom Waits records), he witnessed the downfall of the accordion. "It was 1956 when I took up the accordion, the year that rock 'n' roll got on national television. I remember watching Bill Haley and the Comets, and in their first appearance, Johnny Grande played the accordion... I noticed that after these bands made one appearance with an accordionist, the second time the accordion would be gone. That was because the accordion could not compete with the Fender Stratocaster... The Fender Stratocaster was thin, electric and phallic. The accordion made the performer look fat. Fat was sexy in vaudeville, when the accordion first appeared, because fat meant prosperity. But it wasn't sexy in rock 'n' roll."

As rock music grew, young people who'd taken accordion lessons looked for a way to join in. Local bands like the multi-racial Problem Set from Tennessee Tech had accordionists who'd come out of years of classical training. If you imagine an alternative history where the squeeze-box became a rock mainstay, these bands would have started a new era. Instead they became the last crop of forward-looking accordionists for almost a generation.

☞ Farfisa: The Accordion Heart of the Garage Band Sound

THE ROCK 'N' RACKET that dominated the 1960s was, ironically, backed by an accordion company. Following the British Invasion, Farfisa organs became a central part of America's garage band counterattack. "Farfisa" was short for "**Fa**bbriche **R**iunite de **Fisa**rmoniche," the "United Accordion Factories" founded in 1946 by the combined Settimio Soprani, Scandalli, and Frontalini accordion companies.

The company made accordions for years before branching into other keyboards. Their pioneering work on electronic Cordovox organ accordions (see Chapter 17) led directly to the portable combo (small-group) organs that made their name famous. The company was inspired by (and competed against) the U.K.-based Vox organs that most of the British Invasion groups used. The more affordable Farfisa fueled North America's response.

Immediately after premiering in 1964, Farfisa organs powered up the charts on garage classics by Sam the Sham and the Pharaohs ("Wooly Bully," 1965), and ? and the Mysterians ("96 Tears," 1966). Both were products of Mexican American bands using the organ where they might once have used accordions. The young musicians would have heard conjunto groups from their parents' generation slowly adopt electric organs in the 1950s, when accordions were stigmatized as low-class. Organs built in accordion factories suffered no such disgrace and were embraced by garage bands for years to come.

Garage Band Accordionists

Joey Dee and the Starliters: Squeezing and Twisting

Joey Dee and the Starliters were the house band at the dive bar with the most influential dance floor in the twentieth century. The Starliters are remembered as one of the first integrated rock bands, including at one point a young "Jimmy James" Hendrix on guitar. They were also one of several rock 'n' roll acts that included and then dropped the squeezebox.

The Starliters' first TV appearance in 1956 had Ralph Fazio on lead vocals and accordion. He fronted the band, but you couldn't hear his instrument over the guitar hiding in the back. It was a portent of rock to come—by the time you heard from the band again, Fazio was gone.

In 1960, Joey Dee (now singing lead) had them booked at the Peppermint Lounge in New York. The club started a frenzy as high-class socialites struggled for space to dance the twist. The fad dance was born on what Tom Wolfe described as "a dance floor the size of somebody's kitchen." The Starliters' original one-month engagement stretched for more than a year as they played for celebrity twisters like Marilyn Monroe and Judy Garland. Theirs became the most pivotal real estate in pop history, where more than a century of European couples dances split up.

The accordion had long since left the band when the Starliters had their flash of fame. Half a century later, avant-garde accordionist William Schimmel recalled that near-miss when he covered the opportunistic Starliters' million-selling "Peppermint Twist." "I remember thinking, wouldn't it be great to be a rock 'n' roll accordionist? It would be a chick magnet! So I began taking my accordion to parties, and no, it was not a chick magnet at all."

The Chuckles: Can't Help It

Teddy Randazzo was the accordionist for the Three Chuckles, a New York group whose claim to fame was their appearance in the big-budget ("Color! Cinemascope!") early rock 'n' roll movie *The Girl Can't Help It* (1956). Randazzo's was the sole accordion on screen, and his band were probably the squarest group in an otherwise spectacular show of early rock royalty.

The Chuckles had more in common with teen idols like Dion than with co-stars Little Richard, Gene Vincent, or Eddie Cochran. Rather than the crazier direction rock 'n' roll was taking, they were a pop vocal act (with occasional accordion) that seemed to represent an earlier romantic generation.

Backed with guitar, bass, and vocals (with no steady drummer) the group initially had Phil Bentl on accordion. After Randazzo joined, he played through several charting records but nothing lasting. He split to do solo work but mostly made his fortune as a songwriter with hits by Little Anthony and the Imperials, Frank Sinatra, and others—enough to retire to Hawaii.

Back in the 1950s, the Three Chuckles personified the transition from the golden age of pop music (and the accordion) toward rock 'n' roll. In *The Girl Can't Help It*, the band, like Bill Haley before them, struggled to engage the energy of the new style. In retrospect, they seem tame and amusing rather than threatening, and certainly never pulled off anything like the "out of control" fervor of competitors Jerry Lee Lewis and Little Richard. The Chuckles reappeared with their swinging ballads in rock 'n' roll films like *Rock, Rock, Rock!* (1956) but as time went by, Randazzo and his accordion disappeared and the band itself left little trace.

The Bop-Kats: High School Squeeze-Out

On a Sunday afternoon in October 1960, a New York high school band called the Bop-Kats appeared on television for *Ted Mack's Original Amateur Hour*. Sponsored by Geritol, it was not a rock 'n' roll program. In front of the bemused middle-aged host Ted Mack, phone-in judges picked between the young Bop-Kats, a tap dancer, an eight-year-old saxophonist, three girls dressed like sailors, a young chemistry student (whose act isn't exactly clear), a party-dress-wearing solo accordionist, and a stage-spanning fife and drum corps. The young rockers prevailed.

The Kats played teen rock 'n' roll in the gap between rock's 1950s creation and the Beatles' global takeover. They joined the early wave of guitar bands playing in their parents' basements and edging toward the "garage" sound that decades later inspired punk rock. The quintet sounded fairly traditionalist in their TV appearances, somewhere between rockabilly combos like Bill Haley's and the more extreme sounds of the 1960s. In later recordings like "Here Comes the Fuzz!" they get downright grungy.

The band's accordionist, Ronnie Brodie, was totally inaudible on their TV broadcast. Their tunes, "Whole Lotta Shakin'" and "Be Bop a

Lula," focused on their singer and two guitar players (no bass). Brodie looks like he's having fun, but the band didn't win the vote based on his accordion.

The group was said to have been popular in local dances, but it's not clear how long Brodie's accordion lasted. In later recordings you can hear him playing either Cordovox electric accordion or organ. Without those technological advances he was never going to be the one to squeeze the box into rock.

Gary Lewis and the Playboys Featuring John West and the Cordovox

Gary Lewis and the Playboys were one of the early 1960s pop groups that preceded more adventurous psychedelic outfits like the Turtles. They sold forty-five million records, going head-to-head with the best of the British Invasion, and yet founding member John West's accordion isn't on display in any rock history museum. The Playboys discovered West while he was demonstrating electronic organ accordions at a music shop in Pasadena. He signed up in time for the band's leap to stardom and stuck around until at least 1965, longer than most of the Playboys. By then it wasn't really a band; they'd become "employees" in what amounted to a pop marketing firm.

Assembly-line music in the early 1960s was similar to pop music today, except in place of samplers and electronics, producers hired studio musicians. Savvy promoters always kept their eye out for attention-grabbing hooks, like a drummer who's the son of world-famous comedian Jerry Lewis. All tellings of the Playboys' story, though, begin with the band getting their first gig at the Tomorrowland "Space Bar" at Disneyland without relying on their drummer's inherited celebrity. Not that they weren't privileged. Lewis's mom bought the band's instruments and acted as their manager. Lewis also happened to be neighbors with record producer Snuff Garrett, who stopped by and saw dollar signs. Gary's dad, Jerry, heard the band and said simply, "I only ask one thing, don't grow your hair like those damn Beatles!"

The Playboys remained well groomed compared to their contemporaries and almost immediately had a number-one record in 1964 with the studio-constructed "This Diamond Ring." For two years they cut a remarkable string of chart-topping records, toured, and appeared on *The Ed Sullivan Show* (reportedly after an overt push from Lewis's father).

Despite Gary's best efforts to play his drums in the background, Lewis's name was too big to waste, and he was talked into replacing the band's singer, Dave Walker. Lewis's inexperienced voice got an upgrade using studio techniques, while a significant amount of the band's early recording was taken care of by session players. The Playboys had a hard time reproducing their sound live, and garnered the ignoble distinction of being the first band to lip-sync to recordings on Sullivan's big show. Despite or perhaps because of the trickery on his recordings, Lewis was awarded "Best Male Vocalist" in a 1965 *Cashbox* magazine poll, beating out Elvis and Frank Sinatra.

Compared with the "flying fingers" fireworks of vaudeville players or early TV talent shows, accordions had a hard time finding a musical role in rock. There were never any standout rock accordionists, no big-name artists who raised the bar for young rock 'n' rollers. This is curious because there were so many fine young players at the time, and so much rock music being made by nascent bands in bedrooms, basements, and garages.

In the Playboys, John West's electronic Cordovox accordion wasn't central to most songs, and sounded like an organ ready to shrug off its accordion-shell. Musicologist Marion Jacobson reports that the Playboys' producer Snuff Garrett purposely worked to hide the sound of the accordion to keep it from interfering with the guitars.

It's hard to find documentation on the making of the Playboys' records, and the recordings themselves aren't trustworthy. In the case of the accordion, it's hard to tell what kind of instrument was being played. Did John West's innovative Cordovox accordion make the chimey sounds at the beginning of "This Diamond Ring"? Or was it studio musician Leon Russell on the Lowrey organ, which had virtually the same circuitry inside? It's impossible to know, and really unimportant. Regardless of the sounds on the records, the image of a modernized accordion got its widest dissemination through the Playboys' media appearances.

The Playboys' string of hits ended when Lewis got drafted in 1967. He'd figured to return from the service and step back into fame like Elvis had in the 1950s. His career never recovered. While he was in Vietnam, music shifted toward hard rock and psychedelia. The producers who had shaped the Playboys' hit songs dropped the group as the winds changed. When their contract ran out in 1970, the band broke up. Lewis ran a music store and eventually returned with some success to the "oldies" circuit in the 1980s. By then, one-time accordion rock star John West, along with the rest of the Playboys, had grown up and moved on.

The Angry: Ohio's Accordion Contenders

Accordionists in the 1960s were offered the choice between their grandparents' polkas or cocktail jazz like Art Van Damme. Not enough people heard about the garage champions of Canton, Ohio: the Angry. Drummer Jim Grant met accordionist Hans Stucki in 1962 while playing a local gospel radio broadcast. Hans wanted to start a rock 'n' roll band: "Enough already with the Swiss music ... the gospel music ... the accordion contests." Originally they were the Silvertones, but became the Angry, and then the In Crowd until the Vietnam draft broke up the band.

Their sax player, Ken Stephens, remembered, "Canton in the 1950s and 1960s was referred to as 'Little Chicago' ... because of the less than strenuous enforcement of liquor and gambling laws." The underage Silvertones played school dances and parties and witnessed their first bar fights playing clubs at age fourteen. Like many groups in the early 1960s, they did mostly instrumentals but added vocals under the influence of the British Invasion. Typical set lists included a range of 1960s party tunes like "All Day and All of the Night" and "Love Potion #9." By 1965 they were competing as the Angry with top Ohio groups including the James Gang, which featured future Eagle Joe Walsh.

In 1966, the Angry moved to New York City to try to break into the national scene. They traded in their custom dress-suits for bell-bottoms and "groovy" polka-dot shirts. As they were getting ready to record their debut album with Reprise Records, a combination of the draft board, a car accident, and higher education ended the band. Saxophonist Stephens recalled, "Had times been different and had there not been a war going on that required mandatory military service, the Angry would have had a real opportunity to become a recording success."

One of the distinct advantages British bands had during their invasion is that they weren't under the constant threat of the draft. The Beatles' American contemporaries were all affected by the war. Many, like the Angry, were on the verge of success, only to sink under political and personal pressure.

Hans Stucki remembers taking up the electronic accordion: "I technically didn't play accordion in the Angry." Instead, it was one of the first electronic Cordovoxes, which "sounded like organs when the bellows were locked." These hybrid instruments took the form of heavy, bulky accordions that didn't give players much that organs didn't have. They eventually became an embarrassment. "I even built a 'stand' for it so I could lay it on its back so that it didn't *look* like an accordion," he said. "Sad to say, I was one of those running away from accordions in rock."

On the Silvertones' and the Angry's few surviving demos and live recordings it's impossible to discern whether the keyboard sounds are produced by organ or electronic accordion. Either one could have produced the garage band results on the group's 1965 instrumental rave-ups "Brontosaurus Stomp," and "Red Headed Flea." By then, the accordion's days were numbered. It's likely they would have joined other early 1960s groups that abandoned the instrument if only they'd had the chance.

The Chessmen: Garage Accordion to Canada

Up in Canada, Vancouver birthed another of the rare accordion rock bands, the Chessmen. Most famously, the band featured Terry Jacks, the Canadian pop songwriter who sold ten million copies of his sentimental single "Seasons in the Sun" in 1974. A decade earlier, the Chessmen were a different animal. They were founded in 1963 by students who wanted an excuse to get into frat parties at the University of British Columbia. They were modeled on the Ventures and the Shadows, playing mostly instrumentals in the days before the Beatles.

Their first single, in 1964, contained the instrumentals "Mustang" and "Meadowlands." It was reissued on Seattle's Jerden Records—home of the Sonics' "The Witch" and the Kingsmen's "Louie Louie." Over the next two years, the Chessmen produced a series of pop records held together by Jacks's layered vocals, cascading guitars and the organ-like sounds of Bruce Peterson on Cordovox accordion.

The Chessmen's "Love Didn't Die" stands up against the best of the garage bands. It was recorded 2,500 miles away from Vancouver in Nashville, after Jacks befriended rockabilly chanteuse "Little Miss Dynamite" Brenda Lee at a Vancouver gig. Lee's manager got them a contract with Mercury Records as long as they made the grueling Greyhound bus ride to Tennessee and stayed in a dismal hotel.

Peterson's organ-accordion is layered through the Nashville singles. (They flew down for a second session in 1966.) As in other bands, the Cordovox sound is indistinguishable from any other electronic organ, so pinning down the details about what instrument was used is difficult.

At one point the Chessmen opened for Gary Lewis and the Playboys in Vancouver. It would be interesting to know if Peterson got to compare notes with Playboys accordionist John West.

In 1966, Chessmen lead guitarist Guy Sobell's dad threatened to kick him out of the house unless he went back to university. Off at school in London, England, he sold his Fender Strat to Jimi Hendrix. Sobell's family's opinion of his economic future may have been valid; the Chessmen's final gig in the summer of 1965 paid the band $180. Forty years later, their three singles were collected and reissued with other recordings so we can hear what may have been the first rock band in Canada to use accordion. For a good many years, it was also one of the last.

Galaxies IV: The Accordion That Could Have Played Woodstock

The New York World's Fair of 1964–65 was dedicated to "a shrinking globe in an expanding universe." Fifty million people came to see the future as projected by some of the biggest corporations in the world. The nearby state of New Jersey was represented by a space-age Catholic school quartet, the Galaxies IV.

The band launched midway between President Kennedy's daringly optimistic 1961 proposal that the U.S. put people on the moon and the achievement of that goal in 1969. In an era when punch-card mainframe computers were intimidatingly advanced, the Galaxies' electric guitars and organ accordion plugged right into the future.

The band members hadn't graduated, so they only worked weekends, but over the two summers the World's Fair lasted they played almost a hundred shows. The exposure led novelist James Michener to write about them in the *New York Times* and *Reader's Digest*.

Phil Spector himself judged the Galaxies the winners of a huge "Rock & Roll World Championship" battle between four hundred bands at the 1964 St. John Terrell's Music Circus in Lambertville, New Jersey. Back at the fair in New York, power-broker Robert Moses took a break from highway building (and neighborhood flattening) to declare a Galaxies IV Day in honor of them boosting attendance. The World's Fair still wound up with twenty million fewer visitors than promoters expected, but the boys did their part.

The Galaxies released several singles in 1966, including the lackluster "Till Then You'll Cry," and the pretty darn cool instrumental freak-out "Piccadilly Circus" (a version of the Rolling Stones' "2120

South Michigan Blvd"). As with other groups, it's very hard to tell whether accordionist Charles Brodowitz is playing his Cordovox or some other organ with a volume pedal. Regardless, they pulled off some of the hottest records associated with the garage accordion.

After an appropriately Aquarian name change to Alexander Rabbit, in 1969 their manager turned down an offer to play a certain upstate festival which would have shifted their World's Fair appearance from a career highlight to a footnote. One can only imagine Brodowitz stepping onstage at Woodstock, plugging in the Cordovox (which he'd reportedly already abandoned), and wowing 300,000 hippies with some spacey squeezebox. After missing the biggest show of their careers, Alexander Rabbit recorded one album and split by 1971.

The Devil's Anvil: Eliezer Adoram's Middle Eastern Rock

Swinging through 1960s Greenwich Village, a band called the Devil's Anvil was playing Middle Eastern psychedelic music. Taking their name from the "impassable" desert crossed in *Lawrence of Arabia*, the band were mostly Arab American, but their accordionist was Israeli. Members eventually started the rock group Mountain, which played Woodstock and around the world.

The Anvil began at the Feenjon coffee house in New York City. They attracted rocker Felix Pappalardi, who somehow swung them an album deal with Columbia Records. They delivered a song sequence in Arabic, Turkish, and Greek played on oud, tamboura, fuzz-guitar, durbeki percussion, and accordion. The most commercial track was a cover of the Greek standard "Misirlou" as if played by a world-music incarnation of Cream or the Yardbirds.

The band's ill-fated 1967 record *Hard Rock from the Middle East* was exceptional even in an era when musical boundaries were regularly broken. Unfortunately, it was released on the eve of the Arab–Israeli War, dooming their attempt at musical rapprochement.

The desert-themed album cover features a group-shot with accordionist Eliezer Adoram holding bandmate Steve Knight's electrified bouzouki (perhaps because the accordion wasn't exotic enough). Adoram was an Israeli actor and musician who'd studied in the United States during the folk revival. He'd made waves backing Frances Alenikoff's modern dance interpretations of traditional Jewish music. Born in Israel, he grew up in a kibbutz while his father served in the British army.

Adoram learned Israeli folk songs and became aware of Jewish Yemenite music influenced by Arabian culture. His ability to bridge Eastern European Hasidic, Balkan, and Greek music made him a natural extension of the musical world of the Anvil.

The band arrived during a brief period when record companies were struggling to cash in on rapidly evolving music. The Velvet Underground and Frank Zappa's Mothers of Invention were similarly signed by desperate executives cluelessly stumbling into the avant-garde. The Anvil were one of the more unlikely results of this fertile period, and they inspired few accordion rockers until the rise of world music years later.

Two Paths Not Taken: The Accordion in the Beach Boys and the Band

Beach Boys: Recording Heaven

Of all the attempts to use accordions in 1960s rock 'n' roll, the most sophisticated were probably Brian Wilson's compositions for the Beach Boys. By the mid-1960s, Wilson was less a rock and roller than an unorthodox composer/arranger. His use of accordions and other instruments, including the Beach Boys' voices, was more as layered textures than as recognizable rock instrumentation.

Unlike earlier attempts at rock 'n' roll accordion, Wilson called on virtuosic studio players Carl Fortina and Frank Marocco for subtle effects. He ingeniously wove their accordions into some of his greatest works, including "God Only Knows" on *Pet Sounds,* and the monumental single "Wouldn't It Be Nice."

Wilson encountered the accordion early in life. Mother Audree Wilson remembered, "Brian took accordion lessons, on one of those little baby accordions... At the end of six weeks he was supposed to buy a large accordion, but we couldn't afford it." Father Murry Wilson had been an aspiring songwriter, and the family remembered gathering for the high point of his career when one of his tunes was played on *The Lawrence Welk Show* by the maestro himself.

When they began, the Beach Boys literally rehearsed in their parents' garage. They joined the wave of early 1960s "guitar bands" (Brian played bass) that prepared the world for the Beatles and the rise of rock culture. Brian's later orchestral use of musicians in his "pocket symphonies" was a radical departure. He dragged rock music away from simple dance formats into uncharted territory.

Accordionist Frank Marocco remembered working with Wilson. "On 'Wouldn't It Be Nice' I ended up doing something that was the most difficult thing I've ever done before or since. I came up with this part that was like a triple bellow shake. It was physically demanding, because we had to do it over and over again, and by the end of the session, it was exhausting. I remember thinking, 'I'll never suggest that again!'"

The Beach Boys' accordion-flavored recordings were totally different from other garage-era accordion bands. Whereas young accordionists in most groups tried to compete amidst groups of guitarists, Wilson hired seasoned aces to insert sounds strategically amidst his grand compositions. He told Hollywood's most recorded accordionist, Carl Fortina, "I want you at all my sessions. Every time you play, my records go gold. You're my good-luck charm."

The little squeezebox Wilson played as a child must have stuck with him. But audiences couldn't recognize the accordions hidden in Wilson's masterpieces, and sales of the instrument continued to plummet.

Garth Hudson and the Band's Retro Traditionalism

Elaborate studio creations like Wilson's helped inspire others to head in the opposite direction. Renouncing pop trends, the Band's Garth Hudson played accordion that felt old-fashioned, timeless, and traditional. After backing Dylan's revolutionary "electric" tours, the Band set about subverting rock rebellion. Eschewing extended guitar solos, they incorporated old-time instruments like tubas, mandolins, and accordions. They sounded like acoustic throwbacks to an archaic America.

The Band were one of the last rock groups for years that included even a part-time accordion player among its members. Their country-tinged music was laced together by organist Garth Hudson. "He's the one who rubbed off on the rest of us and made us sound as good as we did," the Band's drummer Levon Helm recalled. Hudson set aside his spiraling Lowrey organ to add reedy accordion to scattered songs by the Band, as well as on Dylan's *Basement Tapes* (engineered by Hudson). His squeezebox connected the group's country rock music with the vaudeville, parlor, and ethnic eras that embodied the instrument's golden age. The Band's work became one of the paramount declarations that inspired the "Americana" aesthetic of North American roots music. Ironic, since most of the band were Canadian.

Hudson grew up in a musical family in London, Ontario. His mom had an accordion and played piano. He learned keyboards as a kid and studied classical music at the University of Western Ontario. At one point Hudson's father bought a reed-organ home and repaired it with his son. With many of the same mechanics as accordions, Hudson recalled, "All these little wooden parts were always breaking, and the reeds needed cleaning. When you buy an antique like that you find that there'll always be dirt in the reeds, so you have to go through and clean all of them." At age twelve in 1949, he was playing accordion in a country band and in high school groups too.

Any number of rockers played accordions in their youth, but few aside from the Band took their outsider stance seriously enough to incorporate such dated sounds. Their acoustic style cut right through the late-1960s electric maelstrom. Before Hudson strapped on his accordion for the back-cover photo on the group's eponymous second album, their sepia-tone reconstruction of American music had already captured other artists' attention. Eric Clapton left Cream to focus on the blues; the Beatles attempted their spare *Let It Be* sessions. The Rolling Stones added acoustic numbers to *Beggars Banquet*. West Coast psychedelic acts like the Grateful Dead turned fully toward country music. Of the many rock bands that followed the Band's lead, almost all bypassed the once-common accordion when digging into their musical roots.

Despite the Band's impression of raw traditionalism, the group's sound was a crafted balance of songwriting, modern recording, and creative musicianship. Hudson constantly stretched his organ's sound with electronic modifications and effects. The accordion seems to have been the most conventional instrument he played. His was often a 1920s model, whose inlayed belly-dancers may have accompanied vaudeville acts fifty years earlier.

Ironically, the Band ended up being among the most forward-looking pop groups, as far as the accordion was concerned. It was roots music that helped the instrument recover after its fairly dismal showing in the rock era. The Band were prescient in their nostalgia, but even a player as skilled as Hudson could not resuscitate the accordion when the rest of rock 'n' roll abandoned it.

17

The Accordion
Exodus

BEFORE ITS PRECIPITOUS decline in the 1960s, the accordion industry was as honed and polished as the instruments it peddled. An integrated distribution and instruction network of dealers, teachers, and sheet-music publishers supported hundreds of student orchestras and clubs. The accordion industry had factories and repair shops scattered across the United States and the world. Aerodynamic designs borrowed from American (and Italian) automakers made accordions as futuristic looking as Detroit's latest chrome fins. After the devastation of World War II, American's desire for accordions literally supported whole towns and regions in Europe.

Promoters of the instrument, not satisfied with purely financial success, had their eye on classical music legitimacy. Some criticized the instrument's lingering ethnic associations as liabilities in a culture where "whiteness" had become a sought-after commodity. By the mid-1950s, the future seemed bright for the increasingly highbrow and ethnically purified instrument.

Then, catastrophe. In less than a decade, from around 1955 into the early 1960s, the accordion not only plunged from popularity, but was effectively banished from trendsetting North American music for what would stretch to be forty years. The once-rising star was branded as the very lowest instrument on the musical hierarchy. In most parts of

America one could not play an accordion without being dismissed with casual ridicule. The only accordion music many people heard was from anonymous Hollywood session players providing Old World charm in films and advertising.

It's tempting to think of the accordion's undoing as the passing of a fad. But the instrument was more than a fleeting trend. Before the fall it had provided entertainment in hundreds of thousands homes for decades. In reality a series of interwoven and possibly inevitable crises deflated the instrument globally during the mid-1960s. The shift in the United States was uniquely brutal. By the 1990s the satirical *Encyclopedia of Bad Taste* opened with a five-page entry on the accordion, and closed with a chapter on Lawrence Welk. Déclassé began and ended with the squeezebox.

Entering the twenty-first century, millennial music fans often can't explain why the accordion was singled out as uncool. Older North Americans remembered Lawrence Welk, Elvis, or the Beatles, but young listeners had seldom heard of Welk, while Elvis and the Beatles were themselves becoming "old people's music."

Ironically, the severity of the accordions' exile would eventually lead to the evaporation of anti-accordion prejudices. The instrument was so erased from mainstream culture that many young people had never encountered it. Without negative experience of their own, contemporary audiences were as often as not intrigued rather than repelled and the accordion slowly emerged from hiding.

Lawrence Welk Didn't Kill the Accordion

People who dislike accordions often associate them with *The Lawrence Welk Show* (see Chapter 7). However, one corny guy with bubbles didn't ruin the instrument for fifty years. Lawrence Welk may have been an accomplice to the accordion's downfall, but he didn't act alone.

Welk was a businessman who carefully tended his audience's conservative nostalgia for the dance orchestras. He responded with pride when critics said he was "old-fashioned." His fans aged loyally with him. Focused relentlessly on satisfying his audience, he became by far the wealthiest accordionist in American history.

Welk's focus on his aging demographic certainly had consequences for the accordion. When millions of rock 'n' rollers took up guitars and

Top Ten Reasons the Accordion
Never Made It in Rock 'n' Roll

1. Early blues players abandoned accordions around 1915, cutting the instrument off from most of the African American music that fed into rock.

2. White folk revivalists dropped accordion-friendly ethnic traditions when they took up Southern blues and folk guitar.

3. European American immigrants' music wasn't invested with enough rebellious energy. The Jewish Polish-American owners of Chicago's Chess Records didn't record loud, distorted klezmer or polkas.

4. Fender's bass made accordionists' left hand (and a lot of other instruments) redundant. "Two guitars, bass, drums" became an efficient money-maker.

5. It was (and remains) formidably tricky to amplify accordions.

6. Guitars were cheap, easy to play, loud, and sexy. Heavy 120-bass accordions were generally not.

7. No one ever saw Clifton Chenier on national television. Rock accordion never had mind-blowing icons like Little Richard or Jerry Lee Lewis.

8. After decades of rising sales, the glut of existing instruments burst the industry's money-making bubble.

9. Lawrence Welk didn't end the accordion on his own—but he helped secure its anti-rock image.

10. With sales already dropping, the panicking accordion industry didn't adapt to the rough and ready new music. Kids knew where they weren't wanted and begged their parents for keyboards, drums, or guitars.

keyboards, Welk's "champagne" pop contributed to stereotypes about the struggling squeezebox. To a degree, baby boomers were conditioned to dislike the instrument when they rejected the tastes of older generations.

On the other hand, the greatest evidence that Lawrence Welk's show didn't trigger the damnation of the accordion was that the same fate didn't follow his pioneering use of electric guitars. Every young rocker who begged their parents for one owes Lawrence Welk a debt for introducing the Fender Stratocaster to America's living rooms. In 1955, he hired young guitarist Buddy Merrill to boost youth ratings, and thus became one of the greatest promoters of Fender guitars until Jimi Hendrix lit one on fire at Monterey Pop Festival.

But by the 1970s, Welk was the last accordionist standing in American music. His show was the final echo of the great ethnic and dance-band circuits of the 1920s. Despite many other nails in the accordion's coffin, Welk's name and image became the symbol of the instrument's downfall long after his final spin on the televised dance floor.

Doomed Solutions to Technical Problems

The history of entertainment is driven by economics and technology as much as by fashion or genius. Major instrumental innovations can usually be traced to practicality. The light-hearted ukulele, for example, was the portable music de jour, the boom box of 1920s. Instruments catch on because they are cheaper, louder, more portable or more musically flexible. They are abandoned for similar reasons: too expensive, too heavy, too quiet.

Back at the beginning of the accordion's run, vaudeville itself functioned as a technology for delivering entertainment across the continent. It went bust due to calamitous innovations beyond its control: the advent of movies, low-cost radio, and records. Through all this the accordion carried on, but things changed after 1960 when the squeezebox simultaneously lost the competition for volume, affordability, and musical flexibility. Electric guitars and amplified keyboards took over because they excelled at each of these.

Accordion vs. Guitar (Part 1, Technology)

In many ways, the accordion crashed because of the accordion itself. The instrument had spread because it was relatively easy to play, cheap, and loud. The features that caused its rise then ushered in its replacements. Electrically amplified instruments were cheaper and much, much louder. It wasn't Lawrence Welk's fault that it was easier to amplify six strings on a guitar than four hundred reeds inside an accordion. The electric guitar, bass, and electric keyboard simply met needs that the accordion no longer could.

Over the last half of the twentieth century, figures like Leo Fender and Les Paul developed and invented devices and techniques that changed not only the instruments they're associated with, but basically all of popular music on Earth. As composer Nicholas Collins noted, "The electric guitar pickup just might be the single most important musical discovery of the twentieth century." The accordion pretty much failed in grappling with these changes. No accordionist ever gained widespread attention using electronic enhancement of their instrument. Without examples to follow, as soon as artists were plugging in, it was easier to switch to other keyboards.

The Accordion Lost the Volume War

One of the main reasons inventors like Les Paul developed the solid-body electric guitar was to eliminate feedback from hollow acoustic instruments. By minimizing unwanted vibrations, they allowed electrical pickups to capture just the sound of a guitar's strings. The accordion's hundreds of reeds presented such a challenge that it never produced a comparable electronic evolution.

Arhoolie Records founder Chris Strachwitz remembered Clifton Chenier playing zydeco in the 1960s: "If you had your loudspeakers behind you, with that accordion plugged into it, because the accordion has a microphone in it, it'll squeal . . . So many joints I went in, oh God, it was squealing constantly."

Electrical amplification was first used for stage vocals. Country and western string players quickly went from simply huddling around microphones to experimenting with contact mics for their instruments. Les Paul attached a phonograph needle to his childhood guitar.

Transferring even the simplest electric pickup to an accordion proved next to impossible. In theory, it would require magnetic pickups that were far longer, heavier, and more expensive than those used in guitars. Wiring would need to be installed for each of the six or more reed blocks inside the instrument. Instead of six strings, it would need to pick up hundreds of vibrating reeds of different sizes. Finally the electronics on the left and right sides of the accordion would have to be connected across the moving bellows, and of course it all needed to remain airtight.

The lack of an easy way to amplify accordions for loud rock 'n' roll was ruinous. After fielding various Cordovox-style organ-accordion designs and a few simple feedback-prone mic systems, accordion R&D departments fell apart along with their industry.

Over the next half-century, the world of audio technology advanced unimaginably. In just one example, for forty years rock iconoclasts the Grateful Dead spent more on audio research and development than the entire accordion industry. By the early 1990s, when Bruce Hornsby played accordion with the Dead, his sound lagged four decades behind the other instruments.

Guitar vs. Accordion (Part 2, Technique)

It's been said that the guitar is easy to play simply, but difficult to play well. To start a garage band in the 1960s a guitarist didn't need to play well. You could play Kinks songs without needing to be Dick Contino. The two chords of "You Really Got Me" laid waste to the arpeggios of "Lady of Spain."

The ease with which beginners can produce simple tunes has always been part of instrument sales. This served the accordion well when it faced down fiddles or bagpipes. Their players were rightfully jealous of novice accordionists. Along with the simple left-hand buttons, promoters of piano accordions could take advantage of the keyboard that was already part of many people's music education. Unfortunately, this also made it easier for accordionists to abandon the instrument for electric organs.

Another factor weighing against the accordion was the dexterity required to juggle multiple tasks. Guitar at its simplest required strumming with one hand and holding notes with the other. Accordions produced musical lines from both right and left hands all controlled by the bellows. If the player wanted to sing as well, this was even more daunting.

Electric guitars simply made more racket for less effort. Lugging around an amplifier suddenly made a guitarist a different creature. Fender historian John Teagle recalled, "Use of echo, and later reverb, goes hand in hand with the popularity of the electric guitar and amplifier... If your electric guitar sounded big you could get away with

☞ Accordion Demographics: The 1960s Youthquake

ROCK MUSIC ROLLED over the accordion when baby boomers came of age in the postwar era. Teen culture wasn't new, but it had lain dormant for a generation. It's often overlooked that there was a drop in birth rates (a "baby bust") during the Great Depression, resulting in an unusually small youth market during the late 1940s and early '50s. As a result, most pre-rock entertainment culture—often starring accordionists—targeted the larger audience of adults. When young people returned to the marketplace in the late 1950s and '60s, the energy of rock 'n' roll felt unprecedented. Youth cultures like flappers, lindy-hoppers, and the 1930s polka craze were more than a generation past, an eternity in the restless eyes of teens.

Industries of all sorts confronted this new youth market. Manufacturers had to traverse the unusually large gap between older and younger generations lest they fade into obsolescence. Unfortunately, the accordion community's strategy seems to have been to hope that rock music would die down and things would return to normal. They didn't realize that their older, more conservative customer base was as much an anomaly as the strange new generation. In the end, teenage baby boomers rejected the earlier accordion revolution and it was swept away.

playing simple licks ... With the right tone, even a kid starting out could sound good."

Acoustic guitarists had developed an expressive language in American music. Hawaiian steel, bottleneck blues, Spanish guitar, and country picking all contributed to its vocabulary. In addition to transferring these techniques to electric guitar, the leap in volume led to a new flurry of innovation. The fuzz-box effects of the 1960s hid some guitarists' skill behind their electronically crafted sound. The endless quest for novelty and personal style propelled the guitar and its tone-shaping accessories into global industries.

The question for young accordionists became, "Can I play the music I want on this instrument?" Even if they could find an instructor ready to teach basic rock 'n' roll (which many resisted), there were few if any exciting rock players to make accordionists cool. And what good was even classical skill on an instrument that was socially worthless?

Staccato: The Attack of the Guitar

Acoustic accordions were ill-suited to the rise of electrical amplification and high volumes. The rhythmic attack of rock music also defied the melodious emphasis of piano accordion development. Acoustic guitars had often been inaudible amidst the rhythm sections of larger orchestras. Amplification added volume and sustain for them to solo, but they continued their central rhythmic role. On songs like 1955's "Pretty Thing," Bo Diddley's guitar serves almost purely as percussion. Besides short distorted solos, there's little traditional melody or chord changes at all. Instead, the song relies only on the guitar-driven "Bo Diddley beat" accompanied by tom-toms, vocals, and Jerome Green's trademark maracas.

Interestingly, the maracas and guitar on Bo Diddley's records closely imitate the rubboard or scraper heard in accordion folk music across the African diaspora. Unfortunately, the upwardly mobile American accordion was oblivious to the energy and rhythms surfacing on R&B and country records during the late 1940s, not to mention regional accordion music like the nascent zydeco. The accordion was simply unprepared for the attack of rock 'n' roll.

Button box accordions had, of course, played tight rhythms in dance music since the 1800s. But the full-size piano accordions that were promoted in the 1950s resisted rock 'n' roll. Compared to the excitement produced by guitarists, inertia alone inhibited a percussive attack when squeezing twenty-five-pound instruments. Accordion teachers had always assigned exercises in smooth volume swells and fleet legato phrases. They neglected Jerry Lee Lewis's machine-gun energy, and the accordion suffered.

The Tiger Combo 'Cordion and the Missing Accordion Power-Chord

Ethnomusicologist/accordionist Marion Jacobson theorized that the density of the accordion's sound clashed with rock music. Electric keyboards, in contrast, cut through loud guitars and could often provide remarkably varied color to support the other instruments. Amplified traditional accordions tended to saturate and muffle the rest of the band.

The Tiger Combo 'Cordion, ca. 1966. *Photo by Laurel Dykstra.*

Blending a full 120-bass accordion into a rock group's sound remains a challenge more than sixty years after players first faced the problem. Manufacturers had dedicated half a century to crafting the distinctive, rich tone of modern accordions. Suddenly, small groups were dominated by bass guitars, which eliminated much of the aural territory where the "orchestra in a box" shone. Something new had to be done to play rock 'n' roll.

Unfortunately the accordion industry mostly headed in the opposite (and increasingly expensive) direction. Jazz accordionist Tommy Gumina's Polytone company created amplifiers specifically designed not to play rock music. His goal was to reproduce the pure sound of jazz instruments without the overtones or distortion of tube amps, removing exactly the features that blues and rock players craved. Gumina's "anti-rock" amplifiers were perfect for his accordion and widely adopted by jazz bassists and guitarists. Nobody, however, put out an amp for accordionists who didn't want to play jazz.

Electric guitarists gravitated toward the simplification of power-chords. Playing as few as two simple notes (the root and fifth) the distortion from tube amplifiers offered even rank beginners an aggressive guitar sound. By comparison, at loud volumes standard accordion chord buttons (especially from multiple reed-bank instruments) could sound muddy or distracting.

The Tiger Combo 'Cordion was one of the few isolated mid-1960s attempts to meet the needs of rock accordion players. Faithe Deffner of the Pancordion and Titano companies worked with Bill Palmer of the famous Palmer–Hughes accordion instruction books to design a flashy, affordable instrument with an internal mic to easily plug into an amplifier.

The Tiger advertised directly to young rockers, saying it would show off the player's "flying fingers" and "flip the crowds" with "piercing leads or swinging chords." The instrument definitely stood out: the standard black and white keys' color was reversed to imitate the Vox Continental organs that were ravaging the accordion market. The keyboard was also dramatically slanted back toward the player, which looked cool and may have improved ergonomics when playing standing up. Breaking the dour 1950s "serious" standard, the Combo 'Cordions came in "sports-car" colors like "Fire Red." Lucky purchasers could even take home a tiger-print gig bag to replace the traditional bulky case.

Internally, the Combo 'Cordions had the unusual register option for the right-hand piano keys to double each note in fifths—similar to rock guitar power-chords. Unfortunately, adding fifths on the piano keyboard produced jazzy "block chords" that weren't very useful in rock. Amplification was regrettably an afterthought on the Tiger, with low-quality microphones that didn't capture the acoustic accordion well and weren't nearly as loud or expressive as competing electronic instruments.

The fledgling Tiger failed before it could develop the kind of following Leo Fender had with guitarists that helped improve his instruments. Accordion designers and promoters never succeeded in connecting with increasingly rare rock accordionists. Deffner recalled, "Teachers of that period did not like rock and were convinced that it was a passing fancy." Her husband joked about the Tiger initiative as "Faithe's Folly." Without an adaptable plan to fit the demands of the new music, the next stage in the evolution of youth-oriented accordion never materialized.

Backing the Wrong Squeezebox

As the accordion market neared the end of the golden age, accordion makers like Julio Giulietti worked tirelessly to raise the status of the instrument. Their strategy was to move beyond pop and folk by targeting the world of "highbrow" concert music and jazz. Anthony Galla-Rini and other sophisticated players premiered challenging material in the quest to distance the accordion from nicknames like "squeezebox" and banalities like the "Beer Barrel Polka." The Titano and Giulietti companies promoted distinct new "free-bass" systems enabling complex left-hand counterpoint bass runs. In the long term, though, the classical world in North America remained resolutely uninterested in these innovations.

Distracted by their quest for classical maturity, accordion boosters lost enthusiasm for earlier pop and folk styles. At their most extreme, sophisticated accordionists expressed contempt for musicians who didn't adequately elevate the instrument. By the time the classical gambit failed, the accordion industry had effectively shed much of its association with folk music. Disastrously, this happened just as the vibrant folk revival of the 1950s–60s brought traditional styles to the fore.

Accordionists were blindsided when the support they'd taken for granted in folk and pop music was swept from under them. Not only did the accordion fail to achieve entry into prestigious concert halls but it lost its place almost everywhere else as well.

Some of the problem was rooted in the accordion's network of schools and teachers. Faithe Deffner determined that accordions lost out in pop simply "because accordion teachers . . . disliked the music and refused to teach it to their students. Consequently, students drifted away from accordion to electric guitars and keyboards on which they could learn the music they wanted to play."

Operation Rock 'n' Roll Accordion!

In 1956 Pietro Deiro's publishing house released accordion sheet music for the "Rock and Roll Waltz," a rather bizarre novelty number about a teenager who sneaks home late at night and finds her parents trying to waltz to her rock 'n' roll records. Kay Starr's recording of the tune went to number one in England and sounds very much like an orchestra trying to impersonate a rock band to amuse grown-ups. This presaged the mismatch between the adult-directed accordion world and the youthful spark of rock 'n' roll.

The accordion industry had several sources of income. First was the sale of accordions, another was from lessons and repairs (both had a part in pushing more expensive accordions), third was the sale of custom accordion sheet music.

Recordings had replaced most sheet music sales to the wider public around 1920. There was still a market for music students, and the popularity of the accordion launched a wave of printed music tailored to the instrument.

Pre-printed accordion music became something of a trap in the age of rock 'n' roll. Teachers who relied on the specialized transcriptions promoted by the American Accordionists' Association had little to offer kids who wanted to rock.

The early 1960s saw very few attempts to capture the energy of the new music for accordion students. *All-Time Hit Paraders* songbooks began publishing in the late 1940s and slowly came to include rock 'n' roll numbers, including editions dedicated to songs by the Beatles. Faithe Deffner lobbied for the Palmer–Hughes instruction series to add "How to Play Rock and Roll" to their archetypical accordion curriculum.

By 1966, Palmer and Hughes were publishing a plea to accordion instructors to unite in a last-ditch campaign, "Operation Rock 'n' Roll Accordion!" They optimistically predicted that rock accordion was "about to take hold in many cities throughout the U.S. [and] on all the national media." But by that time even the instrument's few stalwart rockers had abandoned the instrument. The battle was already lost.

The Accordion Bubble Bursts

In 1950, Mrs. John C. Racki of Buffalo, New York, put an advertisement in the paper to sell her accordion. She received twelve offers and a spot in the paper touting the value of classified ads. Ten or fifteen years later she would not have been so lucky. Accordion shops in the late 1960s were like non-digital camera stores in the early twenty-first century: high-end gear waiting in windows for buyers who never came.

Dutch writer Sander Neijnens posits that the downfall began because accordions were too well built. Mid-century manufacturers simply saturated the market with hand-crafted machines that eventually outlasted many of their customers. Accordions became extinct because they didn't plan for obsolescence.

Millions of new accordions were imported and sold in North America during the 1950s. Eventually there were enough instruments circulating to satisfy beginners. When older players started handing down used ones to younger students, demand fell to the point where manufacturers could not survive. New instrument sales had always supported the rest of the accordion infrastructure. Teachers, clubs, and shops vanished when people stopped buying. The bubble burst and the accordion industry, from manufacturing towns in Europe to individual instructors in North America, fell apart.

The accordion community had always had its share of cutthroat business practices. Promotional catalogs from the 1920s derided unscrupulous competition. Even well-known companies couldn't always be relied on when they changed owners or used different brand names for different markets ("Silvertone" accordions, for instance, were sold through the Sears' catalog but usually made by the Italian Scandalli company).

Some of the more egregious tactics related to the fabled door-to-door accordion salesmen. Notoriously slick and persuasive, these dealers offered free or cheap beginner's accordions and then enthusiastically encouraged the purchase of larger, more expensive models for invariably gifted students. More than one accordion sat in a closet for decades because a salesman sold it with a year's worth of lessons, then skipped town as soon as the instrument was purchased.

The accordion's spike in sales in the 1950s was partially due to shady tactics like these, which produced short-term results but long-term resentment. Lessons designed just to sell accordions did not encourage lifelong players.

When sales began to slack, the industry turned on itself. Manufacturers competed harder to capture a shrinking pool of return customers after new ones dried up. Panicked dealers struggled to offer bigger and better accordions, including the expensive electronic Cordovoxes, to a dwindling number of players. Once-valuable instruments began showing up in pawnshops and thrift stores. Others commenced their long

"The Cordovox Maneuver"

BESIDES THE SHORT-LIVED Tiger initiative, the accordion industry's greatest attempt to modernize was the Cordovox. The idea was to couple space-age organ electronics with accordions. The hybrid instrument could still play acoustically, but would be able to compete in loud bands. For a brief period around 1963–64 a few rock groups used them.

The origins of the Cordovox reflect the complex history of the accordion industry in Italy. In 1946 the Scandalli, Frontalini, and Settimio Soprani accordion companies combined to form Farfisa: Fabbriche Riunite Fisarmoniche, the "United Accordion Factories." Farfisa became famous in the 1960s for combo-organs that drove garage bands.

Before they made organs, Farfisa integrated electronic technology into their accordions. Released in about 1961, the first Cordovox was a full-size acoustic accordion that acted as a controller for an outboard "tone-generator" that produced organ sounds. The whole thing then fed separate amplifier/speakers. All these heavy components were connected by thick cables and fittings custom-made by Bell Labs. The electronics were originally produced by Chicago's Lowrey Organ company, based on their 1961 Holiday Deluxe organ, while the acoustic section of the accordion was built by Scandelli in Italy.

The Cordovox's organ sounds were controlled from an array of tabs on the accordion's front, while a foot pedal controlled the volume (it wasn't necessary to move the bellows). Altogether, early Cordovoxes required seventy or more fragile vacuum tubes. By comparison, electric guitar amps averaged around five.

Organ accordions like the Cordovox (and competing brands Electravox, Elkavox, and Duovox) were successful in creating an instrument loud enough to be heard on modern stages, but they did not save the accordion. They were more compact than full-size Hammond or Lowrey organs, but not as convenient as stackable combo organs. Their technology also dated poorly, with the fatal flaw that each expensive handmade accordion was saddled with proprietary electronics that were impossible to upgrade.

In the end, the sound of the Cordovox was indistinguishable from its slightly less mobile competitors, and the promised freedom of movement was crushed by the bulkiest accordions ever produced. "Ungainly" was not a rock 'n' roll look, and players moved on to keyboards that had to be loaded in and out of gigs, but didn't hang from your shoulders all night long.

They laughed
when I sat down to play the
accordion

and then they heard the rich, warm sounds of a jazz organ; the throbbing beat of rock 'n roll; even the strains of a Hawaiian guitar.

I was in with the "in" group. And I couldn't have done it without my Cordovox.

That's because a Cordovox is the completely electronic instrument. It's more than an organ...more than an accordion. It produces any one of a dozen different musical voices in a split second so that I can play any kind of mood music that the occasion calls for. And, it's amplified to give me a fuller range of sound for any size room.

If you're like me, an accordion player who wants in with the "in" group; if you're a guy who'd like to make a small combo sound like a really big group or if you're in search of a whole new sound...why not try a Cordovox?

It's a heck of a lot more than just an accordion.

CORDOVOX
the exclusive choice of
Fred Waring and the Pennsylvanians

Cordovox is a product of CMI

Cordovox advertisement, ca. 1960s. *Courtesy of Fabio G. Giotta.*

hibernation in the back of closets or amidst the harrowing temperatures and humidity of attics or basements.

Accordion sales were shattered. As late as 1960 there were still 100, 000 accordions sold every year in the United States. By 1976 sales were down to thirteen thousand. The following year the industry journal *Music USA* stopped reporting on accordion sales at all, simply folding them into "miscellaneous other instruments." There were still a million accordion players in the U.S., but by the mid-1970s they were older, with an average age of thirty. Meanwhile there were ten million guitarists and rising, with a median age of twenty-one.

The Exile: Welcome to Hell

After more than a century of expansion, the accordion revolution collapsed in less than a decade. It was baffling and heartbreaking for musicians, dealers, and manufacturers to watch lifetimes of effort evaporate. Worse, accordions didn't simply lose favor, they were culturally disinherited and written out of the will.

While other countries consigned accordions to playing folk music when electric replacements became available, it's difficult to understand how deeply transgressive the accordion became in English-speaking North America. The wildly popular instrument was expelled from mainstream culture and replaced with a caricature. The instrument became so out of fashion that people couldn't imagine a time when it had been *in* fashion. Memories of accordions as modern, versatile, and ever-present were incompatible with this new reality.

This abrupt departure of the instrument went unexamined by a generation of writers, researchers, and historians who were busy revolutionizing the study of vernacular music. Their growing canon of cultural history seldom mentioned the squeezebox. The instrument remains almost entirely missing from American music history, despite its role in almost every phase of the first 120 years of popular entertainment.

The accordion's climb through early pop and vaudeville vanished. Its place in country music was ignored. Accordionists' achievements and aspirations in classical and jazz seemed laughably implausible. The vibrant infrastructure built around the instrument retreated into a sort of subcultural life support. Accordion clubs, competitions, and a few organizations struggled to sustain even memories of the golden age.

You can't blame devotees of the accordion for taking things personally. Their favorite instrument, in many cases their lifetime investment and meal ticket, was buried by what some denounced as "garbage music." Dozens of small-scale domestic factories had closed by the 1960s as manufacturing moved overseas. The remnants of North America's accordion world found themselves with only a few scattered specialty shops supported on faith as much as income. Few apprentices rose to take the place of the local artisans who did repairs into their old age. Their skills that sustained the surviving instruments retired or died with them.

The Bordignon family in Vancouver is typical. After seventy-five years they closed their accordion factory. This left Renzo Faoro, working out of his home, as the city's only technician. In the early 2000s when he retired (in his nineties), no one took his place. In this "post-accordion" age, the few remaining North American retail and repair shops drew visitors from hundreds or even thousands of miles away.

By the early 1980s, most accordion enthusiasts had either retreated into ethnic circuits or entrenched themselves within instruction networks and competitions that were remnants of the golden age. Interactions with classical accordionists in Europe encouraged unheard-of technical proficiency for a few players, but the results were entirely inaudible to most North Americans. The instrument had not scaled the classical or jazz heights that some had hoped would save it. Formal accordion education became largely unavailable outside of very few programs.

Many who awaited the return of the accordion never lived to see it. Rather than a temporary setback, accordionists faced long decades awaiting the impossible: that rock 'n' roll would blow over and something like the old days would return. Some supporters complained about being excluded from popular music while simultaneously admitting they despised it. Accordion festivals remained dedicated to the accordion's fading repertoire. Memorials piled up for once-famous players. A revival did finally rise, but it took decades and was nothing like the glowing future that mid-century promoters had hoped for.

☞ Preserved in Competition

A NETWORK OF national and international competitions survived the accordion's glory days. Originally organized to promote the instrument in the 1920s and '30s, schools with dozens or even hundreds of students competed. Battling accordionists appeared on radio and TV talent shows and "Flight of the Bumblebee" and "Lady of Spain" evolved from contest standards into accordion clichés.

When the accordion industry crumbled, competitions were transformed from part of the wider culture into somewhat insular reminders of bygone days. Unable to expand the accordion's popularity, they served as an underground network of beleaguered enthusiasts keeping their instrument alive.

The competitions drew from the aging accordion standards and a growing number of challenging modern pieces. They became a sort of folkloric structure for passing on skills within the accordion community. The Irish Fleadh Cheoil championships and some classical music competitions are similarly structured to preserve at-risk traditions.

Unfortunately, whereas a few Irish competitors might include "All Ireland Accordion Champion" in their successful professional résumés, North American accordion champions had fewer job prospects. While "reality" TV contests like *American Idol* have returned to popularity, most of the last half-century's pop music developed outside of formalized tournaments. Musical rivalries shifted toward the measurable realms of records and ticket sales where, unfortunately, most accordionists weren't in the same league.

Forty Years Later: A History of the Future

The Accordion (1955) by Toni Charuhas is one of the earliest books about the instrument. In it she spoke loftily of a glowing future that proved disastrously inaccurate in almost every way. She saw the accordion as "a full-grown instrument on the threshold of ripe maturity. Its most fruitful years lie ahead ... In the near future, there will scarcely be a college, university or conservatory that will not accept the accordion as a major instrument ... We may predict from the increasingly favorable attitude and respect with which the modern conductors, musicologist and composers have viewed the accordion, that a happy future is well assured." The triumphs that Charuhas predicted all evaporated; the accordion was instead forced into shameful retreat.

Almost seventy years later we can look back on the accordion's long slow creep back toward normalcy. By the 1980s, the media had begun to periodically "rediscover" the instrument whenever more than a few accordionists gained the briefest attention. The zydeco boom in the 1980s, Nirvana's *Unplugged* set in the 1990s, and the rise of the Decemberists in the new millennium all brought assertions that a Year of the Accordion™ had finally come. In reality, it's probable that no one like Dick Contino or Guido Deiro will dominate pop music again, but a more modest accordion zeitgeist has definitely arisen.

I've tried to relate the first 120 years of the accordion's story in North America. The recent revival would fill another book. In between, a scattering of pop music iconoclasts always held out for the instrument. As the 1980s dawned, "Weird Al" Yankovic, Tom Waits, and They Might Be Giants combined irony with appreciation for the accordion. The Pogues, Buckwheat Zydeco, and Los Lobos brought ethnic styles to rock audiences. Paul Simon's *Graceland* album opened millions of ears (and pocket-books) to world music. Lesser-known aficionados like Brave Combo, Angel Corpus Christi, and Those Darn Accordions paved the way for ethnic mashups, accordion cover songs, and squeezebox agitprop to come. By the 1990s, young aficionados were connecting with elders returning to the instrument of their childhood. Prejudices from both ends of the long exile fell away as people encountered the accordion anew.

There is much to be learned from the tenacious folks who held onto the instrument over the last forty years. Real pain remains, careers were ruined, artists unjustly forgotten. As the instrument returned, there remained a lack of learning resources for players—and few jobs for those with even exceptional skills. Classical accordionists finally did begin to gain long-sought exposure as charming (and somewhat exotic) additions to programs. It remains to be seen whether accordions will be embraced by the conservatories, orchestras, and jazz groups that produce so many top players for other instruments.

Accordion Noir: Taking Back the Airwaves

FIFTY YEARS AFTER the accordion's fall from grace, I was collecting squeezebox records and gathering the stories that eventually filled this book. I asked Rowan Lipkovits (a near stranger I'd met at an open mic) to help start the *Accordion Noir* radio program. He responded that the idea was preposterous, and immediately signed on to the endeavor. We set out with the quixotic goal of returning the accordion to normalcy, or at least reporting on it while it happened.

The show's name was inspired by 1950s crime dramas. We wanted a tough-guy recharge to the accordion's image, replacing joke-book squeezeboxes with street-smart accordions ready to rumble. (You can, after all, fit a lot of hardware into an accordion case.)

I think of *Accordion Noir*—literally the "Dark Accordion"—as an investigation into an instrument that's been suspiciously missing from Anglo-American culture. Around the world people use accordions in ways Lawrence Welk and his audience never dreamed of. But in North America, squeezeboxes had become so deeply square that it was almost radical to appreciate them.

People asked—and we wondered—if we could find enough material to fill an hour-long program every week. More than ten years on, we have an expanding collection of genre-breaching accordion tunes that could play constantly for months without repeating a song. More than a decade of *Accordion Noir*'s playlists provide both a fine accompaniment for this book, and evidence that the squeezebox has returned. Our job now is simply to spread the word.

Accordion Noir Radio and Festival memorabilia. Accordion Noir, *CFRO Co-op Radio,
100.5 FM, Vancouver.*

Formally trained accordionists aren't the only ones lifting up the instrument. Today's accordion encompasses both expert players who have put in years of practice, and DIY punk rockers with the most rudimentary grasp of music theory. Many ethnic and folk traditions are also stronger than ever, enhanced by a growing awareness of vastly different global styles connected by their accordions.

After all this time, the accordion has in effect become a new instrument in North America. Young people don't know why they are supposed to fear it. Many children have never even seen one. Benjamin Ickies told the *New York Times*, "The accordion's in our cultural past, so it sounds somewhat familiar... But for thirty years it's also been a complete outsider, so it also sounds new and fresh. No other instrument has that dichotomy."

Will the Accordion Rise Again?

Will accordions ever dominate pop music like they did in the golden age? The shortest answer is probably "No." But compared to the disdain of recent years, even modest goals are still improvements. T-shirts for Vancouver's Accordion Noir Festival advocated: "Ruthlessly pursuing the idea that the accordion is just another instrument."

Regardless of how cool the accordion becomes, keyboards, DJ mixers, and guitars are still easier options for almost all amplified situations. They're also usually cheaper. That's not to say the accordion's distinctive sound isn't worth the extra effort—and there are situations where accordions still hold their own against competitors.

For instance: without microphones, acoustic guitars are inaudible to all but the most attentive audiences. Even "unplugged" folk concerts aren't usually performed without mics, but when the power goes out, call up the horns, accordions, and drums.

Smaller accordions can still win in terms of portability. Electric guitars and keyboards, with their heavy amps, make for clumsy companions. Musicians lacking a portable generator or a long extension cord may find accordions to be their mobile go-to. Traveling around the world, a little accordion can turn out to be a remarkable doorway into peoples' lives and cultures. Notably, they also fit in most overhead luggage racks.

Expense remains a problem. Because of the labor and complexity involved, accordions cost significantly more than comparable guitars or electronics. If playable survivors from the millions of accordions made between 1940 and 1960 weren't relatively available, the current renaissance would be in dire straits. A hopeful sign is the new generation of technicians who are repairing machines that are often more than twice their age. This work is pivotal to maintaining a playable pool of instruments going forward. Whether it's Skyler Fell working at her Accordion Apocalypse repair shop north of San Francisco, or George Bachich's AccordionRevival repair-tips website and his *Piano Accordion: Owner's Manual and Buyer's Guide,* these are true heroes of the accordion's future.

After years of neglect, the squeezebox is on the ascent. The catastrophe that nearly destroyed the instrument in North America is fading. More musicians are using accordions in innovative ways than any time in the last half-century. The accordion's original revolution spread across the world from 1829 to 1960. Today a global uprising is renewing the squeezebox's story with music in every style and language. Back in 1955, accordion historian Toni Charuhas wrote hopefully about an "accordion of the future" that would rival pipe organs and face "only a handful of bigoted critics." Delayed by half a century, some of her hopeful dreams for the instrument may finally be coming true.

Acknowledgments

The Roots of My Accordion Obsession

The musical seed of this project can be traced to Ian Hill's closing accordion solo on "Di Good Life" (and "Dubbing for Life") from Linton Kwesi Johnson's 1991 album *Tings an' Times*.

Around that time my friend Christina returned from Budapest with a little red accordion. She let me try it, and after one squeeze on a few buttons, I set the instrument down and said, "Lawrence Welk did a terrible, terrible thing." Only years later did I realize my assessment mirrored the maestro's own "Wun'erful, Wun'erful!"

Decades passed and the Galvin family gave me my first accordion with the prescient warning, "Be careful, they multiply." I played that one in the celebratory Thursday march at Seattle's 1999 WTO demonstrations. I hope some of the energy of that day went into this book.

Accordion Noir and the Vancouver Accordion Scene (Holding Down the Bass)

Without my *Accordion Noir* co-host Rowan Lipkovits, I'd be mumbling about accordions somewhere by myself. Meanwhile, the folks at Vancouver's Co-op Radio (CFRO, 100.5 FM, www.coopradio.org), worked to keep *Accordion Noir* on the air since 2006. Thanks to all our listeners and supporters for letting us know you're out there.

Katheryn Peterson, Rowan Lipkovits, and many other people do far more than I to make the Accordion Noir Festival bring the radio show's spirit to life.

The Vancouver Squeezebox Circle (www.squeezeboxcircle.org) meets monthly and includes Alan Zisman, who took charge; Ans, who passed the hat; Andy Fielding, who composed the *Accordion Noir* Theme; Lisan, who watches for upside-down accordions; and many others.

And most recent thanks to my accordion teacher, Meagan Carsience.

Marvelous Pre-readers

These expert readers expanded my vision and caught many errors. Any that remain I kept against their better judgment.

Ruben A. Arellano, Allan Atlas, Nick Ballarini, Alan Bern, Paul Betken, Joe Blumka, Lauren Brody, Joanjett Helen Holtz Emmett Brown, Gerald Cigler, Kevin Coffey, Joel Cormier, Nou Dadoun, Henry Doktorski, Stuart Eydmann, Andy Fielding, Cesar R. Garza, Kurt Gegenhuber, Doug Green, Jim Hiscott, Will Holshouser, Joshua Horowitz, Daniel Kahn, John Krieger, Julien Labro, Josh Langhoff, James P. Leary, Susan Gedutis Lindsay, Marc Lindy, Rowan Lipkovits, Mike Madigan, Joe Maniscalco, Richard March, Joe Markulin, Alex Meixner, Kevin Murphy, Christine O'Neill, George "Ukulele" Pendergast, Cory Pesaturo, Wanda Power, Kim Ruehl, Tony Russell, Henry Sapoznik, William Schimmel, Russ Sharek, Graham Sheard, Paul Silveria, Helena Simonett, Craig Smith, Graeme Smith, Jared Snyder, Gary Sredzienski, David Symons, Jeff Taylor, Michael Tisserand, Russell Wallace, Dan Worrall, Zevy Zions, and Alan Zisman.

The Scholars of Squeeze

Especial Thanks To

Jared Snyder, who has made the old pre-blues African American accordion one of the most well-researched forgotten traditions in American music. The Highlander Center in Tennessee, which suffered a terrible fire as this book went to press. Their archive provided the photo of Zilphia Horton included in Chapter 15. This history is so important, and so fragile. Please support them: www.highlandercenter.org. And my unofficial research assistants, the Vancouver Public Library, with the miraculous international Inter-Library Loan system.

Artists and Scholars We Lost during the Writing of This Book

William Cosby, Régis Gizavo, Lucas Hicks from Rattletrap Ruckus, Len Holland, Allen Juste from Lakou Mizik, Gunther Kablutsiak, Frank Marocco, Pauline Oliveros, Ralph Stricker, Manuel Peña, Jenny Vincent, and too many we've missed. Also remembering Aaron Swartz and his work for open access to academic knowledge, since public scholarship should not be locked away from scholars.

Friends and Individual Scholars

Marié Abe co-produced the *Squeezebox Stories* public radio project and more. Ivan Armsby blogged at *Squeezyboy*. George Bachich wrote the *Piano Accordion Owner's Manual and Buyer's Guide* so I didn't have to. John Beckman helped contact Cornell Smelser's family. Dagmar Anita Binge copied Art Wenzel's "Yodeling Polka." Chris blogged at *Let's Polka*. Kevin Coffey shared from his massive collection of country and western squeezebox. Vera Colley tipped me off about the Nashville accordion conspiracy. The Cornell family of Victoria shared stories of their father and grandfather. Pete Dunk helped me with concertina connections on www.melodeon.net. Sharon Marie shared about her mother Carolina Cotton. Murphy Davis championed Sally Anne Forrester. Gordie Fleming's daughter, Heidi, kept his music alive. Ronald Flynn, Edwin Davison, and Edward Chavez preserved the *Golden Age of the Accordion*. Roy Forbes gifted us Janet Lane's "I'd like a Boyfriend for Christmas." Fabio G. Giota compiled the history of the Cordovox. Denise Gregoire is Johnny Grande's biggest fan. Victor Green's *Passion for Polka* leads the way. Joan Grouman preserves history at the American Accordionists Association Archives. Wade Hall wrote about Pee Wee King. Chris "Zeke" Hand boosted the information we had on Alice Hall. Chris O'Neill blogged at *Accordion Americana*. Ken Hardie loaned his twenty-inch transcription turntable. Richard Harris shared the amazing photo of Josephine and Lena Bergamasco of the Three Vagrants. Marion Jacobson's original "Searching for Rockcordion" article opened up the 1960s squeezebox scene. Mitchell Kezin of *Jingle Bell Rocks* connected us with Roy Forbes. Matsubayashi "Shaolin" Kohji shared Leon Sash's liner notes. John Krieger loaned me button boxes. Jody Kruskal helped with his concertina connections. Kip Lornell recorded perhaps the last English-language African American accordionists. Tony Lupo shared enthusiasm for the Carter Sisters. Richard MacKinnon sent labor solidarity from Cape Breton Island. Ron McConnell provided the photo of the Carter Sisters and Mother Maybelle with Doc Addington and Ron's father, Carl. Ted McGraw introduced me to Anne McNulty's accordions and the Walters accordion company. Mark Miller provided invaluable research on black accordionists from the *Chicago Defender* archives. Pat Missin shared exceptional harmonica history at www.patmissin .com. Celia Pendlebury inspired me to question the whole history of folk dance music. Jay Peterson, Doug Green (Ranger Doug), Jeff Taylor, Joey Miskulin, and Nova Karina Devonie keep western music alive. Annie Proulx showed the way; Rob Richie from Fair Vote helped connect us. Kim Ruehl introduced me to Zilphia Horton. Colin Sannes shared his Wallets. Michal Shapiro produced the *Planet Squeezebox* anthology. Ida Melrose Shoufler, Hall Smith, and Michael Steinman investigated the mysterious accordionist with the Cellar Boys in 1930. Paul Silveria helped inspire the two-version split of this book. Hans Stucki spoke about Ohio's the Angry. Michael Tisserand was court scribe in the *Kingdom of Zydeco*. Keith Titterington interviewed Pedro DePaul. Sherrie Tucker helped inspire the focus on women who play jazz. Suzanne Vance's YA book, *Sights*, was partially inspired by Johnny Grande. Elijah Wald set the bar high. Jerzy Wieczorek compiled accordion sales stats. Sharon Willing shared memories of Foy Willing.

People Working with Institutions

Lorraine Walsh Cashman at the American Folklore Society. Allan Atlas (retired) from the Center for the Study of Free-Reed Instruments at the Graduate Center, City University of New York, and the Deiro Archives. Brittany Carswell's grade 3 class in Saskatchewan. Helmi Strahl Harrington of the World of Accordions Museum. Darcy Kuronen, curator of Musical Instruments at the Museum of Fine Arts in Boston. Jackie Lennon, president, International Women in Jazz. The Library and Archives Canada, and the irreplaceable Virtual Gramophone collection. Memorial University, St. John's, Newfoundland. Tony Arambarri at NAMM for statistics on instrument sales. The Neptoon Records crew (Rob Frith, Jamie

Anstey, & co.) for Vancouver's Chessmen. Jon at the Old Time Radio Catalog. The Ransäters Dragspelsexpo Swedish accordion museum for the copy of Alice Hall's only 78-rpm record. Jude Romualdo of the University of Winnipeg Archives. David Seubert at the University of California Santa Barbara's Cylinder Digitization Project. Aaron Smithers of the Louis Round Wilson Special Collections Library at the University of North Carolina at Chapel Hill. Will Griffin from Smithsonian Folkways. Chris Strachwitz from Arhoolie Records. Toivo Tamminen for the photo of Viola Turpeinen. Karl and Martin from Tempo Trend Accordions. Vaughan Webb at the Blue Ridge Institute & Museum of Ferrum College for their collection of African American and country accordionists.

Publishing Support

Especial thanks to Rony Ganon, Trena White, Peter Cocking, Taysia Louie, and all the folks at Page Two Strategies for their assistance in bringing this book to print.

Every effort has been made to trace the owners of copyrighted material reproduced herein and secure permissions. The author apologizes for any omissions, and will be pleased to incorporate missing acknowledgments in any future editions of this book.

Selected Bibliography

General

Bachich, George. *Piano Accordion Owner's Manual and Buyer's Guide.* Napa, California: Accordion Revival, 2012.

Berner, Geoff. *How to Be an Accordion Player: An Instructional Booklet with Illustrations.* Vancouver: Kolakowski Press, 2006. [Warning: satire, not music lessons.]

Billard, François, and Didier Roussin. *Histoires de l'Accordéon.* Paris: Institut national de l'audiovisuel, 1991.

Ellingham, Mark, et al. *World Music: The Rough Guide, Vol. 1: Africa, Europe and the Middle East.* London: Rough Guides, Ltd., 1999.

Ellingham, Mark, et al. *World Music: The Rough Guide, Vol. 2: Latin and North America, Caribbean, India, Asia and Pacific.* London: Rough Guides, Ltd., 2000.

Elliott, David. *The Concertina Maintenance Manual.* Cleckheaton, UK: Mally, 2003.

Hutchinson, Sydney. *Tigers of a Different Stripe: Performing Gender in Dominican Music.* Chicago: University of Chicago Press, 2016.

Jacobson, Marion. *Squeeze This!: A Cultural History of the Accordion in America.* Urbana: University of Illinois Press, 2012.

Jarry, Laurent, and Olivier Eumont (photography). *Trésors de Lames: Accordéons, Bandonéons.* Paris: Lelivredart, 2014.

Lornell, Kip, and Anne K. Rasmussen, eds. *Musics of Multicultural America: A Study of Twelve Musical Communities.* New York: Schirmer Books, 1997.

March, Rick. "Accordion Jokes: A Folklorist's View." In *The Accordion in the Americas: Klezmer, Polka, Tango, Zydeco, and More.* Edited by Helena Simonett. Urbana: University of Illinois Press, 2012.

Miller, Malcolm, and Basil Tschaikov, eds. *The Accordion in All Its Guises.* Basingstoke, UK: Overseas Publishers Association, 2001.

Proulx, Annie. *Accordion Crimes.* New York: Scribner, 1996.

Ramunni, Angelo. *Accordion Stories from the Heart: A Collection of Accordions from around the World and Their Stories, Inspired by the Extraordinary People Who Played Them.* Canaan, Connecticut: New England Accordion Connection & Museum Co., 2018.

Rippley, LaVern J. *The Chemnitzer Concertina: A History and an Accolade*. Northfield, Minnesota: St. Olaf College Press, 2006.

Shapiro, Michal, ed. *Planet Squeezebox: Accordion Music from around the World*. Ellipsis Arts, 1995, three compact discs and book.

Simonett, Helena, ed. *The Accordion in the Americas: Klezmer, Polka, Tango, Zydeco, and More*. Urbana: University of Illinois Press, 2012.

Wenzel, Haik, et al. *History Unfolds! 100 Years of Hohner Accordions in Pictures* [German/English]. Bergkirchen, Germany: Edition Bochinsky, 2004.

Worrall, Dan M. *The Anglo-German Concertina: A Social History, Vol. 1*. Fulshear, Texas: Concertina Press, 2010.

Worrall, Dan M. *The Anglo-German Concertina: A Social History, Vol. 2*. Fulshear, Texas: Concertina Press, 2010.

African American

Pecknold, Diane, ed. *Hidden in the Mix: The African American Presence in Country Music*. Durham, North Carolina: Duke University Press, 2013.

Snyder, Jared. "Breeze in the Carolinas: The African American Accordionists of the Upper South." *Free-Reed Journal* 3 (2001).

Snyder, Jared. "Garde Ici et Garde La-Bas: Creole Accordion in Louisiana." In *The Accordion in the Americas: Klezmer, Polka, Tango, Zydeco, and More*. Edited by Helena Simonett. Urbana: University of Illinois Press, 2012.

Snyder, Jared. "Lead Belly's 'Windjammer.'" In *Lead Belly: A Life in Pictures*. Edited by Tiny Robinson and John Reynolds. London: Steidl, 2008.

Snyder, Jared. "Squeezebox: The Legacy of the Afro-Mississippi Accordionists." *Black Music Research Journal* 17, no. 1 (1997).

Canadian

Cormier, Joël. "Acadian Accordion Music in South Eastern New Brunswick." Dissertation, University of Toronto, 2011.

Hiscott, Jim. "Inuit Accordion: A Better Kept Secret." *Bulletin de musique folklorique canadienne* 34, nos. 1-2 (2000).

Johnson, Sherry, ed. *Bellows & Bows: Historic Recordings of Traditional Fiddle & Accordion Music from across Canada*. Research Center for the Study of Music, Media, & Place, Memorial University, 2012, two compact discs and book.

Labbé, Gabriel. *Musiciens Traditionnels du Québec (1920-1993)*. Montréal: VLB, 1995.

Le Guevel, Yves. "L'implantation de l'Accordéon au Québec: Des Origines aux Années 1950." *Bulletin Mnémo* (1999), accessed April 18, 2017. http://www.mnemo.qc.ca/spip/bulletin-mnemo/article/l-implantation-de-l-accordeon-au.

Sandell, Greg, and Laurie Hart. *Danse Ce Soir! Fiddle and Accordion Music of Quebec*. Pacific, Montana: Mel Bay, 2001.

Country Music

Berry, Chad. *The Hayloft Gang: The Story of the* National Barn Dance. Urbana: University of Illinois Press, 2008.

Green, Douglas. *Singing in the Saddle: The History of the Singing Cowboy.* Nashville: Country Music Foundation Press, 2002.

Kienzle, Rich. *Southwest Shuffle: Pioneers of Honky Tonk, Western Swing, and Country Jazz.* London: Routledge, 2003.

Kingsbury, Paul, and Alanna Nash. *Will the Circle Be Unbroken: Country Music in America.* London and New York: DK Publishing, 2006.

Russell, Tony. *Country Music Originals: The Legends and the Lost.* New York: Oxford University Press, 2007.

Folk Revival

Cunningham, Agnes "Sis," and Gordon Friesen. *Red Dust and Broadsides: A Joint Autobiography.* Amherst: University of Massachusetts Press, 1999.

Harvey, Todd. *Michigan-I-O: Alan Lomax and the 1938 Library of Congress Folk-Song Expedition.* Dust-to-Digital; Library of Congress, 2013.

Leary, James. *Folksongs of Another America: Field Recordings from the Upper Midwest, 1937–1946.* Madison; Atlanta: The University of Wisconsin Press; Dust-to-Digital, 2015.

Smith, Craig. *Sing My Whole Life Long: Jenny Vincent's Life in Folk Music and Activism.* Albuquerque: University of New Mexico Press, 2007.

Whisnant, David. *All That Is Native & Fine: The Politics of Culture in an American Region.* Chapel Hill: University of North Carolina Press, 1983.

Golden Age

Bove, Bob. *Accordion Man: The Legendary Dick Contino.* Tallahassee, Florida: Father & Son Publishing, 1994.

Charuhas, Toni. *The Accordion.* New York: Pietro Deiro Publications, 1959.

Doktorski, Henry. *The Brothers Deiro and Their Accordions.* Oakdale, Pennsylvania: Classical Free Reed, Inc., 2005.

Floren, Myron, and Randee Floren. *Accordion Man.* Brattleboro, Vermont: Stephen Greene Press, 1981.

Flynn, Ronald, Edwin Davison, and Edward Chavez. *The Golden Age of the Accordion.* Schertz, Texas: Flynn Publications, 1992.

Various artists. *Squeeze Me: The Jazz and Swing Accordion Story.* Produced by Joop Visser. Proper Records, 2006. Four compact discs and book.

Irish and Scottish

Chaoimh, Máire Ní. "Journey into Tradition: A Social History of the Irish Button Accordion." Dissertation, University of Limerick, 2010.

Eydmann, Stuart. "As Common as Blackberries: The First Hundred Years of the Accordion in Scotland, 1830–1930," *Folk Music Journal* 7, no. 5 (1999).

Eydmann, Stuart. "From the 'Wee Melodeon' to the 'Big Box': The Accordion in Scotland since 1945," *Musical Performance* 3, nos. 2–4 (2001).

Eydmann, Stuart. "The Life and Times of the Concertina: The Adoption and Usage of a Novel Musical Instrument with Particular Reference to Scotland." Dissertation, The Open University, 1995.

Gedutis, Susan Lindsay. *See You at the Hall: Boston's Golden Era of Irish Music and Dance.* Hanover, New Hampshire: Northeastern University Press, 2005.

Ó hAllmhuráin, Gearóid. *O'Brien Pocket History of Irish Traditional Music.* Dublin: O'Brien, 2003.

O'Keeffe, Maire. "The Irish Button Accordion: An Overview." *Musical Performance* 3, nos. 2–4 (2001).

Smith, Graeme. "Irish Button Accordion: From Press and Draw and Back Again." *The World of Music* 50, no. 3 (2008).

Vallely, Fintan. *The Companion to Irish Traditional Music.* New York: NYU Press, 1999.

Wallis, Geoff, and Sue Wilson. *The Rough Guide to Irish Music (Rough Guide Music Reference).* London: Rough Guides, 2001.

Klezmer

Horowitz, Josh. "The Klezmer Accordion: An Outsider among Outsiders." In *The Accordion in the Americas: Klezmer, Polka, Tango, Zydeco, and More.* Edited by Helena Simonett. Urbana: University of Illinois Press, 2012.

Rogovoy, Seth. *The Essential Klezmer: A Music Lover's Guide to Jewish Roots and Soul Music, from the Old World to the Jazz Age to the Downtown Avant-Garde.* Chapel Hill, North Carolina: Algonquin Books, 2000.

Sapoznik, Henry. *Klezmer! Jewish Music from Old World to Our World.* New York: Schirmer, 1999.

Sapoznik, Henry. "Klezmer Music: The First One Thousand Years." *In Musics of Multicultural America: A Study of Twelve Musical Communities.* Edited by Kip Lornell and Anne K. Rasmussen. New York: Schirmer Books, 1997.

Slobin, Mark, ed. *American Klezmer: Its Roots and Offshoots.* Berkeley: University of California Press, 2002.

Strom, Yale. *The Book of Klezmer: The History, the Music, the Folklore.* Chicago: Chicago Review Press, 2011.

Strom, Yale. *Shpil: The Art of Playing Klezmer.* Lanham, Maryland: Scarecrow Press, 2012.

Various artists. *Cantors, Klezmorim and Crooners 1905–1953: Classic Yiddish 78s from the Mayrent Collection.* Compiled by Christopher C. King, Sherry Mayrent, and Henry Sapoznik. JSP Records, 2009. Box set, two compact discs.

Louisiana French

Ancelet, Barry. *Cajun and Creole Music Makers: Musiciens Cadiens et Créoles*. Jackson: University Press of Mississippi, 1999.

Ancelet, Barry. *One Generation at a Time: Biography of a Cajun and Creole Music Festival*. Lafayette: Center for Louisiana Studies, 2007.

Ancelet, Barry. "Zydeco Zarico: Beans, Blues and Beyond," *Black Music Research Journal* 8, no. 1 (1988).

Brasseaux, Ryan. *Cajun Breakdown: The Emergence of an American-Made Music*. Oxford and New York: Oxford University Press, 2009.

Brasseaux, Ryan, and Kevin Fontenot, eds. *Accordions, Fiddles, Two Step & Swing: A Cajun Music Reader*. Lafayette: Center for Louisiana Studies, 2006.

DeWitt, Mark. *Cajun and Zydeco Dance Music in Northern California: Modern Pleasures in a Postmodern World*. Jackson: University Press of Mississippi, 2008.

François, Raymond. *Yé Yaille, Chère: Traditional Cajun Dance Music*. Ville Platte, Louisiana: Swallow Publications, 2000.

Savoy, Ann. *Cajun Music: A Reflection of a People, Vol. 1*. Eunice, Louisiana: Bluebird Press, 1986.

Steptoe, Tyina. *Houston Bound: Culture and Color in a Jim Crow City*. Oakland: University of California Press, 2016.

Tisserand, Michael. *The Kingdom of Zydeco*. New York: Arcade Publications, 1998.

Wood, Charles, and James Fraher (photography). *Texas Zydeco*. Austin: University of Texas Press, 2006.

Yule, Ron, and Ervin LeJeune. *Iry LeJeune: Wailin' the Blues Cajun Style*. Natchitoches: Northwestern State University of Louisiana Press, 2007.

Polka

American Folklife Center. *Ethnic Recordings in America, a Neglected Heritage*. Washington, D.C.: Library of Congress, 1982.

Dolgan, Bob. *America's Polka King: The Real Story of Frankie Yankovic and His Music*. Cleveland: Gray & Co., 2006.

Greene, Victor. *A Passion for Polka: Old-Time Ethnic Music in America*. Berkeley: University of California Press, 1992.

Holtz, Dale. *Enemies of Sleep: New Ulm Musicians*. Duluth, Minnesota: Holtz, 2004.

Keil, Charles, Algeliki Keil, and Dick Blau (photography). *Polka Happiness*. Philadelphia: Temple University Press, 1992.

Leary, James. *Polkabilly: How the Goose Island Ramblers Redefined American Folk Music*. New York and Oxford: Oxford University Press, 2010.

March, Rick, and Dick Blau (photography). *Polka Heartland: Why the Midwest Loves the Polka*. Madison: Wisconsin Historical Society, 2015.

Parker, Theresa Cernoch. *Jimmy Brosch Remembers Twenty Legendary Texas Czech Polka Bands*. Katy, Texas: BCP Enterprises, 2011.

Mexico/U.S. Border Acordeón

Burr, Ramiro. *The* Billboard *Guide to Tejano and Regional Mexican Music*. New York: Billboard, 1999.

Dyer, John. *Conjunto: Voz Del Pueblo, Canciones Del Corazón / Voice of the People, Songs from the Heart*. Austin: University of Texas Press, 2005.

Griffith, James S., "Waila: The Social Dance Music of the Tohono O'odham." In *Musics of Multicultural America: A Study of Twelve Musical Communities*. Edited by Kip Lornell and Anne K. Rasmussen. New York: Schirmer Books, 1997.

Gurza, Agustin, Jonathan Clark, and Chris Strachwitz. *The Arhoolie Foundation's Strachwitz Frontera Collection of Mexican and Mexican American Recordings*. Los Angeles: UCLA Chicano Studies Research Center Press, 2012.

Morales, Ed. *The Latin Beat: The Rhythms and Roots of Latin Music from Bossa Nova to Salsa and Beyond*. Cambridge, Massachusetts: Da Capo Press, 2003.

Peña, Manuel. *The Texas-Mexican Conjunto: History of a Working-Class Music*. Austin: University of Texas Press, 1985.

Ragland, Cathy. *Música Norteña: Mexican Migrants Creating a Nation between Nations*. Philadelphia: Temple University Press, 2009.

Ragland, Cathy. "'Tejano and Proud': Regional Accordion Traditions of South Texas and the Border Region." In *The Accordion in the Americas: Klezmer, Polka, Tango, Zydeco, and More*. Edited by Helena Simonett. Urbana: University of Illinois Press, 2012.

San Miguel, Guadalupe, Jr. *Tejano Proud: Tex-Mex Music in the Twentieth Century*. College Station: Texas A&M University, 2002.

Sturman, Janet L. "Preserving Territory: The Changing Language of the Accordion in Tohono O'odham Waila Music." In *The Accordion in the Americas: Klezmer, Polka, Tango, Zydeco, and More*. Edited by Helena Simonett. Urbana: University of Illinois Press, 2012.

Tejeda, Juan, and Avelardo Valdez, eds. *Puro Conjunto: An Album in Words and Pictures: Writings, Posters, and Photographs from the Tejano Conjunto Festival in San Antonio, 1982–1998*. Austin: Center for Mexican American Studies, University of Texas, 2001.

Vargas, Deborah. *Dissonant Divas in Chicana Music: The Limits of La Onda*. Minneapolis: University of Minnesota Press, 2012.

Wald, Elijah. *Narcocorrido: A Journey into the Music of Drugs, Guns, and Guerrillas*. New York: HarperCollins, 2001.

Index

246; leftist politics and, 322–23; Alan
Lomax on accordion and, 320–22; lost
opportunities for accordion, 314–15,
340; missing Upper Midwest, 317–20;
Newfoundland preservation, 225;
polka and, 65–66, 319–20, 347–48;
recordings and, 342; Scottish music
and, 187; Harry Smith and, 324–26;
string bands revival, 341–42; urbane
folk, 340–41
Fontenot, Canray, 162, 168, 171–72
Forrester, Sally Ann, 278, 289, 290–93
Fortina, Carl, 122–23, 368, 369
Fox, Charles, 37
Frain, Gene, 204
free-bass systems, 30, 53, 112–13, 381
free-reed instruments, 13, 16
French Canadian music, *see* Quebec
French music, *see* Cajun, Creole, and
zydeco music
Frosini, Pietro, 51, 53
Funk Serenaders, 280–81

Gabbanelli, John, 175
Gaelic League, 190, 191, 195
Galaxies IV, 366–67
Galla-Rini, Anthony, 58–59, 73, 122,
294, 381
garage bands, 358–59
garage band accordionists, 360–68;
the Angry, 364–65; Bop-Kats, 361–62;
Chessmen, 365–66; Joey Dee and the
Starliters, 360; Devil's Anvil, 367–68;
Galaxies IV, 366–67; Gary Lewis
and the Playboys, 362–64; Three
Chuckles, 360–61
Gardner, Julie, 102–5, *103*, 297, 357
Gentiletti, Saturno, 217
Giles, Hiawatha, 270
Glahé, Will, 71
Godwin, Charles "Knocky," 305
Golden West Cowboys, 278, 286–87,
353, 355
Goldman, Albert, 133
Goodman, Benny, 105, 111, 117
Grande, Johnny, 311, 354, 355–57, *356*

Grand Ole Opry (radio program), 278, 294
Grand Ole Opry accordionists, 285–89;
Helen Carter and the Carter Family,
287–89, *288*; Pee Wee King and the
Golden West Cowboys, 286–87;
Missouri Mountaineers, 278, 285
Graves, "Calico" Ted, 295
Great Big Sea, 224, 225
Green, Archie, 344
Green, Douglas B. ("Ranger Doug"), 298
Greene, Victor, 74, 76
Greensmith, Bill, 269
Griffith, Jim, 158
Grindstaff, Burton, 166
Gronow, Pekka, 70–71
Guard, David, 314
Guidotti, Tito, 106–7
Guillemette, Joseph, 217
Guillory, Kristi, 180
Guillory, "Queen" Ida, 179–80
guitar, 28, 259, 273, 354, 374, 375, 376–
77, 378, 392
Gumina, Tommy, 115, 117–19, 379
Gurza, Agustín, 147, 155
Guthrie, Woody, 79, 260, 323, 332, 335

Hackberry Ramblers, 161
Hale, Grace, 324
Haley, Bill, 310–11, 354, 355
Hall, Alice, 109–12, *110*
Handaeoline/Handharmonika (hand-
harmonica), 16
Handy, Antoinette, 102
Harden, Harry, 246
harmonica, 16, 20, 293, 343
Harper, Joe, 263
Harrington, Helmi Strahl: A World of
Accordions Museum, 22
Harris, "Blind" Jesse, 261
Hartwich, Karl, 70
Hay, "Judge" George, 277, 278, 293
Heavlow, Dorothy, 310
Henry, Murphy, 291, 292
Henson, Matthew, 235–36, *236*
Herborn, Eddie, 193
Hernández, Jorge and Eduardo, 154–55

About the Author

BRUCE TRIGGS spent ten years living with the homeless at the radical Catholic Worker community in Tacoma, Washington. While there he broke his first squeezebox at the 1999 WTO demonstrations in Seattle. For over a decade he has hosted the *Accordion Noir* radio program in Vancouver, British Columbia, and was in on the ground floor at the annual Accordion Noir Festival. After meeting many fabulous accordion players, Bruce decided to write about the instrument rather than learn to play it. He now lives alone in a bachelor pad surrounded by broken accordions. (These things may be related.) Amidst all this he has co-parented delightful and talented twins with their queer moms, an extended family, and their cranky rescue cat.

Made in the USA
San Bernardino, CA
17 June 2020

73687801R00266